This Is That:

Personal Experiences, Sermons and Writings

Aimee Semple McPherson

Must Have Books
503 Deerfield Place
Victoria, BC
V9B 6G5
Canada

ISBN: 9781773237992

Copyright 2021 – Must Have Books

THIS IS THAT Acts 2:16-18
THIS IS THAT which was spoken by the Prophet Joel:
"And it shall come to pass in the last days, saith God, I will pour out of my Spirit upon all flesh; and your sons and daughters shall prophesy . . . and upon my servants and my handmaidens I will pour out, in those days, of My Spirit; and they shall prophesy."

Preface

The realization that Jesus is coming soon and that whatever is done must be done quickly, has put a "hurry-up" in my soul to get the message to the greatest number of people in the shortest possible time by every available means.

Sometimes when laboring in certain portions of the Master's vineyard, we have felt that we were reaching many, but when, under the burden of prayer, the Lord catches us up in the Spirit, and with clarified vision and broadened horizon we see earth's millions who are yet unconscious of the signs of the times and know not that the coming of the Lord is nigh at hand, we are overwhelmed with the desire to speed through the lands, and ring the message forth "Jesus is coming soon prepare to meet him I" Oh, that we might write it in flaming letters upon the sky! It is to this end, therefore, that this book is sent forth.

Part I Personal Testimony simply written and solely for the encouragement of others, knowing that what the Lord has so graciously done for one so unworthy, He is abundantly able and willing to do for all.

Part II "In the mouth of two or three witnesses shall every word be established."

Part III Sermons and Writings contains a message to the sinner; to the born-again soul who has not yet received the baptism with the Holy Spirit, and to the baptized believer who is pressing on to perfection.

Part IV Visions, Prophecies, and interpretations of messages which the Lord has given me in the Spirit and which have been of such value and blessing to ourselves and others; we realize them too precious to be lost.

He bade me go forth taking no thought what I should eat or drink or where with I should be clothed, assured that He who had commissioned me to go into all the world and preach the Gospel knew, and would supply every need according to His riches.

We have never known what it was to have any earthly board behind us or any one person to whom we could look for support, yet God has marvelously supplied our every need.

Will the reader pardon mistakes and look more at the spirit in which the book is written than at errors in composition? It is doubtful whether any other book has been written under similar circumstances. I have had no quiet study into which to retire and close the door to the world and countless interruptions. Each page has been written in spare moments, amidst the stress of meetings, playing, singing, preaching, and working at the altar, besides traveling far and wide with the Gospel car.

The opening chapters were written in Florida, and the work has been continued en route from there to New York, the New England states, and thence across the continent to California.

Though the reader and the writer may never meet in this present life, "this book goes from my and heart with the earnest prayer and hope that we shall rise together to meet the Lord in the clouds of glory, when Jesus shall appear.

Part I.

Personal Testimony

CHAPTER I. MY MOTHER

"The word of the Lord came unto me, saying, Before I formed thee ... I knew thee; and before thou earnest forth ... I sanctified thee and I ordained thee a prophet unto the nations. Then said I, Ah! Lord God! Behold, I cannot speak; for I am a child. But the Lord said unto me; Say not, I am a child; for thou shalt go to all that I shall send thee, and whatsoever I command thee thou shalt speak. Be not afraid of their faces; for I am with thee to deliver thee. Then the Lord put forth His hand, and touched my mouth, and said unto me, Behold, I have put My Words in thy mouth."
Jer. 1: (4-9)

When I was a little girl seventeen years of age, the Lord spoke these words plainly into my startled ears, as I was alone in my bedroom praying one day.

It was a solemn time when He ordained me there to preach the Gospel. At first it seemed too astounding and impossible to be true that the Lord would ever call such a simple, unworthy little country girl as I to go out and preach the Gospel but the call and ordination were so real that, although later set apart and ordained by the saints of God, the memory of my little bedroom, flooded with the glory of God as He spoke those words, has always been to me my real ordination.

It is because the words, "Before I formed thee I knew thee, and before thou earnest forth I sanctified thee" are so true in my life that I must begin my testimony by taking you. Back some twenty years before I was born. Our lives are like a great loom, weaving many threads together, and the first threads of my life are inseparably woven about my dear Mother; it is with her, therefore, that the story of my life really begins.

Returning from school at the age of twelve, she read excitedly of a strange "Army" who were announced to bombard the town and take prisoners for the King. Prevailing upon her mother to risk the danger, they stood in a downpour of rain, awaiting the advent of the army. Presently the word was passed

"Here they come!"

But where were they? Could this be all? Three strangers, cloaked in quiet blue, stepped forth into the square, and knelt in silent prayer.

The humility, seriousness and sweetness of it saved over her heart. She realized the tender drawing of the Holy Spirit, and before a word had been spoken she knew that these were God's people and her people. As they sang

"We are bound for the land of the pure and the holy, the home of the happy, the kingdom of love. Ye wanderers from God, in the broad road of folly, O! Say will you go to the Eden above?"

Her heart, melting in love and adoration, answered

- "I will go."

Her mother had talked much of the mighty power of God manifested in the early Methodist church, and here in the Army she found it again, and it was nothing uncommon to see men and women slain as in the church of John Wesley's day. Her heart was filled with a desire to win other souls for Jesus; the love of Christ constrained her to His glad service, and the all-absorbing purpose of her soul was to prepare in obedience to the divine call.

Soon came the illness and death of her mother, who had talked to her solemnly of the time soon coming when the little girl should be left alone in the world, telling her that she would commend her to the tender care of God and the Captain's wife, who had been her spiritual mother. She did not waver for an instant in answering the call to the ranks of the Army and after quickly packing her simple belongings, my mother left all, friends and home, and native land, to follow Jesus.

The period of service which followed her arrival at the Army quarters in the distant town, brought blessed help and inspiration. The godly life of her leaders, and the prayers of the Captain, who frequently spent whole nights on his face before God in intercession for precious souls, the hours spent in visiting the sick and sinful the trudging five miles to assist in "Outpost" duties, the "War Cry" selling, and meetings, all helped comprise the routine of life.

But again fell the shadows this time an illness which necessitated an extended and work; this meant a painful goodbye to her comrades, and a visit to a country farm.

Then it was, while weak in body, depressed in spirit, and mourning over the loss of a mother's sympathetic hand, that she married, hoping to be able to continue her work for God, but amidst the strenuous and unaccustomed duties of heavy farm work, she was compelled to acknowledge that she was caught in the devil's net, and helpless as far as active service was concerned, and must largely devote herself to the manifold cares of life and home.

Even so environed, she stood true to her Lord, setting up a family altar, and helping with meetings in the homes of the neighborhood, often driving or walking the six miles to the nearest corps, and counted it the one bright hour of her day, even when weary and worn with heavy toil and

7

care. Yet, realizing ever that she had failed the Lord, who had redeemed and set her apart for His glorious purpose, life grew more and more dreary; her spirit grieved sore, with no ray of hope to rectify herself toward God, and the souls she had been called to win.

Ah! Many who read this experience will know how to enter into her feelings, for alas; many grow faint and falter by the wayside, or seek to find an easier pathway, only to discover themselves outside the paths of obedience and blessing.

My mother's pathway, in these days, was hedged about with difficulties. Shorn of her usefulness, fettered by circumstances, she truly did grind in the prison house; but, strange as it may seem, during all the time that her body was fettered, her soul was turning Heavenward. Each hour the longing became more intense to go on with the work for which God had ordained her, and for which purpose she had left home and friends and separated herself unto the Lord. Finally it absorbed her every thought in waking, and became her one dream in repose she must make good her belated pledge.

She must "come back" to the glorious calling of the Cross.

HOPE'S ONE RAY

One day, after reading over and over the story of Hannah, she went to her room, and closing the door, kneeled by her bed, and prayed unto the Lord, and vowed a vow, saying

"Oh Lord, You called me to preach the Gospel, but somehow I have failed You and cannot go, but if You will only hear my prayer, as You heard Hannah's prayer of old, and give me a little baby girl, I will give her unreservedly into your service, that she may preach the word I should have preached, fill the place I should have filled, and live the life I should have lived in Thy service. O Lord, hear and answer me; give me the witness that Thou hast heard me, O Lord, for Thine own Name's sake. Amen."

Turning to the window, she saved back the curtains and gazed wistfully up at the dark clouds shrouding the face of the sky and shutting out the sunshine beyond.

Suddenly there came a rift in the clouds, and a ray of sunlight illumined yonder hilltop, moved quickly down the slope of the hill, reached the valley, the orchard, the house itself, and fell full upon the white, anxious face with its tear-reddened eyes, framed in the window, lighting it with divine radiance, hope and courage, and saved on into the room, flooding it with golden glory.

To the longing little heart of my Mother, as she kneeled at the window, it seemed that surely here was the divine witness from above the sealing of her vow unto God.

Again she read and reread the story of Hannah, and the child she had dedicated unto the Lord. She sat on, gazing far away dreaming of the future years. Over the distant hills the sun was fast sinking, transforming the sombre sky into a glorious mirage of hope, flaming with crimson, purple and gold.

O Hope! Dazzling, radiant Hope! What a change thou bringest to the hopeless, brightening the darkened paths, and cheering the lonely way.

CHAPTEE II. THE BABY

"For this child I prayed; and the Lord gave me my petition, which I asked of Him. Therefore also I have lent him unto the Lord; as long as he liveth he shall be lent unto the Lord."
1 Sam. 1:27, 28

"Hush, my babe,
Lie still and slumber,
Holy angels guard thy bed.
Heavenly blessings without number,
Gently falling on thy head."

There was a B-A-B-Y in the house! A tiny, insignificant little thing; not good for much of anything but sleeping, and crying, and sucking a soft little pink thumb, and it seems that I was that baby.

Mother was rocking the warm little bundle, so carefully wrapped in the big embroidered shawl, and singing softly the childtime lullaby

"Hush, my babe"

The little head was nodding, nodding, n-o-d-d-i-n-g,

"Lie still and sl-"

Tired eyes were drooping, d-r-o-o-p-i-n-g.

"Holy angels guard thy b -"

The tiny fingers were slowly relaxing their clasp,

"Heavenly blessings, without num"

Another final little pat and the baby was asleep.

Outside the dining-room windows the autumn leaves were again drifting lightly to the earth. The late October sunshine was again slanting through the gorgeous foliage of the big maple and locusts that stood as sentries by our door. Fall breezes, rustling through the leaves, shook the branches and sent a veritable shower of gay colored leaves cascading through the air and tapping lightly at the window-pane, as though inviting memory to soar as lightly as they back to the fall, when last these same trees had shaken if their coat of many colors back to the day in her room, when she had prayed for the little daughter that should take her place and preach the good tidings of great joy.

Never, for a moment, in the days that followed, had she doubted God was He not faithful who had promised? Piece by piece the wardrobe had been finished and hidden away cautiously under lock and key. Sitting there, folding the baby in her arms, in memory she again tip-toed lightly up the stairs, and after locking her door, with greatest delight unfolded and lovingly fingered, garment by garment, the wardrobe that was to be for the little girl. Had she not asked God for a "daughter" that would fill her place in His service? Even the morning the little pink-faced, brown-eyed stranger had announced its arrival with no uncertain tones, making the quiet old farmhouse ring and echo, my little Mother had not doubted, but asked confidently

"Where is she? Bring her here."

Then her thoughts saved beyond the past and the present, and soared far away into the future dreaming of the years that were to come, when this wee creature with the turned-up nose, and the "ten tiny fingers and toes," would be preaching the Gospel of Jesus Christ, the Son of God.

Caressing the little fingers, she dreamed of the day when these same little hands, grown stronger, would hold a Bible, and wield the sword of the Word, when these little feet would follow the Lamb

"Whithersoever He leadeth" when these little lips would preach the Word. Ah "Faith, mighty faith, the promise sees, and looks to that alone. Laughs at impossibilities and cries 'It shall be done'."

The great torrent of love and desire for personal service, which had hitherto flooded my mother's soul, was now turned into a new channel the one absorbing, all-important business of her life became the bringing up of the baby in the way she should go. This training, mother felt, could not begin too early in life, and therefore, when I arrived at the age of three weeks, she announced to the horrified nurse, and the astonished household in general, her firm determination to take the baby to a "Jubilee" to the five-mile distant corps.

Much well-meant advice to "Keep that child at home by the fire", followed my Mother to the door. Some declared that the baby would surely have pneumonia. Aunt Maria, who "knew all about babies, "shook her head, and told how they managed their baby at her house, protesting to the last

"You'll kill that Baby! You don't know anything about a baby. Anyone who does not know how to take better care of a baby than that shouldn't have one." (But alas! Aunt Maria's baby, whose natural body they nurtured so carefully, and kept cuddled by the fire, soon took the much-feared cold and died.)

Mother tells me that from the very first meeting I was warmly welcomed occupied the front seat and contributed, without request, my full share to the music and interest of the evening.

At six weeks of age I was promoted to the platform. It was my solemn dedication service in the Salvation Army the hour for which my Mother had longed and prayed the hour of her dreams and hopes the hour wherein she publicly consecrated this visible answer to prayer her little daughter to the service of the Lord.

Thus in my infancy, my precious Mother fulfilled her vow unto the Lord, who had looked upon the affliction of His handmaid, remembered her, and given unto her the child for which she prayed.'

"On Him who watches over all,
I cast my weight of care,
Assured He hears me when I pray,
And always answers prayer.

Sometimes I wait full many a year
Sometimes 'tis then and there,
His answering message I can hear;
God always answers prayer.

Sometimes afar He bids me 'go'
But He'll go with me there;
If He says 'stay', I'm glad 'tis so;
Love always answers prayer.

Tomorrow, perhaps it may be today,
But whether 'tis 'Yea',
Or whether 'tis 'Nay',
God always answers prayer."

CHAPTER III. CHILDHOOD DAYS

(A chapter written for the children - big folks and wise folks should not read, but pass on to Chapter IV.)

"Train up a child in the way he should go; and when he is old, he will not depart from it." Prov. 22:6

"Gentle Jesus, meek and mild,
Look upon this little child;
Pity my simplicity,
Suffer me to come to Thee.
Fain I would to Thee be brought,
Gracious Lord, forbid it not.
Find a little child a place."

"God bless Papa, God bless Mamma, God bless everybody, all over the world, and make little Aimee a good girl, for Jesus' sake, Amen"

So ended each happy, childhood day, with prayers and kisses, and Bible stories. My own childhood days being so blessed with Christian influence and Bible teaching, it has always seemed to me, that the home without a godly praying Mother had been deprived of the greatest of all earthly blessings; that home has been robbed of the greatest of all earthly jewels. The child of that home has suffered an irreparable loss, never to be regained.

On the other hand, the poorest home the humblest cottage in the dell, that contains a godly Mother who day by day dispenses her prayers, tears and smiles, her words of reproof and encouragement, her patience and love, her sunshine, and the lilt of a song that home, though poor as this world counts poverty, is as a casket that contains a priceless jewel.

If anyone should ask me which of my childhood memories I hold most dear, I should skip over the beloved wee lambies, the big Newfoundland dog, the bossies, the colts, the downy little goslings and chickens, my white doves, and numerous other childish treasures of my heart, and should tell of that hallowed twilight hour when, clasped tightly in my Mother's arms, we rocked to and fro in the big old comfy rocker, as she told me the most wonderful Bible stories and sang hymns of the Savior's love.

There was the story of Daniel in the lion's den, ever dear to the heart of a child the three Hebrew children in the fiery furnace - Joseph with his coat of many colors - Moses and Aaron with the children of Israel the life and sacrifice of Jesus, the beauty of that wonderful place called Heaven, which He had gone to prepare. All these and many others were as bright, golden threads woven through my childish training. At the age of five there were very few stories in the Bible I could not rise and tell when asked to do so. So much for an early Christian training.

Did any of you little children ever see the picture of the guardian angel watching over and protecting the tiny boy and girl that ran along plucking flowers at the edge of a great precipice? In the same miraculous way our dear Jesus watched over and protected me that happened again and again.

There was the time I climbed into the big old bucket that hung over the deep, black well with its rows and rows of moss-covered stones that formed its wall down, down, down as far as my inquisitive eyes could see, as I peered over the square, boarded enclosure which stood just on a level with my chin when I stood on tip-top-toe. Sometimes, when the sun was just right, and the bucket was resting on its little shelf just inside the well, I could see another little girl down there, and when I called a friendly little

"Hello!" to her, she would always echo back

"'Lo!" Reaching across the board enclosure that guarded the mouth of the well was the windlass with the crank that turned the roller and let down such yards and yards of big rope, and then drew up the great bucket brimming full of icy water.

The big handle had given me many hard, warning-whacks when I was experimenting with it, and Mother had warned me again and again not to go near the well; but one day when she was having company, I slipped down out of my chair at the table, away from her protecting care, and watchful eyes, and toddled straight to the well which held such mystery and interest.

What fun it would be to get hold of the swinging rope, get into the bucket and go down to visit the little girl I had seen reflected in the water! I had just climbed up on a box, leaned over, and was scrambling into the bucket, when Mother missed me. The silence pervading the air arousing her apprehensions, she flew to the door just in time to see the skirt of a pink dress and a little pair of feet disappearing as I crept over. The handle jarred loose from its holder and was beginning to turn when she caught it and snatched me from the mouth of the well into her arms.

The well was boarded up higher after that, and soon a windmill was put in. There was no more chance to play with the bucket, but surely the Father who watches over all had protected and spared my life. Bless His name.

When you read the next chapter you will see how I slipped from my Heavenly Father's table in just the same way, and leaned far out over the yawning black well of sin, and was just being allured into its depths, and the handle was beginning to turn, when Jesus rescued me and snatched me up into His arms and safety.

Then there was the time Mother had sent me out behind the barn to gather a pail of chips for the kitchen fire. This was one of my daily chores. My Father was a bridge contractor and builder, and there were always such piles of chips where he had been heaving the great timbers.

This particular evening I had on a little white dress with red moons in it, of which I was very proud. The bull, who, with the other cattle, was returning from the fields and gathering about the watering trough, evidently did not like those fine red moons in my dress. He had always been so gentle and harmless that danger from that source was never expected.

I was just at the corner of the barn, opposite a big pile of lumber, and had my bucket almost filled with chips. Frightened at the menacing way in which he advanced, I threw a chip at him and told him to "Go away." Without halting, however, he came on in a business-like, determined way I did not like.

Towering over me, he hit me with his forehead, and every time that I would get up he would bunt me so hard that I would fall down again in the muddy barnyard. Fortunately my Father had sawed his horns off sometime previous, but it was only the mercy of God that kept him from pawing me under his great, angry feet, and that gave me the presence of mind to crawl into and through the hollow place that ran under the pile of lumber, clear to the other end, thus escaping as he waited my reappearance.

I seemed perfectly numb; my mouth was filled with dirt and blood but tightly in my hands I clasped that bucket of chips. Mamma had sent me after chips, and chips I was going to take to Mamma.

Mother heard the sound of my crying but thought I was singing. (This did not speak very well for my singing.) However, she caught a sight of me through the window, and in a moment was by my side, .and when she gathered me up in her arms I was still clinging to the pail of chips, and it was not until she got me to the well and began to bathe me with cold water that I fainted away in her arms, releasing my hold upon them.

Being called upon to endure hardness as a good soldier, and to bring back precious souls for Jesus, no matter how hard the conflict, the Lord has put that within me which causes me to go through, refusing defeat, refusing even to be discouraged, and I often think of the little girl in the bedraggled, red-mooned dress, who brought home the bucket of chips; and someway I know that just as my Mother gathered me with the marks of combat, chips and all into her arms, He will meet me at the end of life's little day and gather me with my tight-clasped, precious burden, into His arms.

Riding the horses on my Father's farm was one of my greatest delights. Here again the Lord watched over me. One time when I was riding a high-mettled horse whom even the men-folks hardly risked themselves with, but who had succumbed condescendingly to my coaxings of sugar and pettings, he became frightened at the rattling of the wire fence, from which I sprang to his back, and began a mad gallop across the fields before I had well gotten my equilibrium.

He was running toward a barbed-wire fence. I knew that if he reached this fence it would ruin the horse, one which my Father valued highly, and decided to cling to his long, flowing mane and spring as he sprang, alighting on my feet, believing that he would slow down immediately. This I had done at other times, but now, unfortunately, I landed on an anthill, which turned my ankle and sprained it badly, severing some of the cords. But my life was spared, praise God, and in spite of crutches and pain I passed the examinations at the head of my class, and came in second for the scholarship, offered the one making the highest grades in the collegiate entrance examination.

During the early years of my life my Mother was Junior Sergeant-Major in the Salvation Army (in other words Superintendent of the Sunday School), and had a great flock of young people under her care. It was often a great effort for her to go to the five-mile distant corps where her work lay. When roads were poor or horse and carriage was not to be had, she would walk; and when roads were good, many's the time (when I was the age of five and six and seven), she carried me on the handle-bars of her bicycle, over hills and dust to the meeting, and kept up her Christian work.

These meetings were to me a great delight. It was a special joy to bring other little children to the penitent form to be prayed for. Very proud was I also of my Mother's imposing title. It seemed very grand and important to me, and not satisfied to await the next meeting at the barracks, I would often convert the big bedroom upstairs into a meeting house. Carrying chairs from other parts of the house thither and lining them up in rows I would conduct a meeting myself, and Mother, listening outside the door, would hear me solemnly announce

"Now, Sergeant-Major will lead in prayer." With this I would kneel and pray.

"Now, the Sergeant-Major will sing a solo."

Here followed the best imitation I knew how to produce of one of her sweet songs.

"Now, the Sergeant-Major will lead the testimony meeting" "Read the Word," and finally all the chairs were solemnly requested to bow their heads while the Sergeant-Major closed in prayer. And so you see God had His hand upon me, and the desires of my heart, .and the aspirations of my mind in these early days. It seemed indeed true that as a child of prayer He had in loving compassion known me, and in tender mercy called me for a purpose. Oh, Hallelujah!

At the Young People's rallies it was customary for the children to wear white sashes with colored mottoes embroidered upon them, and whilst upon the other children's sashes would be such words as "Jesus saves" or "God Is Love" etc., the one my Mother had worked for me read "God's Little Child." and so did she hold me, for the fulfilment of her prayer, through tempest and trial, sorrow and discouragement, that she might claim the promise and bring up the child in the way it should go, that when it was old it should not depart from it.

Tell me, little girls and boys who read this chapter; does your Mamma know Jesus? Does she pray for you that you may be a worker for Him some day, and have you given Him your heart while it is tender and you are in the beginning of Life?

CHAPTER IV. GIRLHOOD

"Foolishness is bound in the heart of a child."
Prov. 22:15

Then came the days of study in the little white school-house that stood on the corner a mile from our home. I was the only Salvationist child there, the other scholars being church members. At first they teased me about the Army with their shouting, their marching and their drum, for they were still a despised people in those days. I finally won over the hearts of the children, however, when I invented a drum from a round cheese box and with a ruler for a drumstick and a "Blood and Fire" banner made from a red tablecloth we marched round the school and played "Army".

Everything went well until it was learned that I had some little talent for elocution. The distance to the barracks being great, and the churches seeming much more popular, I began going to the Methodist church where my father had formerly been a choir leader. Once invited to take part in their entertainments I was soon received in other churches and appearing on the programs the country round.

We received great help and teaching along the lines of elocution, dialogues and plays by the church instructors in this art. After competing with others in the W. C. T. U. work, a silver and later a gold medal was awarded me.

Except for the temperance work, however, very few of the selections or plays were anything but comic. Upon asking preachers whether they would prefer something sacred they would invariably answer:

"Oh, give us something humorous; something comical to make the people laugh. That last Irish recitation was grand. Give us something like, that."

As I recited, the audience would laugh and clap and laugh again until the tears came to their eyes, and I was very popular indeed with the churches in those days, a great deal more so than I am now, mayhap.

As years went by I passed from grammar school to high, and became still more interested in the entertainments of the church. There were the oyster suppers, the strawberry festivals, the Christmas trees, and always the concerts to follow, for which tickets were sold "to help God pay His debts and help support the church, "I supposed then. But I have learned now that our God is so richly able to supply the funds for His work that He need not resort to any such methods.

The praise and applause of the people was very alluring to some of us younger ones, and we often talked together of going on the stage, arguing that the church was giving us a good training on this line and that anyway there was not much difference whether a play or a concert was given in the church or at the theatre.

My next step on the downward path was when I began reading novels from the Sunday School library (for a novel is a novel whether in a paper or a cloth-bound cover). And when I had devoured them I learned where more could be obtained.

The next luring of the tempter came when I was asked by a member of the choir as to whether I had been to the moving-picture theatre that week.

I told her:

"No," that I had never seen any motion pictures outside of the church. She looked at me in such a condescending, pitying way that my pride was stung and I decided to go. I did not tell my Mother, however, and felt very guilty in entering until I saw several church members and a Sunday School teacher there; then I felt better (it surely must be all right if they were there), and settled down to enjoy the pictures.

Athletic, and fond of out-door sports, next in line came costume skating carnivals and then my first college ball. I was now well advanced in the high school. When I brought home the engraved invitation card, Mother flatly refused her permission for me to go and it took a great deal of pleading and coaxing to gain an unwilling consent. My dress and slippers were purchased and I went to my first dance radiantly happy on the exterior, but a little heavy and conscience-stricken on the interior, for I knew that Mother was sad and praying alone at home.

It seemed to be a very proper affair, however. My first dancing partner was the Presbyterian preacher. Other good (?) church members were there - surely Mother must be mistaken or a little old-fashioned in her ideas. How lovely it all seemed, the orchestra, the flowers, the attention paid me, the fine clothes, and the well-appointed luncheon!

Ah, sin, with what dazzling beauty, with what refinement and velvet dost thou cover thy claws!

How alluring are the fair promises with which thou enticest the feet of youth! How cunning are the devices of the enemy! How smoothly and craftily he lays his plans and weaves the net which he draws ever tighter and tighter, illuming the future and its prospects with rose colors and fair painted promises, the fruit of which, once plucked crumbles into gray ashes in the hand of him who runneth after it.

My future and educational prospects looked promising. No effort or labor was counted too great upon the part of my parents to send me to school, and indeed it was no little matter for them ten miles must be covered each day, five in the morning and five at night, on the train or with horse and carriage, despite country roads, with their mud or rain or snow.

There was introduced into our class room at this time, a text-book entitled "High School Physical Geography", which delved into the problems of earth formation, rock strata, etc., and learnedly described the origin of life and the process of evolution. There were quotations from Darwin and other authorities on these weighty subjects. Explaining the origin of life upon this planet, it taught us that from the sea, with its slime, seaweed and fungus growth, insect life appeared. From insect life came animal life, and through continuous processes of evolution at last man appeared who, of course, was higher than the monkeys or any other creature.

How these theories or teachings impressed other students I cannot say, but they had a remarkable effect upon me.

"Man? A process of evolution?

- Why, then God had not created him at all, as the Bible said He did preachers were true when they said there were errors and mistakes in the Bible."

On and on raced the thoughts in my young mind until I reached the point:

"Well, then, if the Bible is mistaken in one place it is very apt to be mistaken in others. Its information is not reliable, and I guess there's no God at all, and that's why Christians act so pious in church on Sundays and do as they please through the week."

"No, I guess there is no God." Even the existence of the big moon and the twinkling stars had been explained by science. The sun, once a great mass of molten lava, had acquired a whirling motion and thrown off all these other planets, earth, moon and stars. Nothing about God, just science and a logical outcome of conditions now revealed, by wise astronomers who had studied it all out through great telescopes (which had cost fabulous sums of money and taken many years to invent); and therefore they knew all about it.

This book raised so many questions in my mind that I delved deeper into other infidelistic theories.

So interested did I become that I wrote an article to the "Family Herald and Weekly Star," published at Montreal, then Canada's leading paper. My inquiries were answered by Archbishop Hamilton and many others. Arguments both for and against the book and its teachings were brought out.

Is it any wonder that our pulpits are filled with infidels and higher critics today?

Out of the letters that poured in for months from England, New Zealand, Australia, and all parts of America, as well as from my own land, each containing a different explanation, not one said:

"Child, the Bible is true. Take the simple Word of God and believe it just as it reads."

The more I read and observed the lives of Christians, the more sceptical of the reality of God I became. (How I could ever have doubted is today a puzzle and a shame to me.) The devil must have blinded my eyes for a time to the genuine Christians about me. All that I could see was empty profession. I saw men singing in the choir or sitting in the pews on Sunday and attending all sorts of worldly functions during the week. I began reading my Bible, to see whether it contradicted itself and how it compared with the books which I had read. Oh, I must know the truth was there anything in religion?

Every time I had an opportunity I questioned and cross-questioned each Christian that I could get hold of. But I did not seem to get far. My first attempt was made upon my Mother. I had been thinking earnestly upon the subject, and just as she was coming up the steep cellar steps with a pan of milk in her hands, I met her with the question:

"Mother, how do you know there is a God?"

Poor dear, she was so surprised that she nearly fell backwards, down the steps. She explained things the best she knew how, bringing forth Scriptures, and pointing to creation with all its wonders as proving the handiwork of a Creator.

Each attempt at explanation I met with the learned words of those books and the superior (?) twentieth-century wisdom of my seventeen summers books and wisdom which left mothers and Bibles far behind. Her arguments seemed to shrink to nothing, and her eyes opened with astonishment as she sat down suddenly on the kitchen chair, unable to get a word in edgeways.

My next attempt was made upon the minister when he came to our house to tea. Mother was out in the kitchen preparing the proverbial ministerial chicken dinner, but I had business in the parlor, ostensibly displaying the family album, but in reality endeavoring to probe him with the questions upon my mind.

"Does the Lord ever perform any miracles or heal any sick folks now?" I asked.

"Why, no child, the day of miracles is over," was his surprised reply. "People are expected to use the intelligence and wisdom the Lord has given them along medical and surgical lines these are really miraculous, you know."

"But doesn't it say, over here in James 5:14, "If any are sick among you to let him call for the elders of the church; and let them pray over him, anointing him with oil in the name of the Lord: And the prayer of faith shall save the sick, and they shall recover'?"

"And is there not a scripture that says, 'Jesus Christ is the same yesterday, and today, and forever and 'He that believeth on Me, the works that I do shall he do also; and greater works than these shall he do; because I go unto my Father"

"How do you reconcile the fact that the Lord no longer does such miraculous things, with these scriptures?"

My questions were evaded, and I was made to feel that I was but a mere child, and therefore could not understand these matters. They were never explained to my satisfaction.

Alarmed over my attitude and questions, my Mother asked me to join some church. When I made excuses she offered to take me to all the different churches, asking me to study the teachings of each of them and to join the one that seemed best. I replied that I felt I was doing enough church work now, with the entertainments and concerts, and added, in a self-righteous way, that I thought I was just as good as any of the others I didn't see any particular difference in our lives, whether I was a member of the church or not did not matter.

"Well, let us go to the Salvation Army special meetings tonight. It is a long time since we have been there together."

Poor Mother! Will I ever forget her face when she found they were having an entertainment there that night, and the first selection rendered after we entered was:

"High diddle, diddle,

The cat and the fiddle,

The cow jumped over the moon!" acted out by one of the local officers, amid the applause of the laughing audience. He was dressed to represent a colored minstrel.

Later we attended the special services being conducted by the Brigadier, his wife and daughter who invited me very sweetly to give my heart to Jesus. I argued with her that there was no God, nothing in the Bible. She seemed to get into deep waters and went for her mother, who also begged me to come to the .altar. Then they sent for the father, and before long I was the center of a group. My Mother on the outskirts, listening with blushing face while I set forth, in my ignorance, my opinion regarding evolution.

Oh, dear Jesus, how could I ever have doubted You when You have been so good, so merciful and so true to me all the days of my life!

19

Mother cried bitterly all the long drive home, and all the reproach she laid upon me was:

"Oh, Aimee, I never dreamed that I should brim up a daughter who would talk as you have before those people tonight! After all my years as a Christian, after my prayers and my work in that corps, you of all people, to talk like this! Oh, where have I failed? Oh! OH!! O-H!!!"

Conscience-stricken, and shamed before her grief, I fled to my room, as soon as we arrived, to think things over. I certainly loved my Mother; to cause her grief and sorrow was the last thing in this wide world which I wished to do "and yet and yet."

Not pausing to light the lamp, I went over to my bedroom window, threw it open wide and sat down on the floor with my elbows on the window-sill, my chin propped on my hands, and gazed reflectively up at the starry floors of Heaven and at the great white silvery moon sailing majestically toward me from the eastern sky, before I finished my broken sentence "I wonder if there really is a God?

Who is right? What is the truth?"

The white mantle of snow which covered the fields and the trees, glistened in the clear, frosty air, and

My! How big that moon looked up there, and how ten million stars seemed to wink and blink and twinkle! I drew a comforter round me and sat on and on, unmindful of the cold, looking up at the Milky Way, the big dipper, and other familiar luminaries.

Surely, there m-u-s-t be a God up there back of them all. They seemed to breathe and emanate from His very presence and nearness.

At school we had studied the planets and how each rotated and revolved upon its own axis, and in its own orbit without friction or confusion. It was all so big, so high, so above the reach and ken of mortal man surely a DIVINE hand must hold and control this wonderful solar system Why! How near God seemed right now!

Suddenly, without stopping to think, I threw both arms impulsively out of the window and, reaching toward Heaven, cried:

"Oh God! If there be a God reveal yourself to me!"

The cry came from my very heart. In reality, a whisper was all that came from my lips but just that whisper from an honest, longing heart, was enough to echo through the stars and reach the Father's throne. Up there, He whose ear is ever open to the cries of His little children, heard me and answered. Bless His Name.

Oh, if every doubter and professed infidel would just breathe that one sincere prayer to God, He would reveal Himself to them as He did to me, for; He is no respecter of persons. Hallelujah!

20

CHAPTER V. SALVATION AND THE BAPTISM OF THE HOLY SPIRIT

"And it shall come to pass, that before they call, I will answer; and while they are yet speaking, I will hear"
Isa. 65:24

Our prayer-answering God who sitteth up-on the throne, whose ear is ever open to our cry, and whose heart is touched by our infirmities, was already answering the cry of this poor, unworthy child. He had set on foot a chain of events which was to lead not only to the salvation and baptism of my own soul, but which was to lead me out into His vineyard and make me a worker in His dear service.

It was just a few days after my prayer at the open window of my bedroom that (my Father having come into school for me) we were driving along Main Street on the way home, eagerly talking over and planning my parts in the grand Christmas affairs and concerts in the various churches and halls then looming above us. How pretty the store windows were in their Christmas dress of green and red and tinsel!

But look! Over there on the left hand side of the street, there was a new sign on a window which I had not seen before, and it read:

PENTECOSTAL MISSION

MEETINGS EVERY NIGHT

ALL DAY SUNDAY

Turning to my Father, I said: "Daddy, I'd like to go in there tomorrow night. I believe that's the place I have heard about where they jump and dance and fall under the power, and do such strange things. It would be loads of fun to go and see them."

And thus it was that the next evening found us seated in the back seats (where we could see it all) of the little Pentecostal Mission which had recently come to town. We were to have a rehearsal in the town hall for one of our plays, later on in the evening. This had just left me time to come in to the Mission.

They seemed to be a very ordinary lot of people, none of the wealthy or well-known citizens of the town were there, and dressed as I was, with the flowers on my hat, a gold chain and locket, and rings on my fingers, I felt just a little bit above the status of those round about me, and looked on with an amused air as they shouted, danced and prayed.

A man, whom I knew to be one of the town milk-men, shook from head to foot under the power, then fell backward and lay stretched out on the floor praising the Lord. At all these things I giggled foolishly, not understanding it and thinking it all very laughable.

Soon a tall young man, (six feet two), rose to his feet on the platform and taking his Bible in his hand, opened it and began to read. I could not help admiring his frank, open, kindly face, the Irish-blue eyes with the light of Heaven in them, and the bushy hair, one brown curl of which would insist on falling clown close to his eye, no matter how often he brushed it back with his fingers.

As he spoke with earnest zeal I took him in from head to foot (little knowing that this young man was soon to be my husband). His text was found in the second chapter of Acts, 38th and 39th verses.

(There is one thing about a Pentecostal meeting. You cannot go there very long without learning that there is a second chapter to the book of Acts. I learned this in my first meeting.)

The evangelist Robert Semple, by name began his discourse with the first word of his text:

"Repent." Oh how he did repeat that word Repent! REPENT!! R-E-P-E-N-T!!! Over and over again. How I did wish he would stop saying that awful word. It seemed to pierce like an arrow through my heart, for he was preaching under divine inspiration and in power and demonstration of the Holy Spirit. He really spoke as though he believed there was a Jesus and a Holy Spirit, not some vague, mythical, intangible shadow, something away off yonder in the clouds, but a real, living, vital, tangible, moving reality dwelling in our hearts and lives making us His temple causing us to walk in Godliness, holiness and adoration in His presence.

22

There were no announcements of oyster suppers or Christmas entertainments or sewing circles made no appeal for money. Not even a collection was taken. It was just God, God, God from one, end to the other, and his words seemed to rain down upon me, and every one of them hurt some particular part of my spirit and life until I could not tell where I was hurt the worst.

"Repent!" The evangelist went on to say that if the love of the world was in us the love of the Father was not there: theatres, moving pictures, dancing, novels, fancy-dress skating rinks (why, it just looked as if somebody had told him I was there, so vividly did he picture my own life and walk), worldly and rag-time music, etc., he condemned wholesale, and declared that all the people who were wrapped up in this sort of thing were of the devil, and were on their way to hell, and that unless they repented and that right speedily, renouncing the world, the flesh and the devil, they would be lost eternally damned forever.

I did not do any more laughing, I assure you. I sat up straight in my seat. With eyes and ears wide open I drank in every word he said. After he had finished with the word "Repent," and explained what true salvation meant the death, burial and resurrection that we would know as we were identified with our Lord, he began to preach on the next verse

"And ye shall receive the gift of the Holy Ghost. For the promise is unto you, and to your children, and to all that are afar off, even as many as the Lord our God shall call."

Here he began to preach the baptism of the Holy Spirit, declaring that the message of salvation and the incoming of the Spirit should be preached side by side and hand in hand, and that for a Christian to live without the baptism of the Holy Spirit was to live in an abnormal condition not in accordance with God's wishes. He told how the Holy Spirit was received in Bible days and how the recipients of the Spirit had spoken in other tongues languages they had never learned as the Spirit gave them utterance.

He put particular emphasis on the "other tongues" spoken of in Acts 2:4, and boldly affirmed that this was the Bible evidence of the baptism of the Holy Spirit.

"Tongues?" Said I to myself "Tongues? Why, I wonder what that is? I never remember having heard of anything like that in the Bible before."

Then, to add still more to my amazement, the speaker himself suddenly broke out talking in tongues, in a loud voice, with his eyes closed and his hands outstretched in my direction.

To me it was the voice of God thundering into my soul awful words of conviction and condemnation, and though the message was spoken in 39 tongues it seemed as though God had said to me

"YOU are a poor, lost, miserable, hell-deserving sinner! "I want to say right here that I knew this was God speaking by His Spirit through the lips of clay. There is a verse in the 14th chapter of I Corinthians which says the speaking in tongues is a sign to the unbeliever. This was certainly true in my case. From the moment I heard that young man speak with tongues to this day I have never doubted for the shadow of a second that there was a God, and that He had shown me my true condition as a poor, lost, miserable, hell-deserving sinner.

No one had ever spoken to me like this before.

I had been petted, loved and perhaps a little spoiled: told how smart and good I was. But thank God that He tells the truth. He does not varnish us nor pat us on the back or give us any little sugar-coated pills, but shows us just where we stand, vile and sinful and undone, outside of Jesus and His precious blood.

All my amusement and haughty pride had gone.

My very soul had been stripped before God there was a God, and I was not ready to meet Him.

Oh, how could I have looked down upon these dear people and felt that I was better than they? Why, I was not even worthy to black their shoes. They were saints and I was a sinner.

We had to slip out early, before the service was over, and how I got through the rehearsal I cannot say, but one thing I knew, and that is that during the next seventy-two hours I lived through the most miserable three days I had ever known up to that time.

Conviction! Oh! I could scarcely eat or rest or sleep. Study was out of the question.

"Poor, lost, miserable, hell-deserving sinner" rang in my ears over and over .again. I could see those closed eyes and that outstretched hand that pointed to my shrinking, sinful soul that was bared before the eyes of my Maker.

I began enumerating the many things which I would have to give up in order to become a Christian there was the dancing. I was willing to part with that, the novels, the theatre, my worldly instrumental music. I asked myself about each of them and found that I did not count them dear as compared with the joy of salvation and knowing my sins forgiven.

There was just one thing, however, that I found myself unwilling and seemingly unable to do. I knew that I could not be a Christian and recite those foolish Irish recitations and go through those plays and dialogues. A child of God must be holy and consecrated, with a conversation covered with the blood of Jesus. My Bible said that even for one idle word (let alone foolish words); we should have to give an account before the judgment throne of God. Yet it was too late now to cancel my promises for Christmas, too late to get others to fill my place. Evidently there was nothing to do but wait until after Christmas in order to become a Christian.

But how could I wait? I was desperately afraid.

I trembled with conviction. It seemed as though every moment which I lived outside of God and without repentance toward Him was lived in the most awful peril and gravest danger of being cast into hell without mercy. Oh, that every sinner who reads these words might feel the same awful conviction upon his soul!

The second and third day I fell to praying something like this:

"Oh God, I do want to be a Christian. I want to ever love and serve You. I want to confess my sin and be washed in the blood of Jesus Christ, But oh, please just let me live until after Christmas, and then I will give my heart to You. Have mercy on me, Lord. Oh, don't; don't let me die until after Christmas."

Many people smile now as I testify of that awful terror that seized upon my soul, but the eternal welfare of my soul was at stake for me it was going to be life or death, Heaven or hell forever.

At the end of the third day, while driving home from school, I could stand it no longer. The lowering skies above, the trees, the fields, the very road beneath me seemed to look down upon me with displeasure, and I could see written everywhere

"Poor lost, miserable, hell-deserving sinner!"

Utterly at the end of myself not stopping to think what preachers or entertainment committees or anyone else would think I threw up my hands, and- all alone in that country road, I screamed aloud toward the Heavens:

"Oh, Lord God, be merciful to me, a sinner!"

Immediately the most wonderful change took place in my soul. Darkness passed away and light entered. The sky was filled with brightness, the trees, the fields, and the little snow birds flitting to and fro were praising the Lord and smiling upon me.

So conscious was I of the pardoning blood of Jesus that I seemed to feel it flowing over me.

I discovered that my face was bathed in tears, which dropped on my hands as I held the reins.

And without effort or apparent thought on my part I was singing that old, familiar hymn:
"Take my life and let it be
Consecrated, Lord, to Thee;
Take my moments and my days,
Let them flow in ceaseless praise."

I was singing brokenly between my sobs:
"Take my life and let it be

Consecrated, Lord, to Thee."

24

My whole soul was flowing out toward God, my Father.

"M-Y F-A-T-H-E-R!" Oh, glory to Jesus! I had a Heavenly Father! No more need for fear, but His love and kindness and protection were now for me.

When I came to the part in the song that said:

"Take my hands and let them move
At the impulse of Thy love"

I knew there would be no more worldly music for me, and it has been hymns from that time forth.

And when I sang:
"Take my feet and let them be
Swift and beautiful for Thee'
I knew that did not mean at the dance hall nor the skating rink. Bless the Lord.

"Take my lips and let them sing
Always, only, for my King."
No more foolish recitations and rag-time songs.

"Oh, Jesus, I love Thee,
I know Thou art mine;
For Thee all the follies
Of sin I resign."

Song after song burst from my lips. I shouted aloud and praised God all the way home. I had been redeemed!

Needless to say I did not take part in the entertainments, and many in our town thought me fanatical and very foolish. Nevertheless the succeeding days were brim full of joy and happiness How dearly I loved God's Word! I wanted it under my pillow when I went to sleep and in my, hands when my eyes opened in the morning. At school, where I used to have a novel hidden away inside of my Algebra and Geometry, there was now a little New Testament, and I was studying each passage that referred to the baptism of the Holy Spirit.

Of all the promises in which I found comfort there was none, I believe, that compared with the simple promises of Matthew 7: 7 to 11.

"Ask, and it shall be given you; seek, and ye shall find; knock, and it shall be opened unto you:

"For everyone that asketh receiveth and he that seeketh findeth; and to him that knocketh it shall be opened." Here He assured me that if I asked bread He would not give me a stone, also that He was more willing to give me the Holy Spirit than earthly parents were to give good gifts to their children.

I would get about so far with my reading, and Oh, the Bible seemed to me all so new, so living and speaking, (and it was God speaking to me), that unable to wait another moment, I would excuse myself from the room, go down to the basement, fall upon my knees and begin to pray:

"Oh Lord, baptize me with the Holy Spirit. Lord, you said the promise was unto even as many as were afar off, even as many as the Lord our God should call. Now Lord, you've called me, the promise is unto me; fill me just now."

The girls found me thus praying and did not know what to make of me, so utterly was I changed.

No more putting glue in teacher's chair or helping to lock him in the gymnasium, or practising dance steps in the corridors at noon hour. A wonderful change had taken place all old things had passed away and all things had become new. I had been born again and was a new creature in Christ Jesus.

Each day the hunger for the baptism of the Holy Spirit became stronger and stronger, more and more intense until, no longer contented to stay in school, my mind no longer on my studies, I would slip away to the tarrying meetings where the dear saints met to pray for those who were seeking the baptism of the Holy Spirit.

What wonderful hours those were! What a revelation to my soul! It was as though Heaven had come down to earth. So much of the time was I away from school that I began to fall behind in my studies for the first time, .and although the final examinations were near, I could not make myself take any interest in Algebra or Geometry or Chemistry, or anything but the baptism of the Holy Spirit and preparing to meet my soon-coming Savior in the air.

Then came the day when the principal of the High School sent a letter to my Mother which told her that unless I paid more attention to my studies I was certainly going to fail.

And to make matters worse, the same day one of the S. A. officers came to call upon Mother, saying:

"Now, Sister, we don't mind so much the other people going to that Pentecostal Mission, but we really are surprised and think you do wrong in letting your daughter go. You being connected with the work for so many years, it sets a bad example to other people for you to allow her to be in any way associated with them. "They told her also that this so-called power was all excitement or hypnotism and false.

When I went home that night Mother was waiting for me. She gave me a very serious talking to, and wound up by issuing the ultimatum:

"Now, if I ever hear of your leaving school and going down to that Mission again, or to the tarrying meetings, I will have to keep you home altogether. I will not have you talked about in this way."

I went to school on the train the next morning as the roads were banked high with snow, and all the way in I was looking out of the window at the falling flakes of snow and praying for the Lord to fix it all some way so that I should be able to knock until He opened or else to baptize me at once.

Walking from the train to High School it was necessary to pass both the Mission and the Sister's home where I often went to tarry for the baptism. As I went past the latter I looked longingly at the windows, hoping that she might be there and that I could speak to her from the sidewalk without going in and thus disobeying Mother's command, but not a sign of her did I see.

I walked slowly past, looking sadly and hungrily back all the way; then finally came to a halt on the sidewalk and said to myself:

"Well, here now, Jesus is coming soon and you know it is more important for you to receive the Holy Spirit than to pass all the examinations in the world. You need the Holy Spirit oil in your vessel with your lamp in order to be ready for His appearing.

"As you have to make a choice between going to school and seeking the baptism I guess you won't go to school at all today, but will just go back to the sister's house and make a whole day of seeking the baptism."

With this I turned and walked quickly back to the house, rang the doorbell and went in. I told the sister my dilemma, and she said quietly:

"Let's tell Father all about it." So we got down and began to pray. She asked the Lord in her prayer either to baptize me then and there or to arrange it some way that I could stay until I received my baptism.

The Lord heard this prayer, and outside the window the snow which had been falling in light flakes, began to come down like a blinding blizzard.

My Heavenly Father sent out His angels to stir up some of those big, old, fleecy clouds of His, and down came the snow and causing the window-panes to rattle, and one of our old-fashioned Canadian blizzards was on. The entire day was spent in prayer and at on going to the depot to see about my train home, the ticket agent said, through the window:

"Sorry, Miss, but the train is not running tonight. The roads are blocked with snow. We are not able to get through." Oh, Hallelujah! I was not sorry, a bit.

Then the thought came "This will not do you much good, for you will have to call Mother on the telephone and she will ask you to go to her friend's home to stay, and warn you not to go near the Mission." But when I went to the telephone and gave the number, Central said:

"Sorry, wires all down on account of the storm."

This time I did shout "Glory "and ran almost all the way back to the sister's home.

The storm increased, and as fast as the men endeavored to open a pathway, the Lord filled it in with mountains of white snow, until at last all thought of getting through while the storm lasted was .abandoned.

Oh, how earnestly I sought the baptism of the Spirit. Sometimes when people come to the altar now and sit themselves down in a comfortable position, prop their heads up on one hand, and begin to ask God in a languid, indifferent way for the Spirit, it seems to me that they do not know what real seeking is.

Time was precious, for while man was working so hard to shovel out the snow, and God had His big clouds all working to shovel it in, I must do my part in seeking with all my heart.

Friday I waited before the Lord until midnight.

Saturday morning, rising at the break of day, before anyone was astir, in the house, and going into the parlor, I kneeled down by the big Morris chair in the corner, with a real determination in my heart.

My Bible had told me "the kingdom of Heaven suffereth violence, and the violent take it by force." Matt. 11:12. I read the parable again of the man who had knocked for bread and found that it was not because he was his friend, but because of his importunity, that the good man within the house had risen up and given him as many loaves as he had need of. Now Jesus was my friend; He had bidden me knock, and assured me that He would open unto me. He had invited me to ask, promising that I should receive, and that the empty He would not turn hungry away. I began to seek in desperate earnest, and remember saying:

"Oh, Lord, I am so hungry for your Holy Spirit. You have told me that in the day when I seek with my whole heart you will be found of me. Now, Lord, I am going to stay right here until you pour out upon me the promise of the Holy Spirit for whom you commanded me to tarry, if I die of starvation. I am so hungry for Him I can't wait another day. I will not eat another meal until you baptize me."

You ask if I was not afraid of getting a wrong spirit or being hypnotized, as my parents feared.

There was no such fear in my heart. I trusted my Heavenly Father implicitly according to Luke 11:11, wherein He (assured me that if I asked for bread He would not give me a stone. I knew that my Lord was not bestowing serpents and scorpions on His blood-washed children when they asked for bread. Had He not said, if your earthly fathers know how to bestow good gifts upon their children "how much more shall your Heavenly Father give the Holy Spirit to them that ask Him?" Luke 11:13.

After praying thus earnestly, storming Heaven, as it were, with my pleadings for the Holy Spirit, a quietness seemed to steal over me, the holy presence of the Lord to envelop me. The Voice of the Lord spoke tenderly:

"Now, child, cease your strivings and your begging; just begin to praise Me, and in simple, childlike faith, receive ye the Holy Ghost."

Oh, it was not hard to praise Him. He had become so near and so inexpressibly dear to my heart.

Hallelujah! Without effort on my part I began to say:

"Glory to Jesus! Glory to Jesus!! GLORY TO JESUS!!!" Each time that I said "Glory to Jesus!" It seemed to come from a deeper place in my being than the last, and in a deeper voice, until great waves of "Glory to Jesus" were rolling from my toes up; such adoration and praise I had never known possible.

All at once my hands and arms began to shake, gently at first, then violently, until my

27

whole body was shaking under the power of the Holy Spirit.

I did not consider this at all strange, as I knew how the batteries we experimented with in the laboratory at college hummed and shook and trembled under the power of electricity, and there was the Third Person of the Trinity coming into my body in all His fulness, making me His dwelling, "the temple of the Holy Ghost." Was it any wonder that this poor human frame of mine should quake beneath the mighty movings of His power?

How happy I was, Oh how happy! Happy just to feel His wonderful power taking control of my being. Oh Glory! That sacred house is so sweet to me, the remembrance of its sacredness thrills me as I write.

Almost without my notice my body slipped gently to the floor, and I was lying stretched out under the power of God, but felt as though caught up and floating upon the billowy clouds of glory. Do not understand by this that I was unconscious of my surroundings, for I was not, but Jesus was more real and near than the things of earth round about me. The desire to praise and worship and adore Him flamed up within my soul. He was so wonderful, so glorious, and this poor tongue of mine so utterly incapable of finding words with which to praise Him.

My lungs began to fill and heave under the power as the Comforter came in. The cords of my throat began to twitch my chin began to quiver, and then to shake violently, but Oh, so sweetly! My tongue began to move up and down and sideways in my mouth. Unintelligible sounds as of stammering lips and another tongue, spoken of in Isaiah 28:11 began to issue from my lips. This stammering of different syllables, then words, then connected sentences, was continued for some time as the Spirit was teaching me to yield to Him.

Then suddenly, out of my innermost being flowed rivers of praise in other tongues as the Spirit gave utterance (Acts 2:4), and Oh I knew that He was praising Jesus with glorious language, clothing Him with honor and glory which I felt but never could have put into words.

How wonderful that I, even I, away down here in 1908, was speaking in an unknown tongue, just as the believers had in Bible days at Ephesus and at Caesarea and that now He had come of whom Jesus had said "He will glorify Me"

I shouted and sang and laughed and talked in tongues until it seemed that I was too full to hold another bit of blessing lest I should burst with the glory. The Word of God was true. The promise was really to them that were afar off, even as many as the Lord our God should call. The comforter had come, lifting my soul in ecstatic praises to Jesus in a language I had never learned. I remember having said:

"Oh Lord, can you not take me right on up to Heaven now? I am so near anyway. Do I have to go back to that old world again?"

"Hypnotism," you say? If so, it is a remarkably long spell and an exceedingly delightful one which has lasted for eleven years, making me love Jesus with all my heart and long for His appearing.

Besides this you must take into consideration that there was no one in the room to hypnotize me. I was all alone when I was saved, and all alone when I received the baptism of the Holy Spirit.

"Demon power" "all of the devil," someone may say. If so the devil must have recently gotten soundly converted, for that which entered into my soul makes me to love and obey my. Lord and Savior Jesus Christ, to exalt the blood and honor the Holy Ghost.

"Excitement," you say? Never! It has stood the test too long, dear unbeliever. In sickness, in sorrow, even in the gates of death He has proved Himself to be the Comforter whom Jesus said He would send.

Hearing me speaking in the tongues and praising the Lord, the dear Sister of the home in which I stayed, came down stairs and into the parlor, weeping and praising the Lord with me. Soon Brother Semple and other saints gathered in. What shouting and rejoicing! Oh hallelujah! And yet with all the joy and glory, there was a stillness and a solemn hush pervading my whole being.

Walking down the street, I kept saying to myself:

"Now you must walk very softly and carefully, with unshod feet, in the presence of the

King lest you grieve this tender, gentle dove who has come into your being to make you His temple and to abide with you forever."

The next day was Sunday. The storm had cleared away; the sun was shining down in its melting warmth. Attending the morning services at the Mission, we partook of the Lord's Supper, and as we meditated upon His wonderful love, His blood that was shed for us, His body that was broken on the tree, it was more than I could bear, and I went down to the floor under the power again. Oh who can describe that exceeding weight of glory as He revealed Himself, my crucified Savoir, my resurrected Lord, my coming King!

School-mates and friends were standing up to look over the seats to see what in the world had happened to me, but I was lost again with Jesus whom my soul loved, speaking in tongues and shaking under the power.

One man was so scandalized to see me lying on the floor that he got up and left the meeting, and going to the telephone called my Mother. (The wires which had been down during the storm, unknown to me, had been repaired and were up by this time.) He said:

"You had better come into town and see to that daughter of yours, for she is lying on the floor in the Mission, before all the people, chattering like a monkey."

Poor Mother! She was frantic to think her daughter should so far forget her dignity -as to disgrace herself in such a manner. She called me to the 'phone, and I heard her dear voice saying:

"Aimee! What in the world is this that I hear about you lying on the floor in the Mission? What in the world does this all mean?"

I tried to answer, but broke out speaking in tongues again.

"What's that?" she demanded. I tried to explain. Then came her voice, stern and forbidding.

"You just wait 'til I get there, my lady; I will tend to you!"

(Just to relieve the tension on your mind I will run a little ahead of my story and tell you that my dear Mother has her own baptism now, and spoke with other tongues ON THE FLOOR, TOO!)

Returning to the Sister's home, I sat down at the organ, awaiting in some trepidation and fear, I confess, the coming of my Mother. To keep my courage up I sang over and over that old, familiar hymn:

"I will never leave thee nor forsake thee;
In my hands I'll hold thee;
In my arms I'll fold thee;
I am thy Redeemer; I will care for thee!"

What would Mother say? Would she understand? Why, it had not been so very long since the power of God used to come down in the dear old Salvation Army. Had I not heard her tell how Brother Kitchen (whom they used to call "the Kitchen that God lived in".) had shaken as he kneeled in prayer, until he had gone clear across the platform and had lain stretched out under the power at the other side? Had I not heard my Father tell how the old-time Methodist Church used to have this same power? Praying God for strength and wisdom, I sang on

"E'en though the night
Be dark within the valley,
Just beyond is shining,
An eternal light."

Six o'clock arrived so did Mother! I heard the jingle of the sleigh-bells suddenly stop in response to my Mother's "whoa!" Then an imperious ring of the bell shivered the tense silence within the house. Slipping down from the organ stool I caught my coat and hat in my hand as I hastened to the door. Mother met me, and with:

"My lady, you come right out and get in here this minute," lost no time in bundling me into the cutter. The Sister and Brother both tried to get a word in edgeways, to reason with and explain to her, but she would hear none of it, and in a moment we were off.

All the way home Mother scolded and cried and almost broke her heart over her daughter

29

that had as she supposed, been cast under some dire spell by those .awful people, who had now been nick-named by the town, "The Holy Rollers." Oh, praise the Lord! No matter what the devil called them he had to admit that they were holy anyway, and that's more than he could have said of many professing denominations, now, isn't it?

Being an only child, loved and petted, it needed only a word of scolding or remonstrance to bring the tears, but now, when she was scolding me more severely and saying more harsh things than she ever had in my life, for some mysterious reason I couldn't shed a tear. I felt duty bound to squeeze out a few tears, out of respect to her feelings, but I could not do it to help myself. All I could do was sing and sing and sing all the way

"Joys are flowing like a river,
Since the Comforter has come;
He abides with me forever,
Makes the trusting heart His home."

The Spirit within rose up and filled me with joy unspeakable and full of glory. Poor Mother would turn to me and say:

"Oh Aimee! Do stop that singing. I can't understand how you can sing; you know your Mother's heart is breaking. Surely you don't call that a fruit of the Spirit." But it did not seem as if I were singing at all: it just seemed to sing itself and came out without any effort.

"Blessed quietness, holy quietness, what assurance in my soul;
On the stormy sea, Jesus speaks to me, and the billows cease to roll."

Upon our arrival home we found my Father sitting by the dining-room fire, with his head in his hands, saying:

"Humph! Humph! Humph!" He always did that when he felt very badly over something. Leading me up to him, Mother said:

"Now I want you to tell your Father all about it. Tell him the way you acted and how you lay on the floor before those people." Well, it certainly did look dreadful to tell it, but Oh, that something kept whispering and echoing in my heart:

"E'en though the night
Be dark within the valley,
Just beyond is shining
An eternal day."

When at last they sent me to my room, I kneeled down quickly and began to pray. It happened that I was kneeling beside the stove-pipe hole and could not help overhearing a part of the conversation between my parents. It was something like this:

"Oh, what shall we do? Those people have got our girl under their influence, hypnotized her, mesmerized her or something."

"It is perfectly useless to argue with her, for no matter what we say, she only thinks she is being persecuted and will hold to it all the more tenaciously."

"Oh, what shall we do?" With this the door closed and I heard no more.

Oh, how can I describe the joy and the glory that had come within my soul? That deep-settled peace, that knowledge that He would lead and guide and would bring all things out right.

When next my Mother permitted me to go to school she told me of the decision which they had come to, namely, that if I went near those Pentecostal people once more they would take me away from school for good, education or no education.

As she told me this the Holy Spirit gave me wisdom to make this reply:

"Mother, the Bible says that children are to obey their parents in the Lord, and if you can show me by the Word of God that what I have received is not in accordance with Bible teaching, or show me any place where we are told that the baptism of the Holy Spirit, with the Bible evidence, speaking in tongues, is not for today, I will never go to the Mission again." I staked my all on the Word.

"Why certainly I can prove it to you," she replied.

"Those things were only for the Apostolic days. I will look up the scriptures and prove it

30

to you when you get home tonight."

Dear Mother she had been a student of the Bible and had taught Sunday School and Bible class for years. Oh, would she be able to prove that all these manifestations of the Holy Spirit's power and presence were only for by-gone days? I was not very well acquainted with the Bible on this subject, yet knew that what I had received was from God.

Assured that Mother would search the Bible honestly, I had pledged myself to stand by the consequences: Whatever the Bible said should stand.

Thus it was that we both turned to the Word of God as the final court of appeal to settle the whole matter.

Mother got out her Bible, concordance, pencil and pad, and with heart and mind full of this one thing, immediately sat herself down at the breakfast table, spreading her books out before her, without pausing even long enough to gather up the breakfast dishes for washing the lamps were not cleaned, and the beds were unmade.

(Oh, if any unbeliever will sit down with an open Bible and an unprejudiced heart, there is no need for us to defend our position, so clear is the Word of God on this subject.)

It was half past eight in the morning when I left home for school. At five-thirty, when I returned, Mother was still seated at the breakfast table, with her Bible and paper before her, and would you believe it? The breakfast dishes were still un-washed, the lamps uncleaned, the beds unmade, an unheard-of state of affairs for Mother, ever an excellent housekeeper.

I waited with bated breath for her decision. My heart softened within me as I saw by her reddened eyes that she had been weeping. Oh, what would her answer be? The smile upon her face encouraged me to ask

"Oh, Mother, what is it?"

Now, dear reader, what do you suppose she said?

With shining face she replied:

"Well, dear, I must admit that of a truth, this is that which was spoken of by the prophet Joel, which should come to pass in the last days!"

She had found that, away back in Isaiah 28:11, He had said "With stammering lips and another tongue will I speak to this people" that the prophet Joel had clearly prophesied that in these last days there should be a wonderful outpouring of the Holy Spirit, likened unto the latter rain, wherein the sons and daughters, the servants and the maids were alike to rejoice in this glorious downpour.

With one spring across the room, I threw my arms about my Mother's neck, squeezing her till she declared I had almost, broken her neck. How happy we were as we danced around the table laughing, crying and singing together

"Tis the old time religion,

And it's good enough for me"

If everyone who is sceptical of the reality of the baptism of the Holy Spirit would take the Word of God and search from cover to cover, he too, would be convinced without the shadow of a doubt that "This Is That."

CHAPTER VI. CALLING INTO THE VINEYARD, AND MARRIAGE

"Come, my beloved, and let us go forth into the field; let us lodge in the villages."
S. of S. 7:11

The chain of events related in the foregoing chapters brings us right up to the place where God spoke to his poor little handmaiden, whose heart was rejoicing in the new-found Savoir the time when He called me to preach The Word, and ordained me in my room as related in the beginning of chapter one.

(If you have forgotten, turn back and refresh your memory.)

An intense, Heaven-sent longing to be a soul winner for Jesus was born of the Spirit within my soul. He had done so much for me; He had plucked my feet out of the mire and the clay. Oh, to be able to win other souls, shining jewels to lay at His precious feet! Oh, to be able to tell of the Redeemer's love to perishing humanity! God spoke within the depths of my being and told me that "Before I called thee, I knew thee; before thou earnest forth I sanctified thee; and I ordained thee."

"Why, you are but a child; no one would listen or have confidence in you," whispered the Enemy.

"What do you know about preaching, anyway?" nodded Self and Common-sense. "Here are preachers, a country full of them, learned, college-bred, who have read books and digested theological studies for years. It is preposterous for you even to think of going out as a worker."

"But not many wise men after the flesh, not many mighty, not many noble, are called: but hath chosen the foolish things of the world to confound the wise; and God hath chosen the weak things of the world to confound the things that are mighty "argued the Word. "Has He not declared that with a worm He shall thrash a mountain that when we are weak, then we are strong and that a little child shall lead them? Has He not said that upon the servants and upon the handmaidens He would pour out His Spirit in the last days, and that they should prophesy? Did He not say that after the Spirit had come out of your innermost being' (not out of your head, intellect or knowledge) (should flow rivers of living water'? You know the rivers are flowing. Just open your mouth wide and He will fill it."

"Yes, but remember in addition to your youth and lack of mental equipment," cried Human Affection, "there is your Mother to be considered. You are an only child, her only comfort and object of affection in this world. Surely you would not consider leaving her out here in the country all alone, after all that she has done for you?"

"Here you have love and home and comfort, all you can wish for. If you went forth as a worker you would have to leave all these," added Love of Comfort.

"If any man love Father or Mother more than Me, he is not worthy of Me," said the tender voice of Jesus.

"No man hath given up houses or lands for my sake and the gospels, but he shall receive a hundred-fold now in this time, and in the world to come eternal life. If you would come after me you must take up your cross daily, denying yourself, and follow Me."

"But, Lord, these Pentecostal people have no earthly board behind them, no salary," cried Prudence and Forethought, "What about shoes and clothes, and necessary expenses?"

"Take no thought for what you shall eat or for what you shall drink or what you shall put on, for the Lord knoweth you have need of these things," calmly interrupted implicit Faith.

"Oh, yes, Lord, by your grace I will take up my cross, 'twill be a joy," sang Consecration. "I will trust you and follow you, come what may. My all is on the altar, have Your dear way with me, whether 'tis 'go' or whether 'tis 'stay let Your perfect will be wrought out in my life. I feel my own weakness and insufficiency know not what the future holds am but a child, but I can hear my Savior calling, take your cross and follow, follow me.'

Oh, here I am, Lord, send me. Such a burden for souls is mine that I would be willing to crawl upon my hands and knees from the Atlantic to the Pacific just to say to one poor, lost soul -

"Dear sinner, Jesus loves you."

"You must go with me, Jesus, you must help my infirmities and speak for me, for behold I cannot speak, I am a child."

But the Lord said unto me, "Say not, am a child, for thou shalt go to all that I shall send thee, whatsoever I command thee thou shalt speak. Be not afraid of their faces, for I am with thee to deliver thee, saith the Lord. Then the Lord put forth His hand, and touched my mouth, and said unto me. Behold, I have put my words in thy mouth."

The battle over, the conflict ended, the consecration made, come what might, no matter who should doubt the transaction that took place in that sacred hour, I had been ordained, not of man but of God.

Day by day the call grew louder, rang more clearly in my ears. Sitting at the piano I would sing, hour after hour, from the fullness of my heart,

"I'll go where you want me to go, dear Lord, over mountain or plain or sea;

I'll say what you want me to say, dear Lord, I'll be what you want me to be."

Tears would roll down my face; my body was there, but my Spirit was far away out in the harvest fields working for Jesus.

So enwrapt was I in the call of the Master that I was often but dimly conscious of my Mother's leaving her work each time I began to play, no matter what part of the house she was in, and coming to the parlor door, leaning against it and wiping the big tears from her eyes on the corner of her apron. God was speaking to her Mother-heart, taking her back to the day of her prayer for the little girl, reminding her of the dedication service when she had promised to let her go where He would send, even to the ends of the earth. She realized that the great divine call had come to her daughter, and that the time for her supreme sacrifice was near. She remembered the words of Hannah:

"Oh, my lord, I am the woman that stood by thee here, praying unto the Lord. For this child I prayed; and the Lord hath given me my petition which I asked of Him: therefore also have I lent him to the Lord; as long as he liveth he shall be lent to the Lord, and she worshipped the Lord there."

Just how it was all to come about, little did we know. The meetings were a feast to our souls.

Workers came freely to our country home, and when the Evangelist, Robert Semple, that blessed man of God who, because of his Christ-like bearing, moved as a prince among men, passed on to another town, he continued to encourage and instruct me in the Lord by many long letters, all of which were filled with scriptures and food from God's storehouse.

Never has it been my privilege to read such letters as those that came from the inspired pen of this saintly man of prayer. He walked and lived and breathed in the atmosphere of Heaven. To know him was to love and respect him.

Then came the time of his return visit to our town and the memorable night when I had volunteered to nurse the two little children of the sister in whose home I had received my baptism. The little ones had been stricken down with typhoid fever, and the mother was fatigued with long care and watching.

Late in the evening, as I was tending the little ones and setting things to rights in the room, the door opened and in walked Robert Semple, offering his services and prayers. After he had prayed, the children fell into a quiet sleep, and we sat down side by side to read the Bible by the light of the shaded lamp. Robert talked earnestly of the Savior and His love, of the work, of the great fields of golden grain, white already unto the harvest, of the need for laborers in these closing hours of the dispensation, of the soon coming of Jesus and the many souls yet to be saved, of what a life of faith meant the sacrifice the joy, the reward then, reaching over he took my hand in his and, telling me of his love, asked me to become his wife and enter the work as a helpmate by his side.

This is the first time I have ever attempted to lift the veil even a little from that sacred, hallowed hour, when we kneeled side by side, hand in hand, and he reverently prayed God to look down and solemnize our engagement and send us forth as true laborers, in obedience to His call, to rescue poor perishing souls from eternal destruction.

While on my knees, with closed eyes and throbbing heart (Why, this was the very room in which I had received my baptism!) the room seemed filled with angels who lined either side of the golden, sunlit path of life that stretched away into the vista of coming days of glorious love and joyful service to our Lord and King.

Here was the visible answer to the call.

Here was the loving human hand sent to un-latch the gate of opportunity and guide my steps into that shining path and start me well upon the way that way that has led through sunshine and shadow, tears and smiles, joys and sorrow, life and death, mountain-top and valley.

Little did I know that night, as I contemplated the shining way that led on and on to the Father's throne, how soon the strong, dear arm that was now about me as we prayed, and led me out into the work, would be removed; that after two years of married life I should be left alone, yet not alone.

The impenetrable mist with which God mercifully veils the future remained unrent, yet, had I known of the little mound of fresh-digged earth that should mark the grave of this dear heart in Happy Valley, Hong Kong, China, I should not have hesitated in that softly whispered "yes," with which I met his question; nor would I have shrunk one instant from the call to stand by his side. I deemed it one of the greatest privileges and honors I had ever known.

Oh, Jesus! Jesus! How wonderfully He hath planned it all for poor, unworthy me! How he had sought and called and chosen me! Is it any wonder my heart sang with rapturous love and praise for such a Redeemer?

The straight-forward, manly way in which Robert went to my Mother for her consent, coupled with the dealings of the Lord in her heart on the subject, made her willing to part with her daughter, though she declared, mother-like, that it took the sunshine and the laughter and the music from the farm and from the home.

I am not going to try to describe the little wedding which took place under the flower-decked arch on the lawn the following August, nor the long tables spread beneath the apple trees for the wedding supper, nor the Mother-face that tried to keep brave and smiling as the little white wedding-dress was laid aside and the newly-clad bride entered the carriage that was soon hidden by a cloud of dust as it sped away to catch the train for Stratford the mission field of which my husband was in charge.

"Were the whole realm of nature mine,
That were an offering far too small;
Love so amazing, so divine,
Demands my love, my life, my all."

CHAPTER VII.EARLY MINISTRY MY BROKEN ANKLE HEALED

"Let us get up early to the vineyards; let us see if the vine nourish, whether the tender grape appear, and the pomegranates bud forth: there will I give thee ray loves."
S. of S. 7:12

The happy days of service for Jesus which followed need not be described in detail.

We had three little rooms in the heart of the city where swirling smoke clouds from nearby foundries saved over the roof and tiny back-yard where I struggled desperately with my first washing. I would wash and rub and rinse, and as fast as I washed the clothes the soot would black them. It was a battle between the smoke and me, and I was greatly troubled, having always heard that the housekeeping qualities of a good wife must be judged by her washing and her biscuits. Cinders would have won the day had it not been for the help and advice of one of the sisters.

Rooms were furnished in an unpretentious way, and even with my eyes filled with smoke from the broken door of the little kitchen range, my first pan of biscuits, hard and brown though they were, were considered a great and triumphant success by the husband who came in, from his toil in the boiler works, at noon. Never were biscuits praised so highly, and it is doubtful whether biscuits ever were quite so hard, but the spirit to learn and try to please was there just the same.

The little assembly was poor in this world's goods, and my dear husband, not willing to lay us as a burden upon them, had accepted this humble position of work, though in other cities he might have commanded a dignified position with a good salary. Like Paul he was not afraid to work with his hands.

The Lord blessed our labors in Stratford, Ontario, swing and baptizing precious souls, leading me on and out in a new way. From Stratford He definitely led us to the city of LONDON, ONT., CAN., where the beautiful home of dear Sister Arm-strong was opened to us. Meetings were held in her parlors until her rooms grew too small, and were then moved to the home of Brother Wortman.

The teaching of Pentecost was practically new in the city at the time when the Lord led my husband thither. Inside of a year, however, over one hundred had received the baptism of the Holy Spirit with the Bible evidence, speaking in tongues, sinners had been saved, and there were several remarkable healings. As a result from the working of the Spirit in these meetings, a large, thriving, centrally located Pentecostal Mission has been built on one of the main streets and the work of God is progressing gloriously to this day.

CHICAGO, ILL.

The Lord began to impress us that we were to go to Chicago, Ill., to attend the meetings of Brother W. H. Durham, and as we were praying for the necessary means, He laid it upon my Mother's heart to provide for the fare and other necessary expenses.

Oh, the teaching and the deepening, and the experiences that were ours in the little North Avenue assembly, where we worshipped for several months, have meant so much in the years which have followed! It was here that the Lord gave me the gift of interpretation.

While praying upon my knees by the side of my bed one day, I was speaking in tongues (when one has received the Holy Spirit and He has right of way, it is difficult to keep from praying in the Spirit, as when the soul becomes just so full that our human mind cannot give utterance to or express its desires, the Holy Spirit within rises and helping our infirmities, prays through us with groanings that cannot be uttered, or praises and glorifies Jesus as the case may be).

This day, as I was worshipping the Lord in other tongues, as the Spirit gave utterance, I suddenly became conscious of the fact that I could understand the words that the Spirit was speaking through me. He described the glorious morning when the mists should be rolled away, the breaking of eternal dawn over the hills, the nearness of the approach of our Lord, which was reaching out and with flaming colors, illuminating the sky with the promise of His appearing. The glory, the beauty, the majestic tread and kingly garments of the Lord were described in wonderful language that I never could have thought of.

When the power lifted from me I was left feeling as though I had had a taste of Heaven.

Not understanding this experience, I did not mention it to anyone, but that night, when seated in the North Avenue Mission, Brother Durham, during his preaching, spoke a lengthy message in tongues. No one in this assembly had had the gift of interpretation up to this time, and they had been praying earnestly for its bestowal upon someone.

As the Pastor spoke, the power was flowing through my being. It just seemed as though the message were rolling in and rolling in and rolling in. The moment the Spirit ceased speaking through him I felt the greatest drawing to spring to my feet and open my mouth, assured that if I did the message would roll and roll forth in English.

I could feel my face growing red; it seemed as though everyone must know I had the interpretation, for I shook from head to foot during the silence that ensued, but even though the Brother pointed over the audience in my direction and said "Somebody here has got the interpretation," I still sat on in my chair, fearful of getting to my feet lest I should be mistaken.

Meeting over, he came down to me and said:

"You had the interpretation, did you not?"

After telling him my experience, he bade me go right to the altar and ask the Lord to forgive me for quenching the Spirit, assuring me that if I did not obey the Spirit I would grieve Him and the gift be taken away.

The next meeting wherein a message in tongues was given through the brother, I yielded to the Spirit, who seemed literally to lift me to my feet, and spoke through me in English, the interpretation of the message which had been given in tongues. I was amazed to find how easy it was: I had nothing to do with it at all. It was almost exactly the same as speaking in tongues, my lips and tongue were controlled by the Spirit in identically the same way. The words did not pass through my brain but came flowing out of my innermost being just as the Spirit gave utterance.

The only difference between this and speaking in tongues was that it came in English. The language was such as I never could have used.

The saints shouted leaped to their feet and the power fell everywhere. Meeting after meeting thereafter, the Spirit gave through me the interpretation. Instead of having the effect of puffing me up, as one might have expected, this gift seemed to humble me more than anything I had ever had. The enemy would strongly tempt me to get up and run from the building when it seemed as though anyone were going to speak in tongues.

One of my severest tests came when a certain message in tongues, seemingly composed of but three or four words, had a corresponding interpretation a couple of sentences long. I knew that the interpretation had not arisen in my mind, but was spoken by the Spirit; nevertheless, not being able to understand the difference in length, and feeling that everyone else must notice it too, I sat down covered with confusion.

Imagine my joy and relief when a man rose in the back of the hall and stated that the message in tongues had been in his own language and that the interpretation exactly corresponded. With a rush of relief I recalled how that in school in our Latin lessons one word in Latin would mean three and sometimes four words in English, and how Daniel's interpretation of the handwriting on the wall varied in length:

"Mene; God hath numbered thy kingdom, and finished it.

"Tekel; Thou art weighed in the balances, and art found wanting.

"Peres; Thy kingdom is divided, and given to the Medes and Persians."

How could I have been so stupid as to have doubted? Yet to this day perhaps some of my readers, when they have heard a message in tongues whose interpretation apparently did not correspond in length, have doubted and condemned.

Today we are made to realize in a very definite way that the Lord is restoring His church to her full Pentecostal glory and perfection, where every gift and fruit of the Spirit is to be manifested.

FINDLAY, OHIO

MIRACULOUS AND INSTANTANEOUS HEALING OF A BROKEN ANKLE

While at Findlay, Ohio, at Brother Leonard's Mission, attending the two weeks' special meetings conducted by Brother, Durham, we prayed night and day for those seeking the baptism, and the Lord met every one. At times the whole floor in front of the altar was covered by the slain of the Lord. Amongst those seeking the baptism of the Spirit was a minister and a doctor of that city.

One evening, being tired in body, from the long-hours at the altar, I went upstairs to lie down, during the tarrying meeting. I had hardly settled down to rest, when, hearing the big bass voice of the minister shouting, "Glory! Glory!!Glory!!!" I bounded off the couch to go and see if he was receiving the Holy Spirit, rejoicing that our prayers were being answered.

In running swiftly down the long flight of stairs I tripped, and, bending my ankle back under me, fell from the middle of the stairs all the rest of the way to the bottom. I could fairly hear the bones crunch under me as I fell. My toes turned towards where the heel ought to be, and my ankle swelled rapidly.

Up to this time, having always enjoyed the best of health, I had never had occasion to take the Lord as my personal healer, although I had witnessed many wonderful healings. Now, as the saints gathered about me and prayed, I must confess that my mind was more occupied with the pain and excruciating agony of my broken foot than with the Lord as my healer; consequently I was not healed that night.

The doctor examined my foot and said the bone was not only cracked, but that in wrenching my foot backwards in my fall, I had completely torn and severed four of the ligaments that move the toes, all being torn but that running to the big toe, thus pulling my toes around and backwards.

As soon as the swelling had been reduced sufficiently to permit a plaster of Paris cast to be put on, Dr. Harrison and his son, also a practising physician of that city, set the bone, drew the bent foot back into place, and put on a heavy cast.

He explained to me that the torn cords could not grow together; that my ankle would, therefore, always be stiff, but by keeping the plaster cast on for four weeks, till thoroughly healed, my foot would be straight. They both warned me not to touch it to the floor, or put any weight upon it.

A pair of crutches was purchased, and by their aid I went hobbling to the train that was to take us back to Chicago.

The afternoon we arrived, I attended the service in the mission, and rested my aching and feverish foot on the platform in front of me. Every jar of the floor sent a stabbing pain through it, and, sick with the pain, I went to my room, a block away from the hall. While sitting there commiserating with myself over the black and swollen toes, which were all I could see of my foot, a voice spoke to me and said:

"If you will wrap the shoe for your broken foot, and take it with you to wear home, and go over to North Avenue mission to Brother Durham and ask him to lay hands on your foot, I will heal it."

The idea of wrapping up a shoe, which was tight-fitting even with my foot in a normal condition, struck me so humorously that I laughed the thought away; but again and yet again came the voice:

"Wrap up your shoe to wear home, take it with you as you go to be prayed for, and I will heal you." The Word says, "My sheep hear my voice," and, at last I reached for my crutches, hobbled over to my other shoe, wrapped it up, and with it tucked under my arm, started clumsily down the winding staircase to go to the mission for prayers.

On the way over the crutch slipped through a hole in the wooden sidewalk, and as my toes struck the hard boards, the perspiration stood in beads upon me, from the excruciating pain that shot up my limb. I felt dizzy and faint as I reached the foot of the steps (Brother Durham lived over the mission). Trembling and white from pain, I felt unequal to climbing the stairs, so two of the brothers carried me up on a chair.

I told them just what the Lord had told me.

There were twelve in the room besides myself, and all but one began to pray. The one who did not pray was an infidel, a brother of our Pastor.

As Brother Durham was walking up and down the room, calling on the Lord, he suddenly stopped, and laying his hands on my ankle, broke out praying in tongues, and then in English said:

"In the name of Jesus, receive your healing."

I suddenly felt as if a shock of electricity had struck my foot. It flowed through my whole body, causing me to shake and tremble under the power of God. Instantaneously my foot was perfectly healed, the blackness was gone, the parted ligaments were knitted together, the bone was made whole. Glory to Jesus! I was healed!

Trembling with excitement and joy, it took me fully five minutes, with the help of the saints, to remove the Plaster of Paris cast. The infidel who was present said:

"Don't be foolish. Leave it on; you will only have to pay a doctor three dollars to replace the cast."

But, glory to Jesus, I was healed. At last the plaster was removed, the absorbent cotton off, my stocking on, also the shoe (which fitted perfectly now), and I leaped to my feet and began to dance and jump on the healed foot.

Everyone in the room was filled with the Spirit, and we all danced and sang and talked in tongues.

Hallelujah! It is no wonder we shout His praises; when we have Jesus we have something worth shouting over.

Suddenly remembering my husband would be coming on the next elevated train, I ran down the stairs, my crutches left behind, and all the way to the station, and told him the wonderful news. My ankle was as strong as ever.

The mission was full to the doors that night, and when the Pastor asked me to step to the platform and tell of my wonderful healing, and the saints saw that the crutches and plaster cast were gone, and that I could leap and dance upon the foot, they shouted and praised the Lord. Many of the Chicago onlookers who knew not the healing power, doubted that the ankle had ever been broken. When the word went back and the healing was announced publicly in Findlay, Ohio, many of the public there who knew it was broken would not believe it was healed. How like human nature. "If they hear not Moses and the prophets, neither will they be persuaded though one rose from the dead."

CHAPTER VIII. CALL TO FOREIGN FIELDS

"And He said unto me, Go ye into all the world, and preach the Gospel to every creature."

Mk. 16:15

It was shortly after our return to Chicago and the miraculous, instantaneous healing of my broken ankle, just related, that my husband and myself were made to realize in a very definite way that the time had come for us to obey the call to China which the Spirit had been laying upon his heart more and more for some time.

We began praying for the fare and clothing which would be necessary. As I have explained, we had no earthly board behind us, no organization to lean upon. We, therefore, looked straight to Jesus, the One who had called us, and asked Him to supply our every need. In just a little over two weeks the necessary clothing and the fare had been donated by the dear saints of God, not by the rich, but by the poor.

We find, all over the country, in our meetings that the rich and the near-rich will come to us and say:

"Oh, I am so sorry that I am not in a position just now to give something. My money is tied up and I am so situated that I am not able to do much now; how I wish I could." And while they are humming and hesitating over it, the poor: step up, and with a glad light in their eyes, grip our hands with a hearty:

"God bless you! Here's a dollar, or here's five or ten," as the case may be; "Oh, I only wish it were more, but I will have more when next week's pay envelope comes in. How proud I am to have this privilege!"

Farewelling in Chicago, we went to Canada, accompanied by Brother Durham, holding revival meetings in different towns and cities in Ontario. In London we found the Lord still graciously pouring out His Spirit and had a glorious revival while there this time.

My home town being but twenty miles distant, I had the opportunity of saying farewell to my parents, but even when Mother waved me off at the depot, she smiled bravely as far away as I could see her waving her handkerchief from the platform. I held my hand out of the window and pointed up, bidding her look to Jesus.

After our last meeting was closed in Toronto, where many were baptized in the Spirit, we boarded the train for St. John's, N. B., and as it was pulling out of the Union Depot, we heard the sweet voices of the saints singing: "God be with you 'til we meet again."

Leaving St. John's, we set sail for Liverpool, England. From there we went to Belfast, Ireland. In Belfast the Lord sent a wonderful revival. In three weeks over two score were baptized in the Holy Spirit and all spoke in other tongues.

Mr. Semple's home, which was in Magherafelt, the North of Ireland, being but a few miles distant, we visited there. His dear father and mother, two brothers and two sisters, each vied with the other in packing the trunk of new clothing and good things for us. When at last the day of our departure had come they said "Good-bye" to their son, and Mrs. Semple (Robert's mother) declared that the Lord gave her the witness right then that she would never look upon his face again in this world. But Hallelujah! "Greater love hath no man than this, that he lay down his life for the brethren."

While waiting in London, England, for the boat on which we were to sail, we were entertained by dear saints who showed us the greatest hospitality and love. In attending Pentecostal, services held in London we found that the Lord was pouring out His Spirit in the very same way as in America, and that hundreds of earnest Christians had been baptized with the same Holy Spirit, speaking with other tongues and praising the Lord. It was here that the Lord gave me that marvelous vision of the Dispensation of the Holy Spirit and the message in prophecy which has always seemed so glorious to me because He gave it.

Standing on the deck, as the boat slipped away from the wharf, we lifted our voices in song with the crowd of saints who stood on the pier. How sweet and encouraging their dear voices sounded as they rang over the ever-increasing distance between us. As far as we could hear they were singing:

"God will take care of you."

And when we could no longer hear them we could see the having handkerchiefs and hats of these precious children of the Most High God.

42

Skirting the edge of the Bay of Biscay, we sailed on to Gibraltar, then in through the blue, sunlit waters of the Mediterranean, to the Suez Canal, and on into the Red Sea, through which the Children of Israel had been led dry-shod. We were surprised at the great width of the Sea, and learned that it was called the "Red Sea" because of the desert wind storms which blow the red sand across the water, giving it at times its red appearance.

Soon we were plowing through the waters of the Indian Ocean. After our visit at Ceylon it was not long until we were nearing our destination at Hong Kong.

En route we gathered good reports of the outpouring of the Latter Rain in Egypt, India, Ceylon, Malta, etc., too lengthy to relate at this time. Suffice it to say that they received the Holy Spirit as well as we, with the same Bible evidence, speaking in tongues. Sick were healed and signs and wonders were wrought in the name of the holy child, Jesus.

On the boat plentiful opportunity for witnessing for Jesus was given us. My husband spent hours and hours each day waiting upon God; the balance in reading the Word. It seemed as though we were being drawn nearer to the Master every day, and belonged less and less to this world.

After weathering a severe typhoon, came the day when we saw, in the early morning sunrise, the mountain of Hong Kong, and beheld the harbor with its numerous busy sampans.

We were met by saints and taken to the Missionary Home, of which Brother Macintosh was at that time in charge. Brother and Sister Dixon and other missionaries were here, and we learned that the Latter Bain was falling in China, as well as in America, as God's little children faithfully proclaimed the truth. Yes, when the Chinese receive the baptism they speak in other tongues just as did the hundred and twenty on the day of Pentecost; the sick are healed and the lepers cleansed. Hallelujah!

In China we felt as never before the need of the Holy Spirit as a Comforter, and found it much more difficult to pray through. It seemed at times as though the air were filled with demons and the hosts of hell, in this wicked, benighted country, where for many centuries devil worship has been an open custom. We have seen Chinese bowing themselves down before their great gods, burning hundreds of dollars' worth of paper to feed their flames of devotion to their gods, and roasting their pigs and offering them with rice and other dainties to the great stone dragons in temple and cave.

Ancestral worship is observed by almost all. It is a peculiar sight to see them carrying food, rice, chicken, candied nuts and fruit, to lay upon the graves of their dead. A missionary once asked a young Chinaman who had recently been saved, when he was going to stop taking food to the grave of his dead. He replied:

"Why, I suppose when your people stop taking flowers as a tribute to the memory of their departed."

43

CHAPTER IX. THE DEATH OF MY HUSBAND

"When thou passest through the waters, I will be with thee; and through the rivers, they shall not overflow thee."
Isa. 43:2

While in China my husband seemed to be drawn nearer and nearer to the Lord each day. He spent hours in prayer day and night. He really travailed in Spirit for the Chinese, and often made the remark that he felt as though he would never return to America, but would rise to meet the Lord from China, carrying precious Chinese souls in his arms to Jesus. He used to sing over and over that little chorus:

"Bringing in the sheaves," only he worded it "Bringing in Chinese, Bringing in Chinese; we shall come rejoicing, Bringing in Chinese."

After the heat of the day, we would often go out to sit on the beach in the evening, and while different workers would be talking together I would suddenly miss my husband. Diligent search would find him hidden away off somewhere behind a boulder or rock, praying earnestly for souls. At other times he would walk through the beautiful graveyard of Happy Valley, reading the inscriptions of missionaries who had laid down their lives for Jesus. How beautiful were flowers and fountains, and foliage such rare beauty as we had never seen!

As we sat many hours studying and reading under these trees, little did we realize that soon dear Robert was to be laid at rest in this very spot in Happy Valley.

The intense heat and the filthy, unsanitary condition of the country in which we dwelt began to tell upon our health. Malaria was raging, and to go out even for five minutes at noonday without a cork helmet and a heavy parasol meant almost certain death.

We were away down the coast at Macoe when my husband was taken seriously ill and was carried, in a very weak condition, to the steamer and back to Hong Kong and up the mountain to an English sanitarium, built especially for missionaries, where care was given free of charge.

Suffering with malaria in its worst form, I went with my husband to the hospital where we could be near (I in the ladies' ward, his ward some distance away), even though we could not see each other except on visiting days.

Robert was just in the hospital one week, and the anniversary of our second year of married life was celebrated during this time by a little exchange of notes sent by the nurse. During the few short visits I was permitted to make to his ward, I ever found his well-worn Bible (the one from which he had preached me under conviction and explained the way of salvation and the baptism of the Holy Spirit), my husband's constant companion. It was marked from cover to cover and his fingers seemed to be always between its pages.

Each day he grew weaker, and although I was confident the Lord would heal him, he felt as though his work were ended, that he had fought a good fight and finished his course, and henceforth there was laid up for him a crown of righteousness.

One evening, at the end of the week, the doctor gave me special permission to sit with my husband, and as my heart leaped with joy at the prospect, little did I dream the reason of this special kindness. I only felt grateful to the doctor, and the thought that my dear one was so soon to be taken from me never entered my mind.

As I sat there by his bedside a great lump in my throat seemed to be choking me as I gazed at the thin, pale face, so changed in these few days, but feeling that I must be brave and encouraging I tried in a pitiful way to talk cheerfully of the soon-coming of the little one we had both planned and hoped for so long.

As we were talking thus I heard the click of the white-robed nurse's heels as she came down the long ward to tell me it was time for me to go back to my own ward now. And O, I shall never forget the sweet smile that lit up his countenance.

Some way a terrible premonition of some sorrow befalling me, an idea vague and unformed, seized upon my heart, and as I clung to the white-enamelled bar at the foot of his bed, I think he must have seen the look that saved across my face, for still smiling encouragingly he looked into my eyes and said:

"Good night, dear; I'll see you in the morning." These were the last words he ever spoke to me, but O, I know there is going to dawn a bright and cloudless morning some of these days, when there shall be

"No more parting, no more tears, No more crying, no more fears," For these things shall pass away when the Lord shall come. Why, it seems that I can almost see the early rays of dawn breaking in the sky just now, and the Spirit softly whispers:

"The morning is at hand; Jesus is coming soon; be faithful just a little longer."

"Good night, dear; I'll see you in the morning."

Oh, dear reader, will you be there in the morning? Will you be ready to meet Jesus on that day?

I returned to the bed in the women's ward with an uneasy feeling hard to describe, and lay for hours staring out into the darkness, listening to the irregular breathing of the other patients about me.

At midnight I sat up in bed with a frightened start. Out of the window at the foot of my bed I could see across the great square court, and in the window which I knew to be beside my husband's bed I saw a bright light burning. Some way a great terror seized upon my soul, as I heard the quick step of the night nurse coming along the corridor connecting the two wards. Straight to my bed she came, and with a tense catch in her voice that I -will never forget, she told me to slip on my kimono and slippers and to hurry to the next ward, that my husband was very ill.

"He's not he's not d-dying?" I managed to gasp through my stiff lips.

"Come quick! He is sinking fast," were the words that sounded like a death knell, as we hurried down the long passage to what?

"Death? O, surely not; it couldn't be," I reasoned. I had never seen anyone die. I was not yet twenty years of age, and away out here on the opposite side of the globe from the Mother who had always shielded and protected me from every wind that blew.

"Dying? Impossible! Why, what of the little one that is to come? Surely he will live to see her clad in the glory of the tiny wardrobe so proudly tucked away?" All these thoughts raced like lightning through my mind. I was as one dazed. My lips were trembling; my knees shook till I could scarcely walk.

Then, as I stood by his bed, and saw that even unconscious as he was, the light of the glory world illuminated his face, I sank down in a heap by his side and clung to his cold hand. He did not open his eyes, did not see me. However, I think he must have been seeing Jesus, so rapt was the expression that lighted up his countenance.

Then, at that moment, when all the world seemed to be crumbling and slipping from beneath my feet, the Comforter, the blessed Holy Spirit, whom Jesus had sent, rose up within me and revealed Jesus in such a precious way, made the will of God so sweet, showed the prepared mansions so real that I shouted "Glory!" by the death bed of Robert Semple, from whom I had never dreamed of parting. Waves of joy rolled over my soul, and I was lifted from earth to Heaven, and it seemed as though I accompanied him right to the pearly gates. "The Lord gave and the Lord taketh away, blessed be the name of the Lord."

When I felt the doctor shaking me by the shoulder, I at last raised my head from the bed, and loosened my clasp on the dear, cold hand. Stooping to kiss the cold forehead for the last time, I realized the great need of the Comforter. He did not fail me, but sweetly spoke in my ears:

"He is not here; he is risen."

O dear friend, never again say that you have no need of the Comforter whom Jesus sent. It is not only in the hour of rejoicing on the mountain-top that you need Him, but in sorrow's dark hour, down in the valley and the shadow of death, you too need the Comforter. Hallelujah! You must not think, when you see us dancing and shouting for very joy in the meeting, that it is all excitement and surface blessings, for this is not true.

Ah no, the Holy Spirit still abides when the feet are led down into the dark waters and it seems as though the floods would overflow then He is there to comfort and uphold; and when we pass through the fiery furnace He reveals the form of the Fourth, like unto the Son of God, as never before.

Oh, how we thank you, dear Jesus, that you ever said: "I will not leave you comfortless; I will send another, even the Holy Ghost."

I was never permitted to look upon the face of my dear one again, as the doctor was

46

anxious to spare me all suffering possible, but Oh, how could I have borne it when I saw them pulling down the shades in hopes that I would not see, and heard the heavy tread of feet as they carried their burden past our windows and down the steps, if it had not been for this precious Holy Spirit?

Our slender funds were well-nigh exhausted and an immediate demand for money and funeral expenses was the next thing to be considered, so I lifted my heart to the Lord who had said: "Take no thought ... I will supply your needs." The afternoon mail of that very day brought a letter from two dear sisters in Chicago, containing sixty dollars. The letter was dated one month previous and stated that the Lord had awakened them up in the middle of the night saying: "Little Sister Semple is in trouble. Rise immediately and send her sixty dollars." They had gotten up and sent the money, and here it was at the spot just when needed. Oh hallelujah! It had arrived long before the hasty cablegram to my dear Mother could have brought the necessary funds from her ever-ready heart.

Morning after morning, of the month that followed, I would wake up with a scream as my great loss saved over me, and I thought of the little one who would never see her father. Then the Comforter would instantly spring up within me till I was filled with joy unspeakable, and my hot, dry eyes would flow with tears of love and blessing.

Then came the little daughter, a tiny mite of a thing, but Oh such a comfort! Here again the Comforter was with me. Truly Jesus is a husband to the widow and a Father to the fatherless. I named the little one Roberta, after her father, Robert. It was in Hong Kong, on the top of the mountain, that my tiny little daughter was born, and when she was six weeks old I sailed to Shanghai.

On leaving Shanghai we went to Japan, Moji, Kobe, Nagasaki. Upon leaving Japan we set sail for Honolulu and the U. S. A., I carrying my precious little burden in a Japanese basket.

Mother had sent money, some of which I had not yet received, and on the boat I kept figuring up and found that there was not enough to take me clear across the continent. Without telling my needs to an earthly soul I kept looking up to Jesus and witnessing for Him every occasion I found on the boat. My feelings on this return trip I will not try to describe, but Oh, there seemed to be such a great big, vast emptiness yawning all about me, and I snuggled the dear little warm bundle, Roberta, closer to my heart.

As I was stepping off the steamer at San Francisco, the purser came running after me, and touching me on the arm, said:

"Oh wait a minute! Here is something for you from the passengers." Opening the envelope which he slipped into my hand, I found sixty-five dollars which had been donated by them.

All through the trip it seemed as though there were not one thing which I needed but the Lord quickly sent. It was nearing Christmas time, and China being so warm, I had nothing but the lightest of bonnets for the baby. I was in my state room, turning the tiny bonnet on my fingers, thinking that I should have a warm one for her when I reached the snow of our own land, when a rap came at my door and a lady's voice said:

"Oh, we have just brought the baby a warm eiderdown bonnet and cape. You are sure to need it,"

At another time I was wishing for a heavy shawl for her. The porter came to the state room, saying that Mr. -- who had gotten off at the last port in Japan, had left this warm woolen shawl, which he declared he would no longer need, with instructions that it was to be given to "that little missionary lady with the baby." It was a beautiful, expensive shawl. How I did praise Jesus!

At another time a thermos bottle was needed.

Without a word to a soul it was brought to my door and quietly handed in. These are only a few of the many things that I might tell you of how He tempers the wind to the shorn lamb and tenderly watches over His little children.

On board the train, which was speeding across the Rocky Mountains and heading toward Chicago, I was afflicted for the first time in my life with train-sickness, and was obliged to remain in my berth for a couple of days. Different passengers had warned me that we had one of the crankiest old conductors on this car they had ever seen, and not to ask any favours of him under any consideration. But Oh, my Lord can make a lion as gentle as a lamb and turn the bitter into sweet, That dear conductor walked the floor hour after hour and took care of the baby for me, even carrying her nursing bottle in his pocket to keep it warm. Praise the Lord!

After a few days' stop in Chicago, we journeyed on to New York City, where my Mother was engaged in Salvation Army work. As the train pulled into the depot she was there to meet me, and I held the baby in one arm, but with the other was still able to point up to the sky to Jesus, just as I had when the train had last pulled out for China. Praise the Lord. When you have the Holy Spirit in your heart He will help you to still keep your hand up and "Keep on praising God."

CHAPTER X.NINEVEH TO TARSHISH AND RETURN

"Then Jonah prayed unto the Lord his God out of the fish's belly . . . And the Lord spake unto the fish, and it vomited out Jonah upon the dry land. And the word of the Lord came unto Jonah the second time, saying, Arise, go unto Nineveh, and preach unto it the preaching that I bid thee. So Jonah arose, and went."

Jonah 2:1, 10. 3:1 to 3

Have you ever had a secret tucked away in the closet of your Christian experience which you shrank from exposing to the sunlight of public gaze and criticism? A spot where somewhere on your spiritual anatomy, so sore that the very thought of its being touched by a curious, probing finger made you wince? A certain period of your life which you would a little rather not have generally known or discussed, all of which has long ago been confessed, forgiven and buried beneath the cleansing blood?

Have you, in telling your experience, been tempted to take a hop, skip and a jump over your deviations from the straight and narrow path of God's best and perfect will for you? Have you felt like leaping over and omitting, when telling your Christian experience, the things which should have been omitted in real life?

Well, that has just been my case exactly.

If this were to be a fine-sounding story of a continued forward march, without ever such a thing as a waver, this chapter would never be written.

The Lord has made me long, however, that each step of my experience may be a blessing and an encouragement to someone. It is easy to tell of the times when we have lived in victory, run the Heavenly race without a single tumble, and when God has blessed us and made us a blessing: the hours of defeat, when we stumbled in the darkness by the way, however, may be of more blessing to the poor backslider who is groping his way back to light, than any other experience could be.

The Lord had been wonderfully with me through the ordeal of my husband's death, subsequent events, and my return to the homeland.

At times the awful waters of loneliness through which I waded, however, seemed as though they would roll over my head, but each time He was with me to comfort and bear me up.

The following year found me battling against the swift, contrariwise tide, struggling to keep my feet, and to take up the broken thread of my life where last left off. My work in the meeting; necessitated taking with me, and .often keeping out till midnight, and as late as two o'clock in the morning, my frail little daughter, who eventually became very ill. I was given expert advice upon her frail condition and was told that I would be responsible for her life if I did not "get her a quiet home and proper food, as the constant moving about and changing food would be the death of the child."

I had come home from China like a wounded little bird, and my bleeding heart was constantly pierced with curious questions from well-meaning people who could not see the will of God in our call to China, and who felt that there must be a mistake somewhere, either in Robert's sudden death or my return home. I could not answer them, not being able to see the will of God in all this yet myself. Wherever I went amongst the dear people who had helped to send us to China, I would seem to feel an atmosphere of questioning (whether spoken or unexpressed), which little by little wore upon me until soon I began to feel like some guilty thing who had no business to be there, but far away somewhere I could not tell just where.

Oh! how I longed for someone who would understand or put their arms about me and help me at this critical moment of my life, and this was just the time that the Lord permitted those I loved best to seem to draw aside the arms that had been before so strong and dependable, causing a little curtain of reserve to drop between us, leaving me on the outside with my baby.

Looking at it in the natural, it is hardly to be wondered at that, like Hagar, with my child, I departed and wandered in the wilderness, and that I lifted up my voice and wept. Pentecost seemed as the mistress, dealing hardly with me and God as Abraham who apparently did not intervene in my behalf.

The loom of life seemed then to be but a tangled maze whose colorings had suddenly plunged from mountain-tops of sunlit glory to the depths of a seemingly endless valley of bewildering gloom. It is only now, after having watched through the succeeding years the steady flying to and fro of the shuttles of destiny, ever guided by the tender wisdom of the Hand Divine, that I begin to see the head and form of the Master being wrought out and woven upon the loom of my life.

50

It was just at the time of my greatest perplexity, when I had begun to lose out spiritually and wander away from the Lord, and was longing to make a home for the baby, that I married again. Before the marriage took place, however, I made one stipulation wherein I told my husband that all my heart and soul was really in the work of the Lord and that if, at any time in my life, He should call me to go to Africa or India, or to the Islands of the Sea, no matter where or when, I must obey God first of all. To this he agreed and we were married under these conditions, and settled down in a furnished apartment.

Disturbed and troubled in my heart, stepping out of the work of the Lord, I turned again to the world, endeavoring to stifle my longings to be reinstated at the banqueting table of my King.

I wonder if there is anyone on earth who is really as abjectly miserable as the backslider? It was such a relief to be able to stay away from the meetings, and yet such a pain to be away from them (if you can analyze that), that I was torn between the two conflicting forces. Some of the saints saw me backsliding and drifting into the world, and my position became still more intolerable.

When my husband received an invitation from his mother to come to her home in Rhode Island I was willing to consent to board the boat in my endeavor to "flee unto Tarshish from the presence of the Lord."

But Oh dear reader, what a great wind the Lord sent out into the sea! Such a mighty tempest was there in the deep that our frail domestic craft was rocked to and fro, so that the ship was like to be broken.

Day by day matters grew worse instead of better; I grieved and mourned and wept for my Jesus and the old-time place in Him. I was a mystery and a constant source of Discomfort to those round about me.

Earthly things - home comfort -oh, what did these matter? I was out of his dear will, and my soul refused to be comforted.

Shutting myself away in my room I would sit on the floor in the corner behind the bed, and cry over and over the one word that I could say when I tried to pray:

"Oh Oh Jesus! Jesus! Jesus!! JESUS!"

Seeing my unhappy, melancholy state, my mother-in-law advised us to rent and furnish a home of our own, saying that the work would occupy my mind and keep me from thinking so much about myself. This was done. With the help of our parents and our own earnings, a well-furnished home was made, containing all that heart could wish B-U-T J-E-S-U-S, and Oh, without Him nothing matters!

"Why can't you be happy and act like other folks, and forget your troubles?" I was asked again and again. Time after time I tried to shake myself from my lethargy and depression and busy myself with household duties. Such a fever of restlessness came upon me that it seemed as though I must wear the polish off the furniture and the floors by dusting them so often. A dozen times a day I would take myself to task as I would catch sight of my tearful face in the looking-glass, saying:

"Now, see here, my lady, this will never do! What right have you to fret and pine like this?

Just see those shining, polished floors, covered with soft Axminster and Wilton rugs. Just look at that mahogany parlor furniture and the big brass beds in yonder, the fine bathroom done in blue and white, the steam heat, the softly-shaded electric lights, the pretty baby's crib with its fluff and ribbons, the high-chair and the rocking-horse. Why aren't you glad to have a home like this for the babies, as any other mother would be?"

"Why, it's perfectly ridiculous for you to think of going out into the world again, and remember if you found it hard with one baby before, what do you suppose you would do now with two?"

Having had it thus out with myself, I would return to my work, half satisfied for a few minutes, saying:

"Well, yes, that's so. I had better give up all thoughts of such things, settle down and get used to my present life."

51

But, Oh, the Call of God was on my soul and I could not get away from it. For this cause I had been brought into the world. With each throb of my heart I could hear a voice saying:

"Preach the Word! Preach the Word! Will you go? Will you go?" And I would throw myself on my knees, tearfully sobbing:

"Oh? Lord, You know that I cannot go. Here are the two babies and here is the home, and here is husband, who has not the baptism and is not even seeking it. I will work here in the local mission, and that will do." But no, the answer still came back, clear from Heaven:

"Go! DO THE WORK OF AN EVANGELIST; Preach the Word! The time is short; I am coming soon."

"Oh, Lord, I am in a pretty state to preach the Gospel, I am. Why, I feel so miserable and down and crushed. I need someone to help me instead of me helping others." At times, lifting my eyes quickly after prayer, I could almost see the devil rubbing his hands and leering at me, saying:

"There's no hope. You might just as well give up. Everyone knows you've backslidden, and would have no confidence in you." Then would ensue another spell of bitter weeping.

My husband and his mother would often say:

"Well, Aimee I don't see what more you want. I don't believe anything could make you happy. It must be your disposition."

(Why, bless the Lord, when in His will I am so happy and full of gladness, my feet and my heart are so light, that they cannot keep from dancing. It seems that no one on earth could possibly be so happy as I.)

My nerves became so seriously affected that the singing of the teakettle upon the stove or the sound of voices was unbearable. I implored the little one to speak in whispers. I hated the sunshine and wanted to keep the shutters closed and the window-shades drawn tightly. The doctors said I would lose my reason if something was not done. I became very ill in body and inside of one year two serious operations were performed. Each time, before going under the surgeon's knife, and during many other times of critical illness, when it seemed as though I were going to die, I would call the saints to pray for me that I might be delivered, but each time they prayed I could plainly hear the voice of the Lord saying:

"Will you go? Will you preach the Word?" I knew that if I said "Yes," He would heal me. But how could I say "Yes?" Difficulties rose like mountains in my path. Oh, now I have learned, that no matter what the obstacles may be, if Jesus says "Go," and I start, by the time the obstacle is reached I will either be lifted over it or it will be gone. God does not ask us to do the impossible. If He tells you to do a thing, no matter how hard it seems, you just start to do it and you will find, like Christian of old, that the lions are fettered and unable to hinder your progress.

After the first operation I was worse instead of better. Complications set in, heart trouble, haemorrhages from my stomach, and intense nervousness among others. The doctors said that another operation would be necessary.

Oh, that home which I had thought to enjoy! Almost all my enjoyment was what I could see from my bed! I wonder if Jonah had nearly as rough a passage as I did when he ran away and disobeyed God. His trip was not as long as mine anyway. We read that Jonah paid his fare, and I certainly paid mine to the uttermost farthing.

The second operation was put off and put off, with some vague hope of trusting God, but how could I trust Him when out of His will, and when every time in prayer I got the answer which throbbed and pounded through my being with every pulse-beat

"Will you go? Will you go? Preach the Word! Preach the Word!"

At last, doubling over with a scream with appendicitis, on top of all else, I was rushed again to the hospital. As I was being prepared for the operating table I prayed earnestly from my valley of despair

"Oh, God, please take me home to be with You. It doesn't seem possible for me to go back and I certainly cannot bear it to go on. I am a misery to myself and to everybody round about me. Please, please take me home to be with You."

But Oh, I am so glad that He spared me. Praise His precious name.

After I had come out from under the ether and the knife, wherein five operations in one had been performed, the poor, unconscious "what-there-was-left-of-me" was put back in the bed and I opened my eyes on the white walls of the hospital-quivering with pain from head to foot, which, instead of growing better grew worse and worse.

Twice my mother had been called by a telegram to see me die. Her heart was torn as the wheels of the train sped over the track, and she prayed that she might be there in time. From the depot she was rushed to the hospital, and chokes up yet, as she sits here beside me and tries to describe her feelings as she entered the room reeking with ether, and looked upon the little form lying on the pillow that had been the center of so many scenes of hope and life and happiness.

She thought of the day she had prayed for the little girl who should go out in the world to preach the Word, the day of the dedication under the banners of blood and fire, the golden future of joyful service, and here was the wreck!

Was this all?

Something within her refused to let go of God and His promises to her regarding me. Whilst the doctors and nurses in the outer room were gravely explaining to her the scientific reasons why I could not live, explaining that mine had been such an exceptional case, and endeavoring to reconcile her to my death, her heart was going out in an agony of prayer to God that her daughter's life would be spared.

Brokenly she wept and prayed, renewing and redoubling her vows to God to help in every way to get me back into the work and keep me there, to do all in her power to help me with my children and in every struggle, come what may.

The nurses, hardened as they were by long training, were frankly in tears and the doctor" herumphed!" and cleared his throat as I came out of the ether, and declared that that hospital had never witnessed such a scene, for I was preaching, telling of Jesus, begging lost souls to come to Him, in that high strong voice which patients have when coming out from the anaesthetic. Broken though I was in body and spirit, the very moment that reason lost her sway, my soul began to sing and preach and pray to my beloved Jesus.

Later Mother came into my room and kneeling down, looked into my eyes and said:

"Mother is here, darling. Mother will help. She understands and will stand by you, dear." In the look which was exchanged it seemed as though a spark of hope and understanding was instilled and glowed in both of our souls, which has never gone out, but has burst into a flame, ever mounting upward as days go by.

One evening, after a nurse and doctor had been in almost constant attendance all afternoon, three young interns came in and gathering me gently in their arms, carried me, mattress and all, into the separate room where people were taken to die.

About two in the morning the white-robed nurse, who had been stroking my hand, saying:

"Poor little girl; poor little girl," seemed to be receding. The fluttering breaths which I could take were too painful to go deeper than my throat.

Everything grew black someone said:

"She's going." Just before losing consciousness, as I hovered between life and death, came the voice of my Lord, so loud that it startled me:

"NOW WILL YOU GO?" And I knew it was "Go," one way or the other: that if I did not go into the work as a soul-winner and get back into the will of God, Jesus would take me to Himself before He would permit me to go on without Him and be lost.

Oh, don't you ever tell me that a woman cannot be called to preach the Gospel! If any man ever went through one hundredth part of the hell on earth that I lived in, those months when out of God's will and work, they would never say that again.

With my little remaining strength, I managed to gasp:

Yes Lord I'll go." And go I did!

I could not have been unconscious for more than a moment, but when I opened my eyes the pain was gone. I was able to take deep breaths without the agony which had accompanied the tiniest breath before. I was able to turn over without pain, and proceeded to do this, much to the alarm of the nurse. In two weeks, to the amazement of everyone, I was up and well, though weak in body. I have hardly known an ache or a pain from that day to this.

On several occasions before and after my return from the hospital, little attempts were made to break the news of my determination to go forth into the vineyard at once.

"Why, what a crazy notion for you to even think of such a thing! Why don't you be like other young women and be contented to stay at home and attend to the housework?" and other outbursts of like nature invariably met my timid, yet firm ventures to gain the consent of the household.

Too weak to argue, I was also too weak to dare even think of disobeying God. That great white whale, the operating table, had thrown me up on the shore. The Lord had spared my life under a definite promise that I would serve Him. Foolish and impossible as the idea might seem, I was going to strike out for Nineveh, without a moment's hesitation, live or die, sink or swim, praying for Divine guidance and filled with a determination to say "Yes" to that call "Will you Go? Will you Go?" I did not know just how or where I was to go, but intended to start anyway and that at once, throwing myself at His feet and trusting Him implicitly. I was assured that He who parted the Red Sea and rolled back the waves of the Jordan would someway remove rivers and mountains for me and take me through the fires unburned.

Mother now being in Canada, I telegraphed there for money; and when alone in the house one night, 'phoned for a taxicab and at eleven o'clock bundled my two babies inside while the chauffeur piled the two suitcases on top, and away we sped to catch the midnight train for home and Mother.

To make a new start and begin all over again it seemed the most natural thing in the world to go back to the starting place from which I had set out before.

God was with me and I was conscious of His leading and support at every step. With my little baby clasped in one. arm and Roberta sleeping in the other, I held them tightly to me as the immensity of what I was doing saved over me. The streets were dark and almost deserted as we rolled along toward the depot.

So here I was setting forth for the second time in my life to obey the great call to preach the Word, but how different it was from the first time how changed the scene!

Scene One. The first time it was high noon and the warm, friendly sun smiled and beamed down upon us from the sky life and hope spread their garments before the little rosy-cheeked bride as she was waved away by tearful but loving and sympathetic friends and relatives, one hundred or more of whom had gathered on the country lawn, some coming many miles to see her off, showering her with flowers, rice and "God bless you's." That time I had gone forth leaning in every way for strength, wisdom and guidance on the strong arm of my husband; blest and victorious in my soul. An open door of ministry lay before us; we were sure of our footing, knew just where we were going.

Scene Two: Setting forth alone at midnight almost running away with my two babies-weak in body empty and lean in my soul no earthly arm to lean upon no visible open door before me no loving friends no flowers or "God bless you's." But Oh, I praise Jesus for the experience! Nothing could tempt me to part with the lessons taught me in those hard places of going through alone with Jesus and thrusting my roots of faith and dependence, confidence and trust down deep into Himself.

My former life in the work had been like that of a vine which twined about the stalwart oak, but when that stronghold to which I clung had been taken away and transplanted into the Heavenly gardens, when my clutch had been loosened and let go there was nothing left of the vine, that had reached so high, but a pitifully broken, crumpled little heap which lay in tumbled confusion on the earth. But now I had found One to cling to and fasten my hold upon who was as the cedars of Lebanon, who would endure forever, from whom I could not be removed one who would never die nor leave me. Oh, it was Jesus! Jesus!!

Yes, thank God for the hard places, for the winds and the icy blasts of winter's storm, for Oh, 'twas there I learned for the first time a little of what it meant to be rooted and grounded and settled to die out and to go through a valley of crucifixion that led to resurrection power and glory.

Did you ever ride along through a tunnel or subway that was pitch dark and seemingly endless? Then all at once, away in the distance, you saw a tiny light which you knew must be the opening of the tunnel and sunlight? That's just the way I felt. I was still in the darkness of the tunnel, but I saw the door, the beacon light of God's dear sunlight His smile of approval, and I was running toward it.

"Here we are, lady, just in time!" broke in the voice of the driver, as the car pulled up at the curb in front of the depot.

I cannot remember now how those two sleeping children and all the baggage were gotten on board, but I do know that a few minutes later, when the train steamed out into the night and sped through the fields and the sleepy towns, we were all on board and the babies sleeping as sweetly as they ever had in their lives in the snow-white Pullman bed.

I was obeying God, and although the enemy was still endeavoring to hound my tracks with accusations and forebodings of future disaster, he had someway lost his grip and his power to overthrow me. When he twitted me with the leanness and the barrenness of my soul, that hurt the most of anything because it was so true, my heart sang within me:

"Never mind, Rebecca's on her way to the well to the fountain-head to the sure source of supply to the banqueting table of the King, and we'll soon be filled up now."

CHAPTER XL. GETTING BACK

"For ye were as sheep going astray; but are now returned unto the Shepherd and Bishop of your souls."
I Pet. 2:25

When the 11:55 pulled into the station of Ingersoll my Father and Mother were there to meet me so was the pony I used to ride. She was only a colt then, but she knew me and whinnied affectionately.

"Suppose she knows you?" said Dad.

"Surely she does I smiled. And as if to remove all doubts on the matter, Fritzie lifted her right front foot to shake hands and quivered all over as she nozzled my cheek with her velvet nose, smacking her lips and pretending to hunt for the old-time sugar lump both tricks I had taught her long ago my, how long it did seem! Was it centuries or was it just years?

Usually Fritzie was quite staid, but how she did pick up her heels and run that day! It seemed as though she couldn't get home and out of her harness quickly enough to play with me. I wondered if she remembered how we used to leap the fences, and the time she followed me right into the kitchen and stamped about, to the dismay of my Mother.

How familiar arid restful and green the dear old fields looked on that drive homeward. Here was the old toll-gate. A mile beyond was the place where I had given my heart to Jesus and cried

"Lord, be merciful to me, a sinner as the sleigh jingled along, drawn by Fritzie's mother. A mile beyond that again was the little white school house on the corner. Every foot of the way was associated with girlhood memories.

No explanations were asked, but Mother informed me that it had all been settled that I was to leave for the Pentecostal camp meeting at Kitchener (then called Berlin) the next day. She herself had planned to attend, but immediately upon the receipt of my telegram had given up all thought of going and had written to engage accommodations for me.

"But, Mother! the children would I be able"

"Never mind the children," she interrupted. "I have taken care of children before and cared for Roberta almost all the time anyway, and Rolf and I will get along fine, won't we, Sonny?" A delighted gurgle and a wide smile, that displayed the new baby teeth, was his response.

"Yes, and we've got the best Jersey milk in the country 'to make him grow like a weed," boasted my Father, as if to conclude the subject.

"But but how can I get back to Kitchener, when I feel so leaked out spiritually? The last time I was there was with Brother Durham and Robert. I was so blest; prayed for the seekers.

What would they think?

"But, I'll go, Mother. Oh, I am so happy, so glad for the opportunity. Are you sure that the extra work will not be too much for you?"

"Too much work? I should say not! Oh, Aimee, nothing is too much or too hard to see you get back to God and back to the place where He wants you. Will you promise me that you will come back in this meeting? We will stand by you, and God will help you."

But I needed no coaxing nor inducement having set my face like a flint, and though all the world were pulling the other way I MUST go through any other course meant death.

Before leaving the next morning for the camp, a telegram was sent to my husband, saying:

"I have tried to walk your way and have failed. Won't you come now and walk my way? I am sure we will be happy."

At Kitchener we were met with the wagon which carried the passengers and baggage to the camp grounds. I soon found myself alighting in the little city of tents, pitched in snow whiteness beneath the green foliage of the forest trees. Glad hands and familiar faces gathered round to welcome me back, but I felt conscience- and duty-bound to make an embarrassed, but hasty, explanation to one and all that I was not where I once was, and said to them

"I prayed for others when they needed prayer. Now I need someone to pray for me and help me get back the blessing and fire of God upon the altar of my heart."

Perhaps some of you can imagine my feelings as I sat in the audience looking up at the platform whereon sat different ones whom but a few years before I had prayed with when they came through the baptism. There they were, shaking and quivering under the power, faces radiant hallelujahs ringing and here sat I, dabbing at my eyes with a wet handkerchief and saying:

"Oh Jesus, You used to bless me like that. I used to shake under the power and praise you just like that.

"Oh, bless me now, my Savior; I come to Thee."

(All through the months of my disobedience to God, the Holy Spirit had never left me, but had prayed through me in tongues many times, and was indeed an abiding Comforter. Oh, the mercy, and the long-suffering of God! How little I deserved it!)

When the call for the altar service came I stole forward amongst the others and bowed at the altar, feeling utterly unworthy to touch even one of the rough planks which formed its floor. All I could do was bow my head and weep. The brother in charge came along and said:

"Now, Sister, lift up your hands and praise the Lord, just as you used to tell others to do." But, Oh no, I felt that I had much to make right with the Lord first that I must beg Him to forgive me and apologize and humble myself in the dust before Him. How little we know after all of the great loving heart of God who runs to meet the penitent soul even as the father ran to meet the prodigal of old.

Brokenly I began to sob:

"Oh, Lord, forgive me" before I could finish the words I felt as though the Lord had put His hand over my mouth and said to me:

"There, my child, it's all right. Don't say anything more about it." This was so sudden and unexpected I could not comprehend it, but thought surely I must be mistaken, surely I would have to beg and plead for hours and it would be very hard to get back to God after having been so disobedient and wandering away. So I settled myself down and tried it again

"Oh Lord, dear Lord, can you ever forgive me" again came the same peculiar sensation as of the Lord stopping my mouth and saying:

"It's all right; it's all forgiven. Don't say any more about it." It was just as though someone had injured me in some way had come to me to ask forgiveness, and I had said:

"Oh yes, that's all right. Never think of it again. Just forget it."

Well, the suddenness and the magnitude of this hearty reception completely bowled me over. It broke my heart and bound me to Him more than any whipping could ever have done. Such love was more than my heart could bear. Before I knew it I was on my back in the straw, under the power, saying:

"Dear Lord, just let me be as one of your hired servants. I do not feel worthy to testify or work at the altar or preach, but just let me love you and dwell in your house, my Savior."

The next thing I knew the Spirit was speaking in tongues through me, giving me the interpretation. A brother from London had a, message in tongues the Lord gave me the interpretation of that and he fell back under the power. I was laughing and weeping and shaking. A little knot of people gathered round to rejoice with me. The Spirit lifted me to my feet and walked up and down praising the Lamb for sinners slain. Palling on my knees I worshipped the Lord again.

A dear old Mennonite preacher who had been seeking his baptism for years was kneeling at the other end of the platform. It had been my privilege to pray for his brother as he came through to the baptism the night before we left for China.

The Lord seemed to guide me to this brother now, and walking on my knees, with my hands outstretched before me, something within me spoke:

"In the name of Jesus Christ, receive ye the Holy Ghost." Immediately the brother fell to the ground and was speaking in tongues almost before he reached it. After all his years of waiting, the Comforter had come in like a flash of glory to abide forever.

The old-time power and the anointing for praying with seekers rested upon me. Many other instances, which I will not refer to here, took place.

But oh, the Lord did not let these wonderful answers to prayer, as I prayed for the seekers, come to puff me up, but to encourage me. It was balm to my wounded, troubled soul.

Never have I worked harder at the altar services in our own meetings than at that camp meeting. We stayed as late as twelve and sometimes two in the morning, praying for seekers and were up again to early morning meeting. He was restoring my soul, He was leading me out to green pastures. I had come to this camp meeting to see God, and Oh, how He did reveal himself to me!

Camp over, I returned to my Mother's to find her happily running the sewing machine on the piazza, making clothes for the children, who were laughing in the hammock that swung beneath the apple trees. Delightedly I repeated the story already written in my letters of the blessing of the Lord upon my soul, and added that I had but one week to wash and iron my things and get ready for the next camp meeting, which was to be held in London, twenty miles away, the very city where the Lord had taken my husband and myself to carry the message of Pentecost some years before.

Happy to do anything to advance my Savior's cause, I had been given the task of painting a great twenty-five foot banner, roping and preparing it to go across the street, advertising the meetings.

Within the house was a little pile of letters, demanding my immediate return "to wash the dishes," take care of the house" and "act like other women." But I had put my hand to the Gospel plow, and I could not turn back. I was going through, and I had the assurance that the Lord would bring my husband also. I certainly never could win him the other way and he would have had to have parted with me for good if I had died, which I surely would have done had I remained out of the work. I was going through; Jesus was with me and nothing in all the world mattered now. My heart was right with God.

Although in many ways the enemy endeavored to discourage, frighten and turn me back, as he did poor Christian in Pilgrim's Progress, and though the tests were hard and his tactics cunningly planned, Jesus held me firm and did not allow me to swerve from my path nor stumble in the way.

The blessed London camp meeting over, the Lord strongly impressed me to accept an invitation from Sister Sharp of Mount Forest, Ont., to conduct Bible meetings there in a little hall called "Victory Mission." The power and the glory of the Lord came down in a precious way. The mission soon became too small to hold the people; we were obliged to hold the services on the spacious lawn between the Sister's home and the mission. Such a spirit of revival came down upon the people that soon a tent was bought, hungry people filled it night after night and those who could not get in stood in rings round its border.

Then came the day when the power fell. It was half past ten in the morning, and in my room I was praying:

"Oh Lord, send Thy mighty power today. Lord, send the power. Send the power, Lord."

Outside, in the tent, two brothers shook hands with each other and said:

"Praise the Lord." As they spoke the power of God struck them both; one fell one way, and one the other, and lay stretched out under the power shouting and glorifying God. Little children began to come in off the street to see what it meant. One look was sufficient and away they ran to bring others to see the strange sight.

Mrs. Sharp's mother, who had a very sore and badly poisoned foot, came hobbling out of the house, her knee on a chair which she used as a means of conveyance. No sooner did she reach the tent that the power struck her and she tipped over (chair and all) was healed, and later danced and praised the Lord.

Sister Sharp came running into the tent, and down she went, the town crier, who used to ring the bell advertising theatres, ball games, etc., came in, and over he went with his bell, and lying under the power added his voice with the others to the praises of the most high God.

It is not necessary for me to go on and relate the wonderful way in which Jesus worked in this meeting, to tell how the town was stirred, how our Sister was healed before the magistrate and liberated, how over a hundred were saved and scores received the baptism, as dear Sister Sharp has herself written an account of the meetings, which you will find related in Chapter One, Part II, of this book.

However, I must tell you the best news of all, for right in the midst of one of the meetings which was held in Mount Forest, my husband landed with his suitcase, to attend the meeting.

So changed was I, so radiantly happy, so filled with the power of God and the unction of the Holy Spirit, that he had to admit that this was indeed my calling and work in life. Before many hours had passed he himself had received the baptism of the Holy Spirit, spoke in tongues and glorified God.

How the Lord does vindicate and honor those who go through with Him! As my husband saw the workings of the Holy Spirit, sinners coming to the altar for salvation, believers receiving the Holy Spirit, and heard me delivering the messages under the power of the Spirit, for truly it was not I, but Christ that lived in me, he told me that he recognized that God had called me into this work and would not have me leave it for anything in the world. And through the succeeding years, though part of the time he is with me and part of the time elsewhere, the Lord has made him perfectly willing for me to go on, whether he is along or not.

The Lord has wonderfully blessed and supplied my every need and the needs of the two children, for food, clothing and travelling expenses. We have lacked no good thing. The way has been growing brighter and brighter day by day. The harvest of souls is increasing month by month.

The work is spreading out and the nets are filled with abundance of fish. Glory! Glory!! GLORY!

CHAPTER XII.REVIVAL FIRES FALL

"And Elijah . . . repaired the altar of the Lord that was broken down. Then the fire of the Lord fell, and consumed the burnt sacrifice . . . And when all the people saw it, they fell on their faces and said, The Lord, He is God."
1 Kings 18:30, 38, and 39

After the meeting at Mount Forest the Lord called us back to the U. S. A. to dispose of our little store of earthly goods and to give me also an opportunity to work with my own hands and feet to help raise the money with which to purchase a new 40x80 Gospel tent which the Lord had shown me definitely it was His will for us to have. We had the assurance that the balance would be in by the time the tent was to be paid for, and true to His word, offerings began to be handed to us in the little meetings.

THE TENT MEETING IN PROVIDENCE, R. I.

The new tent was to have been ready for our camp meeting, which was to begin June first, but the Lord intervened and did not allow it to be completed on time. Knowing little of the winds and power of the elements which have to be taken into consideration when picking out a location for a tent meeting, we, in our ignorance, selected a fine, high hill, on the bluff of the bay where those who came to meeting could enjoy the breeze and the water. That there was a breeze no one who was there and saw the tents go down could deny.

Whatever else the location may have lacked in, the breeze was ever there. If anything could have discouraged us with tent work, surely our experience in Providence would have done so, but praise the Lord, He did not permit our new tent to be completed, and therefore the tent company put up an old tent of their own which had almost seen its day, and cost us nothing for the damage done to it.

But in spite of wind and the hours of struggle to drive the stakes and tie the ropes and keep the tents up, the Lord sent thousands of people to the camp meetings and many precious souls wept their way to Jesus' feet and received the blessed Holy Spirit, the Comforter whom Jesus sent.

Neighbors who were utterly indifferent at first when they saw our valiant struggles with the wind and storms, came to our help and toiled with us.

Then, feeling they had some interest in the tent which they had worked so hard to keep up, came in to hear the message delivered in it, and were brought to the Lord one whole family was saved in one night.

The series of meetings was almost over when one forenoon the last wind storm came, and in spite of all our efforts, down went the big tent with many tears in its rotten old seams which we had worked for hours to sew up, just a short time ago.

My husband, who had worked faithfully each time, was discouraged, and declared that that tent could not be put up again. He had taken a position and returned to secular work, and would not be back that day, but I knew that hundreds would be there for the night meeting. I could not manage that big tent alone, so with the help of a little boy, in the heat of the noon hour, we set to work. We had ten small 10x12 tents scattered about in different places in the grounds; some had been erected; some were still in their bags. These we carried, one by one, raised them on their poles, stretched the canvas and drove the stakes, lashing them, pole to pole, all in one straight row. This had the appearance of one long tent, one hundred feet long and twelve feet wide (if you can imagine how that looked). Then we carried in the chairs. By this time people were arriving and they turned in and helped us.

How the Lord did bless our efforts, this tent was so low the wind could not take it down. Souls were saved into the Kingdom; many danced, shook under the power, and received the Holy Spirit.

Two sisters from Onset Bay, Cape Cod, who attended the meeting, asked us to ship our tent there and, undismayed by the experiences in Providence, we shipped the tent. Although we have lowered our tent several times since, never once have we ever had our tent torn down by the wind from that day to this.

Before going to Onset a short meeting was held at Montwait Camp grounds, Massachusetts, and the Lord blessedly poured out of His Spirit, swing and baptizing hungry souls. The enemy was still testing my faith and endeavoring to draw me back from the work, but thank God, my feet were kept from slipping, even though many times I have had to go through alone.

When the meeting was almost over in Montwait the Lord spoke to my husband, in Providence, E. I., in three dreams, calling him to leave his secular work in the plant where he was employed and come and assist me with the tents.

ONSET BAY

In Onset our new tent was pitched in the Holiness Camp ground, and though the battle was hard, Jesus gave victory. The war against spiritualism, Christian Science, and demon powers was hot and heavy, but we sang and preached the blood of Jesus until the break came and the Lord poured out His Spirit.

COKONA, L. I., N. Y

While yet in Onset the Lord began to speak to me of Corona and different times when praying, would bring the word "Corona" before me. I had been asking the, Lord for a typewriter and thought He was going to give me a Corona as the word kept ringing in my ears, when a letter came through the mail, however, from a dear colored sister, stating that the Lord had directly led her to send for us to come to Corona, L. L, (just outside of New York City) to hold a meeting. My spirit quickened within me as the Lord gave the witness that this was that which He had been speaking of.

The weather now being too cold for tent meetings in the East, we asked the Lord to supply the means whereby we might ship our tents to Florida, where it would be warm enough for a winter campaign, and still praying to this end, we went to Corona.

Upon first arrival this seemed a most discouraging field. No one but this precious colored sister was known to have received the baptism of the Holy Spirit according to Acts 2:4. Though we walked for blocks, not a hall could we find to rent, but I kept praying, and though everyone else doubted my call, I knew that God had sent me.

Finally word came from the Swedish church that we would be welcome to open meetings there during the week.

The second night the church was filled to the door, though church members had been warned by their ministers to keep away from the Pentecostal people and have nothing to do with those folks who talked in tongues. Just one week from the day meetings were opened the break came. A Sunday School teacher from one of the large churches, a man whose sound Christian standing had been known for years, was the first to receive the baptism. The wife of a leading citizen was the second, and when the altar call was given scores from the audience, which was made up entirely of church members, gathered about the altar.

Never having seen a Pentecostal meeting, they were very stiff and did not know how really to get hold and seek the Lord. Knowing that their ministers had warned them that this was all hypnotism, however, I was very careful not to lay hands upon, or speak to the seekers, but prayed by my own chair earnestly:

"Oh, Lord, send the power. Lord, honor your Word just now."

Then it was that Mrs. John Lake, who had risen from the altar and taken her seat in the audience again, suddenly fell under the power, with her head upon her husband's shoulder. In alarm the people said

"She has fainted. Bun and get some water."

But I knew she hadn't fainted, and I kept on praying:

"Lord, send the power. Baptize her just now."

Quite a crowd had gathered round her, but before they could get back with the water, praise the Lord, her lungs began to heave with the power, her chin began to quiver, and she broke out speaking with other tongues to the amazement and delight of all.

On and on she spoke, in such a clear, beautiful language, her face shining with the glory of the Lord. One would say to another:

"What do you think of it?" and others would say:

"Oh, isn't it wonderful, marvelous! How I wish I had the same experience!"

The news of this well-known sister's baptism quickly spread through the town. The next night three were slain under the power and came through speaking in tongues, and thus the meetings increased in power, numbers and results each night.

After preaching in the church one week, Pastor W. K. Bouton invited us to his church to preach on a Thursday night. (After warning his people not to come near our meetings he had come himself.)

The Lord had convinced him of the truth that there was something deeper yet for himself and his church.

The night on which we spoke at his church I had to ask the Lord not to let me be afraid or overawed by the visiting ministers who sat behind me on the platform, and to give me liberty and power in preaching His Word and He never fails. He remembers our weakness, praise His name.

As I spoke, hearty "Amens" and "Hallelujahs" came from all over the church. I felt that I must preach the truth without compromise or fear at least once in this church as they might never ask me again. When finished I took my seat, not presuming to give an altar call in someone else's church.

The Minister rose and said:" How many of you people believe what Sister McPherson has said to be the truth, feel that you have not received the baptism of the Holy Spirit in the Bible way, and would like to receive this experience? Lift your hands."

They tell me that every hand in the church went up. (My eyes were so full of tears of joy I really could not say.)

The people rose from their seats and flocked up the aisles, gathered completely round the chancel rail, inside the chancel, right behind the pulpit, and prayed between the pews and all over the church for the baptism of the Holy Spirit. What a glorious sight it was! This church had been kept clean from concerts and suppers and worldly amusements. Through their consecrated pastor they had been brought up to the place where they were just ready to be saved into the fulness of the Spirit's power.

Three received the baptism that night. One lady fell by the organ, another at the other side of the church. Then two brothers who had not been on speaking terms with each other for over a year were seen talking to each other in the center of the church. One had asked the other, with tears in his eyes, to forgive him, and immediately fell back in his brother's arms under the power of the Holy Spirit. Alarmed, his brother lowered him to the floor.

I do not believe the scenes in that dear church could be described this side of Heaven. Each time someone fell under the power the people would run to that side of the church. When someone would fall on the other side they would turn and go over there. It was all so new and strange.

The Pastor, however, did not run to look as the rest did, but kneeled by his pulpit with his hands over his face, looking through his fingers every once in a while to keep a watch on proceedings. (Laughing over it together later, when he had received his baptism, I told him it appeared as though he believed in the verse that told us to "watch and pray.") He was yearning for the power of God, and yet naturally fearful lest his people should be led into confusion and error.

Seeing the questions and excitement of the people as the power of God prostrated their dear ones, the enemy whispered:

"Well, you will never have an invitation back to this church now. There never was anyone stretched out under the power on that green carpet before. They will never ask you back here again."

Oh ye of little faith, wherefore did ye doubt? At midnight, when the meeting was beginning to break a little, the Pastor touched me on the arm and said:

"Sister, we have talked this over with the officials and the church is yours for as long as you want it, and when you want it. When shall we have the next meeting?"

"Tomorrow night," I replied.

Tomorrow night found the church not only filled to the doors, but the vestry and Sunday

School rooms as well, this night seven received the baptism. The Minister invited me to preach the Bible evidence of the baptism speaking in other tongues as the Spirit gives utterance and to take full liberty in every way.

During altar service he kneeled, looking through his fingers once in a while; at the strange proceedings taking place in his dignified congregation.

Sinners broke down and wept their way to Jesus-feet Protestants and Catholics alike. Such praying and calling upon the name of the Lord, the minister feared would result in the people's being arrested for disturbing the peace.

The third night nineteen received the baptism of the Holy Spirit. Down they went right and left, between the seats, in the aisles, in front of the chancel rail, up on the platform. Oh Glory!

One night, while praying with a young lady who was receiving the baptism, I happened to catch the minister's eye as he was watching and beckoned him to come where he could really see and hear. He kneeled beside the young lady whom he knew well as a devoted Christian worker, and soon saw her face suffused with Heavenly glory as she was filled with the Spirit and broke out speaking with other tongues and praising the Lord. As he watched and listened a wistful look came over the brother's face and without a word he went round to his pulpit again and kneeling down with closed eyes, lifted his hands and began to pray.

"Oh Lord, fill me. Oh Lord, fill me." Over and over he prayed this simple prayer in earnestness and humility before the Lord. The Spirit kept impressing me to go and pray for him. At first I hesitated, feeling my own worthiness, but at last I went and kneeled behind him and began to pray as simply as he:

"Lord, fill him."

"Lord, fill me," he would cry.

"Lord, fill him," was the prayer that filled my soul.

I do not know how long we kept on praying thus, but I do know that when I opened my eyes it seemed almost too good to be true. The minister was swaying from side to side, and soon fell backwards under the power and rolled off the little step and lay under the glorious power of the Lord, just inside the chancel rail.

Someone spoke to his wife, who had been sitting in the audience, and said:

"Oh, there goes William!"

This was too much and with one bound she was in the aisle and ran to the front sobbing imploringly:

"Oh, Will, Will, speak to me. Speak to me."

Kneeling beside her I was praying with all my might that the Lord should baptize this dear Pastor as it would mean so much to the entire church and in fact the whole town. Fearful lest she should disturb him, I said:

"Oh my dear, you wouldn't disturb him while he is under the power, for the world, would you?"

"Oh, but he's dying. He's dying!" she wailed.

"I know he's going to die!"

"Oh no, he is not dying" I hastily explained.

"This is the power of the Holy Spirit, dear. He is safe in the arms of Jesus and if you watch a few minutes you will see him receive the Holy Spirit, I am sure."

"Oh, but I know he is dying! He had a vision once before and he almost died then. Will, Will, speak to me," she implored.

I doubt if I could have restrained her much longer, but just at that tense moment, when the congregation were gathered round in breathless circles, leaning over the chancel rail, some even standing on the pews to see over the other's shoulders, Pastor W. K. Bouton was filled with the blessed Holy Spirit and began speaking with other tongues in a clear, plain language of which the Lord gave me the interpretation, message after message.

People fell to the floor here and there through the audience. Strong men sobbed like babies, and when at last the Pastor rose to his feet he walked up and down the platform, and said:

"Oh, friends, I have to preach!" And preach he did, under the inspiration of the Holy Spirit, telling the people that "This is That," commanding them to be filled with the Spirit, to get oil in their lamps and prepare for the coming of the Lord.

In the two weeks that followed practically the entire congregation from pulpit to the door, besides members who came in from other churches, were baptized with the Holy Spirit and spoke in other tongues.

All the trustees except one were saved through to the baptism. This one held aloof for some time, saying:

"Ok, I don't believe that all this noise and shouting and falling under the power is necessary. I believe in the Holy Spirit, but not in this shouting and talking in tongues."

"Well, brother, even if you don't understand it all now, do not sit back here in the seats. Come up to the altar. You feel it will be all right to seek more of Jesus, don't you?"

"Oh yes, I will seek more of the Lord," he replied. "That's all right," and he took his place with the others at the altar.

It was only a few minutes later while praying with the seekers, and they were going down one by one under the mighty rushing wind of the Heavenly gales that were sweeping from Heaven, that we heard a great shout, and something struck the floor with a thump.

Making my way as quickly as possible to the place where this great roaring was coming from.

I found its source of origin was none other than the trustee who had but shortly before declared that all of this noise and shouting was unnecessary. I doubt if there was anyone in the church who made as much noise as he. He shook from head to foot; his heels beat a tattoo upon the floor; he fairly bellowed and roared forth in other tongues as the Spirit gave him utterance, his face filled with joy and glory.

One brother who had thought it unnecessary to speak in tongues talked for hours after he had been filled, and coming to me as I was on the sidewalk, just leaving for home, said, as he shook with the power:

"S-S-Sister M-M-McPherson, w-w-will I ever b-be able to t-t-talk in E-English again?" and away he went with other tongues again. Oh Hallelujah!

Sometimes the greatest doubters get the biggest baptisms and the people who despise noise make the most noise of all when they receive this old-time power.

Many sick bodies were healed. A young woman daughter of a Catholic family, was carried to the church in a taxicab, and came hobbling in upon crutches, crippled with rheumatism, unable to lift her hands and move the stiffened joints of her shoulders.

Here is her testimony as it was written for publication in the Bridal Call, our monthly magazine:

TESTIMONY OF HEALING

"For the past six years I have suffered from one of the worst cases of rheumatism, known as 'Arthritis Rheumatism' but praise God! He has healed me. For four years I was compelled to use crutches, and the stiffness was just taking a grip on each joint gradually. Until last December I could neither wash nor dress myself, and when one would even try to help me I would weep and moan with pain. My jaw became so stiff I could scarcely get a morsel of food into my mouth unless I broke it into very small pieces. But praise God since I have learned to say 'Glory to Jesus' every particle of stiffness has left my jaws. I have never again used the crutches since dear Sister McPherson's visit to the Free Gospel Church in Corona. Her prayers, together with the dear ones at that church, were answered, and Glory to Jesus.

I have received my baptism with the Holy Ghost and fire.

"I am gaining in strength every day. Today I can wash, iron, sweep, run the sewing machine, and on days when mother is compelled to be away from home, I prepare two meals. I thank God today that we have a Pentecostal church in Corona, and also that God has placed in our midst our dear pastor, Brother Bouton, who is ever willing at all times to serve our Master, and lead his flock in the 'straight and narrow path "

(Signed) Louise Messnick.

I will not attempt to describe to you the wonderful way in which the work is going on day by day in this church. Brother Bouton has written a little of himself. See Chapter 2, Part II.

Now that the work was going on so beautifully here, the Lord told us the time had come to begin our journey to Florida. We announced our expected departure to the people. We did not tell anyone that we were asking the Lord for the means wherewith to ship our tent and pay our fares, but the last night of the meeting Brother Bouton set a table out and was getting ready to ask for an offering for us, but before the song which they were then singing was finished or he could get an opportunity to ask for an offering, the people started. Up the aisles they came, one after another, laying their offerings upon the open Bible.

The Lord sent us, through these dear saints, just the amount needed. As we explained to them that we were called to preach among the poor and go to those who had not yet heard the message of Pentecost, they promised to send us a box of clothing to give to the poor, and ship it to us as soon as possible.

Corona, its dear saints, and our own precious experiences while there will never be forgotten.

CHAPTEE XIII.CALLED TO DWELL IN TENTS

FLORIDA TENT CAMPAIGN, 1917

"For I have not dwelt in an house . . . but have gone from tent to tent, and from one tabernacle to another"
I Chron. 17:5

Our first Florida tent meeting was held in Jacksonville, the gateway to the lower south. A tract of land centrally located was loaned us free of charge, and we immediately set to work erecting tents, buying lumber, building seats, platform, installing lights and making the preparations necessary for each tent meeting. Some twenty-four hours before the meetings were to open all was in readiness, the last bill had been paid, and the piano installed, and we had five cents left over. How happy we were that the Lord had known just how much to give us!

While we were yet speaking of this wonderful way in which God had provided, a poor old colored lady came in, begging clothing, money or; food for herself and children. We told her we were very sorry that we did not have any food to give her (we expected to fast ourselves until the meetings opened and offerings came in) nor any clothing at present, but we gave her the five cents which we had left.

Soon after she had gone, an automobile drove up to the tent, containing workers who had come from Atlanta, Ga. They were hungry and wanted supper right away, and not wishing to tell them that we had neither money nor food, I slipped away in my tent, and kneeling down, told the Lord about it, saying:

"Oh, Lord, if you want us to fast and pray until the meeting opens tomorrow Amen. But if you want me to have something to set before these people, please supply the food."

Rising, I heard a man's big, gruff voice on the street in front of our tent, saying:

"Whoa thar'"

Springing from the wagon, he came in with a cheery smile, carrying a box in his arms, marked "Prepaid," which he deposited upon the ground, with a Right smart heavy box you got here. Sign on this line, please," and he departed.

"Why, here is the box of clothes which the Corona saints promised to send for the poor people! Now I will be able to give some clothes to that dear old colored lady and her children," flashed happily through my mind, causing the thought of supper to be forgotten for the moment, running for the hammer, we pried the top off the box. Sure enough, here was a coat and here were some dresses. The coat felt very heavy, and an experimental shake brought rolling out of its sleeves and pockets cans of corn, peas, salmon and a box of crackers.' Still further search through the box revealed rolled oats, sugar, condensed milk and practically everything that was needed for supper. Oh Glory to Jesus!

This is just one sample of the wonderful way in which the Lord provides for His children when they go forth without purse or scrip taking no thought of what they shall eat or what they shall drink or what they shall put on. He had sent us our supper all the way from Corona, L. I., to Jacksonville, Fla., and had it there right on the tick of the clock, for the bells were ringing six.

The Lord is never late. Oh, aren't you glad He's on time? He's coming on time, too, dear ones. Very soon the floors of Heaven will roll back and He will appear. The two Pentecostal Missions came in with us.

The tent meetings opened with a good attendance, and the crowds increased day after day. The altar was, time after time, filled with seekers for salvation, the baptism, and healing, and the Lord did not turn the hungry empty away.

Practically every state in the Union was represented by the tourists who gathered to this place, and many were amazed as they saw and felt the power of the Holy Spirit, heard the messages in tongues and interpretation, the Heavenly music and singing, and saw the saints at the altar falling prostrate under the power, coming through to the baptism and speaking in languages they had never learned in their lives.

One brother spoke in Hebrew and a Hebrew scholar who was present, heard and understood.

Hallelujah!

Two young men were healed, one of a broken arm, broken at three places, and dislocated at the wrist; the other of a broken hand. Both removed the plaster and the splints before the audience, convincing everyone that they were made every whit whole. One sister was healed instantly of cancer.

Note. As it would be difficult to write from memory of the many eventful meetings which took place, 1917 and 1918, we have selected paragraphs from reports from Pentecostal papers.

CAMP MEETING AT TAMPA, 1917

Glory to Jesus! Glory! Glory! It seems you must almost hear us shouting and praising the Lord away up north. What a wonderful Savior we have! He has taken the foolish to confound the wise, and the weak to put the strong to flight.

He is laying bare His mighty arm. He is separating His people, yea, He is calling out a people from a people. Bless His name!

The Lord is blessing in Tampa. Meetings have increased in number and power steadily. Last night the tent was packed to the farthest corner, many standing and more turned away.

This has been a gathering under unique circumstances with this country standing under the dark clouds of trouble, on the brink of war. Tourists have heard for the first time the soon coming of Jesus and of the latter rain outpouring of the Spirit. With joy many have received the message and been baptized, declaring that they will return to their towns and cities and proclaim the truth.

An entire family from Minneapolis received the baptism the same night.

Great amazement fills the audience as the power of God falls. Many have been slain under the power and began to speak in tongues, prophecy and interpretation.

One lady did not have time to get to the altar. The power fell on her as she stood to her feet, and before she could get to the aisles the Lord had baptized her, as she went. The first sentence was interpreted "Jesus is coming soon, coming soon. Get ready."

Sinners cried out for mercy, and came to the altar without urging. Young men and old have taken out pipes, cigarettes, tobacco and playing cards, left them behind and gone away with shining faces.

A brother a professing Christian and church member for years (without salvation) confessed his sins publicly as the power fell, and running to the altar gave up his beer, tobacco, and many things. He was so filled with joy, which, though he was an old man, he had never before experienced, that he danced and shouted and cried, much to the amazement of his neighbors, for he lives in a beautiful home right across from the tent. This is a wonderful opportunity to work. Just on the eve of Jesus' return to earth, this whole country is waiting with bated breath for they know not what, and we hear His voice beseeching us

"Hasten! Preach the Word, for Jesus is coming soon."

The Lord has given us a Gospel automobile, with which we are able to hold eight or ten meetings a day, distributing thousands of tracts and hand bills, and carrying big display signs of the tent meetings.

PLEASANT GROVE CAMP DURANT

Durant is twenty miles from Tampa, and many of the people here are very poor. Some cannot even read or write, but how hungry they are for God! Yesterday the ground was thick with teams, wagons and automobiles of those who had driven here from a radius of thirty miles around. The Lord is swing and baptizing souls and healing the sick. There are messages in tongues and interpretation. It is a wonderful sight to see. people crowd to the front during altar service, standing on tip-toe on the benches to see the strange sight, men and women, slain under the mighty power of God, speaking in tongues as they are filled with the Spirit.

ST. PETERSBURG

Just a shout of victory from St. Petersburg, Fla., this wicked city where Pentecost has never been preached.

A great celebration was on when our meetings opened. People play cards and gamble on tables by the sidewalk; the streets beside the park and city hall were roped off at night for dancing,

70

and as the band played the people danced in masks and fancy costumes on the public streets.

Our snow-white tent, though comfortably situated, and decorated with palms and flowers to make it attractive, was but a 'poor inducement for such a worldly throng. Standing on the street, giving out hand bills and tracts, I looked at the long lines of automobiles and conveyances streaming by in the parades. This week was something in the nature of a Mardi-Gras and the cars were decorated to represent the state or business of the owner.

Suddenly the Lord spoke to me and said: "Decorate your car and join the parade!" At first this looked impossible. Surely the decorations must cost an enormous sum of money. But the Lord showed me how it could be done. We built a wooden frame just the shape of a tent; then taking a white sheet (which was one of the luxuries of our camp life) we made of it a miniature tent, stretching it over said frame, using cord for guy ropes, and large nails for stakes. On one side of the miniature tent we painted the words:

"Jesus is coming soon;" on the other side

"Jesus saves;" on another side

"I am going to the Pentecostal Camp meeting. Are you?"

Putting down the top of the Gospel auto, the miniature tent, some seven feet long, five feet wide, was lifted up and set over the car so as just to leave room for the driver. The car was also decorated with palms and wild flowers, which we gathered by the way, tied with tissue streamers.

Concealing a baby organ under the tent, I sat beneath it out of sight of the crowd, and the Lord shut the policeman's eyes so that we could slip into the grand parade of cars and get the full length of Main Street with our advertisement. We must get an audience to our tent meeting, even if we had to sail forth with flying colors into the territory of the enemy to advertise our soul-swing business.

Early next morning we got in line with the other cars. The brass bands were going by; the liquor man advertised his business, the telephone, the wheat man and the florist; the butcher, the baker, the tourists representing their different states all were there, having entered and listed their cars.

When it came our turn to slip in, the policeman's back was turned, and he was motioning behind his back for us to come on, and holding back traffic from the other direction with his hand, so in we went. We were far enough behind the bands so that our little baby organ and chimes could be heard distinctly, playing

"Just as I am, without one plea,

But that Thy blood, was shed for me."

and other familiar hymns such as

"Oh get ready, Oh get ready, for the judgment day."

"For you I am praying,

I'm praying for you."

Thousands of people lined either side of the long street, leaning out of their windows, standing on the roofs and after the first astonished stare the people began to laugh and clap their hands and cheer, and that night the tent was packed, and we had no more trouble getting crowds. Sinners were saved, believers baptized. The Salvation Army closed their doors and came in to work with us, bringing their drum and musical instruments.

*Note: DOES THE WORK STAND?

Though two years have passed since this meeting, letters are still coming from Jacksonville, Tampa and St. Petersburg, from those who were saved and baptized during these meetings, stating that they are standing true to this day and going deeper with the Lord

SAVANNAH, GA

This great city, with its hundreds and thousands of living souls, that has never had a Pentecostal mission within its borders, nor heard the message of the latter rain, has been laid heavily upon our hearts.

After shipping our tabernacle, tents, and camping outfit on the railroad, laying hands upon it and asking the Lord to send it right straight through (though freight had been paralyzed by war shipments) we ourselves traveled in the Gospel auto, carrying workers and Gospel literature.

The tent arrived almost as soon as ourselves. The Lord led us right to a spot of land which was loaned to us free of charge, and the first night several came forward for salvation. The second night one of those who had been saved the first night received the baptism. Never have we seen a more hungry, intensely earnest people than these, and although we are unable to stay, we are opening a mission, leaving our benches and fixtures here with Sister Swift of Durant, Fla., whom we brought with us in the car as a worker, and who, with her husband, will care for the work.

PREACHING IN THE COTTON FIELDS

From Savannah, Ga., we traveled by Gospel auto through South and North Carolina, Kentucky, Maryland and New Jersey, preaching as we went, and giving out thousands of tracts. We find this a comparatively inexpensive way of reaching the people, getting to people who never could be reached any other way.

The poor people in the cotton and tobacco field districts, far from Pentecostal Missions, in this way receive the literature and testimony.

At night we run our car into some quiet field or forest, beside a stream of water, pitch our tent, build our camp fire, and put up our camping cots for the night; up and about our Father's business again with the rising of the sun.

We had but eighteen dollars on which to make the trip from Savannah to Long Branch, N. J., the scene of the next camp meeting, but the Lord made either the eighteen dollars or the gasoline to -stretch, for we still had money when we arrived at our destination.

CHAPTER XIV. THE BRIDAL CALL

"Write the vision, and make it plain . . . that he may run that readeth it."
Hab. 2:2

While in Savannah, Ga., the first editions of the Bridal Call, our monthly magazine, were printed. The Lord had been laying it upon my heart to edit such a paper, and gave me, Himself, the name "THE BRIDAL CALL," and the cover design, the Lord appearing in the clouds, and the angels with their trumpets. Over and over the Lord spoke to me

"Write the vision and make it plain, that he may run who readeth it." Hab. 2:2.

At first I hesitated, saying:

"There are so many Pentecostal papers, and more capable writers who are able to give their entire time and thought to the matter. It would be impossible for me, having no office, nor abiding city, holding many meetings, traveling in the Gospel car, mothering the children, and many other things, to write or take the burden of a paper." The Lord replied:

"With me, nothing is impossible." He showed me His exact plan for the Bridal Call; that its, message was not to be one of controversy, fighting, great wisdom or eloquence, but simply what its name implied a call to the bride to prepare for her Heavenly Bridegroom. So whatever reports, testimonies or other matter may be in the paper, we endeavor to have one article making plain the way of salvation, one on the baptism of the Holy Ghost, and one on the coming of the Lord and the preparation to meet Him.

So plainly the Lord spoke, giving me articles to write, in such bursts of revelation, that the tears streamed down my face, while my fingers flew over the typewriter keys.

During our camp meeting in Savannah, the Lord commissioned our consecrated Brother, F. A. Hess (without any word from us), to undertake the printing for several months, charging only for the paper, of which we addressed, mailed and sent out freely from the first issue, two thousand copies.

Later the paper was printed in Framingham, Mass.

Forging ahead into new fields, and having sometimes thousands of people in our audiences, we have secured thousands of new names in outlying districts never before reached by Pentecostal literature.

For two years the Bridal Call has been published regularly. Letters come almost daily, telling of people who have been blessed, saved, baptized, healed, and are on their way rejoicing, through the humble little labor of love the Bridal Call. It has meant many hours of work, often late into the night, but these letters more than repay all the effort that has been made.

The Lord is now opening for us The Bridal Call Publishing House, centrally located at 125 South Spring Street, Los Angeles, Cal., and has commissioned a brother here to print it, so that now we will be able to send the paper promptly on a given date. The circulation is increasing marvelously. Time is short now, and the last invitation to the Marriage of the Lamb must go forth unhindered and multiplied.

We would like our readers to send rolls monthly to your friends, that they may hear the call and prepare to meet the Lord. At present we are sending, monthly, as the Lord supplies the means, thousands of papers, tracts and booklets to prisons, homes, hospitals and struggling, out-of-the-way missions.

A letter from the chaplain of one of our largest penitentiaries, inviting us to send more of such literature, states that he does not want Christian Science or New Thought, but the old-fashioned Gospel, to help sinful men and women back to God. Please pray with us that God will make the Bridal Call a ladder whereon many will climb to life, hope and Heaven. The letters which we receive from the prisoners are very pitiful.

Thank God! How wonderful to be deemed worthy of such a privilege, such an opportunity. Such work should not be stinted for means.

Many doors are open where we could send out thousands. The devil's literature goes forth without stint, and we believe that the Lord will provide means whereby this Bridal Call may be sent- to all the hungry ones whom He lays upon our hearts. All interested please write the "Editor" personally.

CHAPTER XV.EASTERN SUMMER TENT CAMPAIGN, 1917 CALL TO LONG BRANCH, N. J.

"The Spirit of the Lord God is upon me; because the Lord hath anointed me to preach good tidings unto the meek; He hath sent me to bind up the brokenhearted, to proclaim liberty to the captives, and the opening of the prison to them that are bound; to proclaim the acceptable year of the Lord, and the day of vengeance of our Lord; to comfort all that mourn; To give unto them beauty for ashes, the oil of joy for mourning, the garment of praise for the spirit of heaviness."
Isa. 61:1, 2, 3

The Lord witnessed to me concerning our going to Long Branch while in Savannah, Ga., I was waiting on the Lord for direct leadings. A number of letters, each containing a call to some particular city, were spread before me as I prayed.

"Oh, Lord, lead me just as You would have me.

Do not let us get one step out of Your will in any way, or the place that You would have us to be.

This call to Long Branch, N. J., seems to witness in my soul, speak to me, Lord, in some way, if this is of You. If not, take it away from me.

How I wish that I could find out more about the place, its population, etc."

As I spoke, a New York paper was picked up by a little gust of wind and blown across the tent.

Stooping over, still praying for the Lord to direct me and speak regarding Long Branch, N. J., I absent-mindedly picked up the paper and smoothed it out upon my lap, with amazement when, in large letters, printed half way across the paper, this sign met my gaze

"DON'T FAIL TO GO TO LONG BRANCH, N. J."

Beneath this sign was given a detailed description of the place, its accommodation, population, etc., and it wound up, with glaring letters

"WRITE AT ONCE TO LONG BRANCH, N. J., THAT YOU WILL BE THERE."

How wonderful that this New York paper should be away down here in Savannah, Ga., brought into the tent and right to my feet, open at this identical place! The Lord put the power upon me and witnessed that this was no mere accident, but truly another sign that He was leading.

(Condensed clippings and notes from reports.) Showers of blessing are falling in Long Branch, where a tiny band, seven in number, have been praying for revival and an outpouring of the Spirit for years. Brother and Sister W. Martin had grounds ready, soon we had the tent erected and filled with the glory of the Lord.

Workers and seekers have gathered from other towns and cities, crowds increasing daily Sundays people are turned away, unable to gain admission. Many have received the baptism of the Holy Spirit, and scores have come to the altar for salvation, and God is meeting one and all. A number have come out of the churches and received the baptism, and are going on in a precious way with the Lord. We go out daily with the Gospel car, upon which is painted in large letters on one side "Jesus is coming soon;" on the other "Where will you spend eternity?" Twenty and thirty miles of territory is covered daily with literature, street meetings and announcements.

During water baptism service by the ocean, the power of the Lord fell and those being baptized leaped, danced and shouted in the water, while spectators wept and praised the Lord on the shore.

Many of the young people have had marvelous and inspiring visions, some seeing our Savior hanging on the Cross for our sins; others saw our Lord descending in the clouds to catch away His waiting people.

There have been many remarkable instances of healing, one of which we relate: A preacher came on crutches not believing that the Lord could heal as in days of old, and in answer to prayer God healed him instantly, in the middle of the meeting and he ran about the tent, dancing, without his crutches and shouting: "Why, the Lord still heals! He heals as in days of old!"

His wife was so overjoyed she ran up and down the aisles and right up on the platform, shaking my hand and making me dance over the platform with her in such a way that it was impossible to go on with the meeting for a time because of the shouting of the people.

CAMP MEETING, HYDE PARK, BOSTON, MASS

It seemed impossible to ship our tents from New Jersey to Boston, Mass., as the embargo was on.

The Lord opened the way for us, to get a truck; and equipment was rushed through and put up on time. Praise God!

It was impossible to seat the throngs of people, The Pentecostal saints came filled with the glory and fire of God. Their testimonies and ringing songs of praises brought the entire neighborhood on the run to ask: "What meaneth this?" It was a hopeless task to seat the people, though seats were loaned us by the church and every available inch of space packed. Thousands nightly fringed the edge of the tent, standing clear out into the road as far and farther than it was possible for them to catch a word of the discourse.

At first the Catholic element did their best to disturb and break up the meeting, but praise the Lord, He gave us victory.

A policeman who roomed near the tent complained to his chief that he could not sleep for the noise of the people praying and shouting at all hours of the night, and the brethren were asked to appear at the station. They went in the Gospel car, leaving it in front of the door as they entered. The policeman who had made the com-plaint was not in, and the chief told them to sit down and wait for his return. Pacing up and down the floor, he at last went to the window, and looking out upon the car, with its lettered signs, drew back with a start, and said:

"Jesus is coming soon! Coming soon? Well, maybe so. I don't know."

"Are you prepared to meet Him if He should come?" they inquired.

"Have you been born again? Do you know that your sins are washed away, that you have passed from death unto life?"

"No, no, I cannot say that I do." They further invited him to give his heart to Jesus, but this he refused to do, giving several reasons why he could not do so at this time. (This was the chief who refused us proper police protection at our tent meeting.)

Going over to the window several times, he read aloud, in a thoughtful voice: "Jesus is coming soon". Well, well, maybe He is.And indeed He came very soon for this man. That night, the disturbing element, seeing no restraining hand laid upon them, were more disorderly than ever about the tent.

The next day the chief was stricken with heart failure at his desk and died in a few hours.

The news went round that entire section of the town that he had refused protection to the Gospel meetings then being conducted. Thereafter we had three men stationed by the tent at every meeting and perfect order.

Scores have come seeking salvation; the slain of the Lord are many, and deep conviction resting upon the people.

One young lady, a school teacher, came to mock, said she would never be one of those people, suddenly fell to her knees, crying for salvation, was wonderfully saved, and the next night baptized with the Holy Spirit.

Young men who ridiculed, were suddenly stricken with awful conviction while a message was being given in tongues and interpretation. The face of the young man who led the way to the, altar turned white, his knees and hands trembled as he cried: "Lord, be merciful to me, a sinner."

His friends followed him. They were all wonderfully saved and are now seeking the baptism.

A little girl with a paralyzed leg and a stiff knee was brought by her parents, for healing. One leg was two inches shorter than the other. The Lord instantly healed her and she was able to bend her knee and the limb was 'lengthened and became as the other one.

Sunday morning the power fell so no one could preach, the Holy Spirit Himself spoke in prophecy through Sister McPherson. Then she played the piano in the Spirit, and all over the tabernacle pealed forth the Heavenly anthem.

HUNTINGTON, L. I., CAMP MEETINGS

The camp grounds were a beautiful sight, with the many white tents nestled under the tall locust trees.

The meeting lasted ten days, souls were saved, backsliders reclaimed, sick healed, twenty-six received the baptism of the Holy Ghost. One girl who came to the altar to seek her baptism, wore a heavy steel truss around her waist and running down both sides of her limb, it fastened at the bottom of a heavy shoe and strapped down her withered, helpless limb. The Lord baptized her in the Holy Ghost and healed her limb. She removed the truss, brace and shoe, stood up, and walked up and down, perfectly strong and without pain. Her mother wept and saints shouted. Surely we have a right to shout with such a wonderful Jesus.

Among the number who came to the camp meeting from out of town was a lady, educated, refined, a great believer in holiness. She brought with her her little son of about eleven years. She had come to study Pentecost, and analyze this baptism of the Holy Spirit with the Bible evidence, speaking in tongues, its effects, manifestations, etc. She was always asking questions and moving from one to the other as they lay under the power, coming through to the baptism. Sometimes her face would soften and then again the look of a doubting Thomas would come into her eyes and she would want to handle and see.

One afternoon her son, who, without a question, was seeking the baptism, fell under the power, his face, which was always bright, suddenly took on the radiance of Heaven and his whole being seemed to be transformed, as he broke out singing in other languages, clear and beautiful, in poetry, the Lord giving me the interpretation of the song.

When the mother turned around from her investigating and seeking for information, and saw her son, who in his childlike faith had received that which she was questioning, it melted her heart and she herself fell under the power and came through speaking in tongues.

One night, during a severe storm, when the lights went out in the tent, we brought the Gospel automobile up to the edge of the tent, and lifting the side curtains, using the headlights of the car for illumination. This was one of the most wonderful meetings of this series. The Spirit took control in such a way that preaching was impossible.

Two ladies came from a Bible training School, one who had been a Christian worker and missionary for years, was broken in health, and though she did not know much of the baptism of the Holy Spirit, asked to be prayed for healing, during the breakfast hour in the dining tent.

We prayed for her and she fell off her seat and lay on the ground amongst the twigs and leaves, with the ducks, which were a constant source of annoyance to the cook, quacking about her. He does humble His people! No matter how great a worker one has been, everybody must get down.

Hallelujah!

In a few minutes the dear sister had received the baptism of the Holy Spirit and was shaking from head to foot, laughing with joy and talking in tongues.

The last Sunday the floor was covered with those prostrated under the power. Many messages were given with interpretation.

MONTWAIT, MASS

Here precious saints gathered from far and near and met in blessed liberty. The first night three received the baptism of the Spirit and sinners received salvation.

On Sunday nine received their baptism, some were saved and many healed. A dear Methodist minister and his wife and daughter received their baptism. Thirty or more received the Holy Ghost in the ten days' meeting.

WASHBURN, MAINE, CAMP

Since writing the heading of this report, I have been sitting here before my typewriter wondering where and how to begin. It was all so wonderful, it would be impossible for me to describe, but longing to encourage the many poor, hungry saints who are shut away from the meetings, I will do my best.

The Lord was with us from the beginning. The first few days some fifty-four received the baptism, and the number increased daily until within two weeks and a half it was safe to say over a hundred received. Hardened sinners wept their way to the altar; many sat and trembled from head to foot under conviction, and sinners on their way to the altar, fell in the aisles, often it was impossible to preach, the Holy Spirit conducted the meeting; messages in tongues and interpretation came forth from many empty vessels, waves of glory and marvelous singing saved over the audience.

A DRAMA ENACTED UNDER POWER OF HOLY SPIRIT

One night a drama was all worked out in the Spirit, showing forth the ten Virgins, going first with white robes to meet the Bridegroom. They said:

"He delayeth His coming; let us rest."

At first some argued that all should keep awake, for He that would come, would come quickly; but finally all were asleep.

Suddenly a loud cry "Behold! The Bridegroom cometh! Go ye out to meet Him!" Then all the virgins opened their eyes, and examined their lamps in alarm. The five sisters enacting the part of the wise virgins, danced for joy because of the oil, but the foolish begged the wise to share their oil with them. The wise said it was impossible, and sent the foolish to buy oil of Him who had to sell.

Then followed a scene where the foolish knocked at an imaginary door and haggled long over the price they would have to pay for the oil; they wanted to pay only a price which would not inconvenience them or cost a sacrifice, but the man who sold asked for all to give one hundred per cent sacrifice before they could obtain oil. At last the foolish went away, only to find that the wise had been taken up to meet the Lord; then they fell down and tore their hair and wept aloud.

This was followed by a ringing, warning appeal to all to make full surrender, pay the price, buy oil now, for the Bridegroom is at the door.

This was only one of the many wonderful messages and dramas worked out in our midst which were beyond description. On Sundays hundreds of automobiles, horses and carriages filled the fields, and it was impossible to seat but a small part of the people. The altar was full of sinners seeking salvation, and Christians receiving the baptism. Several ministers and their wives received, also many church members and workers, several receiving right in their seats during service.

The fall of the year is coming and campaign in the north and east drawing to a close. The farmers' wagons are busily wending their way between the harvest fields and the barns, as they gather the results of their summer's labor. They mop their hot, perspiring faces, and heave tired but happy sighs.

Many a time, while working at the altar hour after hour, sometimes away into the morning hours, after a heavy day, we have sunk down upon a seat after it was all over and remembered that the Master of the harvest was weary for us. But oh, the joy of it! Row after row of hungry souls seeking salvation, the baptism of the Holy Ghost, divine healing, or a. closer walk with God. The floors have been full of wheat and the vats overflowed with oil and wine. The Ark has been in the midst and we delight our souls in the Lord as we live again the scenes of the past summer campaign.

"Then shall the lame man leap as an hart, and the tongue of the dumb sing: for in the wilderness shall waters break out, and streams in the desert."
Isa. 35:6.

FROM THE NORTHERNMOST TOWN IN MAINE TO THE SOUTHERNMOST CITY IN FLORIDA

The cars were filled with workers as we left Washburn singing and praising the Lord as we journeyed, through the country, and the brothers shouting through the megaphone, the message of salvation and the soon coming of the Lord. Much attention was drawn to the cars by their big gold letters telling of Jesus' soon coming, and asking the questions: "Where will you spend Eternity?" And as we pass through the hundreds of towns and villages on our trips, we sing or testify, or give out literature, meeting many hungry souls. , We traveled all the day, slept by the wayside at night and the Lord always had a place prepared.

We have our Gospel Autos so arranged that we can turn the front seat back and sleep in the car, and the big outdoors is our home. With joy we kneeled by the running board at night to pray and thank the Father for this glorious opportunity of preaching the Gospel far and wide in the otherwise unattainable places.

Oh that you could see the hungry faces that gather around and listen to the Word in the South. Frequently men step out from the crowd during street meeting, and kneel weeping, at the running board of the car, then rise to testify of a determination to go through with Jesus.

All through Virginia, North and South Carolina, and Georgia, we visited many poor homes, cotton and tobacco fields, etc., with the message of love. How eager the poor colored people were to hear the Word and receive the papers! In this way the poor have the gospel preached unto them, and those who could never hear in any other way, of Jesus' soon coming. Precious souls are at stake, no time to be lost and we cry:

"Here am I. Lord, send me." Pray that we may be faithful, unselfish, humble, and quick that we may never lose an opportunity of preaching, instant in season and out of season, the soon coming of Jesus, and what it means to be ready to meet Him. We want to lay down our lives for the Master as He laid down His life for us.

"He who saveth his life shall lose it, but he that loseth his life for my sake shall find it"

Sometimes, while sleeping by the wayside or under damp tents, the enemy whispers of rheumatism, etc., but that is the word we meet him with, and he disappears. He pictures others with comfortable homes and warm beds, and points in scorn to our hard canvas cots, with no home comforts, points to our smoky camp fire, and says the price is great. But, glory to Jesus, there is no desire in our hearts to go back, for we are happy with Jesus alone, and just one glimpse at the altar, filled with seekers after God, more than repays.

Pray for us, dear ones, as we go forth in the life of faith, with Him who said,

"Take no thought for what you shall eat 'or drink, or for what you shaft put on, for the Lord your God knoweth you have need of these things."

JACKSONVILLE

We rejoiced to find converts who had been saved and baptized during the first meeting, still walking with Jesus and growing in grace. The results at the second meeting surpassed that of the first. At times the entire altar was lined with sinners seeking salvation. Many were baptized in the Spirit, and many healed.

The Lord then led us from the Atlantic Ocean to the Gulf of Mexico, preaching and distributing tracts to Durant? Fl., there to conduct the

PLEASANT GROVE CAMP MEETING

God led us, with marching and singing, to en-compass the camp and lay hands upon seats, altar, etc., and claim them for Jesus. The glory of the Lord was in our midst. The tabernacle was filled to overflowing and the groves strewn with autos and teams from forty miles around. A spirit of sweet unity and humility prevailed. There were wonderful messages in prophecy and prophetic song. Dramas were worked out, accompanied by tongues and interpretation. Heavenly music filled the place, and angel choirs were heard.

81

Deep conviction rested on many, and the altar filled with sinners seeking salvation. One dear little girl who received the baptism plead with all, in tongues and English, while under the power, to come to that beautiful city of God.

TAMPA, FLA

With much faith and eager hands upon arriving we set to work getting up the big tent, and several smaller ones, making seats, installing electrical apparatus, painting signs, and advertising. The residence district and business section were visited with handbills, and God blessed our labor, and the tent was filled and a large number stood outside. There were many new faces each night, inquiring "What meaneth this?" Coming closer, and closer to the front, many soon plunged into the fountain.

An elderly lady, from a highly respected family of the city, after hearing Pentecost spoken against in persecuting tones, decided to come and judge for herself. Interested from the start, she attended regularly, later accompanied by her son and daughter-in-law. Soon she was gloriously baptized with the Holy Spirit; then the daughter, a dear, sweet Christian, began very earnestly seeking Him, and her husband said he could barely keep in his seat, the power of God for salvation of his soul was so strongly upon him.

Street meetings were held from trucks and Gospel cars in many parts of Tampa and Ybor City, and from the band stand in front of the City Hall.

A CROSS COUNTRY TRIP TAMPA TO MIAMI VIA OKEE-CHOBEE PRAIRIE WITH TRACTS AND GLAD NEWS

When we left Tampa the car was well filled with tracts and from the west to the east coast t of Florida, a distance of three hundred and fifty miles, we faithfully distributed literature until within a few miles of our destination, when all had been given out, and souls were crowding about the car asking for more.

In this trip we passed through the Okeechobee Prairie, and Prairie City, visiting each house with the first Pentecostal literature they had ever seen.

Our car being heavily loaded this trip, we did not carry a sleeping tent, and learned a little of what Jesus meant when he said, "The birds have nests and the foxes have holes, but the Son of (man has not where to lay His head." The first night we spent in the car; the second night was spent wrapped in a blanket by the camp fire on the prairie near Okeechobee, a new prairie town, where we spread the news of Pentecost. The third night was spent in a fisherman's shanty near Palm Beach, where also we witnessed for Jesus. The next night was spent in a little railway depot to keep out of the driving rain.

All the homes around us had their Christmas trees and fine dinners, but as our tents had not yet arrived, and we did not wish to spend the Lord's money on a room, we built a palm-leaf shanty on the beach, and hung our simple Christmas gifts on a little tree growing near. We kneeled down around it and read the story of Jesus' birth, and after prayer opened our little tokens. Praise the Lord! Though here we have no home and no abiding city, we seek one whose builder and maker is God.

TENT MEETINGS, MIAMI, FLA

The first tent meeting conducted in Miami was held among the white people, the second among the colored saints. To the first meeting thronged the rich and fashionable in their automobiles and fine clothing. A tent meeting was a novelty.

They came to be amused, but many remained to weep and pray. It was a beautiful sight to see the tears rolling down their faces, as they came humbly, and kneeled at the altar, giving their hearts and lives to Jesus in response to the simple message.

Because of the strong racial feeling, the dear colored people did not feel free to attend the white meeting. The Lord put such a love in my heart for the colored race that it was almost

82

impossible for me to pass one of them on the street without such floods of love welling up in my heart that I had to step up to them and inquire:

"have you ever heard of the latter rain outpouring of the Holy Spirit, the baptism of the Holy Ghost with the Bible evidence, speaking in tongues, and of the soon coming of Jesus?"

I think they must have felt my love for them for they flocked about me whilst visiting and distributing tracts in their neighborhoods. Thus it was that after the white camp meeting we moved our equipment to the other side of town amongst these precious people.

MIAMI COLORED CAMP MEETING

The tabernacle was filled, night after night, with precious black pearls to be gathered for Jesus. Picture a great platform thirty-two feet long and twelve feet wide, filled with baptized, colored saints, dancing, singing, clapping their hands, testifying with unction and a clear ring that carried conviction. Picture an audience where the power of God fell till often the evangelist could not minister, but the Spirit took full control; picture the colored saints, old and young, dancing in the aisles, sinners weeping their way to the altar, seekers receiving the Holy Spirit, and talking in tongues, and then you would see only a little corner of this meeting.

At times the power fell till every one raised faces shining with Heaven's light, just shouted, and praised the Lamb for sinners slain, till the noise could be heard blocks away, and people came running to cry: "What meaneth this?"

At other times a holy hush, a spirit of weeping and great heart-searching and humbling saved the people from their seats and they fell on their knees in the aisles, between the seats, and at the altar and are now cleansed whiter than the driven snow, living pure, holy lives for the Jesus who said: "Go, and sin no more."

Drunkards testified to having been delivered from drink, gamblers to being set free from gambling; sinful girls and women of shame testified that the Lord had saved and cleansed them from sin.

Long marches were taken through the streets, and they sang as only colored folk can, played their musical instruments and shouted till people ran to know what had happened. Many danced right on the march and demonstrated to all that

"It is joy unspeakable and full of glory."

Some two hundred colored saints have the baptism of the Spirit in Miami, and many more are seeking and finding.

The people are very poor, and go to meeting in aprons and overalls. Collections very small, and were it not for the dear friends sending offerings in letters, we would have fallen further behind financially than we did. Several times, when we were wondering how to meet the heavy expenses of freight, gas, oil, lumber, lights, groceries, clothing, the needed amount came on the next mail from some child of God whom Father had been telephoning to. Thank God that even in these days, when prices are soaring, it is possible to live a life of faith. It has meant self sacrifice, and in our reports we endeavor to picture the sunny side, to encourage the many who live far from meetings, but fail, perhaps, to show the other side, where sometimes in driving rains, we find our sleeping tents ankle deep in water, our bedding wet, where we struggle to cook on smoky oil stoves and yet keep singing and smiling, fighting the good fight of faith.

KEY WEST FOR JESUS

In the Island of Key West doors opened everywhere. Many begged us to ship our tent here and conduct an evangelistic campaign that would reach every corner of the Island, volunteering their help and prayers, declaring that few evangelists came so far out of the way, and that the whole city would turn out to the meeting.

The grounds of the Harris High School (beautifully located) was chosen as a site for the tent meetings. Every seat was taken nightly and many were standing. New seats were obtained three times and arranged outside of the tent, but it was impossible to seat the large audiences.

83

Ofttimes the tent was filled two hours before meeting was to begin, so anxious were these hungry souls to obtain seats. Men and women came to the altar for salvation, and for the baptism of the Holy Spirit. Sick were healed and the Lord gave me blessed liberty in proclaiming the message of the hour.

My soul was so burdened for the dear colored people that I announced from the public platform that I had done my duty in the Lord toward the white population of the Island, and must risk their displeasure and disapproval now by going to the poor colored folk and telling them the same story. Some remonstrated, but as they saw the earnestness and longing in my heart, almost all agreed to help, and gave us no humbler spot for said meeting than the spacious grounds that surrounded the court house.

Then began earnest visiting among the colored people. At first it was impossible to make them believe that this was a

COLORED CAMP MEETING

or to persuade them that they were welcome to come inside and take seats, but when they really found it was true, how they flocked in!

One dear colored brother, whom everyone, black and white, admitted to be a saint of God, created considerable stir when he came up the aisle, and t after looking at me, voiced aloud the amazement which was written upon his face

"Why, Lawd a' massy! If dar ain't de berry woman what de Lawd showed me in ma' vision!

She hab on de berry same dress her hair am combed de berry same way! Yes, dat's de berry woman de Lawd showed me in ma' vision."

He later explained to us that the Lord had given him a vision, some weeks previous, of a white sister coming, taking him by the hand, leading him through a river of water wherein a dove came down and rested upon him, and later leading him into the presence of the Lord.

It was impossible to keep the white people away. So for the first time in the Island the white and colored attended the same place of worship and glorified the same Lord side by side. We arranged seats for the white people at the sides, reserving the center for the colored people, but so interested became the people in the meetings that reserve was a thing unknown.

The message of the Holy Ghost is new to the dear ones here, some had not heard at all of the Holy Spirit and only one colored sister knew that He had come as a tangible Comforter.

Seven of the most spiritual of the colored workers and preachers have received the baptism of the Holy Spirit during the last four days.

We are not keeping count of the numbers of all that are being saved and getting through to God, but the names are recorded in the Lamb's book of life.

The poor and despised are having the gospel preached unto them, and God is honoring His own Word, preached in simplicity, but in demonstration and power with signs following.

Wonderful visions are seen by many receiving the Holy Spirit. A sister saw a vision of the coming of the Lord, just after she had received the baptism. Leaping to her feet she cried aloud:

"O, don't you see Him? Look! Jesus is coming!

I see a beautiful star rising over the mountains and hills. Jesus is in the center of the star. O, see, he is bursting forth in glory and might!

Jesus! Jesus!! JESUS!!!

Another sister coming for salvation, screamed till she could be heard far away, and the people came running:

"Lord, be merciful to me, a sinner!"

Soon she sprang to her feet, dancing and clapping her hands, her face illuminated with the joy of salvation.

A colored preached seeking the baptism with no one near him, fell prostrate and in a few moments was speaking with tongues and glorifying God.

Suddenly his face convulsed as though in agony, and the Lord took him through the crucifixion scene. He described the death and love of Jesus, the blood trickling from His wounds.

A boy fourteen years old, was gloriously saved, and night after night, pleads and exhorts in the most remarkable manner; many break down and weep all over the tabernacle.

We had expected to close here last night (Sunday, March 10th), but all begged for the meetings to continue till enough could receive the Spirit to open a Pentecostal Mission of their own.

My strength has been holding out in a remarkable way, through this strenuous winter, but at present I am very weak in body, and have to hang on to God for strength for each meeting. Please pray for me, saints, that I do not fail God. Souls are coming home to Jesus. All around are thousands of hungry souls. The harvest is great, the laborers few. As Brother McPherson is away again, I am alone, playing, leading, singing, preaching, and praying at the altar, besides having the Bridal Call to prepare, it is the only power of God that can sustain me. It is still a marvel in my eyes, the wonderful way the Lord helped me while left alone at Key West, to drive stakes, tie heavy guy ropes, and battle to keep the tent up, amidst wind and rain, sometimes preaching all day and sitting up the greater portion of the night to watch the tents and keep driving the stakes in with the big sledge-hammer, as fast as the wind pulled them out, through the night watches, while a three day nor'wester was on.

The wind died down and the meeting closed in triumphant success. The Lord sent a brother to help me take down the big tabernacle, and two colored sisters to assist me in taking apart some two hundred big long benches, pulling the nails and piling the lumber under the blazing sun, rolling the great strips of canvas, getting them into their bags and shipping them to the next place.

Truly He gives His people supernatural strength when they are in the center of His will.

The farewell scene at the depot is a pleasant memory. The station platform was well-filled with both white and colored saints who had got up early to say a. last good bye, bringing little offerings to help us with our fare, and wave us on our way.

Dozens came up and gripped my hand as I stood on the steps of the train, telling how they had been blessed in the meeting.

It was just at the time of my departure from Key West that my dear Mother, with Roberta (whom she had been caring for), joined me. She had told me, when I entered the work, that if ever I needed her help, no matter what it was, she would give it, and now I did need her help as never before. Being left alone so much, with the care of the tents, meetings, and an ever-growing correspondence which really needed the entire time of one person, the Bridal Call subscription lists, shipping of freight, arrangement of new meetings, my strength was giving way.

Sister N (who assisted in duties about the tent) and myself were alone at night in the big: court yard, with drunken men and soldiers, reeling by the tents until all hours of the morning. God marvelously protected and cared for us insomuch that no one came near or molested us in any way.

I was strongly impressed, however, to telegraph for my Mother to come to my assistance, not only because I needed the protection of a mother's presence, but to take hold of the business end of the work, and now, in answer to prayer and the appeal of the telegrams, here she was, sitting by my side as the train sped across the long bridges which spanned the ocean from island to island for the hundred miles back to the coast of Florida.

Mother has been with me from that day up to the time of the present writing. She has never shirked a duty nor one of the responsibilities laid upon her by the work, lifting from my shoulders the entire burden of the correspondence, caring for the long lists of Bridal Call subscriptions, overseeing the care of the children, packing, traveling, and a score of other duties, and I have been left free to give myself continually to prayer, the ministry of the Word, and writing. She has ever been a source of cheer and inspiration. How wonderful that she received the call first that through her call I was brought into the work and that the second time, through my call, she was brought into the work again.

After a short meeting amongst the colored people of West Palm Beach, and the colored camp meeting at Miami, we shipped our tents to Orlando, Fla., and journeyed thither ourselves in our Gospel Auto, distributing tracts and witnessing for Jesus all the way up the coast.

ORLANDO TENT MEETINGS

Our freight was delayed by an embargo, and our time limited, having only a little over two weeks before we must journey northward to prepare for the Nation Wide Camp Meeting in Philadelphia, Pa.

Inquiring of the Lord, as we drove along Main Street in our car, I saw a large, brown tent which would seat at least five hundred people more than our own tabernacle would hold. Inside we found a fine floor, formerly used as a skating rink. The Lord touched the owner's heart to rent us the tent at a small cost for our series of meetings. This was the first time the holding up of our freight had delayed a camp meeting, and Father had a better tent all up, empty and waiting for us, floor and all.

People warned us that Orlando was aristocratic, we need not expect them to come to a tent meeting, but we were sure God had not made a mistake in sending us, so we went to work. Notices were put in the papers, seats engaged, hand bills gotten out and meetings opened. So persistently did we advertise by hand bills, by numerous street meetings, driving up and down the streets, inviting people to come to the tent and hear more about it, that it is to be doubted whether there was anyone within a radius of several miles but what knew that there was a tent meeting in progress in Orlando.

At first many merely lined up their cars in the streets around the tent and listened at a dignified distance, but soon the fire began to fall, and the ice began to melt, and leaving their cars they entered the tent and many, praise God, came to the altar.

The crowds increased daily in numbers and interest. Six came to the altar for salvation the first meeting, and there was not a meeting but sinners were saved and believers baptized with the Spirit, night after night the long altar bench was filled and so were hungry hearts.

Never were we treated with more love and respect, each seemed to vie with the other to help and encourage us. First, (our small living tents not having arrived), a cottage by the lake, with a garage, was put at our disposal free of charge during our stay. The best bakery in town sent their delivery wagon, with such great baskets of bread, pies, cake and cookies, that we had enough to share with our people.

People who owned orange groves brought us fruit by the bushel. The grocer sent boxes packed to the brim with canned goods and vegetables, flour and sugar. People came to our door to tell us of the blessing they had received in the meetings. Oh, it means so much to be in the center of God's divine will. He will open doors and close doors, overthrow the mighty and make your enemies to be at peace with you. Bless the Lord.

The tent, with a seating capacity of nearly fifteen hundred, was filled to overflowing, rows of automobiles, and other vehicles lined the street.

Ministers and workers from various churches attended; some declared that this was the long-lost power their churches used to have. Others scoffed in derision.

Altogether the devil was afraid he was going to lose some of his people. So he had one lady who lived several blocks from the tent go to the police and protest that she could not sleep at night. The next evening a policeman brought a paper to the tent, stating that we must close our meeting at ten o'clock. Toward the end of my sermon I held a watch in my hand and kept looking at it as I spoke. I talked fast as I could, and at five minutes to ten told the people I knew they were hungry and would like to come to the altar, and that there were souls there that should be saved, but that a lady had complained of the noise, therefore we would all rise and be dismissed, and please not to stand or walk but to go out as quickly and quietly as possible.

Will I ever forget the look on those people's faces! Some of them almost owned the town, and for them to be told they had to close a meeting at ten o'clock some of the men snorted at the very thought, and on the way out said:

"We'll see about this!"

"The idea! This place was open as a skating rink for months and was kept open until midnight.

86

Now the Gospel's being preached they want to close it at ten o'clock, eh?"

"The Mayor's a friend of mine. I will see about that. Don't you be afraid, little woman. This thing will be all straightened out by tomorrow night."

Neighbors came up; people who had, up to this time, kept at arm's length and not been quite sure whether they approved of us or not, hesitated no longer, but were our warm friends from that time on.

True to their word they got together in groups on the streets talking it over. Next day a lady who was the owner of a large boarding house, went about the neighborhood and had a petition signed that this order should be cancelled, declaring that the noise did not bother them. This clipping appeared on the front page of one of the Orlando papers next day:

MRS. ROONEY AIDS CHURCH

"Mrs. Bettie Rooney deserves the thanks of all lovers of religious liberty for coming to the rescue and aid of Mrs. McPherson, who is conducting a series of meetings in the big tent.

"It seems that someone, whom Mrs. Rooney claimed lived at a distance, had the city officers close the meeting at an early hour on account of the noise of the speaking and singing interfering with their sleep, when Mrs. Rooney, good Christian woman that she is, immediately secured a petition with the names of twenty-five citizens living right near the gospel meetings, who protested to the Mayor against having the meetings broken up at so early an hour, which of course was acted on favorably, and the disgruntled ones will have to find something else to bring against the meeting.

"The only real charge against the meeting is that they preach the old fashioned GOSPEL, straight from the shoulder, and it makes some of the hifalutin frock-tails, who orate in the pulpit to swell congregations, who look through one eye-glass and wear silk tomfooleries, envious because of empty benches prevailing.

"It would do some preachers good to get religion and pass it on as these people are doing."

Immediately the order was cancelled and the meetings went on, oft-times till midnight.

A young lady who came with a group of others from fashionable families, full of unbelief, was startled and thoroughly convinced when one night the Lord put His power down upon me and gave a message in tongues in the Spanish language, of which I knew not a word. Here is her testimony:

"I was very much impressed at one of the tent meetings, to hear Mrs. McPherson speak in Spanish, and directly afterwards to give exactly the same message in English. She was not conscious of speaking in Spanish. When told later of it she was quite surprised and said she did not know a word of Spanish. I also heard her talk in other languages with which I was not acquainted.

ANNIE L. TREADWELL

When it came time to close the meetings and to move on toward Virginia and Pennsylvania, the town wherein we were told the people were proud and would pay no attention to us, turned out enmasse to the closing meeting. One of the citizens made a speech in behalf of their townsmen, thanking us for our labors of love amongst them, inviting us to come back, saying that they would do all in our power to assist us. A sum of money was presented to help with the expenses of the northward journey.

CHAPTER XVII.MEETINGS IN VIRGINIA AND GOSPEL AUTO NEWS

"Let her glean even among the sheaves, and reproach her not. And let fall also some of the handfuls of purpose for her, that she may glean them, and rebuke her not.
So she gleaned in the field until even, and beat out that she had gleaned."
Ruth 2:15, 16, 17

It was late at night when we neared the state of Virginia, after reaching which we would still have a couple of hundred miles to journey. We all expressed the desire to press on and spend the night on good old Virginia soil. We had heard of the warm hearts of the Virginia people and wondered whether it was really true. Crossing the border we entered a sleeping little town and drew up under the trees by the side of the road to open out our automobile bed and erect our tent covering for the night.

Waking early and peeping out from under the protecting curtains to get our first daylight view of the place, we were surprised to find two houses near us, one just across the street, the other a little, to our right. A man and his wife standing on the piazza of the former were looking toward us talking earnestly, no doubt wondering who we were.

Preparing to continue our journey, we had just finished our roadside toilet, when the man came hurrying across with a silver tray, with a large glass bowl brim full of ripe, crimsoned strawberries, a pitcher of thick cream and a bowl of powdered sugar. Then a little girl came running from the other house with a pan of hot steaming biscuits and a quart of fresh milk from the jersey cow in the field, neither knew what the other had done. This was our first experience of the far-famed Virginian hospitality.

PULASKI, VA. PREACHING ON THE COURT HOUSE STEPS

We were entertained in the beautiful home of Brother Z. Cecil during our ten days' meeting in the town. In order to reach as many people as possible with the message in the shortest time, it was decided to hold daily street meetings in addition to the regular meetings in the Pentecostal Holiness Church. When Brother Cecil went to ask the town officials for permission to preach on the street, they kindly invited us to come in and make use of the court house steps and spacious lawn.

The first night we went in a pouring rain and preached, feeling that time is too short to stop for a little rain. A large crowd gathered and the power fell. Nightly the crowd increased until it was a mass meeting and autos packed both sides of the street. It was a beautiful sight as we preached in God's big out-doors, and the people sat on the grassy lawn around this spacious building.

It was an unprecedented sight to see the power falling in such a place as the saints sang and danced upon the court house steps and down on the pavement. Hearts were touched and tears ran down the people's faces, and crowds followed to the meetings,

IN THE PENTECOSTAL HOLINESS CHURCH

The church was unable to hold the crowds who stood all about the yards and street, trying to hear and see. Several who had been seeking the baptism of the Holy Spirit for years received, new converts just saved also rejoiced in receiving the Comforter.

TWO MISSIONS CONVINCED OF BIBLE EVIDENCE

After the close of the services we had decided to take two days' rest, but the call came to hold some meetings at the colored church. There God led along the line of the Bible evidence of the baptism and made it so plain from His Word that all doubts were saved away, and those who had been conscientiously standing afar off rose to their feet asking the people to forgive them, and stated that they now saw the light, and come what might, would never compromise again.

The leader of another mission invited us to come to his place next night, saying:

"Sister, through that sermon tonight I am convinced that the speaking in other tongues as the Spirit gives utterance is the Bible sign that invariably accompanies the incoming of the Spirit, and I have accepted the light. Come and preach to my congregation that they, too, may receive." The following night found his assembly packed to the doors long before starting time, and God worked and honored His Word. Hallelujah!

The big-hearted people of this town opened their hearts and pocketbooks and our needs and traveling expenses were more than supplied.

ROANOKE, VIRGINIA

Before leaving Pulaski, the Pastor from the Pentecostal Holiness Church of Roanoke called upon us asking us to come to his church. The saints desired the meeting should be held in a tent, but the pastor insisted and on our arrival in Roanoke, we drew up finally at the parsonage where our entertainment had been arranged. We saw a gentleman seated upon the piazza and noticed that his face looked dark and forbidding, and that he did not welcome us in any way. Even when seated later with the pastor and his wife upon the piazza, and he had been introduced as "Brother So and So," he did not say a single "Hallelujah" or "God bless you."

The first meeting was held in the church. The Lord gave me the Wisdom not to go into the pulpit or even on the platform, so I stood quietly in the front and delivered my message upon the coming of the Lord, and the preparation of the Bride to meet Him. Fervent "Amens" came from the audience and tears filled many eyes.

This brother, who sat on the front seat, never looked up, but had the same dark, thunder-cloud look of sarcasm and displeasure upon his face.

When I had taken my seat he rose and gave a, discourse, which was fully as long as that of mine. Someone whispered:

"He is the state superintendent. He has heard about this meeting and come down to stop it."

I cannot repeat his discourse in words, but the substance of it was that if an angel came down from Heaven and preached any other doctrine than that which was set forth in the rules and regulations of their church they were not to believe it; that the message of tonight was all very well, but that he had heard that Sister McPherson taught actual transgressions and inbred sin were all taken out at one time, when we entered the fountain of blood. He said:

"We have the rules and regulations of our church to uphold. Take away our strong teaching of sanctification as a second definite work of grace and you will destroy the foundations and the pillars upon which our church is built."

The audience sat with their faces a mixture of misery and pity, but I was praising the Lord and saying:

"Oh, thank you, Jesus," as He poured the blessings into my soul.

When the dear man had finished speaking I rose and said that it would not be courtesy for me to make any reply in their church; that I had come there under their urgent invitation and would be willing and happy to preach outside, from the Gospel car, or on a vacant lot, anywhere that the saints arranged for me.

I told them that I believed in the finished work of Calvary, believed that sin is sin whether it is actual transgressions, Adamic sin or inbred sin, whatever fancy name you give it, sin is sin; that while man looks on the outward appearance (so-called actual transgressions) God looks on the heart, (inbred sin) and as for holiness, why, without holiness no man shall see the Lord. We must be saved, must be sanctified, but 'tis all through the precious atoning blood of Jesus Christ. "The blood of Jesus Christ, God's Son, cleanses us from ALL sin."

Several leaped to their feet and said they would get a place outside at once. (Both ministers said

"No, stay on for the time of the meetings in the church".) The Lord gave many the witness and the meetings being announced for Sunday, they started out to search for land.

Lots some distance from the church and on the main streets were traced up, but it was impossible to secure them. Every other place was blocked except the lot of land just opposite the Pentecostal Holiness Church. This was given free of charge.

(How those precious saints worked all that Saturday!)

No tent being available, two great strips of canvass were secured and stretched over as large a space as possible. Three assemblies loaned their seats, lumber was hurried to the spot and a platform erected.

Each contributed something towards the erection of the hurried meeting place. One brother gave the electric light wires and fixtures; and though 'twas late Saturday noon the electric company sent out a special car and installed a meter.

A Sister loaned her lovely piano for these out-of-door meetings, told us we were "welcome to the whole house" and paid the drayage on the piano for us. O, for more such consecrated people!

Thousands stood for hours packed all about the tent after every available seat was taken, altar filled, the saints sitting about the floor of the platform till it was almost impossible for me to move about without stepping on someone.

Men were saved, Hallelujah! Sick were healed. Two ministers who had been fighting the outpouring of the Spirit, said:

"We will fight you no longer" and came to the altar.

Street meetings were held every night on the busiest corner from our Gospel car, and the city was stirred. People wept as they stood about the car. A dear man came with the tears rolling down his face and kneeled at the running-board of the car as Brother Dougherty (who arranged all the meetings) prayed with him as he wept his way through to Calvary.

SALEM ASSEMBLY COMES TO OUR HELP

Whilst holding an afternoon meeting in Salem the Pastor of the Salem Church decided to close its door during the balance of the meetings, and with his wife and daughters and flock to come to our assistance. They brought with them their musical instruments, and took charge of the music and were a blessing to all.

When it was time to close the meetings, many business people and Christian workers offered to rent the big auditorium, seating thousands of people, if we would stay another week. We had promised Viola, Del., however, and closed on the Sunday night with thousands of people hungering after God, the long altar benches were filled and refilled.

Virginia is a wonderful field; we trust that we may again visit this beautiful state with its mountains and valleys, and hospitable homes.

GOSPEL AUTO NEWS (July, 1918)

"Never did valiant warrior return with a more conquering tread, or more loyal heart throbbing within, nor more deserving of this public tribute than our faithful 'Pentecostal Gospel Car'."

From the northernmost town in Maine, by the Canadian border to the southernmost city in the entire United States of America, undaunted by mountain or valley, it has steadily and safely carried not only the messengers but the message, and has been indeed and in truth a Flaming Evangel, declaring in letters of gold, that gleam oft-times into the amazed eyes of the onlookers with as startling an effect as did the handwriting on the wall in Belshazzar's palace long ago.

Thousands of persons and vehicles have streamed by the side of the Gospel Car, but free from the man-fearing spirit, and impervious to criticism, instant in season and out of season, the Gospel Car has never hidden its light beneath the bushel, whether the gay bridal party dashed by with lilt of laughter and fragrant orange blossoms, or whether funeral procession, with sombre-plumed hearse, and black-garbed mourners, whether the dancing children rollicked by, or the aged man feebly leaning on his cane, it has solemnly inquired of one and all, "Where will you spend eternity?" declaring that "Judgment day is coming," and exhorting them to "Get Right With God."

Often, as we slow up amidst dense city traffic, it would seem to one uninitiated in Gospel Auto life as though many of the usually sedate pedestrians on the sidewalk, heretofore quietly pursuing their daily routine, had suddenly and involuntarily been transformed into fiery street preachers, who, startled out of themselves, demanded from one and all, in tones which electrify their fellow citizens, "Where will you spend eternity?" Those within hearing distance of the voice

91

look up aghast into the speaker's gaze, they themselves see the car and take up the great question, "?"

Sometimes when we leave the car on some errand, we find on returning that a crowd has gathered about the faithful car which is holding its own street meeting and preaching all by itself; and who can say with what results for eternity?

No member of our party takes a more active part or renders more efficient and obedient service in every branch of the service than does the Gospel Car.

Are there a thousand tracts to be distributed through the byways and hedges, or placed in the B. F. D. boxes? The Gospel Car is ready.

Is there a street meeting to be held? There is one preacher that can always be depended upon Gospel Car.

Is there a pulpit needed? Down goes the top and here is the car for a pulpit. Is there a stand needed? The windshield opens to hold Bible and song book. An altar needed where the penitent may weep his way to Calvary? The running-board does good service, ever ready to receive the copious tears of seeker and worker as they kneel together.

Is there an aged couple, or a mother who has stood long hours to listen with babe in arms, to be taken home? The Gospel car is ready. A heavy burden to be carried? An errand to be run? street megaphone messages to be resounded? The Gospel Car is ready. Is there need of a table upon which to spread the modest evening meal prepared on the campfire by the way? dishes, or a can of food needed? The Gospel Car supplies the need.

Is there a need of bed and bedding for the weary traveler? The Gospel Car carries one folding bed upon its running-board, and another is formed by the front seat, which gently lays back upon its hinges, uniting front and back seats into a comparatively comfortable bed. When prayers and (good-nights) have been said by the flickering of the campfire, the Gospel Car affords protection and rest under the whispering pines. When the editor, hard-pressed on every hand, seeks quiet and rest with Bible or typewriter, it is the Gospel Car that bears her away to some quiet spot apart from the throng.

THE DYING BRIDE

Meetings over, the last lights extinguished in the camp, are the duties of the Gospel Car ended?

May she rest? No! Quick footsteps and an urgent message implores us to come at once to the dying bed of a young bride, who, but a few hours previous, had listened to our message and had later been suddenly stricken and was passing away. It is miles away, on a dark and perilous country road. How can we get there in time? The Gospel Car is ready, and speeds a swift messenger of mercy, never pausing until she stands by the humble cottage door, where the midnight lights and shadowy forms bespeak the presence of the death angel, whose pinions are even now spread to bear away the slender form of the fair young bride.

Through the hours of waiting, wherein the dying and living alike clung to our hands and words for strength and consolation, until the last good-bye was spoken and the sweet voice trailed off into silence with the words: "Meet me in Heaven!" and the last breath fluttered gently away; and on through the hours of morning, while the sorrowing parents were comforted, and the hovering angels rejoiced as the young husband kneeled by the still form of his loved one and gave his heart to Jesus, the Gospel Car stood silently beneath the dews of the light, gleaming softly in the starlight exhorting each neighbor as they reverently left the house with uncovered heads, to remember that for them, too, the "Judgment day is coming: get right with God."

And when again the Gospel Car had brought me back to the home, this time to preach the funeral sermon, as I looked into the sweet face now reposing in the white, flower-wreathed casket, I could catch the echo of her words as she smiled into my face and said:

"Sister McPherson, I'm glad you are here, and I'll meet you in Heaven."

Then on behind the sure-footed horses that drew the hearse and carriages over stony mountain passes (considered too difficult for the other cars) and hills so steep that the nose of the car pointed Heavenward, with a sheer cliff above and a precipice yawning beneath; then down into valleys where we found swollen mountain streams, where the water came over the running-board of the car till someone cried out:

"Surely we can go no further!" But NO, the Gospel Car, with a determined roar from her engines and a quick shift of her gears, emerged from her plunge dripping, panting, but triumphant.

When the little form had been laid at rest beneath the pines on the mountain top, in the sure and certain hope of a glorious resurrection in that land where tears are wiped away, the Gospel Car, having surmounted all difficulties (sometimes axle-deep in mud, again over jagged rocks which cruelly gashed its tires, tested and threatened on every hand), through it all kept up on the return trip till we reached our destination and her work was done, then with a long, expiring sigh, one tired tire sank slowly to the ground. Nevertheless (bathe and rub it as we will), like all other true warriors of steel, the Gospel Car bears its honorable scars of battle, without which no hero is truly decorated.

Gazing upon mark scar of battle, we recall with joyous hearts each scene these scars portray.

Through the many miles of travel the engine has never given us one moment's trouble, yet many a time tires have been patched and re-patched, mended and reinforced until a cheery letter accompanied by a donation meets the pressing need, specifying that this offering was for Gospel Auto Work.

LIVES SAVED BY THE GOSPEL CAR

"Dear Sister McPherson:

"Praise God for sending you and your Gospel Car to our town; if you had not come here, my brother, his wife and sister-in-law would probably have been blown into hell, as my brother had re-solved to shoot both them and himself; but while he was on the piazza he saw God's car go by, and he read: 'Where will you spend eternity?' It held and gripped him. He went in and told his wife (a very wicked woman a saloon-keeper's daughter). She Too-poohed!' and hardened her heart, although she knew him to be desperate.

Only a very short time before they found him in the cellar basement, gas turned on at two o'clock in the morning, unconscious; in five minutes more would have been past all earthly help, the doctor said.

"My brother was wonderfully convicted and has since been saved, and is now seeking the baptism of the Holy Spirit. It pays to pray. After fifty-five years of prayer by Mother, he has at last yielded to God. Bless His Name!" C. A. S.

VIOLA, DELAWARE

We were obliged to drive night and day to make our appointment in time. We found the saints full of faith and good works, and the meetings throughout were at a time of spiritual quickening and up-building. The building was crowded as never before with an earnest throng, listening eagerly to the unfolding of the divine plan of the ages for the salvation of mankind, and the conviction was great; one Catholic brother ran from the building, declaring he would have to go to the altar if he remained longer.

The meeting over, we started for Philadelphia and New York, driving all night, reaching Philadelphia before dawn. We did not pause, but pressed on to Atlantic Beach, where we rested on the sand for an hour, contemplating the greatness of the handiwork of God. Again pressing on to Long Branch to meet some of the dear saints and thence to New York, before we slept.

CHAPTER XVIII.NATION WIDE CAMP, PHILADELPHIA

"It came even to pass, as the trumpeters and singers as one, to make one sound to be heard in praising and thanking the Lord . . . that then the house was filled with a cloud, even the house of the Lord, so that the priests could not stand to minister by reason of the cloud for the glory of the Lord had filled the house."

II Chron..5:13, 14

In the fall of 1917, when we were passing through Philadelphia en route for Florida, it was our privilege to spend two days with the dear saints there and to attend meetings then being held in a large tent. The Lord graciously poured out His Spirit upon one and all, and when scores of saints begged us to come back for a series of meetings, the Lord witnessed in our hearts that this was of Him, and after much prayer and correspondence, a Nation Wide Camp Meeting was planned. Father told me to pray earnestly for money to buy a big Tabernacle tent which would be large enough to accommodate the people. A notice was inserted in the Bridal Call. Friends rallied and offerings came.

The problem was: Where was the tent? The government had commandeered the large tent-making concerns, and even though the Lord assured us that He had the right tent for us, and would deliver on time, I confess that we were anxious as the date for the Nation Wide Camp Meeting approached.

Each time I went to the Lord He would say:

"It is all right. You shall have your tent," but in the meantime my letters here and there to different people brought no hopes. The only tent that would at all fit my requirements was in New York City and was held at thirty-five hundred dollars, and this was out of the question. Sometimes the enemy would whisper:

"You have taken people's money for the tent, suppose you don't get that big tent, what are you going to say to them?" But Jesus said:

"Let not your heart be troubled."

After two years' experience, I had my own ideas of the kind of tent I wanted, its size, shape, seating capacity, texture, and make: One that would shed the rain, be mildew-proof, well roped and guyed, arranged with block-and-tackle system of lowering and raising. Where could such a tent be purchased?

When we arrived in the city of our summer's, work, there was the very tent of my dreams and prayers, in an attic store-room of a downtown building, all tied up in bags, poles and stakes complete, ready for erection. Hallelujah! We went to look at it, climbed the stairs, and as we mounted towards the sky, our hearts mounted also as the tent was described to us, its size and material, ten ounce, U. S. Army duck, double fill and double twist, double stitched, splendid ropes, block and tackle, etc., which had never been erected, worth twenty-five hundred dollars today, and could be had at eighteen hundred cash, but I felt that fifteen hundred dollars was all the Lord wanted us to pay for that tent; and although at first they not accept this, as the man stood in the door and read the sign, "Judgment day is coming, get right with God," his face became thoughtful and he said he would let us know later, and of course Father opened the way.

This tent had been ordered and built for an evangelist whom God was using blessedly in His service. When the baptism of the Holy Spirit was preached, this evangelist refused the light, took a stand against the outpouring of the Spirit, and he became very ill for months.

The tent, which God meant for Pentecost, remained brand new in its bags at the tent-maker's office, with the instructions that it was to be sold only for religious purposes. The news came that we could have it for fifteen hundred dollars, and it was soon up and packed, with throngs of people surrounding it drinking in the message of salvation through the precious blood, the baptism of the Holy Spirit, and the soon coming of Jesus.

Had this tent been purchased in any other city it is very improbable that we would have been able to have had it shipped because of the embargo which at that time paralyzed freight all over the country. And even if it could have been shipped it would have been necessary to have had it sent by express as the time was so short and the delivery charges would have been enormous, so our Heavenly Father planned it all out and had the tent right in the very city where the meeting was to be held.

GLORY OF GOD IN CITY OF TENTS

The beautiful camp grounds were situated on a hill, near the river, and were sheltered by high shade trees. Bows and rows of small tents were erected in squares around the great new Gospel Tent with its snow white canvas.

The dining tents, dormitories, reading and rest tents were erected and soon the grounds assumed the appearance of a well-ordered camp. The leaders themselves rolled up their sleeves and helped with a good will for the future comfort of others. Heavy trucks were rolling up with great loads of cots, beds, seats, dishes, camp equipment, but 'midst all the bustle and the preparation brothers and sisters alike found time to shout and praise God. The trees echoed with the hallelujahs of the saints. As the newcomers arrived they in turn rolled up their sleeves and went to work. Even the night before the camp meeting opened the glory of God seemed to rest down upon the place as we gathered around the big bonfire to play and sing and worship the Lord for what He was about to do in our midst.

The picture of hundreds of saints standing upon their feet with hands lifted toward Heaven, eyes closed, and their upturned faces streaming with tears as they sing, as it were, a new song, and Heavenly anthems voiced by the Holy Spirit through their lips in wondrous harmonic chords of love and thanksgiving, is a never-to-be-forgotten sight, and resembles much the conception that I have always had of what it must be to be in Heaven before the throne of the Most High God.

Oh, if you could but hear them pray, pray as never I have heard people pray before, each one forgetting their neighbor, forgetting all else but the Lord who answers prayer; praying out aloud with all their might, hundreds of them at one time, till no one voice can be distinguished in the midst, for they are all blended in one mighty heart throb of love and desire for God to have His way, which quickly turns into -adoration, and flows forth as a river of praise straight to the throne of God. Needless to say, the answer usually comes before the prayer is finished.

The camp presents a very stirring and inspiring scene every night. After supper in the dining tent; the people move out to prepare for the evening meeting. It is a common sight to see a little group of two or three people kneeling down in the paths, or under the trees, to present to God anything that might be upon their hearts. Then as the evening shadows lengthen, lights are turned on in the great Tabernacle Tent, and. the saints soon fill the shining interior. Soon the night air resounds with the songs and the praise of hearts filled to overflowing with the love of God. After meeting it is not an uncommon thing to hear voices in supplication and praise continued on in the tents.

The night preceding this writing witnessed a scene that melted many a heart. One end of the large ladies' dormitory tent was given over to a children's meeting, and there the little tots were used in a wonderful way by the Spirit. Many a little one glorified God, speaking in other tongues.

A number of parents were there and their hearts just welled with feeling as the Holy Spirit worked upon the children. It was a meeting never to be forgotten.

GOD LOCKS THE LION'S MOUTHS

When the city of tents was first erected on this beautiful hill, where earth and Heaven seem to meet, we found that we were in a neighborhood which was seventy-five per cent Roman Catholic, with institutions and colleges near-by. Gangs of boys patrolled the grounds day and night, keeping watch on everything and everybody, feeling great resentment at our invasion of the hill, which had been their special property since they could first remember. Then when the meetings opened and the power of God began to fall, and there was shouting, dancing and many prostrated, the whole community was stirred to its depths. They had never seen it after that fashion before.

The next night an enormous crowd filled the tent and stood all around the outside. Every time that there would be a manifestation of the Spirit, they would burst forth into peals of laughter, ridiculing and mocking. As an altar service was attempted, the hoodlums thronged into the tent in a body, standing over the seekers, mocking and jeering. The second Monday, night arrived with the worst crowd that we had seen up to this time.

It seemed as if the people were wild with anger, and many came with clubs and cudgels in their hands.

There were organized gangs with leaders, carrying whistles, who gave signals to their men. Detectives afterwards told us that it had been a pre-arranged program to wipe every tent off the ground that night, and open threats had been made to this end.

The devil had carefully laid his plans. A riot took place down in the center of the city that night between the white and colored; there were no policemen available to keep order at the camp meeting grounds. Back and forth, to and fro, the mob surged about the tents. Speaking was impossible, and all we could do was to sing and hang on to God. "Rock of Ages, Cleft for Me," "Nearer. My God, to Thee," "It is Well for My Soul," "Jesus, O How sweet the Name," were among the many hymns sung by the saints, as we all kept in the spirit of prayer.

The meeting was dismissed early, without any altar service. The crowd surged through the tent and over the grounds, like a hive of hornets. One policeman finally came on the grounds, but he was unable to cope with the situation.

The Lord seemed to lay it on me to call an all night of prayer, to settle this matter once and for all. The saints readily agreed and gathered about me. We began to pray one after another for the salvation of these boys and men. We prayed for a revival; prayed for God to have His way.

From this time on there has been no trouble of any kind with the outside people. The opposition has melted away like snow before the summer sunshine.

This outside trouble brought us the support of the different clergymen. One Baptist preacher stood on the platform and gave his word that he would stand by us until the end. Another clergy; man of the Episcopal church said that he had told his boys to be in good behavior, and that if they felt a desire to go forward for salvation, to do so.

Church members, class leaders, and ministers flock to us, and many have received the Holy Ghost since the beginning of these meetings.

We also find there is a large number who have no church home whatever, and many who have never been to church. These are a surprised and interested body of people upon whom God is also moving mightily. Our former enemies as well as our friends, are now asking for our literature, and great numbers of tracts and booklets are being given away.

The policemen who are used to handling large crowds, told us that there were between eight and ten thousand people on the grounds Sunday night, and I have never witnessed better order.

Two young ladies who came to mock, and said it was a shame to keep people lying under the power as we did, suddenly began to weep, crying loudly for salvation, and inside of fifteen minutes were on their backs under the power, speaking in tongues and praising God. Another young lady came to mock, and after the altar call had been given some time, she was deeply under conviction and approached the front. This power struck her suddenly and left her prostrate on the straw in front of the altar. She was saved, and in a very short time began to speak in such a clear flow of tongues that many remarked about it, and then she gave the interpretation and was filled with the glory of God.

A man sprang out of the on-lookers, and demanded that his child should be given to him.

He was invited to lay his hands upon her if he cared to take her, but fear filled his heart and he went away, declaring that he would find someone who would take her. True to his word, he came back with the girl's aunt. She took the child by the hand roughly, led her to a seat, where she spoke sharply to her, and slapped her in the face. At that instant the power of God struck the aunt and sent her reeling to the floor. Who was she that she could withstand God? The aunt left the meeting with the hand of God upon her, supported by two of her friends, and the last that we have heard about her is that she is very ill in bed.

A traveling salesman who witnessed the baptism of this young lady, came out with a declaration that now he had no doubt that this was the power of God, and that he would begin seeking for the same experience.

People of all denominations bring their sick to be prayed for. One father brought his little child emaciated and suffering from a weakness of the body that did not permit of its walking. The little one was prayed for, and when he was placed upon his feet, the proud joy and happiness just shone from the father's face, as the little one began to take steps for the first time in months.

One child who was a pitiful sight to look upon, with a terrible skin disease, and was covered with sores, was instantly healed by the power of Jesus.

One young lady, in writing, says: "Saint Vitus dance and severe nervous trouble had tortured me for many months. My face and eyes twitched so that I was ashamed to sit in a meeting. I was prayed for and the demon rebuked, so that I am every whit whole no twitching, no nervous trouble. Oh what a rest! What a relief! What a Savior!"

One night a young Polish girl ran to the altar, and it was but a short time when she sprang to her feet, and with her face shining with glory, exclaimed:

"I am so happy, I have got it." Later she received her baptism and asked permission to talk with her own people in their language about this glorious Jesus she had just found. Then she told in English the same story while the glory of the Lord filled the tent. A woman who lived in the neighborhood who had come to look on, fell under the power just as she left the tent. A crowd of onlookers quickly gathered, and her son took her away, but the Lord had done the work, and she exclaimed, as she was led away: "I have got it."

Sister Elizabeth Sisson, of New London, Conn., and Brother Cyrus B. Fockler, of Milwaukee, arrived shortly after the opening, and God has wonderfully used their messages in the meetings.

After one morning service, when nearly everyone had gone to the noon-time meal, a little girl of twelve lay unnoticed in the straw. One brother, however, discerned that she was giving messages and interpreting them. He moved over to her, and with one consent others followed, and in the, silence that followed, she spake in tongues and interpreted messages for nearly half an hour.

Messages of exhortation, warning and comfort, beautiful in their construction and completeness, flowed from her lips. She had called a meeting.

One man testified that God had given him a dream the night before in which the little children were shocking the corn. Truly God is using the little ones in this way.

Another little tot of six years, suddenly filled with the power, began to dance in a pretty, childish way. Sister McPherson, led by the Spirit, placed the little one on the altar rail, and for twenty minutes the little girl preached Jesus to a multitude who had come to look upon God's work. It was a sight never to be forgotten as the sweet little face shone with the glory of God, and her childish voice called sinners to know this Jesus whom she knew.

Two young ladies, one a Catholic, one a Methodist, sat scoffing, and pretending to be greatly amused, in an endeavor to hide the real conviction that was in their hearts. Someone told me I ought to speak to them, but all we did was pray.

They seemed to become more quiet after that, and I had forgotten all about them until, while praying at the altar, someone came and said:

"Sister, there are two young ladies over there who want to speak to you."

Making my way through the audience, I found the same two girls with much changed countenances. All laughter was gone, their eyes were red from weeping, and in response to my invitation:

"Oh, girls, don't you want to get right with Jesus tonight? Won't you kneel down, confess your sins, and give Him your heart?" They fell off the chairs on their knees, and began to pray and cry aloud:

"Lord, forgive me. God be merciful to me, a sinner."

Being called to another part of the tent, I, looked around for someone whom I might ask to pray with these girls. Near to me, and looking on was a Methodist class leader and Sunday School Superintendent, with whom I had been talking but a few moments ago, and who had come to investigate Pentecost and see whether there was anything in all this shouting and speaking in tongues.

"Brother, you come over and help pray for these dear ones, that they may be saved," we asked.

Without hesitation they fell on their knees and began praying for the sobbing young women.

How I wish I could make you see the sight that met my eyes when next we returned to this side of the tent!

While the two Methodist brothers had been praying with their eyes shut, the power had come down and the two young ladies had fallen prostrate under the power and were receiving the baptism of the Holy Spirit, and beginning to speak with other tongues.

The little group, many of whom were sinners, that stood round about the girls, were very much impressed with the power and the vision which the girl described, and as we sang about the precious blood which she described, even the Catholic policeman lifted his hands and joined in the song with us.

The Spirit impressed me to ask the Methodist class leader to close in prayer. In his humble prayer, he said:

"Oh, Lord, Jesus, if this is new light for me in these last days, please reveal it to me and baptize me, for Jesus' sake, Amen."

I had just turned to go into the big tent for my Bible, preparatory to leaving for my own tent, when something fell with a thud and a shout to the ground behind me, and all the people began to run and shout. Hastening back to see what it was, I found this same Methodist class leader lying on his back under the power no, I should hardly say on his back, either, for he was really just on his head and his heels, his body raised up from the ground by the power and his feet going round and round.

Before we could reach him he was shouting in tongues and praising the Lord as the Spirit gave utterance. After a time he bounded to his feet and went around the tent leaping and praising God.

The next night he brought nearly a dozen from his own church, and said that his son who was studying to be a missionary to South America, was going to seek the baptism.

NOTES FROM REPORT BY SISTER P. BENT

"Sunday night the crowd was greater than we have ever seen. There must have been thousands without exaggeration swarming the grounds. The tent was so packed that every seat was filled; people were in the aisles, sitting on the platform floor, and stood several deep around the Tabernacle outside the canvas.

"Sister McPherson had a mighty message from God, fresh from the throne, in which she gave us a short glimpse of the Bible from cover to cover, bringing out in great beauty and tenderness the life and death of our dear Savior, Jesus Christ.

"The old Gospel story was not told in vain, but again brought scores to the feet of the Redeemer.

Yes, the space between the platform and congregation was so crowded with men and women seeking the Lord that there was hardly room to put our two feet in any one spot at a time. O, it was blessed to see all kinds and colors at the feet of the same Jesus. We shall never forget that lovely sight. What a wondrous salvation we have to offer to this sad, sorrowing, sinful world of lost and dissatisfied men and women.

"Monday the Spirit was so mightily demonstrated that it was impossible to preach. Several times Brother Fockler endeavored to give out the Word, but there was message after message in tongues, with interpretation following. The Spirit then fell so mightily in baptizing and anointing that nothing so powerful had been seen since the beginning of the Camp.

"At the evening meeting very much the same thing was repeated, when scores had hands laid on them for service, and went down under the power; but previous to that Sister McPherson gave forth one of the most convicting sermons we have ever heard her preach. It was given to her to so vividly show the sinner the meaning of an endless eternity of despair, where there would .never again be the least gleam of hope to brighten the darkness, that many were made to feel the necessity of being prepared to stand before God.

"O, how they again flocked to the altar, big, sound-minded men and women, realizing the awfulness of eternity, and praise God, many must have found the Savior from sin as the swing power fell all around us."

No coaxing was necessary to get the sinners to come to the altar. It was not an uncommon sight to see strong men literally running up the aisle with tears rolling down their faces, throwing themselves at the feet of Jesus and sobbing for mercy.

There are saints here who were born in Italy, Russia, Lithuania, Germany, Sweden, Poland, Finland, Holland, Canada, Ireland, England, and Egypt.

All have come to glorify the name of Jesus.

TESTIMONY

"I have been brought up in the Catholic church, and when I heard that a city of tents was being-erected upon the hill near our home, and that the people there shouted, danced, fell under the power, spoke in tongues, etc., I ran all the way to the tabernacle to see what it all meant.

"When I came to the foot of the hill I looked up through the trees, and saw the tents all lighted up, the brass band was playing; the cornets, trombone, piccolo, piano, bass and snare drum and tambourines were all playing a new song I had never heard. This song I now sing, 'Victory.' When I reached the top of the hill I could see over the heads of the crowd many people dancing and jumping on the platform and in the audience. At the end of the song they all stood on their feet and shouted and shouted and sang the most strange music, which I have since learned was the Heavenly anthem sung in the Spirit.

"I could not get very near the tent on account of the great crowd, so I asked someone near me:

"'What does it all mean? Are these people crazy? What are they dancing and shouting over?'

"The gentleman nodded assent and said yes, he thought they must be all crazy, for such a meeting and such noise he never did hear the equal of in his life. I could have understood it if one or two were crazy, but how could so many be out of their minds? There must have been fifty dancing and five hundred shouting.

"Just then I had an opportunity to press closer and an amazing sight met my eyes. Clear across the width of the tent in front of the altar, and on the platform I saw men on one side of the tent and women on the other side, slain prostrate under this mighty power.

"A young lady near me was crying, great tears rolling down her face, saying:

"O! Jesus, save me; forgive the past and I will follow thee forever.' In a few moments I saw her face become filled with joy, and she fell to the straw and was soon speaking in tongues, strange languages, but O! so clean and plain. This was going on all about in the front of the tent, weeping, singing, shouting, dancing, while I looked on dumfounded. Then from the end of the platform where the sick were being prayed for came several people, dancing and shouting that they were healed. ,

"One man who had been lame jumped so high, well I never saw anyone jump so in my life, shouting and praising God. At midnight the meeting was still going on, but I had to tear myself away.

"The next night found me there again, and I cannot stay away; I have been saved and baptized with the Holy Spirit now, and am O! so happy.

I am laughed at I know, but I am laughing, too, I'm so happy."

"For years I have been an earnest Christian and church member, but always felt a lack and longing for more power in my life. When this camp meeting came to our neighborhood I heard the testimonies and preaching on the Holy Spirit, and the Bible evidence, speaking with tongues. I knew this was what I needed, the Comforter. I went to the altar and began to seek.

"The sister in charge came to me and told me to enter through the gates of praise, and that the day I sought Him with my whole heart He would be found of me. I began to praise the Lord with all my heart, and as she laid her hands upon me and prayed she passed on, but I fell to the floor under the power and saw a great angel with wide spread wings that seemed to reach to the ends of the earth. Then I saw Jesus hanging on the cross and His blood streaming down. I received the Holy Ghost, and He spoke the praises of Jesus in other tongues. Hallelujah! I am so happy I have found my long- felt need.

"For years I have suffered with my eyes; have worn heavy glasses, but still had those piercing pains and failing sight. I was prayed for in this tent three days ago, was perfectly healed, have thrown my glasses away, case and all, and can read the finest print. I give Jesus all the glory."

CHAPTER XIX. MEETINGS FROM MASS TO NEW YORK

"In the morning sow thy seed, and in the evening withhold not thine hand . . . for verily I say unto you, ye shall not have gone over the cities of Israel till the Son of man be come."
Ecc. 11:6; Matt. 10:23

For months the Lord had been burning the message on my heart:

"Go out quickly into the highways and the hedges go into the out-of-the-way places, and declare that Jesus is coming soon."

California rang in my ears, and the Lord had been speaking to us for some time about making a trans-continental, tract distributing-Gospel auto tour The Lord had led us so definitely in the past that we were made to know that it was His voice.

My husband, who had attended the latter part of the Nation Wide Camp Meeting, had gone to Florida again, and it seemed a great undertaking for me to consider driving a car, which had been used as much as ours, myself on such a long trip.

Putting the Lord to the test, I asked Him, if it was His will for me to make this trip to help me to get a new and more powerful car. The committee who had handled all the financial end of the camp meeting said that though the offerings had been good, expenses were so high that there was very little left to divide amongst the numerous workers, so that by the time our own expenses were paid there would be nothing toward the car.

When I mentioned it to Mother she said: "Well, ask the Lord to help you sell the old car at a good figure, and I will pay the balance."

Needless to say, I lost no time in going down the street to see about it. Inside of half an hour I had sold the old car for almost as much as I had paid for it in the beginning, and in a few hours there was a new Gospel Car being lettered with six inch golden letters saying: "Jesus is coming soon, get ready" and "Where will you spend eternity?"

Before setting out for California a chain of meetings was held from Massachusetts and Connecticut to New York.

LONG HILL, CONN

Where a tent had been erected and advertisements issued for a week-end meeting. Saints gathered in from the towns around about and the Lord bountifully poured out His Spirit upon us. Some were saved and several received the baptism.

Amongst the number was one young man who had been seeking for years.

MONTWAIT CAMP

Here we were joined by our dear Sister, Elizabeth Sisson, who had worked so faithfully through the Nation Wide Camp Meeting at Philadelphia, and she traveled with us throughout this entire chain of meetings, blessedly used of the Lord.

The glory of the Lord came down, saints were there from Philadelphia, New York, Boston, Connecticut, New Hampshire, Rhode Island, and many were saved and baptized with the Holy Spirit, with the Bible evidence, speaking with other tongues.

WORCESTER, MASS

A three day convention was held at the Pentecostal Mission of which Elder H. T. Carpenter was in charge, and as the saints who flocked in from out of town lifted their voices in praise with the saints of Worcester the glory of the Lord came down and rested upon the people until they danced and shouted and sang under the power of the Spirit, The Lord saved sinners and baptized believers.

UNITY HALL, HARTFORD, CONN

The saints with their pastor, Brother N. G. Neilson, had engaged one of the most beautiful halls in the city, seating some seven hundred. The Lord had given Brother Neilson the promise that He would pour out His Spirit in this meeting, and praise His name, He kept His word. God blessedly poured out His Spirit, and at some meetings four or five were baptized and a like number saved.

In New York we found that Brother and Sister Vondrann's faith had overstepped the limitations of their assembly hall, and they had rented the large Harlem Casino for the five principal days of the Convention. Brother Vondrann entertained us in the Hotel which is located at 115th Street and Manhattan Avenue. The Mt. Olivet Assembly Hall is located on the ground floor of this building, and we found was formerly used as a dance hall and card room. When they had given their hearts to Jesus this room was turned over for His dear service for the salvation of souls and baptism of believers. Hallelujah!

From the first meeting the glory of the Lord saved down and filled the Assembly Hall. Brother and Sister Vondrann entertained the saints on the free-will offering plan, with a beautiful and simple faith. They later assured us in a testimony, after all expenses for rental of Casino, etc., had been met, that when they opened the Convention they had exactly the sum of six dollars and a half in the treasury.

There could not have been a better location for a Pentecostal Convention in New York City than the Harlem Casino, which is easy of access by subway, elevated, surface cars and busses. The hall seated some seven hundred people. Sunday afternoon, October 6th, when the meetings opened in the Casino, practically every seat was filled and extra chairs were brought in, while the glory of God fell upon each saint.

We had invitations to churches in the city, and spoke at the business men's noonday meeting at John Street Methodist Episcopal church daily.

They gave us liberty to preach the baptism of the Holy Ghost with the Bible evidence, speaking in tongues, and as this meeting was largely attended by Christian workers and ministers, a wide area was reached, and these meetings were truly as a stone dropped in calm waters, sending ripples far and wide in all directions.

Amongst the number receiving the baptism on Sunday afternoon was Mrs. Emma M. Whittemore of the "Door of Hope" work, well known the world over as a blessed child of God and earnest Christian worker of years' standing. Truly God is doing great and glorious things these last days.

Different nights ten and twelve, one night fourteen, came forward for salvation.

One of the crowning joys of the New York convention came when the wife of Pastor W. K. Bouton (who had been seeking earnestly for two years, ever since the power fell at Corona), fell under the power on the platform and came through to her baptism. It seemed that our hearts would almost break with joy as we knelt beside both Brother and Sister Bouton when they received the blessed Holy Spirit. Brother Bouton just leaped and danced for joy. All glory to Jesus!

One woman who had been suffering from rheumatism 'was healed instantly and danced like a young girl. Two were healed of this awful epidemic which is going round. Many were healed from other troubles and afflictions, for which we give Jesus all the glory and praise. There were no numbers kept of those saved or baptized, but we know that they were many, praise the Lord.

Thursday, October 10th, being the last night of the meeting, it had been arranged to have the young folks from the different Pentecostal assemblies within a radius of thirty miles represented in a large mass meeting.

Brother Robert Brown, of 42nd St., was chair-man for this part of the service. The following assemblies were represented by a song or an "on fire" testimony: Glad Tidings Hall, 42nd St.; Beulah Heights Assembly of New Jersey, Sister Robinson's Mission of Brooklyn, The Lighthouse Pentecostal Assembly of Brooklyn, Bethel Assembly, Tottenville, New Rochelle, West New Brighton, Asbury Park and Philadelphia.

Brother Vondrann, representing Mt. Olivet, said:

"When we started our work two years ago, the Lord baptized my wife and myself, and we turned the little hall which had been used as a dancing-hall into the Lords' work... Sister McPherson leaves us tomorrow, but the Lord will remain.

"We started this convention with $6.50, but the first night of the convention brought in $182.00, and my expenses were $181.00. Many thought the work could not live in the locality where our assembly had been opened, but we thank God that many of our guests have been saved and baptized in our hotel. I praise God for the work wrought during this convention, and for the many souls saved and baptized."

Pastor W. K. Boutou, representing Corona, N. Y., said:

"There has been a continuous revival in our Corona Church since 1916. You often hear people say that Pentecostal people are narrow-minded.

That is not true, for wherever there is the baptism you will find a people that are seeking the salvation of souls. I want to say that we thank God He ever sent Sister McPherson to Corona. It is our desire to ever lift up the blood-stained banner of the cross. It is still floating at the mast in spite of all opposition. Though Satan has emptied as it were, the whole battery of hell, God's work is still going on."

Brother Brown, in his closing remarks, said:

"I can speak for all the assemblies and say that our hearts are glad when the Evangelist comes along. God has set them in the church, and I am sure that all of the assemblies here are glad that our Sister has come. I pray that God Almighty will help every man, woman, and child that they may get ready to meet Jesus tonight."

At the close of the sermon many sinners arose to their feet and leaving their seats went to the altar and surrendered to Jesus. A double row of seekers lined the entire front of the hall, several received the baptism and others were healed. "The New York Convention will be a bright spot to be treasured and remembered until Jesus comes, for its many bright conversions, souls baptized, and precious fellowship of the saints."

NEW ROCHELLE, N. Y

During the eight days we were there not one discordant note, or one unkind word or criticism, or tale-bearing did we meet, just Jesus and His praises seemed to occupy everyone. Before the first day was well opened every seat was full and saints were sitting on the floor of the platform and standing in the aisles, but no one minded in the least, and the power came down in streams as they sang the Heavenly anthem and played in the Spirit, etc.

As the meetings progressed many were saved and baptized, many bodies were healed and the last day found the church packed to the doors again and even the ante-room filled.

The influenza epidemic was raging in this city as elsewhere, but the Lord was marvelously good to us and did not permit us to be hindered for a moment in proclaiming the message. Churches were closed up in cities just after we had left, opened in other towns just before we got there, but not a meeting was closed at a time when it would hinder the carrying out of the program which the Holy Spirit had mapped out for us.

In New Rochelle I was stricken with this disease Saturday night, but the Lord kept me up for the three services on Sunday. Sunday night I was taken with violent chills followed by high fever, but in answer to the prayers of the saints and a determined rising up in simple faith, the Lord enabled me to complete the week's meetings so that I lost only one whole meeting.

I went through a severe test, however, when my little daughter took the epidemic which quickly turned into double pneumonia. For two days it seemed the dear little life which meant so much to me must pass on and be with Jesus.

Saints gathered to pray for her, and I was obliged to keep on preaching in spite of the lump in my throat and the weight on my heart. She had come to me in the Harlem Casino and whispered:

"Mamma, may I please give my testimony tonight?" I told her, "Yes," and she stood on the platform and testified, saying:

"I thank the Lord for ever swing me and washing me in the blood, putting upon me the white robes of righteousness. Two years ago He baptized me with the Holy Ghost, spoke through me in-other tongues, and I am going all the way through with Jesus till I meet Him in the clouds."

Staying in the furnished rooms without heat or home comforts, I yearned for a little home where I could care for her properly, and I remembered how before becoming unconscious she had said:

"Oh, Mamma, I do wish we had a little home where I could go to school." I had said:

"Darling, would you want Mamma to leave work and try to get a little home together?" She said:

"Oh, no, Mamma, I don't want you to leave the work; I will try to teach myself." Dear little lamb!

One afternoon someone met me at the top of the stairs and whispered that Roberta was very low.

I could not bear to stay and look upon her; I fell upon the floor and prayed God to spare her life, and the Lord gave me assurance that He would not only raise her up but also poured balm upon my troubled heart by saying:

"I will give you a little home a nest for your babies out in Los Angeles, California, where they can play and be happy and go to school and have the home surroundings of other children. You fixed a home once before out of my will, and it was taken away; now I will give you a home in my will."

He showed me Abraham withholding not his only son, Isaac, laying him upon the altar of sacrifice and being spared the agony of seeing him die; then He showed me that I had yielded up not only one but my two children, had traveled these many months with them from city to city, and town to town, having no home or bed to tuck them into, and that, just as He spared Abraham his Isaac, He would spare me my two children and cause me to joy in His tender care.

It was all so real to me that I could almost see the little bungalow, floors, garden and all.

Brothers Brown and Thompson laid hands upon Roberta, prayed for her, and the Lord touched her body. She soon opened her eyes, and though very weak, knew us all and was able to smile again. I kneeled down and putting my lips close to her, ear whispered:

"Oh, Roberta, God has told Mamma that He is going to give us a little home, where you can have flowers and roses and go to school."

Her face lighted and she answered back in a thin little voice: "Mamma, can I have a canary, too?" And little Rolf, who was listening, said:

"Can I have some rose bushes and a garden?"

Through all the weeks that followed and the four thousand mile drive, the little children talked and planned what they would do when God gave them the little bungalow. Sometimes the enemy sought to test me, and said:

"Now, it is an awful thing for you to build these children's hopes up like this. What if you should be disappointed?" But Father does not disappoint nor break His Word. Praise His name!

CHAPTER XX. THE TRANS-CONTINENTAL GOSPEL TOUR

"And the Lord said unto the servant, Go out into the highways and hedges, and compel them to come in, that my house may be filled."
Lu. 14:23

Pastor S. A. Jamieson of Tulsa, Okla., had been writing us regarding our going to Tulsa to conduct an evangelistic campaign and the Lord had given us a definite witness that we were to go.

Just as we were about to start out, however, in the Gospel Car, a telegram arrived, saying: "Postpone coming. All churches closed and it is not safe for you to be abroad in the land."

Going to the Lord about the matter, He spoke plainly to me:

"Fear not, do not lose a single day. Go at once, and the day you arrive the ban will be lifted and the churches will be open."

(NOTES FROM THE LOG.)

At nine o'clock this morning the last snap was closed, the last strap fastened, the baggage, and the Gospel, testimonies and tracts in place, the last "Good-byes" and "God bless you's" said, and the motor purred softly, (every greasecup had been filled, the tires tested and the gasoline tank filled) , and the car rolled away as quietly and efficiently as though it knew that we had been preparing for this trip for days, and that the hands of many saints had been laid upon it in solemn prayer and dedication. It seemed to realize what was expected of it on the long trip ahead, and importance of its mission, that of being a worthy herald of the great message of love. It seemed as though both our hearts were beating in unison with the thought of the great opportunity which had come into its life and mine.

From our starting point at 115th Street, we went along 7th Avenue to 10th Street, and from thence turned into Riverside Drive. A big policeman, who was leisurely directing the traffic, caught sight of the Gospel Car, and said in a loud voice:

"'Where will you spend Eternity? Well!! What do you know about that?" And as we smiled to ourselves we could not help thinking that if he were going to preach to fashionable Riverside Drive, he could not have selected a better text.

Crossing to Staten Island, thence to New Jersey, we gave out our tracts on the boats, at the ticket offices and to the passers-by.

Five hours' run brought us to Philadelphia, where we rejoiced at meeting the dear saints again.

After attending to freight to be shipped to California, we crossed to Camden, N. J., where Sister Dr. Sharp, had her beautiful bungalow open and warmed to receive us.

After the illness of my little daughter, Roberta and myself, and the hundred-mile drive of the day, the warmth and the light and love and hospitality extended to us in this home made it a veritable haven of rest.

GETTYSBURG, PA., OCT. 26

Glory to Jesus! Gospel Car has left a trail of tracts one hundred and -twenty miles long. How hungry the people are! The searching questions regarding salvation and our teaching, that they ask, reveal the longing in their hearts. At Lancaster, by congested traffic, the Lord held us ten minutes in the main street, during which time scores of men and women pressed about the car, reading the signs and asking for literature.

On through Mountville, York and New Oxford, passing the famous battlefields and reached Gettysburg in time to find the streets filled with soldiers who were off duty, and had a golden opportunity for tract distribution. We are now camping by the roadside, near the Allegheny Mountains.

PITTSBURG, PA., OCT. 27

The tracts which we have been constantly distributing today reach back as a white thread for one hundred and seventy-five miles. We have been climbing the Allegheny Mountains all day. At noon we reached Tuscarora Summit, at an altitude of 2240 feet, and are now outside of Pittsburgh.

We have pitched our camp by the side of the main highway, on the property of Mr.

Carnegie, the great steel magnate, and though doubtless he is unaware that he has guests tonight, the Lord directed us to this spot to camp. Today being Sunday we have had the most wonderful opportunity of distributing our literature to church members and thoughtful, energetic Christian people. No engine trouble, no tire trouble.

CLAYSVILLE, PA., OCT. 28

Not nearly so much mileage today, but bless the Lord, we have been very busy for Him. You remember that the Lord led us to camp right by the main highway, instead of seeking a more secluded spot. Bless the Lord! As we were breaking camp this morning, we heard a rumbling that sounded like the coming of an army, and lifting our eyes we saw great long lines of camouflaged government auto trucks coming down the road, laden with soldiers and material. With "Gospels" and tracts I ran to the road. The Lord put it in their hearts, too, for without exception, every car paused and the soldiers reached for the Gospels and tracts, thanking us and promising to read them, and suiting the action to the word, began at once to read aloud to their companions.

In Pittsburgh we have been busy for the Master. Have had bad road, mud and detours today, and ahead of us tomorrow, but the Lord has taken wonderful care of us, and no accident has resulted.

Passing through Cecil and Claysville, through the great coal-mining section, just as the men were coming up out of the dark underground, their faces besmeared with coal and grime, the electric lights which they had used t in their toil below still burning in their caps, we were privileged to speak and witness for Jesus, leaving them the tracts and literature.

COLUMBUS, OHIO, OCT. 29

This morning we started out over the very bad roads which the residents of neighboring towns had warned us of, lost our way, and came on to a very dangerous mountain pass. One place there was just room for the wheels of the car to pass. A sheer cliff, hundreds of feet deep, yawned below us and rocks hung out above us, but angels seemed to hold the car to the road even though it was wet and slippery. We stopped to inquire of a man the way. He set us right. The Lord gave us the witness that He had sent us this road to reach this man, for when we gave him our message and literature, he brightened and told us of their church on the hill and that the parson would be powerful glad "to know of the Latter Rain." The Lord took us through all the mire and the mud without trouble or skidding where dozens of cars had been stuck in the mud and had been hauled out with horses at great expense and labor. We feel perfectly conscious all the time of a guard of angels that are travelling beside the car, protecting it.

On to Wheeling, W. Va., and then to Zanesville, Ohio, and tonight we are camping by the roadside in a beautiful sheltered spot outside of Columbus, O. Usually the little brooks and streams serve as our wash-basins, but here we have two barrels of rain water, which stand beside a closed summer cottage. We are trusting to be refreshed and rested.

INDIANAPOLIS, IND., OCT. 30-31st

For years I have been longing to meet Sister Etter, and have been talking about it more in recent months. I have longed to hear her preach and be at her meetings we have inquired of those who have read the newspapers, however, and they say that the ban is not lifted.

Blessed be the name of the Lord forever and forever. Oh, how good He is to give us the desires of our hearts. We have travelled some two hundred miles today, and still found time to distribute the literature to many people, also travelling it in the R. F. D. mail boxes.

Through Springfield, O., thence to Richmond, Ind., and we are now in a comfortable room in Indianapolis. Hallelujah! What a luxury it seems! How good God is! Let me tell you the marvelous thing He has done. Well, there was a special meeting of the officials of Indianapolis yesterday, and they decided to lift the ban at midnight tonight, this being just an hour and a half after we arrived. Tomorrow Mrs. Etter's tabernacle will be open and I will have the desire of my heart. Glory!

A day of rest and praise. Called upon Mrs. Etter, and attended the meeting in her tabernacle tonight. We rejoiced and praised the Lord together. The power of God fell; even though there were only a very few at the meeting, the Lord was there showering His blessings upon us. Tomorrow, we proceed on our journey. The command of the Master to go into the highways and hedges is being literally fulfilled. From New York to Philadelphia we followed the "Lincoln Highway," from Philadelphia to Indianapolis the "National Highway"; tomorrow we turn into "Pike's Peak Ocean to Ocean Highway" thence into the "Big Four Highway" for Kansas City.

TUSCOLA, NOV. 1

Have had a glorious day for Jesus, witnessed and gave out literature for one hundred and twenty miles. We are now passing through prairie farms and the great wheat section. We are now camping under the trees. It is very cold and frosty, but God is protecting each member of the party, that none shall suffer or take cold.

SPRINGFIELD, ILL., NOV. 2

Only eighty-seven miles today, for shortly after noon we reached Springfield and the home of our dear Sister Osten, who in loving hospitality held us for the balance of the day; meetings in her parlor tonight, and will send us on our way in the morning refreshed, rested and fed, our lunch box packed with victuals for the journey. Hallelujah!

We are burdened for this beautiful city, the capital of the state, with no Pentecostal Assembly and only these dear ones holding up a little gleam of light in their parlor. They tell us they know of no assembly for a radius of one hundred miles.

How we long to stop over to tell the people the burning message of the hour.

BARRY, ILL., NOV. 3

Just eighty-three miles today, but Oh, the opportunity for distributing Gospels and tracts, and witnessing for the Lord has been glorious. Several young men, who received the Gospels eagerly, told us that they had never had a Bible in their lives.

Today a long funeral procession passed the Gospel Car, and almost all, from the driver of the hearse to the mourners lifted heavy black veils and pressed close to the windows, read aloud,

"Jesus is coming soon, get ready."

We are camping tonight by a wonderful spring of water that flows ceaselessly from a great high rock. Farmers come from miles around, bringing their tanks and vats to be filled from its flow.

Questioning them as we gave out tracts, we learn that all of their cisterns are dry from the long drought and this water from the rock is their only supply. What a privilege to witness for Jesus, the rock from whose river side flows the water of life that never runs dry.

MACON, MO., NOV. 4

The Gospel Car has witnessed and given out literature today for one hundred miles. Oh! that you could see the expressions in the people's faces.

Some look with horror, startled fear, some, with scepticism, spit on the sidewalk and say they "do not believe it." On others belief is written and eager longing to hear more about it. Some say,

"Well, this is just exactly what I have been thinking, that this war, and all these plagues must be a sign of the coming of the Lord. Lady, give us some literature."

Crossing the Mississippi River into Hannibal, people from almost every walk of life gathered about the car, insomuch that as we stopped for dinner, one of the party stayed in the car to dispense literature and witness and answer questions.

A saloon-keeper, a policeman, a traveling salesman, storekeepers, church members, a

109

holiness lady, and many others, gathered about to ask questions and receive literature. The saloon-keeper was much in earnest and we are praying for his salvation. Eternity alone will reveal the fruit-bearing of the seed sown on this trip. Hallelujah!

Traveled until late and the night being raw and cold we paused on a lonely square, wondering where to sleep. A gentleman seeing the car volunteered information, and we learned this was the Mayor of the town. So sorry we forgot to give him the literature.

BKAYMER, MO., NOV. 5

At the restaurant this morning, watching at the window the people who walked around the car, commenting upon its signs and wondering "What meaneth this," one dear old colored brother was so interested that he couldn't leave the car until we returned, and was delighted with the Bridal Call and papers, saying:

"Ah's often he'ad of dese heah Pentecos' people, but Ah's nevah saw any befo'. Ah sho' am glad to get dez heah papahs." ,

As we were about to leave the mayor came up again. Surely the Lord sent him to get his papers. He helped to tie a rope and spoke encouragingly of our work, and received the literature we gave him, gladly. Oh! Lord, work wonders in these dear hearts, we pray Thee.

Hoped to have made more mileage today, but are detained here in Braymer for some adjustments on the car.

OLATHE, KAN., NOV. 6

We realized this morning that "all things work together for good to them that love the Lord and are the called according to His purpose." Our delay of yesterday caused us to pass through the little town of Polo, Mo., by daylight, whereas we would otherwise have passed through unobserved in the darkness. As we passed through this town, we turned and drew up at the filling station. The people trooped after us down the streets, came out of the stores and houses, and crowding around the car, almost made us gasp. They kept us busy giving out literature and answering their many questions about Jesus and our teaching.

One young man said that his mother saw the signs on the car out of the window and told him to run until he caught that car, and bring her some of those tracts that we were dropping by the wayside, and asked us to give him one of every kind we had.

Nowhere on our trip have we met with a more enthusiastic welcome. So eager were the people here that they seemed ready to search the whole car, and dissect all the pockets in the doors, and the boxes before they would be denied. Cries of "These are the Pentecostal people that speak in tongues. I have heard about them and I want to read about them," came from every side of the car.

One dear lady with quivering face, listened as we were praising the Lord, and then, catching hold of my hand, said:

"Oh, tell me how to get the baptism. I have read the Pentecostal literature before." She knew of Sister Sisson, Sister Etter and others, but asked if Brother Simpson upheld this way of receiving the Holy Ghost. She went away laden with literature, exclaiming:

"Oh, what a feast I am going to have today! I am going to sit down and read every word."

One man came running up to the car, telling us he wanted some of these papers for a boy who was going to war the next day and was not saved. On to Kansas City, Mo., thence on to Olathe, Kan., where we are spending the night.

OLATHE, KAN., NOV. 7

Detained by rain today, but have had a quiet time of prayer and spiritual refreshing.

IOLA, KAN., NOV. 8

Have made one hundred seven miles today through muddy roads. Great interest is manifested in the Gospel Car; the editor of the daily paper asked an interview that he might write it for his paper, and gladly received the tracts, Bridal Call and booklets, assuring us that he would be quite an authority on the subject by the time he had read them all, but promising to do so, nevertheless.

OOLOGAH, OKLA., NOV. 9

One hundred and nineteen miles' travelling lands in Oologah, Okla. We are passing through great stretches of prairie country filled with oil wells, and nearing our destination, we are tarrying for the night instead of pressing on to Tulsa, because of the swollen condition of the river, which is flowing over the road we must take. The Lord has promised, however, that when we pass through the waters He will be with us, and through the rivers they shall not overflow us.

TULSA, OKLAHOMA, SUNDAY, NOV. 10

Hallelujah! The Lord took us through the swollen river bottom without mishap. Surely He has given His angels charge over us to bear us up lest even our tires dash their feet against a stone.

In all these fifteen hundred miles we have had but two slight punctures and no engine trouble. The Lord surely tempered the wind to the shorn lambs.

Although the water was flowing over the road and had filled the gullies either side and we could not see which was the road and which was the ditch, the Lord kept us right in the middle of the road for about one-eighth of a mile until the car emerged, dripping but triumphant, at the other side. (May he ever keep us thus in the middle of the King's Highway, through the waters of life.) At noon, looking across the great stretches of prairie, the city of Tulsa came into view, and as we saw the skyline, the buildings and paved streets, after wading through the slough of despond, we shouted and praised the Lord, for it seemed that must be the way it will be when a soul is nearing Heaven, coming up the last lap of the journey the beautiful city, with its walls of jasper looming just before, no more stones, mud, deep ruts or ditches to be avoided, but smooth streets that are paved with gold; no more camping by the way in darkness, for there will be an eternal day.

ARRIVE DAY CHURCHES RE-OPEN

Sabbath morning, as we were driving into the streets of the city, the first service was being held in the Assembly of God Tabernacle. Hallelujah!

Hungry, tired and dusty, after having personally driven and cared for the large Gospel Car, we had but little time for refreshments when meeting hour arrived.

The large tabernacle was well filled, both with people and the glory of the Lord. We found here a strong Pentecostal Assembly, deeply taught and rooted in the Word, clean and free from error, free in the Spirit, and filled with love.

PRAYER PRECEDES REVIVAL

For many weeks, the Tulsa saints were praying definitely for the coming revival. Days of fasting and prayer were observed. With such prayers it was no wonder the Lord brought us through in safety, no wonder the ban was lifted according to the promise God gave me, no wonder seventeen men and women who know not God lifted their hands for prayers and that sinners began coming to the altar from the first night, no wonder the Latter Rain came down in such showers, no wonder sick were healed and some were raised up from death's door, no wonder our tired bodies were rested and refreshed so that we could keep going day and night with scarcely a moment to ourselves. Why, it was as though we had come in contact with a live wire, the faith and hunger and prayers of these dear people. The meetings grew in power and we preached to overflow audiences. Sinners and saints flocked to the altar seeking salvation and the baptism of the Spirit.

SICK HEALED

The epidemic still raging, and many having been weakened and afflicted, we stood hours at a time praying for the sick, and Jesus helped those who came to Him. Praise His name. One man, crippled with rheumatism, insomuch that he could not move without acute pain, walked, ran, danced, and finally danced and leaped, perfectly healed. A man with severe stomach trouble and a sister with running sores, internal troubles, were healed, also influenza, heart trouble, etc.

We were called into houses where poor people were lying so low their eyes seemed glassy, and the rattle in their throats, but the Lord marvelously raised them up. Bless His name!

THE SPIRIT TAKES CONTROL

At times it was impossible to lead the meeting as the place was saved with the praise of the Lord. We witnessed one of the most extraordinary communion services; such melting, such breaking down with tears, such exalting of the blood, messages in tongues and interpretation as the bread and the wine were administered, then the Holy laughter and the shouts of praise as the coming of the Lord w r as preached and that day when we would drink anew with Him the wine in His Father's Kingdom were brought forth.

The Heavenly anthem and the playing under the power of the Holy Spirit were like unto II Chron. 5: 13, 14 (which was engaged by the Victoria Hall Assembly for our larger meetings)

TEMPLE AUDITORIUM ROSTRUM, LOS ANGELES

Ofttimes, just before, during or after the preaching of the Word, the Spirit would break forth with the most stirring, searching and encouraging messages in tongues and interpretation. The people would leap to their feet as one, and throwing up their hands, shout His praises until it seemed that the very Heavens rang.

FIRE FALLS

During altar service one night the power fell in a wonderful way upon several of the young men; one, with his face transfigured with the glory of God, cried in tones that went through every heart," Jesus is coming soon," and another, also in the Spirit, cried:

"Get ready; get ready; get ready!"

Then came a message in the Spirit warning the people that the time was short, the work yet to be done enormous, that self-sacrificing thoroughly consecrated laborers were needed today as never before. The Lord then called many to consecrate and dedicate themselves anew to do His bidding. The power fell, and some who prayed for the enduement of power, the workers laid hands upon them, over fifty fell prostrate under the power. Strong men went down like straws.

To many the Lord revealed Himself and His love in a way they had never known, others saw visions of harvest fields with their need of reapers, others saw Jesus with bleeding hands and feet, and caught a greater revelation of the heart that broke with love and compassion for the lost, others saw great curtains drawn back in the Heavens and Jesus stood revealed before them. Some heard wondrous music, while still others cried out to God as He searched their hearts and showed them things with which He was not pleased, the piano was played under the power and the Heavenly music flowed forth in a stream of melody; saints rose and flocked around the piano, the song was caught up sometimes bursts of melody, sometimes in softest, most sacred tones, declaring the holiness and majesty of the Most High God, swelling until the whole building trembled with the majesty of the triumphant song. We seemed to see the Victorious King leading his triumphant armies, battalion after battalion, banners flying, armor gleaming. When the last quivering note died away a hush fell upon all. It seemed impossible to move or speak, and we were loath to open our eyes or come back to earth again. The saints dispersed on tip-toes. We had been in the presence of the Omnipotent King of Kings.

GOSPEL CAR WHEELS FLY FOR JESUS

The Gospel Car led a busy life in Tulsa. There were ceaseless calls for visiting among epidemic victims day and night. Wherever it went its signs attracted much attention on the streets. The Sunday newspaper printed the picture of the car with its golden sign, "Jesus Is Coming" showing plainly on the head of the paper. There were days of tract distribution, when the seven-passenger car, filled with workers, tracts and handbills, visited neighboring towns and villages, placarding every available window and post with the notices of the meetings and the soon coming of Jesus. Tracts were left in the mail boxes at the farm houses and at the big oil wells, etc.

The Gospel Car also attended noon-day meetings and preached its sermon faithfully at the Tulsa Iron Works while we preached within the foundry to the working men and iron moulders of Jesus and His love, meeting some of these men at the revival meetings, we later had the joy of seeing them give their hearts to Jesus.

Perhaps the most important work of the Gospel Car in Tulsa was street meetings having secured one of the best corners in the city, the top of the auto was put down, and singers, with their musical instruments, filled the car; how those dear ones did sing and testify of Jesus. Illustrated charts were hung from a stand, these charts drew crowds from all about.

Such respect I never witnessed in a street meeting; men removed their hats and stood with bowed heads, and women with tears in their eyes. Then came a call for all who were tired of sin and wanted Jesus for their Savior to lift their hands for prayer. The first night eighteen, the second night twenty-nine raised their hands, indicating that they wanted Jesus as their Savior.

Then came a call to step out and kneel upon the sidewalk by "our penitent form," the running-board, and publicly, before their fellow citizens, surrender to Jesus. Tears were on the faces of many. Two ladies stepped out of the crowd and knelt, their tears splashed on the running-board, as our tears of joy over repentant sinners mingled with theirs. At the close of the last meeting several hundred saints marched out of the tabernacle to the street and formed in circles about the car.

As they sang and prayed the Spirit fell. There were tongues and interpretation as the saints laid their hands upon the car, asking God to protect it and its occupants, and to send a guard of angels with it to keep it from all danger, and prayed that it might ever be a messenger of life and never of death. These dear ones also dropped their offerings toward gas, oil and tracts, inside the car.

God bless them!

TRANSCONTINENTAL TOUR CONTINUED

Leaving Tulsa the Gospel Car turned south by, southwest for Oklahoma City, where we expected to hold a meeting that night. Saints who had been at Tulsa had gone ahead of us on the train to arrange this meeting. While hastening along we found time to distribute tracts through the huge fields of oil wells and in each village and town.

HELD UP AND WAYLAID

Hurrying along, trying to make every minute count, we were obliged to draw up at a filling-station, in the little town of Stroud. As we stopped a man sprang from a doorway and leaped towards the car, shouting: "Praise the Lord." Others came running. In another moment the car was encircled with earnest saints praising the Lord and telling us that they had driven from nine to fifteen miles, having learned that this town being on the highway, we must pass through it today. They had picketed themselves at various corners and doorways, and had waited all day since early morning to ask us to their ten-mile distant mission at Kendrick, for a meeting. We shook our heads and told them that this was impossible, as we had promised to be in Oklahoma City Mission that night, and offering them tracts and literature instead. But they held onto the car and one sister's eyes filled with tears, and she trembled with the intensity of her eagerness and hunger. Kendrick was a little place and off the beaten track, and no evangelist or Pentecostal workers ever came that way, and they were not going to let us go by without coming if they could possibly help it.

113

Our arguments that we must keep our first promise gradually weakened under the steady fire of their pleadings, until we consented to telephone and call up Oklahoma City as a test, that if the saints there were willing, we should stay.

The Oklahoma City saints replied that Tuesday would be just as good, that they would have more time and could get a larger crowd together. While I was 'phoning, the saints were lined up praying.

How their faces brightened as the Gospel Car was turned from the highway and out through the country ten miles away, where a hot supper was steaming on the table and preparations for our comfort had been made!

It was only a little village, but this seemed to be the largest building in it, and even before we got there we could see the lights shining inside and out and people standing outside looking in through the door. The seats were filled and some standing in the back as we sang and praised the Lord together. After a simple message an altar call was given, and one dear sister received the baptism of the Holy Ghost, speaking in a clear, beautiful language.

Next morning we pressed on to Oklahoma City, having left a goodly supply of tracts and Bridal Calls. As we traveled we were talking of and marveling at the great need of workers throughout the country and in the out-of-the-way places.

OKLAHOMA CITY

The saints were ready and waiting for us. The Lord gave us a precious meeting, pouring out His spirit upon us without measure, and another dear sister received the baptism of the Holy Spirit that night. There were many calls for us to remain, holding meetings amongst the Indians; round-houses were offered us free of rent, but the season was late and the weather getting cold, great snow storms had been reported farther ahead in the mountains and we hastened on our way.

Our first point of compass was Amarillo, the last town in Oklahoma. From Amarillo to Tucumcari, New Mexico, and thence on to Santa Rosa. As we journeyed, Sister B and my dear mother gave out tracts through fields of cotton to the gangs of road workers, bridge builders, farmers, tent encampments by the way, and to the white-topped caravans as they lumbered slowly on their way.

Although there had been a heavy snow storm just a week before, and roads were heavy, we got along without any difficulty until after we had left Tucumcari. Here the roads leading to Santa Rosa became more and more dangerous, mud, snow, deep gulches, and steep mountain passes. Had we stopped to inquire about roads ahead (we afterwards learned), drivers would have told us this road was impassable in wet weather.

Miles and miles we traveled, where the only sign of life was an occasional prairie-dog or rolling tumble-weed. Deeper, ever deeper the wheels cut in the soft mud till it was flying clear over the top of the car. I got out and put the skid-chains on, and on we went. Santa Rosa was only nine miles away, and our eyes were constantly on the speedometer, as we sighed with relief each new mile we covered.

Darkness had now overtaken us, but with the good lights of the car we crept on in low gear, the two sisters walking, Roberta and Rolf, my two children, asking how they could help me drive. The wind was sweeping over the prairie in icy blasts when the car at last settled down to the fenders.

Our first thought was to search for lumber to jack the car up on, but not a tree had we passed for a hundred miles. Sister B and myself at last set off over the plains to search for help, and the Lord directed us to the home of a Mexican, who came with team and labored till two a. m. without avail. It dawned upon us at last that the Lord did not want us to go on that night, and though we have always taught and believed that ALL THINGS work together for good to those who loved the Lord and were called according to His purpose, we could hardly see that this was one of the "all things."

The two sisters spent the night in the two-miles distant Mexican adobe house, I and the children (now asleep) in the car. I spent the night in prayer, and just at daybreak came the Mexicans in their wagon with more boards, and the first time trying we were out of the mud and on our way.

We had not gone more than a mile when we saw God's reason for holding us back; deep wash-outs and gulches had to be crossed, where only good light, and careful driving could have saved the car and its passengers. But the Lord was with us and the guard of angels was never more real to us, and though water came over the fenders at times, we never had to stop again.

SANTA ROSA

Beaching the town, cold, hungry, wet and muddy, the Lord had a blessed surprise for us. As we reached the square a young couple rushed across the street crying:

"Praise the Lord! Won't you come right to our house? O, we are so glad to see some Pentecostal saints, haven't met any for over two years! Come and stay a week, can't you?"

How wonderful, here in a wilderness, where we never would have expected to meet a soul who had received the Holy Spirit, They welcomed, fed and warmed us, washed our muddy car, gave us dry clothes while ours were washed. Even the sister's shoes fitted our feet, and her children's, clothes fitted the little ones. How we sang and prayed and the power fell; their hearts were starved, they needed us and we needed them, and we all needed the Lord, and He satisfied the need. Hallelujah!

From Santa Rosa we journeyed across the state of New Mexico, via Socorro. We had expected to go by the northern route, over the Datil Mountains, but found the passes so full of snow that we turned down on the southern trail to Deming, N. Mex., thence to Tucson, and on to Phoenix, Ariz.

Many miles of desert with no signs of life; the giant cactus towered above the car and occasional coyotes skulked in the distance. Houses were sixty and eighty miles apart, and so our kind and thoughtful Father sent us through this long-stretch of road with three other automobiles, making the party of four in all, the other cars being seasoned travelers with kind-hearted men and women who offered assistance and encouragement all the way, one of them even driving the car for two days to rest my arms.

From Phoenix we were advised to go north to Needles, Cal., thus striking the old National trail again and avoiding the deep sand of Yuma and other southern points. This stretch of sand and stone took us over the last of our poor roads, for at Needles we struck a boulevard which ran through the desert to the top of the mountains, through the mountain passes leading on down the long grade, where we were able to coast for many miles through the winding grades and beautiful scenery, until we came to San Bernardino, Cal.

After the prairies, plains, deserts and mountains this was like a new world. For a week past we had been passing through great mining sections where the mountains were yielding gold, silver, amalgam, zinc, iron, copper and other minerals, but now all this was past and we were in the land where thousands of acres were filled with beautiful fruit trees, oranges, lemons, grapefruit, etc., hanging in abundance.

We hastened on to Rialto, Upland, Glendora, and Arcadia to Pasadena, and from Pasadena to Los Angeles, arriving Saturday noon, finding the saints prepared and waiting to welcome us. Every arrangement for our comfort and accommodation had been made by these precious children of the Lord, and Sunday the revival meeting opened.

We were able to luxuriate in the surroundings of home comforts after our long journey and tract-distributing trip for Jesus, but as we looked upon the beautiful country, the welcoming glow in the faces of the saints, and attended the first meeting, where the power fell in showers, we could lift our hands and say truly,

"The toils of the road seem nothing since reaching the end of the way."

CHAPTER XXI. MIGHTY DOWNPOUR AT LOS ANGELES

"Shout; for the Lord hath given you the city."
Jos. 6:16

*NOTE: (The following account of meetings is taken from a report written for the Pentecostal papers during the Los Angeles revival.)

THIS IS A REAL REVIVAL.

A real revival spirit fills the people. It sprang, as all other revivals have, from the sure deep roots of much travailing prayer and intercession before the Lord, and it came suddenly as God's answers usually do. As the saints were praying here, and asking of the Lord great things, the Lord was answering.

"Yes, Yes, My children, Yes. I will take the weak to confound mighty, and things which are not to bring to naught things that are. I will take a worm to thrash a mountain."

True to His word, the Lord spoke to this weak little worm of the dust who feels the weakest of God's children, and burned into my heart the call to Los Angeles. The call was so strongly impressed upon me that we set forth and a band of angels seemed to accompany us all the way, lifting us over the stony places, upholding us through the swollen streams and bringing us safely to our journey's end. But for this revival we wish to give Father, Son and Holy Spirit all the Glory. Paul may plant; Apollos may water, but 'tis God who giveth the increase.

Christmas week was a week of preparation. Crowds grew steadily and by the end of the week the people were not able to get into the hall; prayer room filled, rostrum, seats and stairway filled, and scores being turned away. Such weeping and singing and dancing!

The windows of Heaven were opened; sinners were saved, believers baptized with the Holy Ghost, ofttimes from twelve to twenty in a single meeting.

The shouting and the Heavenly singing of the people, with its attendant cloud of glory, so filled the tabernacle that at times the priests and the Lord's ministers could not minister.

People complained that they were not able to get into the building, large as it was, so The Temple Auditorium with its rows of galleries, besides the pit and great rostrum, (seating some three thousand five hundred people), was rented for the larger Sunday meetings without a moment's hesitation, even though the price was one hundred dollars for every three hours. Pastor Fisher and Brother Blake, with their band of workers, did not count any price or trouble too great, but threw themselves heart and soul into the work.

NEW YEAR'S EVE

While the world was jubilating outside with their noise-making devices, the Lord had a few noise-making devices within who were having a R-E-A-L jubilee, and Victoria Hall was packed to its doors.

The Lord led me to preach that night on the valley of dry bones, and point the way for each dried-up soul to get back to the place of power and blessing. When the call for the altar service was given the prayer room was filled to overflowing, the rostrum, the entire altar (and even though the seats were moved back to make room) all round the building and in the aisles scores were praying for salvation, believers receiving the Baptism of the Holy Ghost, sick healed and such dancing and rejoicing as the lost came home!

It was estimated that over one hundred were slain under the power on this one night alone. With much weeping, many confessions were made; differences melted away as the saints threw their arms about each other; tears of love and praise were mingled.

Many who had lost their first love came to be prayed for that they might be so charged with the power that they might be workers for Him in the coming revival. As the workers were prayed for they fell, one to the right, another to the left, and some lay for hours under the power as God dealt and spoke with them. They forgot the music, and the shouting, forgot the hall in which they lay, and were caught up like Paul of old into the third Heaven. Many of them had visions; some saw the harvest fields white, heavy heads drooping low for the gleaner's hand, and heard the great call for reapers to stop fighting each other with their sharp sickles and go out into the field and gather in the grain, because Jesus is coming soon.

Others saw visions of souls going down into eternal perdition without God and without hope, and heard their cries and shrieks as the Lord bade them go rescue the perishing and snatch the sinners as brands from the burning. One saw the Lord walking through the orchards with His axe in His hand, cutting down fruitless trees by the root, casting them into the fire, and transplanting fruitful trees to their places, and gave a message in the Spirit.

God spoke and revealed Himself to others in a marvelous way until they declared that they saw into the depths of His great heart of love and compassion until their own souls throbbed with His as never before with yearning for the lost.

Strong men and women wept like children; a broken, contrite mellow spirit seemed to fill everybody.

Just as the midnight hour was approaching, someone went to the piano in the Spirit and played "Victory Ahead" and saints joined in and marched round and round the building in such numbers that the aisles were choked as they took the place for God; All joined hands, forming one unbroken circle about the entire hall and prayed with such fervor and zeal that it seemed the very Heavens dropped fatness and honey. Missionaries, evangelists, ministers and Christian workers heard of this great outpouring hundreds of miles away and came by train and boat that they might themselves be revived and be a blessing to others.

In all the month's meetings held under the auspices of Pastor Fisher in Victoria Hall and the Temple Auditorium, not one drop of rain fell outside, even though it was the rainy season, no jar was felt, and no lack of unity or love was displayed. The Spirit took absolute control of the meetings.

As the Sunday afternoon services in the great Auditorium were dismissed, the audiences flocked to Victoria Hall, many of them not waiting for supper, so that by five o'clock every seat was taken; by six o'clock there was scarcely any standing room left, and by seven o'clock hundreds were being turned away from the door, some weeping with disappointment because they could not get in. There were messages in tongues and interpretation; there was Heavenly singing and music in the Spirit, Often before preaching, several have received the baptism in the overflow meeting held in the prayer room, while during the sermon others come through, speaking in tongues and magnifying God.

This revival is truly not man-made or woman-made, but has come down from the Father of lights, for whether the message comes forth in burning inspiration of the Holy Ghost or is given in just a few simple, plain words explaining salvation, the baptism of the Spirit and the coming of the Lord; or whether there is no preaching at all?

Results are just the same, scores come to the altar and believers receive the Holy Ghost.

It is impossible to describe the many wonderful cases wherein we have seen our God work. A husband and wife who have not lived with each other for seven years, both got saved and ran and threw their arms around each other; she received the baptism. Another couple who hadn't spoken for several years got back to the Lord, and the little girl came with such joy to tell how papa and mamma were going to have a happy home.

Another fine-looking man came, crying like a baby, asking us to pray for him, he wanted to be saved. We prayed for him, his face was bathed in tears, and in less than fifteen minutes the man was under the power, speaking in other tongues.

A young lady, a beautiful violin player, came to assist in the music, was gloriously saved, and lay stretched out under the power of the Lord, very near her baptism. Many who were here say they have travelled the world over the last twelve years, since the latter rain began to fall, and that they have seen great revivals, but all declare that they never saw a revival like this, and all agree that it outshines even the wonderful days of old Azuza St., of which they all speak with rapt faces; such a unity and melting together of workers, such a laying aside of quibbles and hair-splitting doctrines, such a going out together for poor, lost sinners, God cannot help but bless.

BETHEL TEMPLE. G. N. ELDRIDGE, PASTOR

Sunday afternoon, January 19th, after the close of the meeting in the Temple Auditorium,

118

meetings opened in the beautiful Bethel Temple, the entire orchestra came from Victoria Hall with violins, cornets, a guitar, etc., and half an hour before meeting was opened people were being sent back to the overflow meetings or down to the basement, where an earnest prayer meeting was in progress. The Heavenly singing rose, swelled to a cloud of glory and a mantle of adoration enfolded the people. One after another people from the age of six to the old man who boasted of his seventy-eighth birthday, sprang to their feet with quick, burning, definite testimonies.

After a simple message from the Word and an earnest altar call, sinners and believers were on their way together to the basement, where seats had been removed and the great floor cleared for a prayer and tarrying meeting. Ere long the floor was covered with the slain of the Lord and many workers, evangelists and missionaries were passing from one to the other, praying with and rejoicing over those who were coming through to their baptism.

After the week at Bethel Temple we again took up the revival meetings in Victoria Hall. The seats were filled long before meeting, then people stood wedged tightly for hours. Ushers struggled to keep the aisles open to conform with the fire laws; children and younger people sat on the floor in front of the altar, even on the platform itself, and every available foot of space was taken until the speaker found it hard to move to and fro without stepping upon someone. They raised the windows and stood on the window-sills; seats were put on the elevation that covers the baptistry, many stood in the halls and the corridors; overflow meetings were held in other parts of the building, one in the prayer-room, where the singing and praising would be echoed in to us in the larger hall as believers received the baptism. One night eleven received the baptism during the preaching. Pastor Fisher had thrown open his office suite of four rooms for an overflow meeting. Here many were filled with the Holy Spirit, others were in earnest prayer before God for conviction to rest upon the entire audience of the larger service.

The floors of the prayer room were filled; they fell on the platform where the sick were prayed for; many sinners who came up the aisles for salvation and lined and relined the altar across the front were saved and struck down under the power of God as soon as they reached their knees. One night it was thought remarkable by many of the workers who were looking on, to see eleven out of one group of twelve which had come to the altar for salvation, not only saved, but baptized with the Holy Spirit.

The singing of the Heavenly choir, the messages in tongues, and interpretation, were indescribable.

Such a sweet spirit of unity and love prevailed, such a mantle of worship and adoration fell upon and enveloped the people that many times it was impossible to preach; even testimonies would be drowned out by the bursts of praise and song which would sweep from the pulpit to the door. Again the audience would arise and with uplifted hands praise and worship the glorious One who had caused the desert to blossom as a rose, and pools to spring forth in the wilderness, and give floods in the dry land; Hallelujah!

The messages in tongues and interpretation also vividly described the coming of the Lord, the approaching darkness sweeping o'er the land, the rising up of the beast out of the sea, the great red hand over the horizon, ascending in the sky, reaching over the earth, and gripping it so tightly that blood oozed forth between its fingers.

Ofttimes the messages were more than the sinners could bear, and as the sufferings of the Lord were described sobs would be heard, men and women from many parts of the building rose and came to the altar for salvation. Although no effort was made to keep track of the number saved or baptized in these meetings, we know the angels rejoiced one night at the spectacle of forty men and women coming to the altar for this glorious salvation. An entire Catholic family were saved the same night.

Two women who came in drunk and were saved at one o'clock in the morning, praised God each meeting for having been saved from a life of sin and shame, and filled with the Holy Spirit. Needless to say, everyone who received the Holy Spirit spoke in other tongues as the Spirit gave utterance, even the man who had been born deaf and dumb.

He came to meeting day after day writing with pencil and pad. He sought the baptism of

119

the Holy Spirit and of course in order to baptize him the Lord must enable him to speak. After seeking five nights, the Holy Spirit suddenly came to His temple. It would be hard to describe the shouting and the joy of those who gathered round him as he received the Holy Spirit and came through speaking with other tongues in an audible voice.

When he rose from under the power the voice had not left him. Bless God! We praise God for many cases of healing and deliverance. All through the meetings praise has been given to the Father and to His Son Jesus Christ, and to the Holy Spirit. No man or woman has either taken or been given the glory, for all has been so manifestly done by God through weak vessels of clay.

CHAPTER XXII." THE HOUSE THAT GOD BUILT."

"Yea, the sparrow hath found an house, and the swallow a nest for herself, where she may lay her young."
Ps. 84:2

During the week at Bethel Temple the Lord had spoken this command with the promise:

"Go to Victoria Hall Sunday night. I am going to do something wonderful in Victoria Hall Sunday night." And Oh, He did keep His word!

All this time the Lord had continued to assure me that He would provide for me a little home for the children. He spoke to other people throughout the city on the same lines insomuch that they were calling me up on the telephone with the word that God had been showing them that the little children should have a home and place to go to school.

Now this particular Sunday night of our return to Victoria Hall, the place was packed to the doors with people when a young lady sprang to her feet, saying,

"The Lord shows me that I am to give a lot to Mrs. McPherson. I have four lots of land and do not need them all. I am not called to preach the Gospel, while she is, and by giving the land that the little ones may have a home and she may be free to come and go in the Lord's work, I will share in her reward." A brother sprang to his feet, saying:

"Yes, and I will help dig the cellar." Others chimed in with: "Yes, I will help lay the foundation," "I will do the lathing," "I will do the plastering," "I will furnish the dining room," and so it went on until even the little canary bird was promised.

A lady promised rose bushes. Now the canary and the rose bushes touched my heart and caused me to shout more than all else, for small as the incidents may seem, I could see God, for the canary and the rose bushes were the two things the children had asked for beyond all else. The Heavenly Father had not forgotten.

When all was arranged a day of dedication and earth-turning was set, and after singing and prayer the saints formed a long line and marched round the lot single file, asking the Lord for the needed means with which to erect the little home.

Away back yonder, when out of the will of God, how I had struggled to get a little rented flat furnished, and what misery I had gone through, but now God is Himself planning a home which would be our own, a home given and built by the saints, where every tap of the hammer drove nails of love into the building and into our hearts.

Perhaps none of my readers who have always had a home for their little ones, a pillow of their own at night, could enter in with me into this wonderful joy in their behalf.

Brother Blake was a builder by trade, and he undertook to oversee the erection of the little home.

Soon the brothers were digging the cellar and doing the work either entirely free or at a very low figure. One brother who offered his services was tested by the enemy, who said to him:

"Now you know you should be working somewhere where you could earn a good day's pay to take home to the wife and family."

He knew God had spoken to him, however, and toiled away at the foundation. On his way home one night it began to rain, and right at his feet lay fifteen dollars. God had richly paid him for his two days' labor. Hallelujah!

This is just one instance out of many where God has blessed every undertaking about this little home. It was a wonderful thing, also, that the lot of land, just on the suburbs of Los Angeles, while away from the influence of the city, should be just across the street from a fine school. Let everybody that reads say "Glory." We ourselves are so full of thankfulness and praise we can cry with David," Oh, where, my soul, shall I begin to praise the name of Jesus?"

CHAPTEE XXIII. LOS ANGELES TO SAN FRANCISCO

> *"The plowman shall overtake the reaper, and the treader of grapes him that soweth seed; and the mountains shall drop sweet wine, and all the hills shall melt."*
> Amos 9:13

Leaving Los Angeles at noon, via the San Fernando Valley, we passed through the citrus and olive ranches, through the Newhall Tunnel and on to Saugus with its great fields of oil wells nestling at the foot of the mountains, losing no opportunity with tracts and literature.

From Saugus we climbed the mountain grades of the San Francisquito Canyon, skirted the edge of the great lonely Mojwe Desert spread like a vast, silent emptiness far away into the blue distance. Then up and up the mighty Tejon Pass with its rocky cliffs and precipices (Mt. Whitney in the distance). From the snowy summit we dropped to plains whereon a straight road stretched before us like a long, shining ribbon.

Speeding over this highway, sunset found us in the town of Bakersfield.

There was no Pentecostal work in Bakersfield, so we decided to spend the night there. We distributed tracts, and also held an open-air meeting at one of the principal corners, from the Gospel Car. Here we found special need for the little Gospels, which we gave freely.

On the journey toward Oakland and San Francisco, a blinding rain made driving not only difficult but dangerous. Hurrying along with side curtains buttoned securely and the windshield misty with the falling torrents, we failed to see an approaching- freight train until within twenty feet of the track. The train was going too fast to stop, and had I slammed on the brakes the car would have skidded ahead into the train. Quick as a flash the Lord gave me presence of mind to whirl the car to the left and up the side of the track, thus avoiding the train and coming to a stop without injury. Hallelujah!

We prayed for dry weather; soon the sky cleared, and as we crossed the bay on the ferry from Oakland to San Francisco the sun smiled down upon us from a clear blue sky, as a promise that the Lord would send down upon us the showers of blessing and the sunshine of His love whilst in this city.

Brother and Sister Robert J. Craig, with their workers, were waiting to welcome the Gospel Car and its seven rejoicing passengers.

GLAD TIDINGS HALL

From the first meeting to the last the glory of God rested upon the people. The manifestations of the Spirit's power increased daily, hungry souls came from far and near and were filled with good things from Father's table. Crowds increased daily, and even though an extra gallery was built, the last meeting found the crowds standing clear out onto the sidewalk.

The way in which sinners rose to their feet in response to the altar call and came from the galleries and from various parts of the hall to the altar was a sight to warm the heart of any soul-winner. At the close of each preaching service the long prayer room would quickly fill from one end to the other with earnest seekers for the baptism of the Holy Spirit. The prayers of seekers and workers went up with such unison and in such accord that their voices sounded like the rushing of many waters. Many were prostrated on the floor under the power of God while they received their baptism, others were filled with the Spirit while kneeling or standing upright on their feet, with hands and face upturned to Heaven.

These after meetings ofttimes continued until five and six in the morning. Among the many baptized with the Holy Spirit during these meetings were two ministers, church members and a number from a nearby Salvation Army corps.

FIRE FALLS IN WATER

As the new converts took a firm stand for the Lord and were buried 'neath the water in baptism, the fire fell in the baptismal fountain till Pastor and new converts danced and shouted, talked in tongues with interpretation.

Throughout our meetings everywhere we have put the ministry for the soul first, then the ministry for the body, nevertheless miracles of healing have been wrought in almost every meeting.

Among those who were healed in the San Francisco meeting was a child whose throat was to have been operated on the following day, instantly healed in answer to prayer. The doctor bade the mother take the child home, saying that she was perfectly whole.

A lady who had suffered with internal trouble and rupture for eighteen years was instantly made whole by the Great Physician, Jesus, in answer to the prayer of faith, insomuch that the truss has been removed and she leaps and dances and praises the Lord, absolutely free from pain.

A brother whose knee and ankle had been stiffened from a severe accident, was touched by the Hand Divine, and his joints loosened up so that he danced and leaped for joy, his limb made whole and sound as ever.

An elderly lady afflicted with neuritis in head and face, insomuch that for a number of years she had not had a sound night's sleep, came to ask for prayer. So tender was her head and face that she held her hands over it while we prayed, as though in terror lest the lightest finger touch should reach it. She was instantly healed, and through the entire balance of the meetings continued to praise God that all pain and tenderness was gone, and she slept soundly, free from suffering.

What a wonderful Savior is He who has borne not only our sins but our sickness in His own body upon the tree, and by whose stripes we are made whole. Here is the testimony of a sister:

HEALED OF TUMOR

"I had been afflicted with a tumor on my wrist for a number of years and had never had a permanent healing until now. Sister McPherson and a brother prayed for me and I am thoroughly healed. I work at my stenographic work every day and there is no soreness in the wrist at night, which shows it is a perfect healing. Praise the Lord. I was healed of internal trouble which made my life miserable, and my sight, which had been affected from my nervous condition, was also healed, so I am now made perfectly whole."

B. L. L.

Brother and Sister Craig, who have stood as pastors of this work for seven years, are precious, fire-tried saints of the Lord. Through the many doctrinal issues and contrary tides that the enemy has brought to bear against the children of -the Lord in these last days, they have stood firm and true. The kindness, hospitality and love extended to us by the dear ones of San Francisco will never be forgotten.

After the farewell service, saints and pastor gathered about the Gospel Car, and prayed and sang ere we departed to our next field of labor.

OAKLAND, CAL.

Mrs. Carrie Judd Montgomery, who, with other Oakland saints, attended many of the meetings at San Francisco, having the work of Oakland on their hearts, asked us to hold a series of revival meetings in that city. As this was out of the question, every date having been promised far ahead, Sister Montgomery arranged two special afternoon meetings, which we sandwiched in without interfering with those of San Francisco.

The first meeting was conducted in Ebell Hall, the second in the great ballroom of the Hotel Oakland.

Both meetings were well attended by members of all denominations. Several ministers who were there expressed their longing for a deeper work and a melting of the coldness in their churches.

A Methodist minister and a Methodist Episcopal preacher both gave cordial invitations to us to come and preach the next Sunday morning.

SAN JOSE "THE GARDEN CITY"

Pastor J. H. Sparks and his assembly, who had been preparing and looking forward to this special effort for months, had all in readiness. The Liberty Hall was filled with people. All were hungry for the meetings and eager to help.

The way in which these California saints go to work to advertise a meeting is an inspiration. Almost every trolley in the city carries a big revival meeting banner outside, besides the cards within. The windows of the shopping districts have been placarded in every direction. The city has been mapped off and visited from house to house with personal and printed invitations.

In addition to the daily street meetings, automobiles bearing signs and banners go through the streets. Singers with guitars and banjos and big base drums are within, whilst a brother sits astride the engine and shouts through the megaphone of the soon coming of Jesus, and bids the astonished populace come to the Liberty Hall and hear all about it.

Our first convert was a poor old man who had spent Saturday night in jail. Sunday he was saved and the following Monday found him on the front seat with a shining face and a glad testimony. He had found work, and promised to be true to Jesus.

One dear Catholic woman who had heard about the meetings came fifty miles to be saved. With uplifted hands and radiant face, she joined in the march about the building, shouting and praising her new-found Savior.

A newspaper reporter attended every meeting and printed the greater part of every sermon in the daily newspaper. Ministers and church members alike came to hear the message; souls were saved and the glory came down.

WELCOMED HOME

"When are you coming home? Will meet you" was a message recently received over the phone from the Los Angeles assembly. "Home," why, 'tis the first time in years we have had such a message or a place that we could really call home.

Thus we had our first glimpse this week on a hurried trip to Los Angeles, of the little house which we have beheld by the eye of faith from the day the land was dedicated, and it is going to be just what we need, nothing elaborate in any way, but it will be a home nest and the dear saints who have toiled at it faithfully, have been so Spirit-filled that with the hum of the saw and the tap of the hammer have gone up songs of praise and victory, and prayers that God's blessing would follow and bring us safely home.

It has been indeed a labor of love, and our hearts are overflowing with gratitude to the precious Father who hath remembered the low estate of His handmaiden and fulfilled His promise and hath done exceedingly abundantly above all that we could have asked or thought. We are looking forward today with greater courage and lighter hearts than ever before to the work of winning souls and spreading the message of the soon coming of the Lord, as we think of the little ones coming home from school, singing and playing happily about the bungalow and praying for the Mother as she comes and goes in the Master's service, in obedience to the command of Him who raised her up from a dying bed to preach the Word. All glory to Him who has kept us within His tender care until this day.

And as we are looking forward now to taking our children to this haven of rest which loving hands have prepared, we know that if we are faithful a little longer we shall someday receive a wireless message to come to the home over there which our Lord has gone to prepare, and shall rise with souls who have been redeemed through obedience in preaching the Word our spiritual children that there we may enjoy together the building made without hands, that fadeth not away, eternal in the Heavens.

Part II. Testimony of those touched by God in our Meetings

THE MIGHTY POWER OF GOD MANI FESTED AT MOUNT FOREST, ONTARIO.
SISTER E. SHARP

"Blessed is she that believed, for there shall be a performance of those things which were told her from the Lord."

These words were given to me while we were talking over the work of our mission that the Lord led us to open, four months previously, in the town of Mount Forest, Ont., Canada, in the year 1915. The plougher, the sower and cultivator had done their work, and now we were expecting some fruit from our labors. As believers, we were looking for the signs following.

Hearing of a great Pentecostal camp meeting at Kitchener, Ont., about sixty miles from us, I went there, and at that meeting met Sister Aimee Semple McPherson, whom God was using mightily among those hungry seekers my heart was greatly drawn to her, and one night while we were praying in a tent with five young girls who were receiving the Holy Spirit, the Lord spoke to me, saying:

"There is the one for your work, the one I shall use in the revival I promised you." I spoke to her at once, and the next day she received the assurance and confirmation from the Lord that she was to come.

At this Camp meeting the Lord used her to encourage and pray with my Mother, who received the Spirit, whom she had been seeking to receive for three years, also my brother and a niece were baptized with the Holy Spirit at this meeting through her ministry.

Before the close of that Camp meeting my loved ones, with myself and about sixty others, followed the Lord in water baptism, in the river, while multitudes of people thronged the banks. Sister McPherson gave a soul-stirring message to them, while still in her wet garments. About seventy people or more were baptized with the Holy Spirit in that meeting, through her instrumentality.

Two weeks later a number of my loved ones planned to attend a Camp meeting at London, Ont.

My daughter was anxious to go, after hearing that so many young children were filled with the Spirit at Kitchener. (We had never been taught to believe that children could expect to receive the Holy Spirit.)

During these two weeks, in answer to prayer, God had deepened a hunger in the soul of the preacher in our mission, so that he, with my loved ones, went to this Camp meeting to receive this part of "that which was spoken of by Joel the prophet." I received a letter from them that he and my daughter received the Spirit at the same time, both speaking in tongues as the Spirit gave utterance, also that my nephew had been baptized with the Holy Spirit in the previous meeting, and my brother-in-law and his father both were filled with the Spirit in the same meeting, after Sister McPherson had almost carried the father there to hear his son speaking in tongues. A sister-in-law also received the Holy Spirit in the same Camp meeting.

While I was reading the wonderful news I began to shout and praise the Lord in such a way that my seven-year-old boy closed the doors and windows lest I should scare the neighbors and wake up the town. It seemed as though the floodgates of Heaven were opened on my soul, and I began at once to plan for our own meeting.
SISTER MCPHERSON ARRIVES AT MOUNT FOREST

The Lord would not let me advertise these special meetings as I did before; I just announced that Sister McPherson would be with us for a short time, the meetings to commence on Sunday.

On Saturday evening, on my way to the station to meet the Sister, who was to arrive on the train, I asked the Lord for a confirmation if this was the beginning of the revival He had promised me a year before, if so, would He just baptize someone that evening. The Sister, on her way up, asked the Lord for a promise. The Lord said: "Everyone that asketh receiveth."
THE FIRE BEGINS TO FALL

On our return to our home from the train, which was about 9 p. m., we found the home unexpectedly filled with young people. We at once began to pray and sing, and presently my boy, ten years old, fell across another young man, and began to speak in a language he had never learned. My husband, now convinced of his need, received the gift of the Holy Spirit on the following Monday morning while at family prayer, and he began to shout in other tongues. A few days later a younger boy, seven years old, received the Spirit, and spoke in Chinese, as the Spirit gave utterance. One week later I had the joy of seeing my husband and three children, along with many others, obey "The Word," by being buried with Jesus in water baptism.

MULTITUDES COME RUNNING TOGETHER

Very soon our mission could not hold the crowds, and for some nights Sister McPherson stood on our front piazza and preached to the enormous crowds that filled our lawns. In answer to prayer the Lord gave her a 30x60 tent, which was erected on the lawn.

Shortly before this, during a testimony meeting at the mission hall, while we were singing, the mighty Comforter came upon me with power and set the joy bells ringing, and at the same time the Holy Spirit fell on a young man who began shouting:

"Glory to Jesus!" while I shouted "Hallelujah!" The young man began to shake and to shout louder. The church people who had gathered for the meeting became alarmed and terrified, and left, telling men on the streets that I was hypnotizing this young man. Presently the hall was filled with mockers and scoffers, and with professional and business men of the town, inquiring, "What meaneth this?"

THEY WERE ALL AMAZED

One doctor pulled the brother off the chair, opened his shirt and applied a piece of ice, wrapped in a towel, to keep the fire from burning.

Still he shouted:

"Glory, glory, glory to Jesus!" and I shouted:

"Hallelujah!" The lad's parents were sent for, as they were told "Jim" was dying. Meanwhile I was shouting, and two doctors busied themselves one of them placed his knees on one of the young man's arms, and the other doctor placed his knees on the other of the young man's arms trying to hold his hands quiet, but he shouted all the louder, until his father came and dragged him home, and our meeting closed that evening without any testimonies, but has never been dismissed.

This had been the first time the Power of the Holy Spirit had fallen in our mission hall or in any public place in the town.

THE LATTER RAIN FALLS

When the meetings began at the tent it was noised abroad, and multitudes came from different parts of the country, from villages, towns and cities, and we had to meet every train. The promise, "Everyone that asketh receiveth" was truly fulfilled. In those blessed days of blessing and outpouring of the Spirit, many did not even ask, but only desired the gift, and the Lord baptized them with the Holy Spirit.

What times of rejoicing we had in our home at the rear of our tent, where we set apart our large sitting-room for hungry souls, to weep their way through to Calvary and Pentecost. We joyfully took the spoiling of our goods, to see the dear tear-stained faces weeping on our fine upholstered chairs, couches, rugs and sofa cushions. When I look at them now they look sacred, even to touch, in loving remembrance of those hallowed hours, when we tarried with them, when we heard the Heavenly choir singing, as we joined in the praise and worship of the King of kings.

Our Sister had wonderful visions, and the Lord gave us many songs through her while she

129

was "In the Spirit." The Lord gave me messages in unknown tongues, and gave Sister McPherson the interpretation, which put a holy fear on those who had wandered away from God, and many were convicted of sin and came to Jesus.

HEALING IN THE NAME OF JESUS

One day my Mother came to our home with her foot badly poisoned; she had suffered much for weeks, but the Lord Jesus gave victory and healed her.

One man, the town-crier and bill-poster, had three running sores on his ankle for years; the doctors could do nothing more, and wanted to amputate the foot. When he heard of the healing power of God he came along to have some "Mission Ointment," as he called it, applied. We told him we had no mission ointment but the healing ointment of Calvary. We prayed and laid hands on him, and anointed a cloth with oil in the name of the Lord Jesus, and wrapped it around his leg and ankle in Jesus' Name. He came back the next day and told us he felt like needles pricking all his toes and ankle. When we removed the cloth we shouted "Glory to Jesus," for he was perfectly healed, and all the blackness gone he walked without a limp. He was a living testimony in the town, for everyone soon heard of his healing.

THE OLD-TIME POWER

One Saturday morning, about 10:30, while my hands were in flour, preparing to bake, and another lady worker was sweeping, with a big apron and dust-cap on, we were asked to come out to the tent to see my husband, slain under the power of the Spirit on one side of the altar, and the town-crier, who had assisted him in the tent, with the benches, etc. slain under the power of the Spirit on the other side of the altar.

I began to shout:

"Glory to God," and the sister shouted and waved her hands. Next my Mother came to the tent, and she, too, commenced to shout. Then came our preacher, and my daughter, and Sister McPherson. Everyone of us was slain under the power of the Spirit. The tent rapidly filled with Scribes and Pharisees, scoffers, policemen, doctors and hotel-keepers, all inquiring what power was this, or who was the cause of all these people being mesmerized and hypnotized. Even the preachers did not recognize the "Old-time Power" which they had been praying for so long, to visit their churches; it had come so rapidly to the little crowd of humble people whom they despised.

In a short time the whole town was stirred, and all rushed to see, while the power had lifted from all but the town-crier, who was made the subject of much criticism and examination by the doctors.

All the while Sister McPherson, who had regained her feet (she had been slain under the power of the Spirit, too) was preaching.

"This is that which was prophesied by the, prophet Joel, and the same power that dear John Wesley felt in his meetings, before the 'Amen Corner' left the churches." She preached the Gospel in its simplicity, decisively, and convincing many that this was the same as in Acts 2.

Others, however, mocked and said: "They are mad, only fit for the asylum."

HALED BEFORE THE MAGISTRATES

We shouted and praised God until far in the afternoon, when I was served with a summons to appear before the magistrate that evening at 7:30, which hour was our specified meeting time, for praising Jesus with a loud voice. Oh what glory filled my soul when I took that paper from the police constable for the sake of Jesus. The Lord was good to me; I danced around the constable in the Spirit. This brought Sister McPherson, who, when she saw me dancing, began to dance around them also. He went away remarking to others:

"We cannot do one thing with these women."

The Lord was with us in the Courtroom, while listening to the charges against us. Of course I had to plead guilty to the charges made by the scribes and the Pharisees, some of them being Methodist Church people among whom I had, been a worker for years.

It was true there was such drawing power at the tent it caused people to look out of the photographer's window so that he could not get them to pose for their photos, and he was consequently losing money.

The printers and compositors in the pressroom were also attracted so that the editor was losing money.

The dressmaker was a loser, for the singing got on the nerves of the people, and she had to go home, ill.

The grocer felt so bad that he felt like shouting, too.

But a dear Catholic expressman would not put in any charge against us; he said they should just let us go and obey God rather than men.

The Word of God was fulfilled in many ways. The Holy Spirit gave us, at that hour, what we should say, and we testified to the wonderful works of God in our own souls and homes.

The Lord sent us a fine man, Rev. J. Clark, a Methodist minister, who had been baptized with the Holy Spirit at Winnipeg, to witness in the courtroom that evening, and to convince the magistrate that this was of God.

While we were in the courtroom, Sister McPherson, with a band of young converts, conducted a meeting at the tent, which was packed, and an immense crowd outside, of a furious, angry mob. God gave her the message of:

"What meaneth this?" and "This is that" - gaining them every moment, and the Holy Spirit stilled the tempest, and the meetings were advertised far and wide, for afterwards large crowds came to "see and hear."

I, hitherto, had possessed a man-fearing spirit, and shrank from noise and manifestations, but I praise the Lord for sending Sister McPherson into my life, as she taught me how to praise the Lord and to get out of bondage to man, and to take my liberty in the Spirit, for "whom the Son makes free is free indeed."

She left aside all doctrines, but lifted up Jesus, and magnified the Blood, truly honored the Holy Spirit, and preached the soon-coming of Jesus, as we had never heard before, and our dear Lord honored her messages by swing and baptizing many. The effects of these meetings will reach to the uttermost parts of the earth. This year missions have been opened in different towns by dear ones who received blessings at that Camp meeting.

The Lord gave us many precious songs through Sister McPherson, in the Spirit, also the messages in prophecy: Awake, O Earth!" and "Jesus is Coming Soon," were given through her during the last few weeks of those meetings, before she and her husband left for his home in Providence, R. I., where they together began their work in the large tent donated by the saints of that place.

Surely we have seen "the arm of the Lord revealed," and the Holy Fire came from Heaven with slaying power when our floor appeared like a battlefield that even unbelievers looked on in wonder.

"He that goeth forth and weepeth, bearing precious seed shall doubtless come again with rejoicing, bringing his sheaves with him."

TESTIMONY OF PASTOR W. K. BOUTON, FREE GOSPEL CHURCH, CORONA, N. Y.

After preaching the Gospel for about twelve years with marked success, I began to realize there was something needful in my life, but did not know just what it was. I would often say to my people: "God is about to do some strange thing in our midst, but what it is I do not know." I felt a need, but thought I was in possession of all that God had for me, except that I must go on and "grow in grace and in the knowledge of the Lord daily, line upon line, precept upon precept, here a little and there a little." I never dreamed of the Baptism of the Holy Spirit. I thought those days were passed; in fact, I was taught by the teachers under whom I studied, that we need never look

131

for supernatural things, those days were over and gone forever. Whenever I heard anything about the Baptism, or people speaking in other tongues, I would say it is an error and would warn my people to have nothing to do with it. We were having very good meetings, and scores of souls were saved. We hardly ever had a service at our church, especially on Sundays, but what God was wonderfully blessing and swing souls.

NEW LIGHT

About this time one of our members came and told me of a woman who was preaching in the little Swedish Church here in Corona, He said:" You ought to hear her, she speaks in other tongues, and it seems the Spirit of God is wonderfully using her." I warned this brother to keep away from these meetings and told him he would be sorry if he became entangled in such a bondage. A day or so later, a sister came to me with the same news and told me to be sure and hear this woman. I warned the sister likewise.

Then two other members of my church came and told me how wonderfully God was using this woman, and said one of our members had received this strange blessing and also spoke in other tongues. I said: "If she does this kind of thing she will have to leave our church for she cannot come to our church with this nonsense." Soon two or three others, all members of our church, came to see me and said I must hear this woman.

All these things made me very curious and so I determined to hear her, not because I believed in what she said, but because my curiosity was aroused. The first time I heard her she impressed me as being honest and sincere and of having a great knowledge of the Scriptures. After hearing her the first time I came home and told my wife how I felt about this matter. My wife said: "You be careful; you warned others; now you look out, or you will be ensnared in some of these latter day errors." But I found myself at the meeting the next night, vastly interested. I was saying "Praise the Lord!" and "Amen" to many of the things she said. When she spoke of the falling away of the churches I could say Amen, when she spoke of the coming of the Lord I could say Amen, likewise when she spoke of the tribulation to come upon this whole earth. I could also give my Amen when she stood for a clean church and for a people wholly set apart for the service of God. But when she told of the way God would baptize us with the Holy Ghost and fire with the outward sign, namely, speaking with other tongues as the Spirit gave utterance, I must admit I could not say Amen, for I did not believe it. When I reached home I "searched the Scriptures to see whether these things are so," and to my great surprise in nearly every place where the Holy Spirit was poured out I found they spake with other tongues. I was sorry to find these things, because I had been preaching to the contrary. I continued to go to the meetings; somehow I could not stay away. One night Sister McPherson spoke of the Baptism of the Holy Ghost and the gifts, from the 12th and 14th chapters of I Corinthians. This settled it all with me; I was sure this thing was of God and that the Lord was still baptizing people today, as He did in the days of the Apostles. After this meeting was over I invited Sister McPherson to come to our church. I had not consulted any of the Trustees, nor any members of the church. I simply took it upon myself to invite her. She readily accepted the invitation.

THE BAPTISM OF THE HOLY GHOST

The next night the meeting was in our church. In her first talk Sister McPherson proved beyond doubt that down through the ages the church had lost the gifts of the Spirit, and she likewise proved that God was going to restore them and was restoring them now. She said nothing in particular, however, about the tongues. We opened the meeting again the next night and told Sister McPherson to say anything she felt led to, and immediately she preached on the Baptism of the Holy Ghost, with the signs following. That night the Lord began to pour out His Spirit in a way we had never seen before. All over the church people were lying prostrate, the altar was filled all around the rail and down the aisles. I confess I was a little afraid. I had been praying to see these things and now as my eyes were beholding them I was half praying that God would stop. I feared

132

we might all be arrested. I think eighteen or nineteen people were baptized in one of the first meetings. I used to plead for people to come up and give themselves to the Lord, but now we had to beg folks to leave the altar and make room for others. This continued for two weeks, every night, until one and two o'clock in the morning. People were receiving the Baptism and coming through speaking in other tongues. Sunday School Superintendent, teachers and people from other churches came in, God making no difference, but baptizing all alike. Most everybody in our church received this blessed Baptism, all the officers included, except myself. I could tell others to praise the Lord and lift up their hands, but when it came to lifting up my own hands and praising the Lord I realized in what a bondage I was. Nevertheless, I was determined to have my Baptism, so on the 26th day of November, 1916, after the meetings had been going on for some time, I sought the Lord. After having my hands extended for about fifteen or twenty minutes, and "seeing no man save Jesus only" the Lord poured out the Holy Ghost upon me, and I, too, began to speak with other tongues as the Spirit gave utterance. It seemed as though Heaven had opened and I had entered into the city; I heard and saw things which completely revolutionized my life.

DIVINE HEALING

So in two weeks our church was thoroughly transformed by the power of the Holy Ghost and we began to see new things. God was healing people. Numbers, which time would not permit me to speak of, were healed immediately. One man came, into the meeting with heart disease.

He had had many doctors, but none could help him. After prayer and the anointing with oil the Lord Jesus healed him. Two sisters with very large tumors came for healing. One of the two sisters was to have an operation in a week.

The tumor was on the back, a little below the neck.

After prayer and anointing with oil I placed my hand upon the tumor. I could feel it getting smaller under my hand. So I called her mother and asked her to feel it. She did so and immediately threw up her hands and praised God, for the tumor had diminished. O, there is power in Jesus' blood, and the "prayer of faith does save the sick." Praise the Lord! The other sister felt that all pain had left her and she said she was healed. Another brother had a disease for years and the doctors were unable to help him. While we were anointing him with oil the Holy Ghost came upon him and he began to speak in other tongues, and testified that God had immediately healed him. Another sister with a very, very bad case of catarrh was instantly healed. One sister had a cancer on her intestines, of which an X-ray picture had been taken. Two local physicians of this town had diagnosed her case. Her bed was prepared at Flower Hospital, but Glory to Jesus! in the twinkling of an eye God healed her. This was nearly two years ago and no sign of it has ever returned. Praise the Lord! There are scores of others which could be mentioned, but suffice it to say that the prayer of faith does save the sick and the Lord does raise them up.

These things have been going on in our church for nearly two years; there has been no stop, and the power of God is manifested meeting after meeting. God is still swing and baptizing people.

At the present time of writing, twelve souls were saved at our last service. When God has His way, souls will be both saved and baptized in the Holy Ghost.

FAITHFULNESS REWARDED

Let me say in closing, that wherever there is an honest heart, God will always reveal Himself to such a one. Wherever there is one "hungering and thirsting after righteousness, he shall be filled." Truly, if "we first seek the kingdom of God and its righteousness, all things will be added unto us." God has proved this to me over and over again. I was a poor boy, compelled to work for a living at the age of eleven, and I know what it is to be hungry and to want the necessities of life. I know what it is to be without shoes on a cold winter's day, walking the streets with the snow water oozing out of the tops of little shoes which had no soles on them. I know what it is to go to school with my sister's waist on and the other boys all laughing because I had so many buttons down the back. But I sought Him. and not only that, but He sought me, and praise His Name! He found me. Today I have my own home and most everything heart could wish for, and am the Pastor of a spiritual church, "who love not their lives unto death," but Jesus first and last.

O, how thankful we are that God ever permitted Sister McPherson to come to Corona. God through her has done a work which will redound to the glory of God; and the revival is still on. Sept. 23, 1918.

MEMORIES OF THE CAMP, BY ELDER GEORGE LLOYD

Ever since the blessed Camp at Philadelphia the Spirit has prompted me to write and try and tell of some of the wonderful things witnessed there. And that is the most difficult part, to tell of the most wonderful things, for it was all wonderful, and our God was there in mighty power.

It was not the great number of definite and glorious healings that we witnessed that appealed to the Spirit most urgently, for we know that our God is a mighty God, and we know that Jesus Christ is the same, yesterday, today and forever.

Praise His glorious name! And we know that Jesus can and does heal, and that He loves to heal all that come to Him in true penitence and faith.

And then there were the many soul-searching messages in tongues, with prompt and beautifully true interpretations, many, many of them. And then came the Heavenly drama, with various and beautiful acts of the Holy Ghost, shown forth by the precious saints, for they were in the Spirit.

Glory to Jesus.

And the great number of converts, it was glorious, for we never witnessed so many cases of clean-cut salvation before, where the dear ones would come weeping their way to the altar, some falling under the power on their way. And when they had prayed through they were ready to testify to a salvation that saves.

One blessed scene comes before us often, and we can see that great congregation of blood-washed saints, with uplifted hands, pouring out their hearts to God in earnest prayer, until the sound resembled the rushing of a mighty river of waters, in its volume. And when the spirit of prayer had continued many minutes, there was heard a new sound, and the prayer was changed to a song of holy adoration, even praises to our King.

Hallelujah!

And as the holy anthem broke forth, Sister McPherson seemed to float toward the piano, with uplifted hands and transfigured face, and commenced to play and sing in the Spirit. We had heard spiritual songs before, but never like this; never such tones from a piano had our ears heard before, and as verse after verse of the holy anthem was given to our Sister with tongues and interpretation, and the saints who were in the Spirit would all join in the glorious chorus, we were transported with ecstasy, and we were in the Spirit and were singing the New Song without any effort on our part.

Oh, the precious, Heavenly music! Who can in any way describe it? We could only compare it to an Aeolian harp with its rising and falling cadence, and its sweet, blended harmonies, only far sweeter and more pure in tone than the finest pipe organ, for this was the Holy Ghost playing upon God's great instrument not made with hands. Glory to Jesus!

So the glory seemed to increase over the white city of tents until the last great day of the feast, and on the last night of the blessed meetings, when the last "God be with you" had been sung, and the congregation was dismissed, there remained a large class of disciples who had tarried for their anointing for service to our King. The dear ones took their places in line, waiting patiently and prayerfully their turn for their anointing for service until the early morning hours, and God was very near with mighty power, and we pray that the anointing received by the dear ones shall go with them to their different homes and assemblies, and kindle the Pentecostal fires anew and keep them brightly burning until Jesus comes.

As for myself, I just praised God for the anointing that remains with me, for I am conscious of a new power such as I never had before, and a determination to give all that I have and all that I am into His glorious service. And as we left the blessed tabernacle and went to our tent and cot for an hour of needed rest before our journey homeward, we looked up to the starlit morning sky and praised our dear Heavenly Father for the glad privilege of spending twenty days in Heaven, in Whose precious Name be glory forever. Amen.

A MONDAY NIGHT MEETING. BY PHOEBE C. BENT

One week of the Nation Wide Pentecostal Camp Meeting had passed. The truth had been working in the hearts of the rough element that lined the outside of the big tent each night in great numbers. The crowd of young men and women from the neighborhood had come to mock and jeer the work of God this Monday night. The very air was charged with the opposition of the evil one which drove many a saint to get under the burden and lift it with prayer. If the adversary was carefully marshalling his forces, the Master was more carefully organizing the saints of God for the great struggle to come; and the Master has never lost a battle.

As the singing progressed, Sister McPherson, inspired by a revelation from God, arose to her feet and gave a stirring exhortation that the saints move more unitedly together against the evilness around them. Then the Holy Spirit, knowing what was needed for the situation, changed the order of the service.

It has often been said that one of the charms of a Pentecostal meeting is that there is never any monotony. You never know what is going to happen next, praise His name. So it was announced that a number of leaders would give their testimonies. have you noticed in the accounts of the great struggle over the sea, that the secret of a successful offensive lies in the ability of the attacking army to hurl fresh troops into the fray.

So it was this night, that the Holy Spirit threw one leader after another to the front with their testimonies. Some were not even allowed to finish their story before they were moved off, but the Master had His way, praise His name. It was a hard battle. A feeling of a weight almost too heavy to lift settled over the saints.

Then came the sudden orders to dismiss the meeting abruptly. This would seem like defeat, yet the Lord knew just what was needed. The crowd soon melted away, after the benediction, disappointed in their purpose of having a good time.

Then Sister McPherson called for an all-night meeting of prayer, asking for those who would pray through to victory. Sister Sisson arose and said that

"The people shall become our bread. This opposition on their part has driven us to our knees in this all night of prayer. 'Why do the heathen rage, and the penile imagine a vain thing? The kings of the earth set themselves, and the rulers take counsel together against the Lord, and against His anointed. He that sitteth in the Heavens shall laugh.' Yes, God laughs He has given us a chance to get His coin. Can't you hear His coin clink? Help yourselves, children."

With common consent every one sank to his knees in prayer, and for two hours hearts poured out their cries to Heaven. Who could doubt that those in prayer moved God on His throne in behalf of His saints? The Holy Spirit placed a mighty soul-travail upon one sister, who wept and moaned with sounds "which only the Spirit can utter."

When the praying had ceased, Sister McPherson, in that simple way of hers, said:

"Now, dear ones, just let us be quiet and see what God has for us." From the silence that followed it could be seen that the Spirit worked this way and that upon different ones. Sister McPherson had retired to one end of the rostrum, where she swayed back and forth in a peculiar step or dance. This continued for some time, when suddenly she moved rapidly to the great upright piano, and began to play in the Spirit. The moment the first strange chord was struck, all eyes were riveted upon her. Wonderful music flowed from the keys as her hands flew rapidly to and fro. Strange, and sometimes weird Heavenly chords were struck, that never man could produce in the natural chords that struck to the very soul. After a wonderful prelude, she sang a song about the Lord's coming, that was perfect in rhythm, rhyme, and metre.

135

She then arose and gave a message in tongues, using certain things to emphasize her words. She took a megaphone which stood near at hand, and filled it with flowers from a vase on the pulpit, which typified the "horn of plenty." Next, placing the flowers on the floor, she watered them from a pitcher, showing that His saints would be revived and watered with the Latter Rain, which would soon fall upon them, and then closed with an exhortation to get ready for the soon oncoming of King Jesus.

Immediately after the message followed a tableau of the crucifixion. Sister McPherson took the outstretched hands of another sister that moved in the Spirit, and made the motions of driving the spikes through her hands and feet, into the cross. Then she laid her down, as in the tomb, then raised her up as in the resurrection.

After a message in tongues, she gave the interpretation of the tableau that had just transpired before them as follows:

"Behold, the Lord is calling. He is searching for a people for Himself. He is calling; who will follow Him? Who will be willing to go all the way? Such a one will reign with Me. Wilt thou, wilt thou follow me? Behold the way is long; the night is dark; the road is thorny; yet trust thou Me. I will be with thee. Behold, wilt thou follow me, wilt thou go with Me through Golgotha? Wilt thou go with me through the lonely way of Calvary?

"Behold thy hands thy hands that are busy with the cares of this world they must be nailed to the cross. Art thou willing to have thy hands nailed to the cross? Thy busy feet, that have walked for this world, must be nailed to the cross. Thy heart, that has beat for this world, must be pierced for me. A new heart will I give thee. Who will follow me? Who can bear the crucifixion of this world? Can you live for me alone?

"He was laid in the tomb then did His enemies mock Him. Then did the resurrection come. Behold! He will come again. He will give thee a crown eternal. Rejoice in Me, for the City is in sight. I will present My people perfect to the Father. Many members from the East and from the North and from the West and South shall become one body. Little children, will you follow Me?"

This tableau finished as the first early signs of (lawn were breaking,' and the great prayer of consecration which followed from the heart of Sister McPherson, seemed not only to take in her own soul, but the souls of the whole camp. It was a time in which the hearts around her melted with that sweet sadness that only a contrite heart knows. This prayer seemed to close that wonderful Monday night of prayer; and as each saint departed there was not one who doubted that a great victory had been won for God. To Him be all the praise. It was little that we did; He did it all-glory to His name!

SOME THINGS WHICH I SAW. BY ELIZABETH SISSON

Yes, things which I saw in Sister McPherson's tent:

A brother injured in an auto accident, for months unable to use one leg, instantly healed, leaping and dancing on the platform, after hands had been laid upon him with the prayer of faith.

A blind brother was so far recovered that he could walk about the tent and grounds, could see the buttons and trimmings on a lady's dress, and said he kept seeing more all the time.

A sister who came into the camp on canes, had also a cancer, has been walking for days without sticks, and told me she felt the healing thrills go through and through the cancer. A sister very ill with serious heart trouble was instantly healed as she went forward to be prayed for; the healing came before the hands were laid on. Another left off her glasses, got her sight so she could thread a needle; also all her teeth were loose, and they have come in tight and sound.

A Roman Catholic lady came in to be prayed for, gave her heart to Jesus and was healed. But it is impossible to keep track of the cases, they so multiply on our hands.

We had two thousand chairs in the tent. These were all filled an hour or so before preaching service began. Then all around the tent they stood, ten, fifteen deep, in profound attention for an hour and a half or two hours. Crowds composed of every nationality; all the Protestant denominations, and the Roman Catholics, with a good sprinkling of clergy, and a large crowd of non-church-attendants. God certainly advertised the goods. The power and demonstration of the Spirit was wonderful. That "joy of the Lord" which is "our strength" filled the place, beamed on every face, and danced in the eye of every saint. The "slain of the Lord were many." The whole altar was filled with them from end to end, daily the most wonderful baptisms in the Spirit. Altars at night were full of unsaved, seeking and FINDING salvation.

WONDERFUL DOWNPOUR AT VICTORIA HALL. BY PASTOR W. W. FISHER

The Latter Rain in great abundance has been coming on the saints since the sister opened her campaign. Old, dried-up cases, where the individual has been seeking the baptism for years, have been falling under the power of God and coming through speaking in tongues. Backsliders who failed God have been saved back into life and are now singing His praises. I never, in all my extended ministry, saw so many slain under the mighty power of God as have been observed in the prayer room after the call was given for seekers. It has seemed so easy for the people to yield themselves to the Spirit. In some instances the Evangelist had only to lift her hands and the power would tumble them over.

In the large Auditorium Sister McPherson held the vast throng of nearly three thousand for over an hour with the Gospel message, and many followed her to get under the showers. In all a great revival has started in our midst. The people are letting go of issues and doctrines and are joining in with smiling faces, so that old grudges are being settled and the saints are getting the love of God restored in their souls.

The messages of the Lord, as given through our sister are witnessed to by the Spirit. They are the kind the church is in need of today. They are just the kind of messages that are needed in the city of Los Angeles, where much spurious doctrine has originated, and where the Saints are in such bewilderment they scarcely know what to believe.

The Latter Bain is falling, some say even more copiously than the former rain, and we are exceedingly glad to be in the showers.

SAN FRANCISCO REVIVAL. BY ROBERT CRAIG, PASTOR

It was a glad day for the Kingdom of Christ in this place when the Lord directed our Sister Aimee Semple McPherson to hold a series of meetings in San Francisco.

Literally towering mountains of prejudice against the Pentecostal movement have been saved away under the same candid and forceful presentation of the claims of the full Gospel Message.

How many, many times church people have said:

"This is just what we have wanted and is just like the power fell fifty years ago, except for the speaking in tongues."

Scores who had grown faint of heart over the coldness and indifference of the denominational churches have had their hearts gladdened and their spirits refreshed and warmed at these Pentecostal fires.

Oh! How many church members, and among them many dear Scandinavians, have been swept thru into their baptism.

Many Salvation Army people, touched by the power of the Spirit, have come and received the Baptism of the Holy Spirit, Acts 2-4. Among them several officers and ex-officers. Though it may mean expulsion for them, yet, praise God, they bear the reproach joyfully, counting it a privilege to thus fill up a measure of His suffering which remains.

From every possible angle the work of the Lord at Glad Tidings Mission Auditorium has been greatly strengthened, deepened and settled, for which we praise our Heavenly Father.

One splendid Baptist minister, who will now devote his life to the Pentecostal Ministry, received, his Baptism as did also Evangelist A. C. Stevens, whose testimony now rings clear and strong for Pentecost.

Just how many have been gloriously converted in these thirty-three days eternity alone will reveal. It has been a deep work and we believe that the fruit will remain forever.

The Healing power provided in the Atonement has also been graciously manifested.

Quite a number of city ministers came to listen, wonder and view the marvelous work of God in the large prayer room strewn night after night) with the slain of the Lord, and hear them burst into new tongues. Pity the man who goes back to his church to fight against this gracious Heaven sent Revival. He will be writing his own epitaph.

Toward the close of the campaign the prayer room was much too small and little prayer-groups could be seen in various parts of the building pointing sinners to Christ. This beside the ofttimes crowded altar.

Part III. Some Sermons and Writings of Aimee Semple McPherson

"COME now, and let us reason together, saith the Lord;, though your sins be as scarlet, they shall be white as snow; though they be red like crimson, they shall be as wool. IF ye be willing and obedient, ye shall eat the good of the land. BUT if ye refuse and rebel, ye shall be devoured with the sword, for the mouth of the Lord hath spoken it."

(Isa. 1:18, 19, 20.)

C-O-M-E; I-F; B-U-T; How much is expressed in the three opening words of the three above verses. The whole Gospel is embodied and expressed through these concise, plain statements of God. First of all let us take the word C-O-M-E.

Dear sinner, Jesus loves you. His arms are outstretched toward you, His voice is calling you, He has prepared a glorious Salvation for your body, soul and spirit, and His great heart and love and life are composed of one great, loving c-o-m-e! c-o-m-e! c-o-m-e!

No matter how deep you may have fallen into sin, Jesus says, "Come, I will forgive you and wash you whiter than the driven snow."

No matter how black and vile your heart may be, no matter how evil your mind and filthy your appetites, or how strong your sinful habits, COME, and I will take away your sin-filled heart and give you a new heart a clean heart filled with pure, holy thoughts; I will fill your mind with thoughts that are in Heavenly places, and your mouth with praises; I will break the fetters of every evil habit and cause you to walk forth a free creature in Christ Jesus.

"No matter if you have been a moral professor, striving to live well in your own way you must come to Me just as you are," says Jesus. "You must be born again; nothing but the blood can save. All your righteousness is as filthy rags."

Let the little children come, the aged with their white heads and misspent years, the colored and the white, the yellow and the brown come unto Me, all ye ends of the earth, and be ye saved.

COME! COME!! COME!!! The call goes forth to the Queen upon her throne and to the poorest wretch in the convict's cell alike; all have sinned and come short of the glory of God; all have need of His great salvation.

Come, let the weeping tears be dried and the discouraged, hopeless soul take new courage, and find new hope, for Jesus is the hope of the hopeless. Plunge beneath the crimson flood that flowed from His wounded side, and thou shalt know that there is indeed balm in Gilead, and gladness in the house of the Lord.

Let the giddy, laughing, thoughtless sinner, dancing on the brink of Hell, be sobered and come to Jesus in repentance, confessing his sins, or he will be eternally lost in that land where laughing and dancing are never known. The invitation is extended to all mankind, irrespective of race, creed, color or age; all alike need Jesus, and without Him are undone; it will wail nothing to gain the whole world and lose one's own soul. "Come, now, and let us reason together," saith the Lord, "though your sins be as scarlet, they shall be as white as snow; though they be red like crimson, they shall be as snow." No matter how great or how small your sins may be, Jesus will forgive and pardon you, and, better still, He will remember them against you no more if you will turn to Him today whilst there is yet time.

"If ye be willing and obedient, ye shall eat the good of the land." I-F dear sinner, Jesus has done His part, He has sent forth the great call, "Come," throughout the world; He has laid down His life and shed His blood to redeem you; He has prepared a great and glorious feast and builded a glorious, Heavenly city for you to live in. But now we come to the great, middle word of our test, "I-F." It does not look like a very big word to read it, yet it is of such gigantic proportions and looms up such a mountain that your whole soul's eternal salvation or damnation depends upon that one .little word "IF."

God has left you a free-will, moral agent; He will plead with you to come; He will endeavor to win you to His salvation and love, but He will never force you to accept it. There must be a willingness upon your part to accept this Savior as your Lord and King, a willingness to let Him give you a new heart, and shape your life and pattern it after our great example, Jesus. Here, then, is the whole key to the situation:

"If ye be willing, and obedient, ye shall eat the good of the land." ' First Willing; Second Obedient, then ye shall eat the good of the land; there is nothing too good for the Lord's children. Has He not told us that "AH that I have is thine" and that "no good thing will He withhold from them that walk uprightly"? The good of the land, with its joy, its peace that flows like a river, its Heaven for evermore, are yours IF ye be willing and obedient to the calling and commands of the

141

Lord. And O, His yoke is easy and His burden light. Hallelujah!

B-U-T.

But, then we come to the only other alternative, the solemn, dark, grim punishment of the wicked.

"But if ye refuse and rebel, ye shall be devoured with the sword; for the mouth of the Lord hath spoken it." There are only two paths: one leads to life, the other to endless death; one leads to hope and joy, the other to despair and utter darkness.

God hath no pleasure in the death of the wicked, but longs that all should turn from the error of their ways, hearken to His great, eternal invitation, expressed in the word C-O-M-E, be willing and obedient, and inherit life everlasting. But, if you refuse His invitation, and rebel instead of obeying, you choose your own path, and thereby seal your own doom, signing your own death warrant, and shall surely be overtaken with God's sword of judgment, which will fall upon all who have rejected Jesus the Christ.

If ye be willing and obedient, and become a child of King Jesus by being born again and accepting His salvation, you will dwell in the courts of His glory forever.

But if ye refuse and rebel, and choose rather to remain in sin, and continue to walk on as the devil's child, you will, of course, share in the devil's home and reward, and be devoured with the sword. The mouth of the Lord hath spoken it, and no matter who has tried to tell you destruction will not come, nor sorrow overtake those who refuse and rebel, they cannot change the true facts of the case, for the mouth of the Lord hath spoken it.

O, dear sinner, heed this simple message today. Come to Jesus as you are. Will you not kneel down just where you are this moment, and cry out "O, Jesus, you have invited us to come, poor, wretched, sinful, vile. O Lamb of God, I come.

Forgive my sins, create in me a new heart, make me obedient and true to You forever. Take all desire for the world, the flesh and the devil from my life, and create a right Spirit within me, and I will follow You wherever You may lead me, dear Savior." You will feel His cleansing blood applied and His Spirit will bear witness with your spirit that you are a child of God, and with His great, eternal arms about you, a new life will open out before you, and you will find your feet in the path that leads on through the gates of pearl and the streets that are paved with gold.

May God bless you, and help you to accept this great invitation at once? for today is the day of salvation. O, harden not your heart.

WHAT SHALL I DO WITH JESUS?

"WHAT shall I do with Jesus?" Clear and imperative rang out the voice of Pilate above the clamor of the throng assembled in the Judgment Hall.

"What shall I do with Jesus?" The question was flung forth over the mob of frenzied, upturned faces.

Fair and square, demanding an immediate, decisive answer, this question of momentous importance resounded through the court room, and hung suspended in the tense, tragedy-laden air. From the murmuring sea of anger-tossed accusers was born a mighty, unquenchable tempest of bowlings and ragings, while dark faces grew darker still with blood-thirsty fury against the still, calm figure standing so meek and sweet in his robes of flowing white.

It was Jesus this pure, mild man, standing there friendless and alone in the midst of this howling rabble. How out of place He looked like a tall, sweet, fragrant lily in the midst of thorns and briers; like a pure little lamb in the midst of a pack of hungry wolves, with bared fangs. Dear Lamb of God, innocent, and unresisting, before the great judgment seat of Pontius Pilate he stood, awaiting the verdict of those arrayed against Him.

"What shall I do with Jesus?" What decision would they render upon this question this momentous question this greatest and most important question that has ever been decided since the world began? There were only two possible ways of answering only two courses of action open: there was no neutral ground, for had He not declared that

142

"He who is not for me is against me"? Either they must accept Him as the King of Heaven, Jesus, their Savior, or they must crucify and drive Him away from their hearts. Either they must accept Him as their Messiah, their Redeemer, or they must reject and put Him to an open shame.

Louder, and with ever increasing determination, rose and fell the cry of the people; "Away with Him! Crucify Him! Crucify Him!

"We have no King but Caesar." They had rendered their decision, their choice had been made; they had given their irrevocable answer, and had de-determined to crucify and put their Lord to an open shame.

Harsh hands fell upon the gentle Nazarene, and rushed Him from the court. Mercilessly did they tear His garments from Him, and bared His precious back to the smiters. He meekly bore the cruel lash to the last, stinging blow that by His stripes we might be healed. A crown of thorns was thrust down upon His brow; a purple robe put upon Him in mocking derision. He was led to Calvary's Hill, bearing His cross, and crucified by cruel men.

They crucified their Lord; they gave Him vinegar and hyssop to drink; they spurned and rejected Him to the last. And He bowed His head and died He who would have gathered them to His bosom He who would have been their King, and have taken them up to reign with Him on His throne.

Pilate's Judgment Hall the very name calls to memory that shameful scene, and our hearts cry out:

"How cruel, how foolish those Jews were to reject and crucify their Lord to let Him stand there on trial alone, with no one to accept Him and stand on His side!"

Yet, did you ever stop to realize that the border of Pilate's Judgment Hall has been enlarged and its walls have widened and widened, till today this whole world is a judgment hall Jesus is still on trial, and the Spirit is echoing and re-echoing the question:

"What will you do with Jesus?"

The whole world is obliged to answer this question, as did the Jews of old. Each living soul, irrespective of race, color or creed, must take sides either for or against Jesus. There are today as in that day of old but two courses of action open.

Each heart must answer individually and definitely whether he, too, will cry:

"Away with Him! Crucify Him." Or whether he will open his heart's door and let Him enter as King of Kings and crown Him with love and allegiance.

Perhaps some reader cries out in horror:

"Oh! We would never crucify Jesus we would never think of driving the nails in His hands!"

But consider a moment, dear one. If you have not accepted Him as your Savior from all sin and unrighteousness, if you have not come to Him in repentance and had the blood applied to your heart, you have done just that crucified your Lord afresh and put Him to an open shame.

Remember he who is not for Him is against Him neutral you cannot be;

Each time you go out of a meeting unsaved; each time you go to bed unrepentant; each new day the sun rises and finds you unprayerful, un-thoughtful of your soul's salvation, you are crying out:

"Away with Him! Away with Him!" O, perhaps you do not say it in words. But actions speak louder than words, and even though your mouth may speak much love, if you have not unconditionally surrendered your heart and life to Him, and permitted Him to rule on the throne of your heart, you are unconsciously answering the question "What shall I do with Jesus?" by saying:

"Away with Him! Crucify Him! I have no king but self and the world; I want my own way. Away with Him! Away with Salvation." And another voice is added to the throng rejecting Jesus. "In what way am I saying 'Away with Him'?" you ask.

Why, can you not realize, dear unsaved soul, that every step you take every foot-fall that resounds along the corridors of time, apart from Jesus every step towards worldliness in sin is crying out, louder than you could ever speak;

143

"Away with Him; I choose the world; I have no king but self." Each time you put off Salvation and say:

"Not tonight," you are adding another thorn to the crown which you are making of your life and placing it on His dear brow.

We are all making a crown for Jesus out of these daily lives of ours, either a crown of golden, divine love, studded with gems of sacrifice and adoration, or a thorny crown, filled with the cruel briers of unbelief, or selfishness and sin, and placing it upon His brow.

Each new day lived in holiness unto the Lord; each new sacrifice of praise, is just another gem in the royal diadem with which the Christian is constantly crowning the King who sits supreme on the throne of his heart.

Each new day lived in sin and indifference to Jesus is just another thorn, another cruel brier the sinner's life is weaving into the crown he is placing upon the brow of the friend and King he has rejected and driven away from his heart.

Then they put upon Him a purple robe, crying,

"Hail, Jesus, King of the Jews," and smote Him with their hands. Many today are still living lives of hypocrisy, mockery and pretence; many are putting upon Jesus a purple robe of outside formality; they go to church and sing "All Hail the Power of Jesus' Name but by their lives they smite Him with their hands.

And He, bearing His cross, went forth unto Golgotha, and there they nailed Him to the cross.

The great, rugged cross was stretched upon the ground, and Jesus' dear body stretched upon that cross. O, sinner, behold that man the Son of God with the kind, resigned, tender eyes, waiting to be nailed there for your sins: See those rough, heavy hands seize the nails and place them to the palms of Jesus' hands. Hear the great, ringing blows of the hammer, as the nails are driven deep crunching through flesh and sinew and bones deep into the wood of the cross for your transgressions. Dear hands - hands that had fed the multitude hands that had blessed the children, healed the sick, raised the dead faithful hands that are knocking at your heart's door just now as you are reading these very words they nailed them to the cross. It was your sins, and my sins that nailed Him there. Are you still pushing His hands away from your life, and piercing them with nails of scorn, and unbelief, and pride?

Then they drove the nails through His feet the feet that had travelled so many weary miles to bring hope and cheer and light and He was lifted up high on the cross, up and up, suspended upon those cruel nails till at last the cross sank with a thud into the hole that had been digged for it. And there He hung, the King of glory, between earth and Heaven, in shame, alone, for us.

Sinner, dear, how high you have lifted Him in open shame others have seen you reject Jesus! O, won't you receive Him just now as your Savior? Will you not love Him who first loved you?

See that beautiful face, more marred than the face of any other man. Hear His cry:

"Lo, I thirst! Give me to drink." They offered Him vinegar and hyssop the bitterest of their hatred and unbelief. But ah! He thirsts for the sweetness of their love and adoration and acceptance. What are you giving Jesus to drink sweetness or bitterness? love or rejection? Our lives are as a sponge, either absorbing vinegar and hyssop from the world and the devil, or sweetness and fragrance and the water of life from Jesus and His Word.

Jesus is calling anew today:

"Lo, I thirst!" Dear one, what have you to offer Him today from your life acceptance or rejection?

Jesus cried: "Father, forgive them; they know not what they do." Oh, sinner, it does not seem possible that you could have realized what you were doing in refusing to accept Jesus, and persisting in crying;

"Away with Him! Crucify Him!" Perhaps you never quite realized that you were crowning Him with thorns, and crucifying Him afresh, and that he who is not building up for Him is tearing down.

What will you do with Jesus today? How will you answer this eternal question? Jesus is standing before you awaiting the verdict. You must judge; you must render your decision, for or against Jesus or the World, Life or Death.

Judge, and choose ye this day, for soon this whole scene will be changed forever. The sinner will be removed in a hurry from his judgment seat, and Jesus will mount the judgment seat to judge the nations. The graves shall be opened, the sea shall give up its dead, and all the dead, both small and great, will stand before Him whom they have judged.

Everything will then be quite reversed. Instead of it being a question of "What shall I do with Jesus?" the question confronting each sinner will be, "What will Jesus do with me?" In that great day those who have accepted Jesus and made Him ruler in their lives, will be accepted of Him and sit with Him on His throne, but all those who have rejected Him, and cried:

"Away with Him from my life, I have no time for Jesus will be rejected then by Jesus. He will Himself echo the sinner's own words;

"Away with him; 'depart from Me, I never knew you.' Depart into the home prepared for the devil and his angels."

Those who gave Him to drink of the sweetness and wine of their love will drink anew with Him the wine of His Father's Kingdom, but those who gave Him naught but rejection, and the gall of bitterness, must drink the cup of their own sin and death to the dregs.

What will you do with Jesus? O, accept Him now; seek Him whilst yet He may be found; call upon Him while He is near. Put away the evil of your doings; cease to do evil; learn to do well; wash you; make you clean. Accept Him as your Lord and Savior just now. He is calling you who are weary and sick with sin; seeking you in tenderness. He is whispering; Come unto Me all ye who are weary and, heavy laden, and I will give you rest. Him that cometh unto Me I will in no wise cast out. Today is the day of Salvation; tomorrow it may be too late, for He is coming soon to earth again, coming with power and great glory.

Get ready to meet Him.

WHICH ROAD?

ONLY TWO ROADS IN LIFE: UPON WHICH ARE YOU?

SEARCH where you may, the wide world over, there are only two roads to be found in this life.

One road leads to Heaven; the other road leads to Hell. The first road leads to everlasting life, the second to everlasting death. The one to joy and peace and eternal day; the other to eternal sorrow and darkest night and destruction.

Every man, woman and child in this world, irrespective of race, color or creed, is at this very moment traveling either the one or the other of these two roads. In other words, every individual living is either on the road to Heaven and life, or upon the road that leads to Hell and death.

I am just a plain body, that believes in stating a plain fact in plain words. It is time that preachers stopped sugar-coating and misconstruing God's Word; time they stopped preaching politics and oyster suppers and began to preach these plain facts that are so simple that even a fool need not err therein.

First of all let me give my text, and we will see what the Lord says' about these two roads, their destinations, and the pedestrians thereon. Jesus says, "wide is the gate, and broad is the way that leadeth to destruction, and many there be which go in thereat; because straight is the gate and narrow is the way that leadeth unto life, and few there be that find it."

This statement, if understood, would surely revolutionize the ideas of a great many so-called broad-minded people, who have always believed that living a moral life or being a church member would be a sufficient passport into Heaven. Being a church member is no longer a despised way, but quite the opposite; it is now considered quite the fashionable and proper thing to do. Many think this is all the Lord requires of us; but upon this erroneous belief falls the Word of God with a startling blow that overthrows all such false security.

Narrow is the way that leads to life and few there be that find it. O, that Christians, as well as sinners, and cold professors, would awaken to the reality of this fact and get one glimpse of the countless millions pouring into eternity every day without God and without hope! They would spring from their beds of ease and rush into the highways and hedges to compel men to come into the narrow way, and get right with God before it is too late.

The Word of God shows us where these two roads start. "All were born in sin and shapen in iniquity." "All have sinned and come short of the glory of God." We are also reminded that as God "cannot look upon sin with the least degree of allowance," "the soul that sinneth, it shall die."

But Jesus took our place, He died in our stead, thereby opening a new and a living way, the narrow way, into the presence of the Father.

O, sinner friend here tonight! O weary, heavy-laden pilgrim! halt a moment and consider. Which road are you on? Are you traveling towards Heaven or Hell? We all entered life by the one and self-same road, that is, we were all born in sin, and shapen in iniquity.

Figure one on the chart shows us just a little of the circle which represents the earth. All having been born under the curse of sin, and, having need of the second birth ("Except a man be born of water and of the Spirit, he cannot enter into the kingdom of God." John 3:5), enter the infancy of life on the wide road marked by figure two on the chart.

Many anxious mothers ask the question:

"Sister, what do you think becomes of the little babes, and children who die before the age of accountability?" I answer promptly, and without a moment's hesitancy

"I believe they are taken to be with the loving and compassionate Jesus, who said: 'Suffer the little children to come unto Me, and forbid them not, for of such is the kingdom of Heaven'."

But there comes a day, possibly most of you can look backward along the road of time and recall that day for yourself when the little heart and mind begin to know the difference between

146

right and wrong. The young pilgrim, after running along carelessly from infancy, suddenly sights in the distance a great, old, rugged sign post, that has stood the storms of many generations, but still stands firm and unmovable. This sign post the Cross of Calvary stands just at the parting of the way.

Did you ever notice the peculiar and wonderful shape of the cross? The foot points to the earth and humility, and to the fountain filled with blood, as though it were saying

"Come, poor, tired, troubled, sin-sick soul. Lay down your burden; plunge into the fountain filled with blood. Here is cleansing for the filthy, pardon for the sinful, rest for the weary, peace for the troubled, relief for the oppressed, freedom for the captive. Just throw yourself down at the feet of Jesus and He will make you whole."

The top of the cross points upward toward the sky and Heaven, as though saying

"Lift up your head, poor, weary pilgrim; lift up your eyes to the Heavens above you; lift up the hands that hang down; strengthen the feeble knees; say unto them that are weak, 'be strong and of good courage, for He who died upon the tree has gone up yonder, beyond the clouds of glory, to prepare a place for you, that where He is there you may be also

The two arms of the cross are outstretched as though to gather the whole world into the loving embrace of Him who said:

"Come unto Me, Oh ye ends of the earth, and be ye saved."

Thank God for such a sign-post to reveal the way of pardon and point out the narrow Heaven-bound road to the sin-sick soul.

Figure three on the chart shows. us where the two roads divide. Oh, let your feet pause here, dear one, at the parting of the way. Don't make a mistake, for this is the most important decision you will ever be called upon to make in your whole life. Which road will you take? One turns to the left, the other to the right. One leads to Heaven, the other to hell.

Look carefully at the two roads as depicted on the chart, and you will notice that the broad road which leads to destruction is a crooked road, so crooked that he who walks upon it is always unable to see just what lies ahead. Each new turn of the road he finds himself committing sins more vile than his conscience would have permitted a month or a year before. Were the road not crooked he would be able to see the flames of hell and hear the weeping and the anguished cries of the lost who call:

"Go back! Go back!" He would run for his life to the refuge of the cross.

"Why is the road crooked?" you ask. Because it is the trail of the serpent. The same serpent that deceived Eve in the garden is deceiving the nations today.

"Why is it crooked?" Why, because it is impossible for a serpent to crawl straight. The devil is crooked and he will deceive you at every turn of the road till at last he has plunged you into destruction.

Now while the trail of the serpent leads into hell, 'tis the way of the cross that leads home to the glorious land of Heaven. Oh 'tis a Heaven to go to Heaven in when we walk in the shadow of the cross. Hallelujah!

The broad road, that leads to destruction, looks inviting to your feet. It is strewn with flowers and worldly pleasures. The so-called broad-minded man who lives on the broad way can tell you of worldly pleasures, theatres, dance halls, fashion, love of money, popularity, music and sin to be found at every turn of the road.

They could tell you, if they would, of broken hearts too, of drunkards, and harlots, of empty hearts, and misspent lives. They could whisper, too, with white faces and scared eyes, of ghastly deaths they have witnessed of those who found the wages of sin were death, and went into the presence of their father, the devil, and to the home prepared for him and his imps.

But no, they will not tell you of these true facts, but tell only of the light surface, and the tinseled, varnished side.

THE BROAD WAY

147

That downward road (figure four) is broad and easy to enter. Just a little disobedience, a little lie, forgetting to pray, wandering from God, whatever it was that came first into your life you remember it when you began your downward career on the broad way that leads to destruction.

Perhaps you did not really mean to go far on that downward path, but somehow it all seemed so easy. One sin led to a greater one, till soon you were so tangled up and slipping so fast it seemed impossible to stop and go back.

It is so easy to go down to hell and destruction, just a toboggan slide, till at last you shall awaken to find it is too late, unless you listen now to the warning and stop and return to the cross, that dear old weather-beaten sign-post, and weep it all out at Jesus' feet.

THE END THEREOF IS DEATH

It is a dreadful thing to go on to the end of the broad, sinful road. I have gazed with wide, horrified eyes into bleary, sinful eyes and bloated faces. I have marked the lines of sin upon the face and oftener upon the heart. I have seen the great chains of appetite, the prison doors of evil, I have stood at the death beds of those who had rejected Christ, and such a message as you are now hearing, and held their hands with a shudder as they passed out into the dark, without God, to reap their reward. I have heard those who would never seem to sober down and think before, when asked to accept Jesus on their death beds cry out:

"Too late! Too late! I'm lost!" I can tell of weeping and wailing and gnashing of teeth, as they died.

The proud and haughty sinner, the infidel, they who have declared in their learning that there was no God, no hell, no Heaven, shall have to pass with the drunkard and the harlot through the jaws of death (figure five) into that awful home prepared for the devil and his angels. There shall be weeping and wailing and gnashing of teeth. Their not having believed there was such a place will not have moved it or taken it away. "The wages of sin is death."

DYING WORDS OF THE UNSAVED

Here are some of the dying words of the unsaved:
"Hell is a refuge if it hide me from thy frown."
- Altamont.
"I would gladly give thirty thousand pounds to have it proven there is no hell."
- Charteres.
"Give me more laudanum that I may not think of eternity and what is to come."
- Mirabeau.
"Oh, my poor soul! what will become of thee? Whither wilt thou go?"
- Cardinal Mazarin.
The atheist Hobb's last words were: "I am taking a fearful leap into the dark."
Voltaire was a noted, wealthy infidel, yet his last words were: "I am abandoned by God and man; I shall die and go to hell."
Death in that awful place where their worm dieth not, and the fire is not quenched.

"Oh", you say, "If God is a God of love He would never cast a soul down into hell." No, God will not willingly cast the sinner into destruction, and if he goes to hell he will have to go over the body and blood of Jesus Christ who died to save him; rejecting the love of the Savior who did all in His power and shed every drop of His blood to redeem him from that place which was built, not for the sinner, but for the devil and his angels.

Those who live in sin, with the devil as their father, in this world, will live with the devil as their father in that home which has been prepared for him; but the children of God who have owned Him as their Father here below, will live with Him in His home in peace and joy for evermore."

THE NARROW ROAD

148

The other road (figure six), the narrow road, blest road of light and life, begins at the cross.

Jesus is the door; there is no way to enter but by Him, and the blood He shed for the remission of our sins. It is a narrow road, there is no room to take earthly things with you; there is just room for Jesus and you. If any man would follow Me, let him deny himself daily, take up his cross and follow Me. It means a right about face. It means being born again and being made a new creature in Christ Jesus, so that the things we once loved we now hate, and, Hallelujah! the things we once hated we now love.

In order to enter this narrow road that leads to Heaven you must repent of all sin, make things right, straighten up your back tracks as far as possible, ask Jesus to cleanse you from all sin and unrighteousness, and "though your sins be as scarlet, they shall be as white as snow; though they be red like crimson, they shall be as wool."

Isa. 1:18. "For he who cometh unto Him, He will in no wise cast out"

Those who travel upward, for it is a steady climb, can tell you of joys untold. They can tell you of a peace the world cannot give nor take away. They can tell you of broken hearts that have been healed, and sad lives made glad. They will testify to you of salvation from all sin, and deliverance from all bondage, of broken chains, and captives made free in Christ Jesus. They can tell of the baptism with the Holy Ghost (Acts 2:4) and the gifts and fruits of the Spirit in their lives.

I have in this road also looked into eyes and faces, but they were filled with the glory and love of God. Instead of evil and wariciousness, they were filled with tenderness and tears of gratitude to the blessed Savior who grows sweeter as the days go by. Glory! Glory! Glory! Each step you take in this road brings you one step nearer Heaven; one foot says "Glory!" and the other says "Hallelujah!" and with a pure heart and a clear conscience you are on your way to Heaven. O, sinner, where have you such joy as this?

THE END THEREOF IS LIFE

Here, too, I have stood by death beds and instead of convulsed, fearful faces of sinners, I have seen calm, peaceful faces of those just going to rest in the arms of Jesus. Blessed are those that die in the Lord, and go shouting home to glory.

Here are the dying words of a few of the saved:

"Lord Jesus, receive my spirit." - Stephen.

"I have fought a good fight, I have finished my course, I have kept the faith.

Henceforth there is laid up for me a crown of righteousness, which the Lord, the righteous judge, shall give me at that day; and not to me only, but unto all them also that love His appearing." II Tim., 4:7 - Paul.

"The best of all, God is with us." - Wesley.

"I am sweeping through the gates, washed in the blood of the Lamb." - Cookman.

"I am in perfect peace, resting alone on the blood of Christ: I find this sufficient to enter the presence of God with." - Trotter.

"The battle is fought, the battle is fought; the victory is won." - Dr. Payson.

The cross-bar of the cross (figure seven), represents the river of death through which so many saintly feet have trod. Oh, what a wonderful thing to have Him bear you up that the floods do not overflow, and to be able to cry with Catherine Booth:

"The waters are rising, but so am I; I am not going under, but over."

Just beyond the waves of death a glorious crow r n is waiting. Will there be any stars in your crown? Do you not long to be a soul-winner for Jesus? How pitiful it would be in that last day to have lived the most of our lives for the devil, to have given Jesus but the few closing hours of life's little day, and to be obliged to go empty-handed without a single soul with which to greet the Master, not a trophy nor a jewel to adorn the crown that you lay at His feet.

Beyond lies the glorious city of Heaven whose twelve gates are each composed of a solid pearl, whose street is made of pure gold, as it were transparent glass and the foundation of whose

149

wall is garnished with all manner of precious stones. The building of the wall is of jasper, and the city of pure gold like unto clear glass. That land has no need of the sun, neither of the moon to shine in it, for the glory of God doth lighten it, and the Lamb is the light thereof.

Here there shall be no sickness nor crying, no pain nor death nor sorrow, no misunderstandings and no heartaches, and there shall in no wise enter into it anything that defileth or that worketh an abomination or maketh a lie, but they which are written in the Lamb's book of life.

Ah! the toils and thorns of the way are naught to be compared with one glimpse of the glory that awaits us in that beautiful city where Jesus wipes all tears from all faces, and there is no more night. Hallelujah! the very thought of seeing Jesus sets my whole soul on fire.

Who ever heard a sinner saying, "O, I'm so glad that someday this life will be over and I am going to die and go to hell and destruction." NO!

You never hear them anxious to talk about death and punishment. But the true child of God loves to think of the day when he shall lay down the cross and receive the crown.

Between Heaven and hell is a great gulf fixed.

There is no possibility of crossing from one to the other after death. As a tree falls, so shall it lie. Today is the day of salvation tomorrow may be eternally too late.

Now sinner, stop, and decide just now, which road you are on, and which road you choose to journey on from this time forward; decide which home you will dwell in forever where the fire is not quenched and the worm dieth not, or where no weeping shall ever be heard, but singing and rejoicing and joy unspeakable forever and forever.

You are a free-will agent; you must decide for yourself. Jesus has opened the way, and He is holding the gate open wide for you just now. O come tonight, dear ones, come just now. Never, never blame Jesus, or say He sent you to hell, for if you refuse to be saved and enter in, you send yourself there; He has done His part. How He will help you and carry you through if you will only let Him. Just now, wherever you are, He is whispering,

"Behold, I stand at your heart's door and knock." Open to Him just now. Say, "I will arise and go unto my Father." Today is the day of salvation. You have no lease of tomorrow.

Come just now.

"Angels are lingering near,
Prayers rise from hearts so dear,
O wanderer, come."

BEHOLD, THE MAN!

"Then came Jesus forth wearing the crown of thorns and the purple robe, and Pilate said unto them, Behold the man"

John, 19:5.

JESUS has promised us in His Word that He, if He is lifted up from the earth, will draw all men unto Himself, and before beginning this subject today I cried out to the Lord to help me to sink out of sight and to lift Him up above the earth until you should see no man save Jesus only.

BEHOLD the man! Behold THE man! Behold the MAN! I would like to repeat it over and over again, until I catch every wandering mind and bring each straying thought into captivity. Behold the man. Just close your eyes to all else for a few moments.

STOP beholding your business your pleasure your home your earthly cares and duties your neighbor whatever it may be that has been absorbing your attention, and Behold the Man, Christ Jesus.

If you have never stopped long enough before in your busy life to behold the man, the Lamb of God, the one who loves you more than any earthly friend loves you, I want you to behold Him NOW.

I am sure that if you could only get one glimpse of that face which is the fairest among ten thousand, if you could only catch one cadence of His voice, sweet as the rushing of many waters, if you could only gaze for one moment into the depths of those tender eyes filled with understanding and sympathy and love, the tears of love and gratitude would spring to your eyes, your heart would fill with praise till you would never wish to cease from beholding and adoring and worshiping this Man, Christ Jesus. As the shades of darkness and unbelief are driven back by the light of the sun of righteousness, and as you behold the man, you will find new beauties, new attributes and graces unfolding themselves before your astonished and adoring eyes each moment you behold, till your heart bursts forth into singing,

"Since mine eyes were fixed on Jesus, I've lost sight of all beside, So enhanced my Spirit's vision, Gazing at the crucified."

As we sweep back the curtains of the centuries and look back through the undimmed corridors of the past, we behold the Man seated with His Father upon his throne. He was with His Father from the beginning the brightest jewel in Heaven, the joy of the Father, the delight of the angels, the light of the temple, the only begotten Son, worthy of praise upon harps of gold, and the angels fell prostrate at His feet as He sat in His kingly robes and splendor in their midst.

Behold the Man, with His Father when He spoke the world into being, and set the sun, the moon and the planets in the sky.

Behold the Man, filled with sorrow on that memorable day when our ancestral parents fell into sin and because of that sin were banished from the sight of God under penalty of death. And when there was no eye to pity, no arm to save, none that could pay the ransom price for their redemption, we Behold the Man, saying: "Father, send me, I will pay the price. Without the shedding of blood there is no remission of sins; I will shed my blood, Father, I will be the bridge to span the gulf between man and God." Then we read that "God so loved the world that He gave His only begotten Son that whosoever believeth in Him should not perish but have everlasting life."

Behold the Man, standing up to take leave of the Father, leaving the songs and the adoration of the angelic hosts, laying aside His royal robes, His sceptre and His crown, stepping down from the throne and coming all the way from Heaven to earth for you and me, that we might not perish but have everlasting life.

Behold the Man, conceived of the Holy Ghost, born of the virgin Mary, coming to a world that found no room for Him in the inn. Behold Him born in a manger amidst the most deplorable and humble surroundings, coming to reach the loavest and the poorest of sinners.

Behold the Man living and growing up with Mary, His mother, and. Joseph, in the carpenter shop. Behold Him at the age of thirty, baptized of John in the river Jordan, ready to begin

His ministry. Behold the Man rising from a watery grave as the Heavens opened and the Holy Spirit descended upon Him and the voice of God spoke aloud saying, "This is my beloved Son in whom I am well pleased." Thus He entered upon His ministry with divine authority and the power of the God-head resting upon Him and abiding with Him.

Behold the Man tempted in the wilderness for forty days, tempted in all points like as we, and yet without sin. Behold Him turning the water into wine, preaching the gospel of the Kingdom, healing the sick, cleansing the leper, raising the dead, opening the eyes of the blind, unstopping the deaf ears, feeding the hungry multitudes, calming the troubled sea, weeping over Jerusalem, forgiving the sinner, giving water to the thirsty, healing the broken-hearted.

Behold the Man the King of Glory walking in humility upon this earth, footsore and weary.

Behold Him praying alone, night after night on the mountain side, praying for you, dear heart, and for a sleeping world who would never appreciate nor understand. The birds had their nests, the foxes their holes, but the Son of Man had nowhere to lay His head.

Behold the Man, at the last supper when even though His heart was aching, even though He knew the hand that would betray Him, and the disciple that would deny Him, even though He knew that all would forsake Him and flee away, His thoughts were for you and for me when He vowed that He would drink no more of the fruit of the vine until He drank it anew with us in His Father's kingdom, saying:

"As oft as ye do this ye do show forth my death 'til I corned Oh, glorious bridge that spans the long, silent years from the day of His death till the day He shall come.

Behold the Man, praying in the garden alone while His disciples slumbered and slept. Behold His agony and the travail of His soul as He cried: "Nevertheless, not my will, but thine, he done. And being in an agony He prayed more earnestly: and His sweat was as it were great drops of blood falling down to the ground."

Behold the Man bending low over His disciples in His sorrow, crying one understanding heart to watch with Him. But He found them sleeping and said unto them: "Why sleep ye, rise and pray." "And while He yet spake, behold a, multitude," pressing on through the gray dawn of morning, coming with staves and swords to take this Man this Jesus of yours, and mine.

Behold the Man, led as a sheep to the slaughter, and as a lamb before his shearers is dumb, so He opened not His mouth. Behold Him despised and rejected of men, a Man of sorrows and acquainted with grief. Behold Him bearing our griefs, carrying our sorrows, wounded for our transgressions, bruised for our iniquities. He was taken from prison and from judgment.

Behold the Man, condemned to die by the multitude He loved and longed to gather in His arms. Behold Him, beaten with stripes and nailed to the cross. The crown of thorns was placed upon His brow, the Roman spear pierced His side. But, Oh, beloved, hear Him cry, "Father, forgive them, they know not what they do!" Then when the debt had been paid, when He had borne our penalty (death) in His own body on the tree, hear the glad triumphant words that rang through the sky that hour, and still resound through the earth today:

"IT IS FINISHED." Then behold the Man as midst rending rocks and darkening sky, He bowed His head and gave up the ghost.

Behold the Man, lying wrapped in the cold silence of death in the tomb. Then in the early dawn of the third day, as the first gold and purple rays of morning rose in glad triumph above the hills of Jerusalem, an angel from Heaven spread his great white pinions and, sweeping down from Heaven to earth, rolled the great stone away from the mouth of the sepulchre.

Behold the Man resurrected, rising and coming forth again to look upon the world His world, purchased by His blood. Behold Him again, living and loving, walking and talking with His people, feeding the hungry, encouraging the downcast.

Behold the Man, leading captivity captive, ascending on high to give gifts unto men, saying:

"It is expedient for you that I go away, for if I go not away the Comforter will not come. But if I go away I will not leave you comfortless, I will send another, even the Holy Ghost. If I go away I will come again and take you unto myself that where I am there ye may be also, "and the clouds received Him out of their sight.

Behold the Man seated again at the right hand of God the Father. Behold Him standing at your side just now as revealed by the Spirit, hear Him say: "Behold, I stand at the door and knock, if any man will open to Me, I will come in and sup with him and he with Me." Let Him in, dear heart, draw nigh to Him and He will draw nigh to you. Receive the Holy Spirit which He has sent to lead you into all truth. Be faithful a little longer. Then soon, yea, very soon, you will BEHOLD THE MAN, coming in the clouds of Heaven with power and great glory to take you to Himself, where in the midst of joys unbounded as the waves of the ocean, we will behold the Man by the glassy sea, and worship in adoration at His throne, our Redeemer, bur Bridegroom forevermore. Open your eyes just now, dear heart, Oh!

BARABBAS

"And they all cried out at once, saying, 'Away with this man, and release unto us Barabbas.'

Now Barabbas was a robber, who for certain sedition made in the city, and for murder, was cast into prison." Luke 23:8, 19; John 18:40.

JUST these few vivid, gripping incidents - nothing more is told us of this man Barabbas.

The thick shroud of mystery that envelops both the beginning and the ending of his life is undispelled by the light of the scriptures, but these few bright crimson drops, wrung from the very heart of his story, as it were, seem to cry aloud the tale of innocence pursued by Temptation. Temptation overtaken by Sin. Sin pounced upon and condemned to die by The Law. Stern Law conquered and its grip loosened by. Jesus, the Substitute and Redeemer who died in the sinner's place.

Such a striking type is Barabbas of the whole human race, and of ourselves individually, that, as we stand looking down upon the incomplete story of his life, it seems like some wondrous, fascinating, unfinished texture stretched upon the loom of life, its riotous colors bespeaking sunshine and shadow, joy and sorrow, tragedy and triumph, threads frayed and hanging from the ending, threads loose and dangling at 'the beginning, as though inviting the onlooker to pick them up and weave again the history of the whole human race, as embodied in the study of Barabbas.

CHILDHOOD DAYS

About the spring time of every child we love to weave the white threads of innocency, a godly, praying Mother, and the picture of a little white-robed form learning to pray at mother's knee.

The home that has robbed its children of a praying mother has deprived them of one of the richest treasures that it is within its power to bestow, a memory which money could never buy, nor time destroy.

Whether Barabbas had a praying mother or not we do not know, but we long to think of her as instructing him in the old laws and the prophets, weeping and praying for him as he wandered into bad company and the paths of temptation. As he grew older we do not know whether or not he was married, but there may have been woven into the loom of his life with golden threads of love, a wife and a beautiful baby boy, but one thing we are certain of, and that is that he was led into sin, ever deeper and deeper, while God was speaking to him and the angels were warning him, saying,

"BARABBAS, BE SURE YOUR SIN WILL FIND YOU OUT"

Doubtless, Barabbas meant to call a halt sometime in the near future. He never meant to go so far into sin as to be caught, cast into prison and condemned to die. Every dark cloud of warning that the Lord put into his way was doubtless tinted rosy with promising colors of golden wealth and remuneration by the devil, as he was led on and on from one sin to another, until at last

we read that
"BARABBAS WAS A ROBBER"

In all probability his robbing started in some seemingly simple and trivial way, some tiny, childhood theft for which his conscience troubled and accused him. At the second theft, a little larger than the last, his conscience did not seem to trouble him quite so much, and unbelievably soon, his soul was hardened, until he became the leader of a band of robbers and started up insurrection in the city. He may have chuckled to himself and told his colleagues that they were clever enough to evade the law, and that they never would be caught, as many another sinner assures himself. But once more came the last and final warning:

"Repent; be sure your sin will find you out. Whatsoever a man soweth, that shall he also reap. The soul that sinneth, it shall surely die."

(Oh, Barabbas! What a striking type you are of our foreparents who, in the Garden of Eden, when first tempted by this same sin, stole and ate the fruit from the forbidden tree. No doubt Satan, in the form of a serpent, whispered in your ear, as he did in the ear of Eve, saying:

"Eat thereof. Ye shall not surely die." And then, guilty and sinful, you sought to hide yourself behind the trees of deception, and to assure yourself that neither God nor the Law would see nor punish you there.

But just as surely as Adam and Eve, shrinking guiltily behind their covering, heard the firm footfalls of Almighty God, walking through the garden to meet them, in the cool of the day, just as surely as God called out, saying:

"Adam, where art thou?" just as surely as He discovered, condemned, and punished their sin; just so surely did the footsteps of the law seek and overtake you, Oh Barabbas!)

Cunningly the devil led him on and on until one day he found himself the ringleader of an insurrection made in the city streets. Then, blinded with demoniacal rage, his blood surging in tumultuous riot through his veins, his reason overstepped her bounds, and quick as a flash a heavy blow was struck; the limp body of his victim fell with a sickening thud to the ground; a deep-dyed thread of crimson was shot through the texture upon the loom of life, and
BARABBAS WAS A MURDERER

Swiftly the heavy, relentless hand of the law fell upon the shoulder of the guilty wretch, staging with horror upon the work of his hands.

Escape was impossible. Mercy was out of the question. The Law must take its course. Doubtless the trial that followed was fair and square in every respect. Barabbas was G-U-I-L-T-Y.

And there were many witnesses to prove his guilt, both as a robber and as a murderer. No power could avert the penalty of the law, nor hinder it from descending upon him.

To and fro, back and forth flew the shuttle of time across the loom of life, now weaving threads that were dark sombre mournful. Was it with bated breath and blanching cheeks, or was it with a thin veneer of bravado that he heard the awful sentence pronounced upon him:

"Barabbas, you, with your two thieves, who conspired to work under your leadership, are condemned to die, and shall be hanged upon three crosses of wood on Calvary's hill till you are dead."

And when, plunged into the blackness of the dark dungeons beneath Pilot's judgment hall, chains clanking upon the damp flagstones as he writhed in the anguished throes of remorse, did he cry aloud?

"Oh, bitter thongs of the law! Oh, bands and chains of justice! Is there no escape from thee, e'en though I see my awful error and now repent?" And did the voice of firm, relentless law, with face like flint, echo from the haunting memory of mother's teaching, "An eye for an eye, a tooth for a tooth; the Murderer shall surely be put to death." Sitting there in the darkness of sin, unable to help himself, beyond the help of mortal man, the chains of approaching retribution already biting into the flesh of his body, condemned to die without hope, nothing to look forward to but death, what a picture is Barabbas of the whole human race.

BARABBAS A PICTURE OF THE HUMAN RACE

By Adam sin entered. The first sin recorded was that of theft; Gen. 3:6. The second sin to be recorded was murder. Gen. 4:8. God, in His infinite holiness, could not look upon sin with the least degree of allowance; the soul that sinneth, it must die. Death and eternal despair followed in the wake of sin. A great gulf had been fixed between man and God, the strong arm of the law fell heavily upon the human race, and after a fair trial the verdict, G-U-I-L-T-Y, was brought in. The sentence of "death" was passed, and man was plunged into the dark prison of captivity beneath the judgment hall waiting the hour when judgment should be executed upon him.

Oh! that someone would come to open the prison doors of those who were bound. Oh! for an arm to save, one who would bear the griefs and carry the sorrows of a sin-stricken race, one who would be wounded for the sinner's transgression and pay the sinner's debt!

Who knows the thoughts that throbbed through the aching brain of Barabbas during the days that followed, the stabbings of remorse, memories of other days, and thoughts of what might have been, the sleepless nights, the hopeless days, not one ray of light to pierce the gloom! Did that awful voice that had pronounced the sentence in the judgment hall keep ringing in his ears:

"Thou shalt be hanged upon a cross of wood on Calvary's hill, thou and thy two thieves, till thou art dead"? Did he lose all track of time, till his ears were ever straining to hear his name called and the great door to be swung wide, the hour when the dark silence would be broken, and midst the roaring of the voices of the rabble, and the piercing light of day, he would be led forth to die that shameful and ignominious death? In the silent darkness of his cell, with no other sound than the drip, drip of the sweat drops which came from the ceiling and fell like tears upon the flagstones at his feet, did the vision of the cross, his cross, rise before him, ever drawing nearer and nearer as the hour of his crucifixion approached?

Steadily on and on the shuttle flies across the loom in sombre and desolate colorings. Oh! what is this! The threads of wild terror and panic are being shot across the loom! Barabbas, sitting stock upright, rigid as though turned to stone, listens with every nerve tense.

Hear it? There it is again; it is his name they are crying:

"Barabbas! Barabbas! Release unto us Barabbas. Bring forth Barabbas! Barabbas! B-A-R-A-B-B-A-S!"

'Tis the voice of a multitudinous rabble, ever growing and swelling in volume. But how could he hear it away in this dungeon? The doors must be open. Yes, footsteps are echoing along the stone corridors that lead to his cell, nearer and nearer they sound, swords singing, keys jangling on their rings, and ever as a background, comes the imperative roar of the mob in the judgment hall above, a roar that is now settling into a steady chant brooking no denial.

"Barabbas! Barabbas! Release unto us BARABBAS!!!!

Louder and plainer comes the tread of the soldiers, until, at the sharp word of command, they halt before the cell. The rattle of the ponderous key in the door, the grating of the lock, the creaking of the heavy door, and then the expected words:

"Come forth, Barabbas, another is to die in your place today. You are a free man."

Tell me, O weaver at the loom, did a faint ray of hope dawn in his heart, or did he shrink back and cry, from the anguish of his soul?

"Oh!! Do not laugh at my calamity, and mock when my fear cometh. I know that I have had a fair and square trial. I know that I have been proved guilty and am worthy of death. I will go to my death upon the cross, but Oh! don't, don't mock at my calamity and jeer at my hour of sorrow." And did the keeper reply:

"'Tis neither jest nor mocking, Barabbas.? Tis true, thou art a free man. For one named Jesus is to be stretched upon your cross on Calvary's hill, 'twixt the two thieves today. With mine own eyes have I seen Him tied to the whipping-post in the court without, His back bared to the smiters, the blows of the cruel lash raining upon His shoulders. They are now leading Him up the

155

hill to be crucified. Come forth! Barabbas!

Come forth! You are free! He shall be bruised for your iniquity, and the chastisement of your peace is to be upon Him. He will die in your stead."

A FREE MAN

Free? FREE?? F-R-E-E??? Surely his ears could not hear alright! Surely this must be some horrible dream rising up to torment him.

"Make haste, Barabbas, come forth!"

Ah! the chains were loose at his feet. His hands were free. The biting iron that had long lacerated his flesh was gone. One trembling step two three and he was almost to the door, but no restraining hand had fallen upon him, no voice had jeered:

"Ah, Barabbas, come forth and pay the price.

Thy sin hath found thee out." Four five six he had gained and passed the door. Seven - eight - - nine - steps. He was groping his way along the corridor, stumbling blindly toward yon distant ray of light. True, the soldiers were marching behind him, but they were making no effort to seize him. What did it all mean? Surely they would seize upon him at the last moment. But, no, they are turning off in another direction and he is left alone, walking into the ever-growing light that pierces his unaccustomed eyes.

When at last, reaching the yawning doorway, clinging to its portals with one trembling hand, and shading his eyes with the other, what were his thoughts as he gazed once more upon the sunlight, and once more heard the singing of the birds, and the voices of children round about him? Were the golden threads of hope and new resolution already being woven into the texture, even amidst his bewilderment?

Oh these dangling threads that hang loose from the end of the texture, tell me, just how was the story finished? Did Barabbas catch sight of the throng wending their way to Calvary's hill? Did he hear the hissings and the jeerings of the multitude, and see yon lovely Man, in robes of white, fall beneath the burden of the cross? Did he run, perhaps, to the old cottage home, and clasping his amazed wife and little boy by the hand, cry:

"Oh, come with me, and let us go and see the man that is dying in my place. Today was the day set for my execution. Today I was to be hanged upon the cross and die a felon's death, but another man, an innocent man, is dying, dying for me. Oh, come and let us go and look upon His face that we may fathom the mystery of such love."

LET US GO AND SEE THE MAN

And did they push their way together through the throng and up the hill, ne'er stopping till they reached the foot of the cross, where sobbing women mourned the grief of Him who bore our sorrows? And as Barabbas gazed into that face most fair, and saw the nails, and the blood drops streaming down from brow and hands and feet, as he looked into those eyes of deep, unutterable love, and heard the words:

"Father, forgive," falling from those anguished lips, did he cry:

"Oh, Jesus, thy love has won my heart! Yonder are the two thieves, one on the right, one on the left, but there is the middle cross, the cross upon which I should have died." And stooping down, did he take his little son up in his arms, and pointing to the cross did he sob in his ear:

"Oh, Sonny, look, that is the cross your Papa should have died upon; that is the place where I should have hung, the death I should have died, but yon lovely Man, whom they call Jesus, is dying in Papa's place. Oh, wife and son and Oh, my heart, let us ever love and live and work for this Jesus who gave Himself for me"?

As Barabbas gazed steadfast into the eyes of Jesus, did .the face of the Lord turn toward him?

Did their eyes meet, and was there a look of understanding exchanged between the two that broke Barabbas' heart and held him captive by the chains of love forever? Did he fall upon his

156

knees, crying: "Jesus, how can I ever thank you?

    Drops of grief could ne'er repay
    The debt of love I owe;
    Here, Lord, I give myself to Thee,
    Tis all that I can do."

Was he there when the mangled body of Jesus was lowered from the cross and laid within the tomb? Was he there upon the morning when Jesus appeared to His people and ascended up in the clouds unto His Father's throne? Was he among the hundred and twenty on the Day of Pentecost who received the gift of the Holy Ghost and went forth proclaiming the message of Jesus and His power to save?

We know not of a certainty, but one thing we do know, and that is, that when this whole world of ours was wrapped in darkness and imprisoned by sin and death, the Spirit of the Lord was upon Jesus, anointing Him to preach the gospel to the poor, to heal the broken-hearted, to preach deliverance to the captives, recovering of sight to the blind, to set at liberty them that are bruised, and to preach the acceptable year of the Lord. We do know that Barabbas was no greater sinner, nor more devoid of hope than this whole world of lost sinners, and that Jesus came and was wounded for our transgressions, bruised for our iniquities, the chastisement of our peace was upon Him, and by His stripes we were healed; that when we like sheep had gone astray, and had turned everyone to our own ways, the Lord laid upon Him the iniquity of us all. He was oppressed and He wm afflicted, yet He opened not His mouth. He was taken from prison and from judgment. He was cut off from the land of the living. For the transgression of the people was He stricken. He made His grave with the wicked and with the rich in His death, yet He had done no violence, neither was there any deceit in His mouth. He was numbered with the transgressors, and He bare the sin of many and made intercession for the transgressors.

MANKIND, IN THE DUNGEON OF DESPAIR. AWAITS DEATH

By one man sin entered into the world, and death by sin; and so death passed upon all men, for all have sinned. Rom. 5:12.

What a hopeless, miserable dungeon, man had placed himself in by his sin, and disobedience to God. No matter how he might search, there was no way out. The great, massive DOOR OF MERCY was the only hope. The Law, stern jailer that he was, refused to open that. Because of one man's sin Death reigned supreme up-on his throne from Adam to Moses. (Rom. 5:14.) Sitting there within the prison cell of despair, there came the day when the people which sat in darkness saw a great light, and to them which sat in the region and shadow of death, light sprang up (Mat, 4:16.)

The footfalls of Deliverance were heard coming along the corridors of time, Grace (Heaven-sent turnkey) bore the key of divine, sacrificial love that turned the lock of condemnation and swung wide the ponderous door of mercy.

Mercy and Love (inseparable pair) stepped within the prison cell, and, loosening the bands of Despair, and breaking the power of Sin's strong chains, called to all mankind:

"COME FORTH."

"You are free men; another has died in your place, one named Jesus has borne your cross and paid the price of your redemption. Come forth, come forth. Oh! trembling souls, why sit longer in the valley and in the shadow of death? Can you not understand? The door is open, the chains are broken. Barabbas, BARABBAS, COME forth!" What would you have thought of Barabbas, had he refused to leave the dungeon, choosing chains and darkness rather than liberty and light? What opinion would you have had of Barabbas had he been such an ingrate, so void of appreciation and gratitude that he did not even take the trouble to climb blest Calvary's hill to see and thank this Jesus who died for him?

Jesus died for you; your prison door stands WIDE, the Spirit calls: "Come forth, the sunlight of God's love and mercy awaits you, pardon and peace are yours for the taking. Will you turn just now to Calvary, wend your way to the cross and gaze into the face of your Savior, that face which was more marred than the face of any other man?"

There are your two old companions, Sin and Death, hanging upon the two crosses beside your Lord; for the first thief y sin, there can be no allowance, no excuse sin must die to you and you to sin. For how can we that are dead to sin live any longer therein?

As for the second thief, at the eleventh hour his pardon came, when death was swallowed up in victory. For the sting of death is sin, and when our old companion, sin, is dead, then it is that the sting is taken out of death, and the ransomed soul can cry: "Oh! death, where is thy sting?" Whether the body sleeps or wakes matters not. To be absent from the body is to be present .with the Lord. Verily, I say unto yon, this day shalt thou be in Paradise with Me.

Yes, dear sinner, Jesus paid it all, all to Him you owe. Turn to Him just now. Thank Him for His great love and for the shedding of His precious blood, and as you gaze upon Him your heart will be melted, the tears will fall from your eyes, and you will break forth into singing:

"My Jesus, I love thee, I know Thou art mine: For Thee all the follies of sin I resign; My gracious Redeemer, my Savior art Thou; If ever I loved Thee, my Jesus, 'tis now.

A CERTAIN MAN WENT DOWN

Luke 10:30-35.

THE message which the Lord has laid upon my heart to bring to you, whilst directed to all sinners, is intended more especially for the backslider.

Oh, there are so many backsliders in the world, so many who once walked with the Lord, but have some way or other let go of His hand and have wandered far away. There is not a man or woman on the face of this earth more miserable than a poor backslider, who, once having walked in the presence and joy of the Lord, feasting upon the dainties from His bountiful hand, goes down into sin and seeks to drown the achings of his longing heart in the swirl of this world's gaudy, tinseled pleasure.

It would be impossible for one who had never been a backslider to fully understand or sympathize with the mute agony, shame, and longing in the backslider's heart was a poor, discouraged backslider just once since my conversion, and I know the miserable yearning and crying of the heart to be back in the sunlight of His dear smile the leaking out the trying to cover up our backslidden condition from those round about us the plunge into the world to try to stifle and satisfy the restless longing that nothing but Himself can satisfy.

How desperately I longed for someone who could enter in and sympathize with and help me, and had there been someone to make a real effort to reach out and help me back to victory and the security of His Love, I would have escaped much suffering and buffeting at the hand of the enemy.

And so tonight my whole heart goes out to the backslider, and I long to reach your hand and help you back to Jesus and the city of Jerusalem.

The first step toward getting back to Jesus is made by realizing and frankly admitting that you are a backslider.

We are going to read tonight about a certain man who went down, and I want each of you to watch, as we follow him in his journey, and see whether his case is not very similar in every respect to your own. First of all let us refresh our memory by reading the whole story. It is found in the tenth chapter of Luke, beginning at the thirtieth verse:

"And Jesus said, A certain man went down from Jerusalem to Jericho and fell among thieves, which stripped him of his raiment, and wounded him, and departed, leaving him half dead.

"And by chance there came down a certain priest that way; and when he saw him, he passed by on the other side.

"And likewise a Levite, when he was at the place, came and looked on him, and passed by on the other side.

"But a certain Samaritan, as he journeyed, came where he was; and set him on his own beast, and brought him to an inn, and took care of him.

"And on the morrow when he departed, he took out two pence, and gave them to the host, and said unto him, 'Take care of him; and whatsoever thou spendest more, when I come again, I will repay thee'."

Now as we go through it word by word, and follow the picture on the chart, let every backslider and sinner put themselves in the place of, the "certain man" and find their location in this picture. There are many of the certain men and women who have been "going down," here in this room tonight, but let each forget the other forget that there is another "certain man" in the room, and narrow the words down to his own individual case.

Oh, "certain man" here tonight, you who have been wandering away from God, how easy it is to go down. The road to destruction and eternal sorrow of hell is just one long, swift toboggan slide. There is nothing to boast about in being a sinner or a backslider. Anybody could go down, any coward could become a sinner, but it takes the real courage and grace of God, and every spark of manhood and womanhood there is in you to go up the steep incline to Heaven. A dead fish can

159

float down the stream, but it takes a live one to swim up against the current. Any poor, spiritually dead soul can float down to destruction; it does not require any swimming or resistance. Nothing but the divine life and power of the Lord, however, can take him up again.

Went down! Oh, the depths of the precipices and pits of sin that are conveyed by that one word d-o-w-n.

FROM JERUSALEM TO JERICHO

Let Jerusalem, on the chart, stand for all that is holy and pure and Christ-like, for all that is embodied in the New Jerusalem that is soon coming down from God out of Heaven, and Jericho for all that is sinful and profane and ungodly.

How you, dear certain man, ever came to pass out through the gate of Jerusalem and start on your long downward journey, I do not know.

Perhaps it was lack of prayer it may have been a failure to read God's Word (you can not dwell in the presence of the Lord without prayer and the Word any more than you could live without breathing. When you pray you are talking to God when you read the Word He is talking to you) it may have been that you allowed the cares of this life to press heavily upon you.

With me it was the taking away of the dear one who had led me to Jesus, and upon whose strength I had ever leaned instead of allowing the Lord to teach me to grow in Him and be able to stand the storms. When my earthly support was suddenly transplanted to Heaven's garden, I was left like an ivy, stripped from the oak to which if had clung. Oh, what a poor little, fallen, tumbled heap I was! But now, bless His dear name, I have YOU TAKEN THIS JOURNEY?

I have learned to cling to and lean upon Jesus a support that will never die nor leave me alone.

Be the primary cause what it may, the fact remains that the certain man went down from Jerusalem to Jericho AND FELL. Oh, you cannot walk one single step without Jesus, no matter how strong you are; or how many years you have been a Christian; the moment you let go of His dear hand, that moment you will cease to stand, and you will fall AMONG THIEVES.

It is not long after the backslider has begun his downward journey that he discovers that he, too, has fallen among thieves.

These thieves that we are reading about did two things to the certain man before they left him:

I. THEY STRIPPED HIM OF HIS RAIMENT.

II. THEY WOUNDED HIM AND DEPARTED, LEAVING HIM HALF DEAD.

and that is exactly what the thieves have been doing to you.

Did you ever stop to realize just what constituted the raiment which used to clothe you in Jerusalem (the city of salvation) this priceless raiment and attire of which the enemy has stripped you?

Let us look at the chart and see what sort of raiment the holy life in Jerusalem stands for, and what you have lost.

Those who walk and live in the presence of the pure and holy Son of God must be attired in the raiment clean and white which is the righteousness of the saints.

Each individual that goes into the marriage supper of the Lamb must have on the wedding robe Jesus has prepared worldly garments and the?

cloak of self -righteousness and morality will not suffice but will vanish before His gaze.

J stands for JESUS: When we walk with Him He clothes us with Himself, and the garments of His righteousness. (Rev. 3:18)

E stands for ENJOYMENT: His presence is fullness of joy. (Ps. 16:11.) He has poured the oil of everlasting joy upon the heads of His people, (Isa. 35:10.)

R stands for REST: In the presence of Him who said: "Come unto Me and I will give you rest." (Matt. 11:28.) "The weary find rest for their souls." (Jer. 6:16)

U stands for USEFULNESS: Those who walk with the Savior, who said: "Work while yet

160

'tis day, for the night cometh when no man can work," will long to be soul-winners and wear the cloak of service.

S stands for SALVATION: Ah, dear backslider, do you not remember how you used to go forth, glad in the beautiful garments of salvation, which had been put upon you by Him who was "your light and your salvation"? (Ps. 27:1.)

A stands for ADORATION: Where is there a soul that could behold his glorious Redeemer without bowing at His feet in adoration and praise? Did you not feel a great loss when the thieves stripped from you the garments of adoration and worship?

L stands for LOVE: When we dwell with the GOD who IS LOVE (1 John 4:8), and He "hath set His love upon us "(PS. 91:14), we will imbibe and partake of His nature until the first fruit of the Spirit, LOVE (Gal. 5:22), shall spring forth from our lives.

E stands for ENRICHMENT: No mortal tongue can tell the great, inexhaustible store of riches to be found in the Christ who became poor that we by His poverty might be made rich.

M stands for MERCY: The child of God who abides beneath the blood is covered with the MERCY (as a garment) that is "great above the Heavens "(PS. 108:4), and TRUTH (the girdle which fastens the garment about him) of PS. 85:10, these meeting together to form His raiment.

What a dreadful loss it was when the thieves stripped YOU of YOUR raiment. It was impossible to go without the secure walls of the city of His love and to begin your downward journey toward Jericho without losing those beautiful garments. It was indeed a sad day when you were stripped of your robes of Christlikeness.

Gone was your Jesus; gone your Enjoyment, your Rest. Taken away was your Usefulness, your robes of Salvation, your Adoration, Love, Enrichment, and Mercy.

The first stroke of the enemy which left you denuded of such garments was bad enough, but, Oh, the second thing that happened to the "certain man" was far, far more sad, if that were possible, for T-H-E-Y W-O-U-N-D-E-D H-I-M, and departed, leaving him half dead.

What wounds the devil and his imps (the thieves who rob you of salvation, rest and happiness in this world and the world to come) can inflict upon the backslider and the sinner! When the garments which Jesus purchased for Him by his blood are taken away there is nothing left to protect the sinner from the blows rained upon him by the enemy.

The backslider, wandering far from God, who has been thus stripped and wounded, is in a critical condition indeed. The wicked old thieves nod and wink to one another as they pick up their booty and DEPART, LEAVING HIM HALF DEAD.

The mile-posts by the way now point toward JERICHO, and each mile-post the certain man reaches on his downward way means just another wound to burn and sear its way into his very soul.

Let us look again at the chart and see what these mile-posts that lead to Jericho stand for First:

J stands for JOLLIFICATION. "Not a serious wound," you say, "just a little amusement, no serious harm in that, a little gossip, an idle jest, the theatre, novel or a game of pool." "Young folks must have entertainment," says the enemy. Who hearkens will find that jollification has left a wound and hastened him to the second mile-post

E which stands for EVIL. I have seen the serious wound reflected in the sinner's eyes, in the lines of his face, and have heard the words of profanity rise from his heart but O, the eyes of God look right down into the depths of that soul, and from Him there is nothing hid.

R stands for RESTLESSNESS. Instead of rest which was once his, when he loved the quiet hours of prayer "alone with God," there is now a driving, irritating restlessness that goads him day and night. Anything to get away from his own thoughts is a welcome diversion.

I stands for INDIFFERENCE. The heart that once responded to His every leading and sprang to obey His call, is now indifferent to His voice.

C stands for CALLOUSNESS. The indifferent heart soon becomes calloused and hard. Once so tender that he melted in contrition before the Lord, he now listens to the tender story of the Crucifixion, the warning thunder of coming wrath unmoved.

H stands for HATRED. When the devil has gotten his victim into the place where he hates the Spirit, who endeavors to rouse him into sense of his peril, hates good and loves evil (Mic. 3:2), he rubs his evil hands and a smile of demonic joy twists his countenance as the poor, duped soul draws near the city of eternal Woe.

O stands for OBSTINACY. When one receives this wound he obstinately refuses to be warned of his danger or flee from the wrath to come. He walks out of the meeting, goes home and to bed, hard, unyielding, obstinate.

What a deceitful old traitor the devil is! He smiles and tricks and fools the soul along while it has life and strength and means, but when it is down and out, helpless, dying and alone, the devil does not even take the trouble to pretend that he is his friend.

Half dead thank God he is not altogether dead, for whilst there is life there is hope! Helpless, unable to drag himself one painful step toward the city of salvation, the sin-sick soul is left lying in the road. "The whole head is sick and the whole heart faint; from the sole of the foot even unto the head there is no soundness in it, but wounds and bruises and putrifying sores; they have not been closed, neither bound up, neither mollified with ointment." Isa. 1:5, 6.

What a picture, not only of the individual, but of the whole human race, that wandered from God.

"THERE CAME DOWN A CERTAIN PRIEST THAT WAY"

Surely this priest, who typifies the L-A-W, will be able to lift, heal and restore the sin-sick soul.

But no, there is nothing to hope for from him, for,

"HE PASSED BY ON THE OTHER SIDE"

And Paul explains to us that "The law made nothing perfect." Heb. 7:19. Moreover the law entered that offenses might abound.

"And likewise a Levite, when he was at the place, came and looked on him." Surely one would be justified in expecting help from the Levite who is filled with his good works and self-righteousness, but no, the Word tells us that all our righteousness is but "filthy rags "(Isa. 64:6), and that "a man is not justified by the works of the laic "(Gal. 2:16). Turning over a new leaf or signing your name to a pledge can never lift you nor heal the wounds of your sinful soul, and thus we read of the Levite: "And he passed by on the other side."

In what a deplorable, perilous condition humanity found itself. Is it any wonder that the helpless soul should cry aloud:

"Oh, wretched man that I am, who shall deliver me from the body of this death?" Rom. 7:24. Is there no arm to save? Is there no eye to pity?

Ah, yes?, glory to Jesus, there is one who sees and approaches from the distance.

Who could it be but Jesus this good Samaritan filled with compassion and tender love for lost, wretched humanity, groveling in the dust of humiliation and despair?

Oh, what a journey Jesus took in order to reach poor, fallen souls who lie bruised and bleeding on the road to destruction. What a journey! All the way from Heaven to earth He came; all the way from the manger to the cross He went, and from the tomb to His Father's throne.

"As He journeyed" no distance was too great to go, no soul too far out of the way for Jesus to reach him with His love and proffered help

"CAME WHERE HE WAS"

Yes, this good Samaritan who was none other than the King of Glory, never rested, once He had seen the fallen condition of the world, until He had laid aside His crown, divested Himself of His kingly raiment, taken upon Him the form of man was not contented even with standing by the sinner's side, but must come where he was, taking his place, and hanging upon his cross, paying his penalty, and dying his death.

162

"For what the law could not do, in that it was weak through the flesh, God, sending His own Son in the likeness of sinful flesh, and for sin, condemned sin in the flesh:

That the righteousness of the law might be fulfilled in us, who walk not after the flesh but after the Spirit." Rom. 8:3, 4.

Was ever such love, such mercy as this known in this universe of ours? "Came where he was." Why, dear sinner, dear backslider, there is not one of you who has wandered so far away whose wounds are so obnoxious and horrible but Jesus has come where you are.

Was humanity poor? Jesus became poorer than they all.

Were any despised? He was more despised than they.

Was there any friendless and alone? He prayed on the mountain-side, sweat great drops of blood in the garden alone, and groaned upon the tree.

Was any filled with sin and laden with iniquity?

He bore their sins and their sickness in His own body on the tree.

Oh, how I love those words, love to repeat them over and over:

"As He journeyed. He came where he was." Why, sinner, look! Can you not see Him just now? He is standing right beside you. If you put out your hand you can touch Him and feel His nearness. "They should seek the Lord, if haply they might feel after Him, and find Him, though He be not far from every one of us." Acts 17:27.

Just the faintest little cry for help, uttered or unexpressed, and He will reach down His great arms and place them about you. Praise His name!

"And it shall come to pass, that whosoever shall call on the name of the Lord shall be delivered: for in Mount Zion and in Jerusalem shall be deliverance, as the Lord hath said, and in the remnant whom the Lord shall call." Joel 2:32.

"Call unto me, and I will answer thee, and show thee great and mighty things which thou knowest not." Jer. 33:3.

"AND WHEN HE SAW HIM"

What an awful and yet what a wonderful thing it is to know that Jesus sees right down into the depths of the heart, and the intents of the human mind that nothing is concealed from Him that everything is laid bare and open in His sight.

Oh, what will this good Samaritan do when He looks down into your heart? Will He shake His head and walk away when you confess your awful sins? Why, no, the Word tells us that when He saw him

"HE HAD COMPASSION ON HIM"

No matter what your mistakes, your failures; no matter how vile your sins have been; if you will but truly repent and obey the Word of the Lord He will have compassion upon you. If man were your judge there would be very little to hope for or to expect but punishment, but His heart is filled with compassion. He knows the many times that you have wept upon your pillow; He knows the heartaches and the longing; He remembers the weakness of your frame, and pities you as a Father pitieth His children. It was that great heart full of compassion that caused Him to weep over Jerusalem and cry upon the cross:

"Father, forgive them; they know not what they do."

"AND WENT TO HIM"

Jesus has come to meet you, not half way, not three-quarters of the way, but all the way. He has come to you just now with pleadings and tender mercy. Just one word and He is right at your side with hope and succor.

"AND BOUND UP HIS WOUNDS"

163

Yes, those painful, cankerous wounds are the first thing that demand His attention. All infection must be cut away and sin destroyed. He can bind every heart-bruise so gently, pouring in oil and wine.

"But, oh!" you say, "I don't seem to have the feeling and the tender desire for the Savior which I should have. My heart seems hard, and my conscience dulled." Yes, I know; that is because of those dreadful wounds indifference, callousness, and obstinacy, but do not let this discourage you from calling upon the Lord, for when He comes He will bring with Him his cruse of oil and will soften every hardened wound, making your heart tender, and flooding your soul with the old-time love.

"Oh, but I do not seem to have any strength. My spiritual energy seems to be so faint and at such a low ebb." Well, praise the Lord! He brings His wine with Him also. He will revive and bring back life and strength by the quickening of His Spirit.

"AND SET HIM ON HIS OWN BEAST"

How many poor, timid souls, halting between two opinions, trembling at the sight of the yawning pit before them, and yet fearful to trust themselves to the Lord's tender hands, say:

"Oh, I do so long to be a Christian, but I am afraid I could not hold out. I am afraid I could not hang on to my profession." Why, Hallelujah!

I have such good news to tell you. This is a salvation you do not need to hang on to it will hang on to you. This is a Savior that you do not have to uphold and keep from falling; He will uphold and keep you if you will but put your trust in Him.

"They that trust in the Lord shall be as Mount Zion, which cannot ~be removed, but abideth forever." Ps. 125:1.

What would you have thought of this good Samaritan had He turned to the wounded man and said:

"Now come, my man; I have bound up your wounds. I have poured in oil and . Here beside you stands the little beast (salvation), the sure-footed little animal that can climb the most rugged mountain without slipping or making a misstep. I want you to pick up this beast, put it on your poor, bruised back, walk back all the many weary miles to Jerusalem with this burden upon your shoulder, and mind you do not let it fall."

Was this what he said? NO, Never! He did not ask the man to carry the beast, but He brought the beast to carry the man. Therefore He set him on His own beast

"AND BROUGHT HIM TO AN INN"

The inn is the place of shelter and security where his wounds shall be ministered unto in other words, the church of God. It was the good Samaritan Himself who brought him to the inn; not by his own struggles and weak efforts, was he carried thither. Put your case in the hands of Jesus and He will bring you forth by His own hand and lead you in a way you know not of.

Mountains that seemed impassable in your own strength will be surmounted, and you will be borne up upon wings as of an eagle over every difficulty.

"AND TOOK CARE OF HIM."

have you ever sang that chorus:

"God will take care of you,
Through all the day, o'er all the way, He will take care of you.
Be not dismayed, whatever betide;
God will take care of you;
Within His arms of love abide;
God will take care of you"?

The tender, loving solicitude and care of the good Shepherd over His little lambs of the good Samaritan over the wounded soul, can never be described. His patience and His love are boundless. He will supply every need of body, soul and Spirit.

"ON THE MORROW WHEN HE DEPARTED"

Yes, there came the day when, after Jesus had journeyed all the way from Heaven to earth, and from the manger to the cross; after He had fed the multitudes and healed the sick, and comforted the broken-hearted, and taken the sinner's place, and shed every drop of His blood for the redemption of a lost world, conquered death and the grave, He fulfilled the word which He had spoken to His disciples, saying:

"Ye have heard how I said unto you, I go away and come again unto you. If ye loved me ye would rejoice because I said, I go unto the Father, for my Father is greater than I." John 14:28.

"It is expedient for you that I go away; for if I go not away, the Comforter will not come unto you; but if I 'DEPART I will send Him unto you." John 16:7. And thus it was that on the morrow, "while they beheld, He was taken up and a cloud received Him out of their sight" But before He departed the thoughtful Savior, who was ever providing for our good,

"TOOK OUT TWO PENCE"

(Salvation and the Baptism of the Holy Ghost).

Two pence was a day's wages at that time; so He has left enough to supply the need for this entire day. Praise His name.

"AND GAVE THEM TO THE HOST:"

Has the host of your inn, the preacher of your church, been faithfully spending and preaching these two pence, dispensing all that they provide for your comfort? Many hosts hold back one penny and feel that when they have preached salvation and repentance they have given the man all that he has need of, and is for his good. If this is what your preacher has been doing you should go up to him and ask him what he has done with that other penny, why he is not preaching the baptism of the Holy Ghost according to Acts 2:4 Peter, who acted as host to the three thousand on the day of Pentecost, dispensed the two pennies freely as he said:

"Repent, and be baptized, every one of you, in the name of Jesus Christ, for the remission of sins" penny number one;

"And you shall receive the gift of the Holy Ghost" penny number two. Acts 2:38.

"AND SAID, TAKE CARE OF HIM"

Stewards, hosts, and pastors, you are responsible to God for the way you preach the Word.

There is power enough, encouragement and grace enough in the Word of God to take care of and support all them who come beneath your teaching, if you preach the Word in its entirety, and they will but obey.

"WHATSOEVER THOU SPENDEST MORE:"

These words open to us such a vista of glories, such unlimited acres of promised land, with the fruits of the Spirit, the luscious grapes, and the land that flows with milk and honey, such a boundless and fathomless ocean of blessing, such heights and depths, such lengths and breadths in the great unsearchable love of God, that we cry out

"The half has never yet been told."

"Whatsoever thou spendest more"; why, dear heart, salvation and the baptism of the Holy Spirit are just the beginning just the first few toddling steps of the new-born child into the realm of the Spirit just the a, b, c's of the gospel. To live without salvation through the blood of Jesus and the baptism of the Holy Spirit according to Acts 2:4, is to live in an abnormal condition nowhere recorded in the Word of God. Ahead of you are the gifts and the fruits and the graces of the Spirit, and a life that He longs to change from glory into glory until He has brought us unto perfection and can present us to the Father faultless, without spot or wrinkle.

165

"WHEN I COME AGAIN"

Why, beloved! He is coming again!! Did not He whose promises are known never to fail say:

"If I go, I will come again, and receive you unto Myself"? John 14:3. And when the disciples had watched Him until the clouds had received Him out of their sight, did not the two men who stood beside him, clothed in white apparel, say:

"Ye men of Galilee, why stand ye gazing up into Heaven? This same Jesus, which is taken up from you into Heaven, shall so come in like manner as ye have seen Him go into Heaven." Acts 1:11.

Did not the apostle Paul declare that "The Lord Himself shall descend from Heaven with a shout, with the voice of the archangel, and with the trump of God: and the dead in Christ shall rise first:

Then we which are alive and remain shall be caught up together with them in the clouds, to meet the Lord in the air: and so shall we ever be with the Lord." I Thess. 4:16, 17. Did He not tell us to comfort one another with these words?

Did not the Lord, speaking through John on the Isle of Patmos, say:

"Surely, I come quickly." And is not the Spirit speaking today throughout the whole world, through yielded vessels:

"Behold, Jesus is coming soon; get ready to meet Him"?

"When I come again" Oh, what a glorious day that will be when we shall gaze with open face upon the beauty of the good Samaritan, our Redeemer and Savior divine. "And when I come again

I WILL REPAY THEE"

Why! Just one glimpse of His beautiful face fairer than the lilies, brighter than the sun just one smile from His tender eyes just one "well done," and we would be a million times repaid for any little labor of love that is naught but our reasonable service when all is said and done.

Oh, dear backslider, and Oh, dear sinner, will you not speak the word just now:

"Lord, save me." He is standing right beside you. He will hear the faintest cry; His glorious salvation is ready to carry you to the safe refuge of the inn. He is waiting to care for and watch over you, and at last, when He comes again, to take you to dwell with Him forever.

"Come, weary soul, by sin oppressed, There's mercy with the Lord;
And He will surely give you rest,
By trusting in His Word.
"Only trust Him; only trust Him;
Only trust Him now.
He will save you; He will save you;
He will save you now."

IT WAS just after I had finished preaching the other night, that during the altar service, while an invitation song was being sung, I went down through the audience inviting sinners to the altar. Amongst others with whom I was dealing I came to a young man who answered my invitation to give his heart to Jesus by saying:

"O, Sister, if I could if only I could believe!

But I have never seen or felt the presence of the Lord in my life; I have never heard His voice or been conscious of His dealings with me."

Soon after that the Lord gave a message in tongues and its interpretation that set me to thinking a great deal. How slow of heart and how slothful of understanding the whole world has been, when it came to recognizing the presence, leadings and dealings of the Lord!

"The ox knoweth his owner, and the ass his master's crib: but Israel does not know, my people doth not consider." For thousands of years God has walked with His people, but they have not understood or recognized His presence. The world today, and even many of the Lord's children, fail to recognize the stately steppings of the King.

Away back in the garden of Eden, God walked with Adam. He longed to walk with him and commune with him in unbroken communion; but both Adam and Eve failed to comprehend the great plan and purpose of God, and miserably disobeying Him, lost the garden of Eden.

God walked with the children of Israel as Moses led them through the Red Sea. He walked with them through the wilderness; revealing Himself by the pillar of fire and the cloud. He came unto them as manna from Heaven; He was made manifest to them as a Rock which followed them, and from which gushed forth the clear, living water of life. He thundered forth His voice from Mount Sinai, but His people failed to really understand and to recognize the leadings and manifestations of the great, omnipresent God. They murmured and rebelled, and lagged behind until they fell short of the Promised Land.

God visited Pharaoh, and walked in his land.

He walked through his palace, and visited the humblest home. When Pharaoh would not listen to His voice, God spoke through plagues and pestilences. God walked through his land with no uncertain step, leaving the imprints of His feet in every home; but all failed to understand, or recognize the dealings and presence of Jehovah.

Someone says, "O! but if I could only see Him, or some plain, unmistakable manifestation would be wrought in my sight, I could believe." But, dear one, if you cannot recognize Him through His Word, and present' day manifestations, you would not believe even though one should rise from the dead.

Jesus came and walked with His people, came away from His Father's throne; all the way from Heaven to earth. He walked in a fleshly, visible reality among the people of this earth, but the world would not recognize or believe in Him.

He was born in a manger. He lived in His Father's home for thirty years, but the world roundabout were not stirred into belief they did not understand. He walked into the midst of the teachers in the temple at the age of twelve. They marvelled at His words, but with all their wisdom and learning, even they did not recognize their Lord. He walked through the throng, and into the river of Jordan to be baptized of John, but even though the Spirit descended upon Him in bodily form as of a dove, and even though the Father's voice spoke aloud from the Heavens, "This is My beloved Son" still they did not understand but slow of heart and slothful of understanding, they said, "An angel spake" or "It thundered."

For the three following years Jesus walked in the midst of His people. He wrought signs and wonders; He healed the sick, cleansed the lepers, raised the dead, yet, through it all the unbelieving world failed to understand, or believe, or recognize the pure, spotless Lamb of God, moving in their midst. He passed through the city's throng; He entered the lonely home; He preached on land and sea to the multitude, and to the lone woman at the well; but few, O so few, recognized Him and believed it was the Lord.

He stood in plain sight in the midst of the rabble throng, as a Lily among thorns, a Lamb among wolves, but they did not understand. Pontius Pilate was near the truth when he asked the question: "Art thou the King of the Jews?" The high priest was near the light when he asked:

"Art thou the Christ, the Son of the Blessed?" but neither of them really recognized or understood the import of Jesus' reply, or knew He was the Son of God.

He walked up Calvary's hill, bearing His cross.

He was lifted high between Heaven and earth as He prayed: "Father,, forgive them, they know not what they do." But though the rocks rent, and the earth did quake; though the veil of the temple was rent in twain from the top to the bottom; though many graves were opened, and the bodies of the saints which slept arose; though the sun hid its face and the Heavens were filled with blackness, still, unbelievable as it may seem, the spectators in Jerusalem at large did not understand or believe this Jesus to be the Son of God.

With what piteous ignorance and utter incomprehension they sealed His tomb, and stationed the Roman soldiers to guard the door of the grave of the Lord of Heaven and earth. Then, though the stone was rolled away, and the very earth gave up its dead, and the soldiers themselves were slain by the power of God, the people round about refused to recognize the Lord.

Even Mary, when first meeting Him in the garden after His resurrection, failed to recognize her Lord, and mistook Him for the gardener. How many times today, even those to whom He is dearer than all else, fail to recognize His form and step, as He Comes walking through the garden of their lives.

He walked with His disciples by the way, but their eyes were hold en, and they did not know Him; even though their hearts did burn within them as He talked to them by the way, they failed to recognize Him. Thomas refused to believe the evidence of his own eyes and Jesus had to bid him thrust in his hand, to handle Him and see that it was really He Himself, before he would believe.

He was seen of above five hundred brethren at once, after His resurrection; He was caught up and a cloud received Him out of the sight of those watching below, and yet after all there were only about one hundred and twenty who really followed to the Upper Room to tarry for the Holy Ghost.

How patient He has been with our stupidity, and slow, unbelieving hearts! How His heart must ache when even today the world rushes blindly on to destruction over His crucified body, and refuses to understand. Hear Him say:

"O Jerusalem! Jerusalem! How oft would I have gathered thee as a hen gathereth her brood beneath her icing, but ye would not!"

He is speaking today with the voice of ten thousand thousand cannon. He is speaking through plagues and pestilences, through blood, fire, and vapor of smoke. His footsteps are echoing on the hilltops and through the valleys with no uncertain tread. He is walking through the city streets. In the mansion His hand is again taking the firstborn and in the tenements, mothers' hearts are bleeding for the sons slain with the sword. His footsteps are falling with heavy tread through the battlefield, among those tortured with shot and shell; His feet are treading softly through the long, darkened wards of blood and moans and death. He is leaping upon the hills. He is standing behind our walls. He is looking in at the lattice. He is standing beside you just now as you read these words. He is speaking to your heart, "Believe in Me and thou shalt be saved."

HAVE YOU FAILED TO UNDERSTAND

Failed to recognize the Son of God failed to recognize His dealings in your life? He speaks sometimes through sickness, sometimes through the taking away of a loved one, sometimes through trial and sorrow. Oh, have you recognized your Lord so long with you and thou hast not known?

He is calling you just now to repentance, calling you to put away The evil of your doings, to be washed in the blood of the Lamb. He is calling you to be filled with the Spirit and to prepare to meet Him in the air. Once your eyes have been opened you will see Him on every hand.

If the world cannot see Him in this present crisis, if it cannot hear His voice now in the din of battle, it will never understand till it awakens to stand before the Judge of the quick and the dead. Then men will call for the rocks and the mountains to fall on them and hide them from the face of Him that sitteth on the throne.

O dear heart, tear off the bandage the devil has put upon your eyes, and see Jesus NOW. Open your ears and hear Him calling YOU, that you be not partaker in the punishment of those who having ears hear not? and having eyes fail to see Jesus their Savior, the Door of Escape.

LIBERTY BONDS "OVER THERE"

(Inspired by Our Country's Call for the Third Liberty Loan, April, 1918.)

The Great World-Wide War The Need of Sacrifice and Funds Patriotic Talk Will Not Suffice; Actual, Literal Giving Necessary The First, Second and Third Call for Liberty Loans Liberty Bonds, or Devil Bondage Liberty Bonds and Interest Bearing Security - The Only Way to

Get "Over There"

PRACTICALLY everywhere one looks today are grim reminders of the world-wide war, its horrors, and the need for sacrifice and loyalty at this trying hour. Service flags wave to us from the doors of homes whence loved ones have taken their departure from "over there." Posters call to us from the windows of stores and offices. The call to buy Liberty Bonds speaks aloud to us from the page-wide adds of every newspaper, reminding the citizens of our fair land of the vital necessity of sacrifice and of making liberty loans to the government.

In return for each liberty loan a liberty bond is given to the subscriber. This liberty bond is an interest-bearing security, with the United States of America behind it. It is being realized more and more every day that this war cannot be conducted without sacrifice and money, for back of the great armies of this nation now going to France, standing as the great bulwark upon which the tempest of this war must spend itself, is the financial strength of the IT. S. A., whose true, active, numerical terms are Liberty Bonds. Actual giving is necessary; even the most patriotic talk will not pay the debts incurred by war. Sacrifice and giving are absolutely essential.

The herculean struggle the battle to the death now going on in the worldly realm is analogous with that now going on in the spiritual realm.

The great, age-old war between righteousness and unrighteousness is being brought to a final climax in these last days. We fight against a mighty, a wily and a deceitful foe one who would deceive the very elect, if that were possible.

Ever since he appeared to Eve in the Garden of Eden, disguised as a serpent, speaking fair words and weaving lies, he has been fighting, lying and deceiving all who would hearken unto his words.

Although the enemy has put up an unceasing fight from the beginning, there has never been a time when his demonic troops have been mobilized and fighting in massed formation as today. The old devil's time is short, his days of rule and power are numbered, for King Jesus will soon overthrow his earthly throne, strip him of his power, bind him with chains, and cast him into the bottomless pit. In the meantime the battle will rage with ever increasing fervor and intensity, as a whirlwind, gathering momentum as its weeps on and through the stricken world.

We are in this war as soldiers of Jesus and as citizens of that land over there. This war will tax each overcomer to the utmost. We can only win as we abide in Jesus and sacrifice ourselves, our all, freely to His service. We are going to win, but not easily not without paying the price, and fighting the good fight of faith. We who have determined by the power of the Spirit to overcome and conquer till we get over there, must win by a whole-hearted sacrifice by making great "liberty loans" unto the Lord and receiving our "liberty bonds" as eternal security of the promised land "over there."

Our King Jesus is calling for LIBERTY

LOANS from all His loyal subjects who intend to go "over there" to rule and reign, crowned as overcomers, so therefore:

BUY of me gold tried in the fire,
 A crown of righteousness, which the
 Lord shall give you at that day.
Stand fast, therefore in the
LIBERTY where with Christ hath made you free.
And above all things put on charity,
 which is the
BOND of perfectness.

He who lendeth to the Lord is wise. He is calling upon His people to subscribe liberally of their time, their love, their means, their praise, their loyalty and patriotism to His kingdom, their bodies, souls and spirits. Just as our country is sending out the call for the third liberty loan today, so, through the Holy Spirit the third call for liberty loans and the buying up of liberty bonds is going forth in the spiritual realm.

THE FIRST CALL FOR LIBERTY LOANS

169

Went forth during the dispensation of the Father.

Many subscribed liberally of their lives, love and sacrifice, and in return secured eternal liberty bonds guaranteeing infinite thousand-fold interest in that glory land "over there." In response to the appeal of the Father, many stepped forth, counting no sacrifice, no loan too great.

Abraham when called upon to contribute of his unswerving loyalty and obedience to the call divine, manifested his supreme love and willingness to sacrifice by laying his only son, Isaac, upon the altar.

Daniel entered the lions' den.

The three Hebrew children entered the fiery furnace.

Joseph endured the prison.

Job endured suffering and bereavement. And so we might go on and on enumerating those who, during the dispensation of the Father, responded to the first call for liberty loans and received in exchange eternal interest-bearing Liberty Bonds.

We are reminded also of the enormous interest that was paid on those bonds even in this world.

ABRAHAM made his liberty loan and, instead of keeping his own liberty and saying:

"No, Isaac is mine, my time is mine; I will not give this liberty of mine away, but will keep my son and my life and my time to myself he gave his all as a Liberty Loan unto his God, and received in return a Liberty Bond which began to bear immediate interest, for the angel declared:

"Because thou hast done this thing and hast not withheld thy son, thine only son, in blessing I will bless thee, and in multiplying I will multiply thee, thy seed shall be as the stars of Heaven, and in thy seed shall all the nations of the earth be blessed, because thou hast obeyed my voice."

DANIEL. In return for Daniel's great sacrificial Liberty Loan, wherein he loaned his all, body, soul and spirit, unto his God and entered the lions' den, he received a Liberty Bond, an interest-bearing certificate. This interest began at once; not only was he liberated, but was given honor and "prospered in the reign of Darius, and in the reign of Cyrus."

THE THEEE As for the three Hebrew children, HEBREW they, too, received instant interest CHILDREN, on their liberty loans. They entered the fiery furnace in Nebuchadnezzar bonds, but through their sacrifice and obedience their bonds fell away, and they were brought out of the furnace with none other bonds than Liberty Bonds whose interest began immediately when the King promoted them in the province of Babylon.

JOSEPH. Joseph's sacrifice and liberty loan, whereby he lost his liberty and was cast into prison, purchased a Liberty Bond which also paid wondrous interest. Pharaoh said unto Joseph:

"Thou shalt be over my house, and according to thy word shall all my people be ruled" etc., and Pharaoh took off the ring from his hand and put it upon Joseph's hand.

JOB was true to God? and made his great Liberty Loan, through pain and sorrow, through bereavement and earthly loss, till he, too, received his Liberty Bond with interest, "for the Lord gave Job twice as much as he had before. So the Lord blessed the latter end of Job more than his beginning; for he had fourteen thousand sheep, and six thousand camels, and a thousand yoke of oxen, and a thousand she asses. He had also seven sons and three daughters. So Job died, being old and full of days" and went "over there" to reap his reward and dwell in joy forever.

HANNAH. The great Liberty Loan of Hannah, when she lent her son, Samuel, unto the Lord, and many other instances too numerous to mention, flood our minds as we think of that first call for Liberty Loans which went forth during the dispensation of the Father.

SECOND CALL FOR LIBERTY LOANS

During the dispensation of the Son, the second call for Liberty Loans went forth. Those who responded and left all to follow Jesus received interest on their sacrifice immediately. Those who left their fish nets received something far better; they became fishers of men. To those who left

170

houses and lands and friends to follow Jesus, He said:

"Everyone that hath forsaken houses, or brethren, or sisters, or fathers, or mothers, or 'wives, or children, or lands, for my Name's sake, shall receive an hundred fold, and shall inherit eternal life." Instead of claiming a right to their own fleshly liberty in this world, liberty to live their own self-centered lives, the disciples and followers of Jesus made their liberty loans unto the Lord that the great battle might be waged, and that they might attain unto that most excellent glory "Over There."

Many are called but few are chosen, and although this call went out to many, comparatively few responded. The rich young man who was invited to make his Liberty Loan by selling all he had and giving to the poor and following the meek and lowly Jesus henceforth, "went sorrowing away."

JUDAS, for a petty earthly gain, sold his right to the eternal Liberty Bond, and his right to reign "Over There."

Through the short ministry of the Savior in this world, however, there were a few who heard and responded to the call for Liberty Loans, and left all to follow Him. Out of this number we might cite a very few cases recorded in the Word.

PETER yielded his liberty unto the Lord, and leaving all to follow his Master's leadings, secured his Liberty Bond, the assurance of reigning with Jesus; and neither whippings, manifold stripes, imprisonments, nor even death, head downward on the cross, could make him part with that Liberty Bond, and his hope of going "Over There."

STEPHEN made his Liberty Loan unto the Lord, contending even unto death for his freedom and liberty "Over There," a freedom and liberty purchased by Jesus on the cross. Shortly before he kneeled upon the ground and the stones were flying through the air, and raining with a sickening thud upon his valiant body, his soul, gazing through the windows of his vision, saw "the Heavens opened, and the Son of man standing at the right hand of God" He had seen a vision of the land "Over There."

PAUL made a Liberty Loan unto the Lord, and instead of reserving his liberty to live his own life and walk in favor and honor with the people of his land, he gave up this liberty for the Savior who had called him "as one out of due time." He received in exchange his Liberty Bond as security and declared that "neither death nor life, nor angels, nor principalities, nor powers, nor things present, nor things to come, nor height, nor depth, nor any other creature should be able to separate him from the love of God, which is in Christ Jesus our Lord;" and rather than part with his Liberty Bond, his written agreement and promise of an inheritance incorruptible, "Over There," as revealed through the Word of God, he endured the lash, the prison chains, the dungeons, the nakedness and the peril, yea, even death itself, rather than be disloyal to his Heavenly country and King. He besought his brethren that they should present their bodies a living sacrifice, assuring them that this was their reasonable service.

On and on we might mention case after case of those who made Liberty Loans unto the Lord, giving freely of their love, their praise, their time and means during the second call for Liberty Loans.

THIRD CALL FOR LIBERTY LOANS

Just as the third call for Liberty Loans is going forth in our land today, so it is in the spirit realm that the third call is going forth.

With the ushering in of the dispensation of the Holy Spirit began the sounding forth of the third call for spiritual Liberty Loans. For nineteen hundred years the Spirit has been sending forth the call for men and women who would present themselves unto the Lord, men and women who would sacrifice their liberty unto His cause, men and women who instead of using their liberty to do as they pleased and live selfishly unto themselves alone, would forego this liberty and make it a Liberty Loan unto the Lord, reckoning that they were not their own, but were purchased by a price, not of silver nor gold, but the precious blood of Jesus.

171

This in all probability will not be the last call for Liberty Loans sent forth from the government of our nation, but it will be absolutely the last call sent forth by the King of Heaven.

With the closing of this dispensation, the time to purchase Liberty Bonds for eternity will have been fulfilled, for once the good man of the house has risen up and shut to the door, no man will ever be able to open it again. Banking hours will be over, and the Lord will say:

"Wherefore then gavest not thou my money into the bank, that at my coming I might have required mine own with usury Luke, 19-23.

The time for making Liberty Loans unto the Lord, and securing these eternal Liberty Bonds, is almost over, and those intending to surmount every difficulty by His grace and press on to the victor's reward and the marriage of the Lamb, "Over There," should today subscribe to the very utmost of their ability, of possessions, time, love and praise, that they may secure their liberty bonds entitling them to be among the number when the brave soldiers of the cross come marching down the golden streets of the New Jerusalem, for those who are unwilling to leave father and mother, houses and lands for His sake are not worthy to be called His disciples.

Since this great third call for Liberty Loans has been sounded forth through the power of the Spirit, thousands have responded and given up all for Jesus. Martyrs have been burned at the stake fed to the lions tossed to the bulls in the arenas torn limb from limb on the rack guillotined eyes burned out tortured in unspeakable ways, yet through all the dangers they have stood firm and fought the good fight of faith, and have marched on as a glorious army "Over There."

THE LAST GREAT FIGHT BETWEEN THE HOSTS OF DARKNESS AND THE HOSTS OF LIGHT IS RAGING TODAY

as never before. Victory is coming, through our Lord and Savior Jesus Christ, for the "kingdoms of this world" shall "become the kingdoms of our Lord and His Christ, and He shall reign forever and ever." Rev. 11:15.

If you long to be over there when the soldiers go sweeping through the gates, and up the golden streets in triumph, while the angelic host of Heaven cheer, and the bands of music are bursting forth into the triumphant march If you would join the everlasting song of the redeemed.

If you lay any claim to the right to salute the blood-stained banner of Jesus Christ no price will be too great no sacrifice too costly no Liberty Loan too great to make for the cause of Jesus Christ today.

You will make your Liberty Loan freely, and with the "love that seeketh not her own." You will give all your body, soul and spirit to His service today, and cling to your liberty bonds, yea, you will "stand fast therefore in the Liberty wherewith Christ hath made you free" and will not be again entangled with the yoke of bondage.

(It is either Liberty Bonds or Devil Bondage.) You will secure your Liberty Bonds not because they pay big interest, not because they are the safest investment on earth, but because of love for Him who died for you and gave Himself freely for your redemption, Heaven's greatest. Liberty Loan Jesus.

MODERN WARFARE - "OVER THE TOP"

MARCH, 1918

Enlistment Good-bye to Everyone - Change of Garments - The Training Camp - Embarkation on the Battleship of Faith - Enemy Ships - The Submarine - The Airships - Munitions and Supplies - Trench Digging - Mortars for the heavy Artillery - Poisonous Gas and Gas Masks - Over the Top to Victory.

THE GREATEST battle the enemy has ever waged is being fought today. This battle is raging between the children of God who have, determined to go through with Jesus, and every demon in hell, for all are arrayed against them at this time. The enemy, knowing that his time is short, is putting forth every effort within his power and it is only as we keep low at the feet of Jesus and under His blood that we will ever be able to withstand his terrific onslaughts.

Every known tactic and device of modern warfare is employed in this great final struggle of today. The consummation of the age is at hand, and whatsoever the enemy is going to do must be done quickly. Therefore, now as never before, we should watch and pray, be wakeful, be vigilant, and obey our leader, the Holy Spirit, who was sent by the Father to endue us with power during this last herculean struggle.

ENLISTMENT

Everywhere one turns today, posters calling for enlistment into the Army and Navy are to be found. The children of God are called upon by the Holy Spirit to enlist in the Army of King Jesus and fight as good soldiers who are sure of certain victory. The Lord is not calling for conscription or forced service in His army, but demands voluntary, whole-hearted enlistment into His service.

GOOD-BYE TO EVERYONE

Those who have heard the call and are willing to obey it must say good-bye to their old world, good-bye to the old realms of sin, good-bye to worldly companions, good-bye to pleasure, business, relations, everything that would hinder or deter their going forth unhampered into the Army of the Lord.

MODERN WARFARE

It is a call to a life of separation, a life where we are in the world and yet not partakers of its worldliness or frivolity.

CHANGE OF GARMENTS

After saying good-bye to old associations, we are called to strip off all civilian clothing. Each earthly and sinful garment must be laid aside forever, whether it is a robe deep-dyed with sin stains, or a white- washed cloak of morality; they must be left behind before the whole armor of our God is put on.

"Wherefore take unto you the whole armor of God, that ye may be able to withstand in the evil day, and having done all to stand. Stand therefore, having your loins girt about with truth, and having on the breast-plate of righteousness; and your feet shod with the preparation of the gospel of peace; taking the shield of faith, wherewith ye shall be able to quench all the fiery darts of the wicked, and take the helmet of salvation, and the sword of the Spirit, which is the Word of God."

Ephesians 6:13-17.

THE TRAINING CAMP

Next comes the life in the Training Camp. This training camp may be in our kitchen, in the office, in the shop or in the field, but it is just as truly a training school as though it were filled with barracks and parade grounds. Long, tedious days may follow; days of drilling and marching; days of practice and study; days of doing the same thing over and over again until we learn to do it well and in perfect union and harmony with the rest of God's soldiers; days when spiritual muscles unused to withstanding the enemy will ache and cry for rest. But through all the tests and the severest trials, if we so see His hand leading and guiding, if we so lift our eyes and behold "His banner over us is love" so that there is peace and contentment and a longing to learn our lessons well, we are spurred onward to be good soldiers and victorious in every battle. Oh, those grilling Training Camp days! when we are taught that "he who ruleth his own spirit is greater than he who conquers a city." Our Captain is taking each one through this experience.

EMBARKING ON THE BATTLESHIP OF FAITH

Finally there comes a day when we set sail on the Battleship of FAITH. All land is out of sight and we feel our helplessness and utter dependence upon Him as never before. The Spirit warns us that there are enemy ships lurking behind yonder fogs of doubts and carelessness, and a constant lookout and the setting of a constant guard is necessary.

ENEMY SHIPS

Suddenly as we gaze through the glasses of discernment and care we see a great battleship bearing down upon us, painted drab, and so innocently melting into the surroundings that without the warning of the Spirit we should not have recognized it until too late.

On it Comes belching death and defeat at every loophole, but the returning shots from the broadside of the Word of God is sufficient and terrible enough when fired by the big guns of "FAITH" and "HUMILITY" to sink any ship that can come against the children of God.

THE SUBMARINE

At times the enemy comes openly, riding on top of the waves of our daily life; but more often, as the perilous, evil days continue, he comes to us beneath the waves in a hidden, subtle, submarine manner. It is only the earnest, wakeful child of God whose eye is searching the wave that will detect the rising of the little periscope, as the enemy seeks to find his range, and discharge his torpedoes of discouragement, doubts and overwhelming temptations. But Hallelujah to Jesus, He has a few submarine destroyers that can divert and explode every trick of the devil.

There is the submarine destroyer of "Prayer,"
the destroyers of "Hope," "Faith," and "Love,"
the destroyer of "Praise," and the great Word of God, these put every foe to flight, and without these protectors you cannot withstand one attack of the enemy in these last days.

Ships are sending up distress signals, ships are sinking all about us today because of their lack of watchfulness, or because of their lack of prayer.

There is no escape, no other pathway that leads to the overcomer's goal, for the only pathway leads through the war zone. God is calling overcomers, not cowards, to reign with Him upon His throne.

Watch and pray. Pray without ceasing and in everything give thanks. Let your eyes be anointed with spiritual discernment, and no matter how the enemy may seek to camouflage his ships or territory, you will never be deceived.

THE AIRSHIPS

At times the sky above you on land or on sea may be filled with aeroplanes of the enemy, for the principalities and powers of the air are today arrayed against us as never before; but if we abide in Him and obey Him in humility, there is not an enemy who can swoop so low or drop a bomb of deceit, evil suggestions, false teaching or discouragement but will be brought low and caused to fall in flaming defeat by the guns of watchfulness and prayer mounted on the power of Jesus' name and turned Heavenward.

There are days when we reach the land, and our pathway leads over shot-torn battlefields. There, with saddened hearts we see the remains of many a former comrade lying strewn about us, but our Leader speaks, saying, though a thousand may fall on one hand and ten thousand upon the other that He will take us through if we will seek His face and hide in Him.

MUNITIONS AND SUPPLIES

Before entering the great battlefields we should make sure that we are taking with us plenty of ammunition and plenty of solid nourishing food.

Light surface blessings and effervescent joys do not make good fighting food for soldiers. Wheat and fats are necessary. Be sure you take with you, therefore, a goodly supply of the wheat of God's Word, and are feeding in a fat pasture upon the deep things of God.

TRENCH DIGGING

There will be many long days of trench digging as you go down in humility and prayer, hiding in Him. There will be days of seeming inactivity when all that can be done is to watch and hide ever closer in His depths. There are days of quick action and storming the enemy's trenches; but locked in this struggle as His people are today, Jesus will prevail against all the powers of the enemy and cause those who put their trust in Him to be more than conquerors.

MORTARS AND HEAVY ARTILLERY

How we need the guidance of the Spirit and His strength in all things, whether our fighting is done with the long distance guns of faith and intercessory prayer, or whether it is a hand-to-hand fight with the bayonets of patience and long-suffering and love amidst trying circumstances. In firing off the heavy artillery be sure that you have laid a solid mortar foundation, for if your guns of faith and prayer waver in uncertainty you must not expect to hit the mark or rout the enemy. Do not place your guns upon selfishness or self-centered aims, for this foundation will never hold.

POISONOUS GAS AND GAS MASKS

Beware of poisonous gases of spiritual slumber and slothfulness, drifting over on the winds of deception from the enemy's trenches. These poisonous vapors of smoke are foretold in the Word and would cause you to sleep, as did the ten virgins of old and as the disciples in the garden, until you forget to watch and pray and cease your constant vigilance. When you see these clouds of poisonous gases of carelessness coming toward you put on the gas-mask of triple-plied wakefulness, prayer and praise and you will be unharmed.

Never exalt or raise yourself high in your trenches, as when your head appears above ground you will be a sure and certain mark for the enemy's missiles. Keep low at Jesus' feet and you will be safe.

OVER THE TOP TO VICTORY

Finally be of good courage, fellow-soldiers, for there is nothing to fear, while you watch and pray and live in obedience to the commands of our leader, who will surely win the day.

Someday, very soon, the battle will be over, the last grim foe conquered, and the crown will have been won. Someday, if we are faithful and have overcome even as He overcame, He will take us in triumph to reign with Him upon His throne forever and forever.

Throw aside all weights, all slumber, and press on "Over the Top." Why, the end is in view! The victory is in sight already.

THE RED CROSS

No Man's Land - The Shell-torn Battlefield High Explosives and Means of Death - The Red Cross the Only Hope of the Wounded Stretcher Bearers - First Aid Equipment - The Ambulance of "Prayer" - The Red Cross Hospital Atop Calvary's Hill Its Door Open, Cleanliness, and Skilled Tender Hands Removing Stained and Muddied Garments - Bathing the Wounded Soft White Robes Operations, Amputations and Probing for Hidden Shot and Shrapnel - Ever Constant Vigilance - Food and Rest, Love and Safety of the Red Cross - "Let ME be a Red Cross Worker."

BLEAK, barren, filled with deep shell holes and constantly churned and harrowed by tons of high explosives poured into it from the fortifications of the enemy, there lies a narrow strip of country between the front line trenches of the Army of Righteousness and the front line trenches of the devil and His Satanic hosts that might well be termed No Man's Land, for those who are found in this land do not belong to Jesus, nor yet does the devil fully own them in the strictest sense of the word, till he has conquered body, soul and spirit, and cast them into the dark, eternal prisons of Hell.

The great battle (wherein hostilities were opened and the first shot fired when Satan was cast out of Heaven; and the second when Satan ruthlessly attacked God's dearest creation, Mankind, in the Garden of Eden) has never abated, but has saved on and on like a tornado, gathering strength and momentum and ever growing in intensity.

Throughout the length and breadth of the entire spiritual "War Zone" there is no region so filled with danger, so unprotected, so saved with shot and shell; for whilst the soldier of King Jesus digs deep and securely entrenches himself in the strongholds of his Savior's love (Psalm 61:3) and of His power, the sinner is left alone in No Man's Land at the mercy of the enemy, whose heavy artillery, machine guns, shrapnel, barrage fire, liquid fire and poisonous gases pulverize, scorch or choke all who come within their reach.

High overhead the shells of overwhelming evil, pressure and influence from the devil's heavy artillery, scream as they tear through the air, intent on some mission of destruction and death.

Shot from the rapid-firing machine guns of incessant temptation whine and spit in the dust on every side. "Not a pleasant place to dwell," you say? Yet this is just the position of every sinner.

Each moment spent outside of the lines of the Lord's Battalions is fraught with the gravest danger of death yes, death eternally.

Whenever the devil can get a favorable wind (evil influences or companions) blowing in the sinner's direction, he sends out his poisonous gases, causing all who breathe them unprotected by the gas-mask of resistance in Jesus' name, to strangle and finally pass into the slumber from which few awaken. Through the smoke-laden air can be discerned the dead and the wounded. The former lie still and cold; the latter sprawl painfully and helplessly, torn, bleeding, some with eyes put out with shrapnel, others with limbs torn away, shattered shoulders and thighs, some wounded in the head, while in others the shot has buried itself deep into the flesh. There they lie, unable to help themselves, unable to help each other. In order to reach them with aid and succor one would need to be willing to sacrifice his own life. WHO will go?

THE RED CROSS HOSPITAL ON CALVARY'S HILL

Many of the wounded have lain, mangled and bleeding, for long hours, longing for someone to come who could bring relief and carry them to some place of refuge. REFUGE? Could there be a place of R-E-F-U-G-E within traveling distance of this bedlam of suffering and death? Ah! Yes, just back of the lines .of the Army of Righteousness stands a hill called Calvary, and its top is crowned with a glorious hospital where woes are wiped away, and the balm of Gilead is applied.

This hospital is known as the Red Cross. It is none other than the old, rugged cross, stained red with the blood of Him who died that we might live, whose heart was broken that He might heal all broken hearts, who was wounded on the blood-stained cross that He might heal, through His wounds, forever, all the wounded who came unto Him. (Jer. 30:17). Yes, there in the "open door "(Rev. 3:8) stands the great Physician Himself; but who will go after and bring in the wounded and dying from the great shell-torn battlefields of No Man's Land?

THE CRYING NEED OF RED CROSS WORKERS

It is an easy matter to rescue those who are wounded or fall behind the lines (Psalms 37:24), but who will be willing to go without the camp, and outside of the lines, willing to lay down his life to rescue the wounded brother and become a worker for the Red Cross? The hospital cannot come to the wounded, therefore there is vital need for human instrumentality, Red Cross workers with the Red Cross seal upon their foreheads and upon their left arms, and equipped with bandages, lint, gauze, sets of tourniquets, splints, restoratives, etc., go forward with the ambulance of "Prayer" and the stretcher of "Faith."

Out there, on the fields of sin of No Man's Land lie hundreds and thousands of wounded souls (Isaiah 1:6) , looking, calling perishing, dying for the need of Red Cross workers to carry them to Jesus in Faith and Prayer. There are those amongst the wounded who cry aloud in agony of spirit, and there are those who keep back the cry of suffering between set teeth, that the onlooker should not know the secret torture. Others lie unconscious of their grave danger and nearness to eternity's black night, without Jesus.

THE COMING OF THE AMBULANCE

Shot and bursting shell fragments are falling all around, threatening to extinguish the last spark of life and hope. Will no one heed the call? "Ah, Yes!" cries a voice, "I see a little procession coming down from Calvary's Hill. They are coming with their ambulances and help."

"How do you know it is not some ammunition, or supply conveyance?" asks another sufferer, grown sceptical from long waiting.

"I know it is help coming speedily because I see the sign on the side of the car. It is composed of a pure white background (the spotless righteousness and purity of Jesus) and on the white background is a big RED CROSS (Col. 1:20).

Nearer and nearer the ambulances come. Other cars and supply trucks have dashed by on the other side unheeding (Luke 10:31-32), but the ambulance comes right to the spot where the wounded lie (Luke 10:34) . Leaping from the car, the workers of the RED CROSS, bearing their stretcher of faith, pass by the dead, now beyond aid (Jas. 1:15) and press on to the wounded (Matt. 22:32). Opening their "First Aid" equipment, they kneel beside the soul suffering from the wounds of the devil.

First and most important, the worker of the RED CROSS carries a set of tourniquets of all sizes.

These are made to adjust to any part of the wounded man's body where an artery may spurt.

The first glance at the wounded man tells the bearer whether blood is being lost in dangerous amount. The bearers have instructions to lose not a second where this instrument can be used.

Prevailing prayer, coupled with the Word of God, and the authority and power in the mighty Name above every name, can be so firmly wrapped about the wounded limb that the life-giving flow that is ebbing away will be stayed. There is a portion of God's eternal Word and a prevailing prayer that can fit any part of the body or soul, no matter what conditions or circumstances may be.

An array of mental splints formed of Faith, Hope and Love is second in the bearer's pack.

Often the wounded man is so shattered that he cannot be moved without killing him unless reinforcements are attached to his mutilated limbs.

Lint, gauze and bandages (Ezek. 34:16) supplement these. Each bearer should have a thorough training in bandaging (Rom. 12:15), (Isaiah 1:6).

Restoratives (Jer. 30:17) are administered and the wounded man laid gently upon the stretcher of "Faith," carried to the ambulance of "Prayer" and the motor of "Love," whose power is supplied by the oil of the Spirit is started. The car is turned toward the Red Cross hospital on Calvary's Hill. Tender and skillful handling and driving are necessary, as often rough handling and unwise treatment kill the little spark of life left in the patient.

Up and up, nearer and nearer the dear old Red Cross Hospital on the Hill, in the Ambulance of Prayer, the wounded man is carried till at last he is brought to the "Open Door "(Rev. 3:8), where the Great Physician (Mark 2:17) is standing with a smile of tenderness to receive the suffering, sin-sick soul. Within, all is shining with immaculate cleanliness, for this

HOSPITAL FOR THE HEALING OF BODY, SOUL AND SPIRIT

is none other than the "Fountain of Blood" drawn from Emmanuel's veins.

Tender yet firm hands are ready there to help the weak soul and support him within the interior of this refuge, while his sin-sick soul is throbbing forth the prayer:

"Blessed be the fountain of blood, To a world of sinners revealed,
Blessed be the dear Son of God,
Only by His stripes we are healed.
Saviour, to that fountain of Thine,
Leaning on Thy promise I go,
Cleanse me by that washing of Thine,
And I shall be whiter than snow."

Upon his arrival at the Bed Cross Hospital (the fountain of blood that flowed from the blood-stained cross of Jesus) before much treatment can be given, or wounds be dressed, the verminous, stained and muddied garments of sin and un-cleanliness must be removed (Jude 23). Gently each garment of the world is taken or cut away.

(Workers of the RED CROSS should use great care in performing this task, and deal gently, ofttimes leaving this work to the Head Physician Jesus Himself for if rough handling is given and the earthly garments and habits jerked off in our conscientious, but crude, unwise way, death may result to the weak man. Jesus can remove each garment that is stained by sin, and strip him almost painlessly, if the patient will be pliable and yielding in His dear hands.)

THE OPERATING ROOM

As soon as the old worldly garments have been stripped away, the patient is bathed and thoroughly cleansed from head to foot, and indeed the blood of Jesus cleanseth from ALL SIN. Many a time the wounded man has to be placed upon the operating table and portions of shot or the devil's shrapnel that have been buried within the flesh, must be probed for, no matter how painful, till all foreign matter has been removed. But as the Physician applies the knife and the probe He whispers, "Be still, My child, faithful are the wounds of a friend (Prov. 27:6) and I wound that I may heal." And He probes deeper and deeper till the shell is reached and removed.

AMPUTATIONS

There are times when some member of the body, perhaps an arm or a limb, has to be amputated (something that has marred and hindered our spiritual life, perhaps a dear one or a treasured possession) but through the pain the Physician explains while the hand or foot is being cut off that "It is better for thee to enter into life halt or maimed than having two hands and two feet to be cast into hell." Many have had one eye so badly blinded or hurt that it had to be removed, but through it all the Savior's voice goes on:

"It is better for thee to enter into life with one eye, rather than having two eyes to be cast into Hell." (Matt. 18:8,9.)

Sometimes as His dear hands are dealing with the injured man, cleansing wounds,

178

applying His ointment, and assuring him that he will heal him of his wounds (Jer. 30:17) and applying the bandages, according to Psalms 147:3, which says He healeth the broken in heart, and bindeth up their wounds, the patient looks up and sees that the hands of the Great Physician Himself are wounded, and he cries out in amazement: "What are these wounds in thine hands?" Then He answers: "Those with which I was wounded in the house of my friends." (Zach. 13:6.) "Not only my hands, but my feet, my side and my brow were wounded for your transgressions." And shamed before His great sacrifice and love, his murmuring dies away and he cries: "O Lord, continue your dealings, no matter what it means I trust you, Lord."

REST AND FOOD

The operating room experience over, the patient is soon placed in bed to rest (Psa. 23:2), but first he is arrayed in fine linen, clean and white (Rev. 19:8). Then as the weary finds rest, wounds bound and beginning to heal already, clean in body and soul, he whispers: "I will lay me down in peace, and sleep; for Thou Lord only maketh me dwell in safety." (Psa. 4:8.)

Here in the Red Cross Hospital are found food and rest and love and safety. The Physician is always on call, and ever watches in vigilance over him, for He never slumbers nor sleeps. (Psa. 121:3.)

(The food for convalescents, nurses must remember, should not often be given as strong as to well people, but the milk of the Word, the wine of the Kingdom, the bread of Life, and later, as the patient grows stronger, the strong meat may be given under the direction and supervision of the Great Physician.)

Those who dwell within the fountain of blood, which is indeed a hospital where woes are soothed away and broken hearts healed, located at the foot of the red, blood-stained cross of Jesus? are safe and immune from danger (Rom. 8:38,39).

Above it, unfurled to the breeze, flies the blood-stained banner of the cross, the Red Cross on its background of the pure white holiness of Jesus, and though the devil's airships, principalities and powers of the air may soar aloft above us, though demons may rage, and great long-distance guns may fire their great explosives and shell all about us, he is safe who abides under the protection of the blood, the unfurled banner of the cross, and the protection of Jesus, his Lord.

"LET ME BE A RED CROSS WORKER"

Then (growing stronger day by day) with the return of strength, Comes the great over-whelming love of the RED CROSS and all it has meant to him.

The shuddering, awful thought of the field from which he has been rescued the firing of the cannon, the smoke of battle, the moans and heart-rending cries of misery fill the soul with a new-born desire and determination to himself be marked with the insignia of the RED CROSS.

Provided with an ambulance of prayer and the stretcher of Faith, carrying the Word of God, and his First Aid to the wounded kit, he would go forth to sacrifice even life itself. The cry of his whole heart is, "O that I might go and bring in other souls, even as I was brought to the cross!

O, that others might know of the balm of Gilead, and the hospital atop blest Calvary's Hill! O, Dear Savior, let ME be a Red Cross Worker!"

179

THE TWO HOUSES

THE HOUSE ON THE SAND AND THE HOUSE ON THE ROCK

EVERY man, woman and child throughout this world is erecting a building. "Except the Lord built the house, they labor in vain that build it." Ps. 127:1.

The great army of house-builders is divided into two classes, namely, the sinner and the saint.

(Bight here let us make it plain, that each individual is either a sinner or a saint. It is impossible to be both; it is impossible to be neutral; there is no half-way business with God. Either you are the child of the Lord or you are serving the devil there is no middle territory.) Just as there are only two classes of house-builders, just so there are but two foundations, the sandy foundation of sin and unrighteousness, which lies in the devil's domain, and the solid Rock, which is Jesus Christ.

THE MAN ON THE SAND GATHERS HIS MATERIAL

The sinner is building day by day. His mind is not troubled by the lack of foundation. He does not deem it at all necessary to dig deep, but begins erecting the edifice of his life by bringing up the stones of unrepentance, and wilfulness; the stones of sin and unbelief; and piling them, moment by moment, hour by hour, day by day, year by year, one upon another, on the sands of this life.

The stones of evil thoughts and distrustfulness are piled up day by day. The stones of pride, selfishness and hardness of heart toward God take their places in the building, which is growing moment by moment into a life and structure which will surely fall in the great day, when God's judgments are poured out upon the world.

THE MAN ON THE ROCK DIGS A FOUNDATION AND GATHERS HIS BUILDING MATERIAL

While in New York City sometime ago, I was very much impressed with the great world-famed sky-scrapers. For many weeks, yes, months, I saw a high board fence built around a certain lot.

Behind this board fence, and above it, I could see great cranes and derricks, and hear the steel drills.

Dozens of men were working there, drilling and digging, and blasting down into the solid rock; down, and down, and down they went, digging a foundation for the great steel sky-scraper which was soon to be erected, and one of the men assured me that the higher the building was to be the deeper the foundation must be sunk into the solid rock.

After having been away for a short visit and returning again to the city, my eyes opened wide with surprise as I saw the steel building so quickly taking shape, and towering with imposing grandeur above its neighbors. Why, it really seemed that it took longer to build the foundation than to put the steel frame-work of the building together.

This is a very apt illustration, it seems to me, of the Christian's life, as he prepares to build upon the solid Rock, Christ Jesus.

First of all he digs a deep foundation of repentance, and goes down in humility into Jesus, his Lord. He plunges into the fountain filled with the blood. He falls prostrate at the dear, pierced feet of his Master; for indeed the way down is the way up, in our spiritual life. "He that Humbleth himself shall be exalted."

His neighbors may laugh at him and tell him this digging deep, this weeping and mourning over his sins is not at all necessary; but the work goes on. The great boulders of hindrance must be blasted by the love and power of God. Every obstacle must be removed, and a solid, settled, foundation made. He must dig deep into the atoning work of Jesus, before the building of his Christian life can be constructed. "But every man take heed how he buildeth thereon, for other foundation can no man lay than that is laid, which is Jesus Christ."

The foundation having been laid, the building begins to take shape. Upon the stones of repentance and Godly fear, are laid the stones of mercy and divine tenderness. The boundless grace and love of Jesus Christ, the stones of sincerity and truth, the stones of thanksgiving and glorious praises to the Lord of his salvation, are added to the building. Love, joy, peace, long-suffering, gentleness, goodness, faith, meekness and temperance are piled moment by moment, day by day, year by year, one upon another.

The stones of love and unselfishness, a longing for souls, and a yielding to the will of God, a desire to live like Him and abide in His presence are added again to these; and so the work goes on, by each word, and deed and thought, here a little and there a little, precept upon precept, line upon line, tier upon tier.

"Jesus Christ being the chief corner stone, the building is fitly framed together, and groweth into a holy temple in the Lord, for a habitation of God through the Spirit."

Next in importance in the house comes the door through which admission is gained into the house.

As for the sinner who builds upon the sand "Sin lieth at the door" the devil, who is the controlling agent of his will-power, is the door-keeper; thus the door swings on its hinges to admit the worldliness, and sin, and evil thoughts and companions, who occupy the rooms within.

The door is ever shut and locked against God as He is manifested through the great love of Christ ever shut and barred to the wooings of the Spirit and the rappings of that gentle hand. His ears are closed to the voice that is saying, "Behold, I stand at the door, and knock; if any man wilt open, I will come in and sup with him and he with Me" closed to the warnings of the Savior who would plead with him to leave this sandy foundation, and this perishable building, which can never stand the storm, and to the invitation to him to come over and build upon the solid Rock, Christ Jesus.

The door of the child of God who builds upon the rock, is not so; but righteousness, through the power of the Spirit, standeth as doorkeeper. The blood of the slain Lamb is sprinkled upon the door-posts and the lintels. The door is ever open to admit the leadings of the Lord, the dealings of His Spirit, His righteousness, and all His blessed will, and swings shut to bar out the things of the world, the flesh and the devil, which are displeasing to the Lord, his Maker. Thus his rooms are occupied by faith, and hope and love.

Next in importance come the windows in the two houses. The windows of the sinner are darkened with the things of this world, and his vision impaired. He cannot realize his own danger, and his viewpoint is distorted. He cannot foresee the awful storm of wrath which is soon to break.

"When the keepers of the house shall tremble, and the strong men shall bow themselves, and the grinders cease because they are few, and those that look out of the windows be darkened"

The windows of the saint are illuminated with the glory of God, as revealed by the Spirit. His view is clear as he gazes into the future and beholds that

"There's a land that is fairer than day, And by faith he can see it afar,

For the Father waits over the way,

To prepare him a dwelling-place there."

Those who stand without his walls see the light of the Lord shining through, for

"Behold, he standeth behind our wall, He looketh forth at the windows, showing himself through the lattice. Song of Sol. 2:9.

In his dining-room the sinful man who is building upon the sand, is feasting upon the things of this world; he says to his soul: "Soul, thou hast much goods laid up for many years; take thine ease, eat, drink and be merry." But God is saying unto him:

"Thou fool! This night thy soul shall be required of thee; then whose shall these things be which thou hast provided." Luke 12:19-20. He feasts upon things that can never satisfy the hunger of the soul that is crying after God. He is as one that "dreameth, and behold, he eateth; but he awaketh and his soul is empty." Isa. 29:8.

In his dining-room, the child of God is feasting on the milk, and the honey and the wine. The fruits of Canaan are spread before him. The bread of life is his, and for him the glorious crystal waters flow from the throne of God. The voice of the Bridegroom is heard speaking:

"I am come into my garden, my sister, my spouse; I have gathered my myrrh with my spice; I have eaten my honeycomb with my honey; I have drunk my wine with my milk: eat, friends drink, yea, drink abundantly, beloved." Song of Sol. 5:1.

While the sinner is feasting upon the applause of his fellow-men, and the treasures of this world, the children of the Most High are dining at the table of the Lord dining upon his righteousness and love; upon the joys and fruits of the Spirit, and their souls are filled to overflowing, as He leadeth them through the green pastures of His Word.

The inmates of the house which is builded upon sand are dancing to the tunes of this world and its applause dancing to the strains of earthly popularity, and self-centered aims. Outside, threatening storm-clouds of death's dark night are gathering, and the rolling thunders seem to cry aloud in warning.

The wrath of God is soon to be poured out, but unheedingly they dance on and on, ever nearing the brink of destruction and hell.

The inmates of the house on the rock are dancing, too. You remember as the brother of the prodigal son approached his father's house, he heard the sound of music and dancing. Some folks seem to think the devil has a monopoly on all the dancing and joy; but dancing and joy really belong to God, and as the devil cannot steal it he has tried to counterfeit it.

Within the heart of him whose hopes are built upon the solid foundation of Christ and His righteousness, there is joy unspeakable and full of glory, for: "His mourning has been turned into dancing," Ps. 30:11, and "There the virgins rejoice in the dance, both old and young together." Jer. 31:13. They "Praise Him with the tambourine and dance," Ps. 150:4, and cry: "Let them praise His name in the dance." Ps. 149:3. "For the children of the Lord have a right to shout and sing, For the way is growing bright, and our souls are on the wing, We are going bye and bye to the palace of the King.

Glory to God, Hallelujah!"

As for the sinner his bed is so short that he cannot stretch himself upon it, and the covering so narrow that he cannot wrap himself in it. Isa. 28:20. When he lies down at night there is an unrest in his heart, for he is unprepared to meet his God; his conscience is troubled as the Spirit of God strives with him, assuring him that "Whatsoever a man soweth that shall he also reap" and his covering of self-righteousness and excuses cannot cover or conceal him from the eye of God.

As for the child of God, his rest is sweet in the Lord. He hears the voice of the Psalmist ringing down through the ages: "I remember Thee upon my bed, and meditate on Thee in the night watches" Ps. 63:6. Let "the saints be joyful in glory. Let them sing aloud upon their beds." Ps. 149:5.

O, the peace that belongeth unto the child of God, to know that if his eyes never open again,

"to be absent from the body is to be present with the Lord," and "to live is Christ, and to die is gain."

The Word tells us that "Where your treasure is, there will your heart be also." The worldly man is storing up treasures of this world's goods, heaping to himself riches, houses and lands. He tears down his barns and builds greater, and there bestows his fruits and goods. He bids his soul take its ease, because he has much goods laid up for many years. But God is speaking to him through His word, saying: "Thou fool, this night thy soul shall be required of thee: then whose shall these things be, which thou hast provided?" He has laid up treasure for himself, but is not rich toward God. "For what shall it profit a man if he gain the whole world, and lose his own soul?"

The worldly man takes no thought of the great tomorrow, and does not seem to realize that he cannot take one penny away with him. Born into this world naked and without a penny, he will have to enter into the next world in the same condition.

The child of God is laying up treasure above "where moth and rust do not corrupt, and where thieves do not break through nor steal" The poorest child of God, who lives in the humblest cottage in the dell, and has laid up treasure in the world beyond is richer than an ungodly king that sits upon his throne, with all his splendor, for his riches are laid away in Heaven, and will not pass away throughout the endless ages of eternity.

The Lookout Tower of the sinner, and the Lookout Tower of the saint are totally different. Both look out upon life, but from very different viewpoints. The Search-light of the sinner's vision goes through all the earth, searching for earthly possession, earthly treasure, earthly pleasures and popularity. From his lookout tower, the searchlight of the sinner's eye is ever turning expectantly and inquiringly, from one end of the land to the other Searching, searching, ever searching for new amusement, new pleasure or gain, ever seeking something to still that gnawing hunger that is eating into his heart; ever endeavoring to satisfy the longing in his soul, which, if he but knew it, nothing but God can satisfy.

DARK CLOUDS APPROACHING STORM GOD'S WRATH

The dark clouds of the approaching storm of God's wrath are filling the sky above the sinner's head. He refuses to see them, for he has eyes only for earthly things. Then, though the thunders crash with deafening roar about him in these last days of war and tribulation though the lightnings flash and strike round about him he refuses to believe that this is more than a passing shower, and his search-light still continues to wander restlessly throughout the earth for new achievements and honors.

The wise man, who has built his house upon the rock has his search-light constantly turned upward toward the Heavens. God is his high tower, in which he is safe from the enemy. He has set the watchmen of Vigilance and Prayer upon his walls, of whom he is ever enquiring:

"Watchman, what of the night?" Is. 21:11. The watchman's answering voice can be heard saying:

"The dark night of God's wrath is breaking over the whole world. The hour of storm and tribulation is at hand; the great ocean of God's love, which has floated on, calm as a river and deep as the sea, through the many centuries of sin and unbelief, is now being churned into a mighty storm of wrath."

The storm signals are all set, the danger signals are up, and woe to that man whose house is built upon the sand. Everything that can be shaken, will be shaken, and only those things that cannot be shaken will remain.

"Watchman, what of the night?" and again the answer comes:

"Wars and rumors of wars, plagues and pestilence, blood and fire and vapor of smoke." The storm is raging, but the children of the Lord are preparing for the coming of their Redeemer.

Upward, ever upward, turns the searchlight of the child of God, searching, ever searching. In each new cloud that brings sorrow to the sinner, he sees another sign of the coming of the Lord, for has he not said: "When ye shall see these things come to pass, rejoice, for the coming of the Master draweth nigh"?

The rain is falling falling upon the just and the unjust. The rain increases to a downpour.

Unto the man whose house is built upon the sand the rain brings terror and is destruction, and the beginning of the wrath of God; but to the man whose house stands on the rock, it brings floods of blessing. It is to him the Latter Rain falling on the earth, and "his heart is filled with song, and praise and mirth."

The clouds of darkness that are gathering over the sinner are bright clouds to the saint. He is looking for Jesus to come in the clouds, and fully expects to be caught up in the clouds to meet Him.

The lightning of God's wrath which brings sure and certain destruction to the sinner, brings power and glory to the child of God. God sitteth on His throne. Out of the east proceedeth forth thunder and lightning. The sinner quails beneath this power, but the man whose house is built

183

upon the rock sings aloud:

"O Lord, send the power just now, And fill us, every one."

And through all the storm the child of God is in his watch-tower of prayer and vigilance, his searchlight ever gazing above:

"He is looking for Jesus from glory to come, That Jesus who died on the tree,

A cloud of bright angels to carry him home, To that glorious eternity."

He seeks to warn the man who has long been building upon the sand, but the latter refuses to take warning. Ah, if he could but see already the great billows that are sweeping over this earth today, lashing at the stones of his shaky foundation, causing even kingdoms and thrones to totter and fall!

Each sinner, both small and great each soul who has rejected God, and failed to build upon the solid rock? Christ Jesus shall surely fall in ignominious shame and death, and the place wherein he stood shall know him no more, but throughout the endless ages of eternity he will mourn his disastrous folly in neglecting to build upon the solid rock: "For what shall it profit a man if he gain the whole world and lose his own soul?"

HOUSE ON THE ROCK STANDS ETERNALLY SECURE

And though winds may blow and the storm may beat upon that house, it will not fall, for it was founded upon a rock:

"All they that put their trust in God Can never be removed,

They stand secure like Zion's mount,

By many ages proved.

Though fierce the storm in fury beat.

And awful thunders roar,

The children of the Mighty God

Are safe forevermore."

While the sinner's house sinks down to the lowest pits of hell, the house of righteousness, founded upon the rock, will stand eternally in the Heavens, in that land where storms never come and tears never flow.

LOST AND RESTORED

AS I SAW IT IN MY VISION

THE following message was given under the inspiration of the Holy Ghost, in London, England. The text, which was given by the Spirit was as follows:

"That which the Palmerworm hath left hath the Locust eaten; and that which the Locust hath left hath the Canker-worm eaten; and that which the Cankerworm hath left hath the Caterpillar eaten."

Joel 1:4.

"And I will restore to you all the years that the locust hath eaten, the cankerworm, the caterpillar, and the palmerworm, My great army which I sent among you." Joel 2:25.

While in London, England, waiting for the boat in which to embark for China, I was asked by a certain preacher one day if I would not speak to his congregation that night. Inquiring of the Lord, I felt it was His will, and told the man that I would go. That evening a beautiful limousine, with liveried attendants, called for me, and I entered with weak and self-conscious steps, crying: "Oh, Lord, do help me do Thy will tonight."

On the way I gazed upon the beautiful streets and buildings, till at last the car stopped in front of an imposing and spacious edifice.

As we went up the steps and into the side door of this immense building, I remember taking a hurried glance at its size and vaguely wondering whether some small room therein was used for a mission. Great was my surprise therefore, when being led through the door and on the platform, I found that this whole building was packed with people, and I was to speak to them at once. My attendant whispered into my ear that we were late, and then I heard the voice of the man on the platform saying: "Now our sister will speak to us and bring the message."

Before I realized it, I was standing, dazed and confused before the largest audience I had ever spoken to. The gallery, the balcony, the pit and the rostrum were all filled; and to add to my confusion, just then the footlights flashed into brilliancy all around me? And there I stood, a slip of a girl, with my Bible in my trembling hands. I had prepared no sermon, trusting God to speak through me at the moment. But not a thought came to me. Lifting my heart to God in silent prayer, I said:

"O God, if you ever helped me in my life, help me now!"

Just then something happened The power of God went surging through my body, waves of glory and praise saved through my soul, until I forgot the throng of eager faces that had, a moment before, seemed to swim before me, forgot the footlights, and the learned men with their long-tail coats, forgot that I was only a child of eighteen, and that many there with their gray hair knew more in a moment than I in the natural course would know in a lifetime, and "I was in the Spirit."

All this takes a long time to write, but it happened in a moment, for those who put their trust in God shall never be put to shame. My mouth opened; the Lord took control of my tongue, my lips and vocal organs, and began to speak through me, not in tongues, but in English. The Spirit spoke in prophecy, and as He spoke, I did not know what the next word was to be; certainly the water did flow, not from my head but from the innermost depths of my being, without my having aught to do with it.

As I spoke thus for one hour and a quarter, there did not seem to be a stir in all that vast audience, and as I spoke I saw a vision of a great circle, composed of ten smaller circles, as shown in the preceding picture. This big circle seemed so big that its top reached the sky; it was the dispensation of the Holy Spirit, from its opening on the day of Pentecost to its closing at the coming of the Lord Jesus. The vision was so indelibly stamped upon my mind that I have had my husband draw it from my description that all may see it as simple and plain as the Lord showed it to me.

Before starting to speak, I opened my Bible with closed eyes, trusting God for my text, and my finger was guided to a certain verse; when I opened my eyes and read it this was the verse the Lord had given me:

"That which the palmerworm hath left hath the locust eaten; and that which the locust hath left hath the cankerworm eaten; and that which the cankerworm hath left hath the caterpillar eaten." - Joel 1:4.

Just so when I came to the bottom of the circle, and the dark ages were pictured in their horror, my hand automatically turned the page over to the second chapter and placed my finger upon the following verse:

"I will restore to you the years that the locust hath eaten, and the cankerworm, and the caterpillar and the palmerworm, My great army which I sent among you." Joel 2:25.

I have, in the following pages, written the message as it was given. It is He, not I, who is worthy of praise forever.

JUST as there are three in the Godhead: Father, Son and Holy Ghost, so there have been three separate and distinct dispensations or periods of time.

First came the dispensation of the Father, as recorded in God's Word throughout the Old Testament, from Genesis to Malachi. Throughout the dispensation of the Father, He promised that at the close of this dispensation He would bestow a great gift, even Jesus, His only begotten Son, upon this earth, as our Redeemer and the propitiation for our sins. At the close of that period of time God the Father kept His word, and true to His promise, gave Jesus, as His great Love Gift to the sinner.

Secondly came the dispensation of the Son, as recorded in the four Gospels, Matthew, Mark, Luke and John. Now, just as the Father had a gift to bestow upon the world, even as Jesus, who is our salvation, tells us over and over again that He longs to bestow a gift upon all those who believe on Him, even the gift of the Holy Spirit. All throughout His ministry upon this earth, with ever increasing emphasis, Jesus depicted to His followers the importance of their receiving this gift which He was to bestow upon them when He went away.

Jesus seemed, to a certain degree, to be limited in the scope of His ministry, was sent only to the lost sheep of the House of Israel, was able to be in only one place at a time, etc., and declared in John 16:7: "It is expedient for you that I go away, for if I go not away the Comforter will not come unto you; but if I depart I will send Him unto you." Plainly Jesus thought it more important for us to receive the Holy Spirit than for Himself to stay upon this earth. Thus, just as the Father kept His promise and sent Jesus, His love gift to the sinner, so now in turn Jesus kept His word and prayed the Father to send the Holy Spirit, His gift to the believer.

Thirdly came the dispensation of the Holy Spirit, which opened on the Day of Pentecost. (Acts 2.) This dispensation we are still living in and will be living in until Jesus comes for His waiting Bride.

The days of Jesus' tender ministry upon earth were over. He had eaten the last supper. He had been tried in the sinner's stead and had died in the sinner's place. He had been laid in the lonely tomb, resurrected in power and triumph, had walked forty days upon earth after His resurrection. He had promised for the last time that He would not leave His little ones comfortless, but that He would pray the Father that He would send another Comforter, even the Holy Spirit, who when He was come would in His office work take of the things of Jesus and reveal it unto them (John 16:13); lead them into all truth (John 16:13); not speak of Himself but of Jesus (v. 13); show them things to come (-13); glorify Jesus (-14); reprove of sin, of righteousness and of judgment (-8) teach them all things (John 14:26) testify of Jesus (John 15:26); endue them with power from on high (Luke 24:49); pray through them with groanings that could not be uttered. The last words of Jesus before His ascension, before the clouds received Him out of their sight, as recorded in Luke 24:49, and Acts 1:8, were concerning the importance of tarrying for and receiving the Comforter whom He would send.

TARRYING FOR THE COMING OF THE HOLY SPIRIT

With glowing hearts, and the Master's command, "Tarry until ye be endued with power from on high" still ringing in their ears, the little flock of about a hundred and twenty wended their way to the "upper room" in Jerusalem, to await there the advent of the Holy Spirit, the opening of this great, new dispensation of the Spirit sent from Heaven. For ten days they waited. They "continued with one accord in one place in prayer and supplication." One accord, O what unbroken harmony is depicted in these simple words! Thomas was not saying to Peter:

"Peter, what are you doing here. You denied the Lord thrice, you cursed and swore; the Lord will never baptize you with the Spirit." Peter was not saying to Thomas:

"Well, Thomas, what are you doing here? You always were an old doubter anyway; don't think you will receive anything from the Lord." Ah, no! they were with one accord in one place in prayer and supplication.

THE COMING OF THE HOLY SPIRIT

(Acts 2:4.)
"And when the day of Pentecost was fully come they were all with one accord in one place. And suddenly there came a sound from Heaven" (and bless God, there has been a sound ever since when the Spirit falls and comes in). "From Heaven" (Yes, thank God, in spite of what man may say, undoubtedly this sound is from Heaven). "Like as of a rushing mighty wind, and it filled all the house where they were sitting. And there appeared unto them cloven tongues like as of fire, and it sat upon each of them. And they were all filled with the Holy Ghost, and began to speak with other tongues as the Spirit gave them utterance."

186

I have often tried to picture the sudden consternation and excitement which surged through the streets of Jerusalem when the hundred and twenty men and women were filled with the Holy Spirit, and burst out shouting and talking in other tongues, so filled that they acted like drunken people (Acts 2:13). I can seem to see the crowds running up this street, and that, windows flying open, heads thrust out, doors opening, everybody running, devout men gathering up their long ministerial robes and forgetting their dignity, running with the rest to swell the one great question:

WHAT MEANETH THIS?

"And when this was noised abroad the multitude came together, "(Beloved, if the Holy Spirit is falling in your midst you will not need oyster suppers or box socials or Xmas trees to bring the multitude, your only trouble will be to find seats for the people) "and were confounded, "just as you have been, perhaps, "because that every man heard them speak in his own language." They were amazed, they marvelled, they were in doubt. Sober-minded folk asked the question:

"What meaneth this?" Mockers declared:

"These men are full of new wine" O, what an uproar! What an excitement! you dear people who dislike confusion, and demand things to be done "decently and in order" would have been scandalized.

"But Peter" a new Peter, no longer afraid of the opinions of people, "standing up, "(the Holy Spirit, when He endues you with power, puts a real stand up for Jesus spirit within you, and takes the cowardice out) "said: these are not drunken, as ye suppose, but this is that which was spoken by the prophet Joel. And it shall come to pass in the last days, saith God, that I will pour out of My Spirit upon all flesh." Then as Peter preached that mighty sermon under the power of the Holy Spirit, among other things he told his vast audience to

"Repent and be baptized, everyone in the Name of Jesus Christ, for the remission of sins"

and that they, too, would "receive the gift of the Holy Spirit" Furthermore, just as though he looked away ahead through the coming years, and saw the doubts in some of your minds, Peter declared that "the promise is "not only "unto you" but "unto your children and unto them that are afar off" that means you, brother, sister, for he goes on to say, "even as many as the Lord our God shall call." Now, if God has called you, the promise is unto you. How glad I am that the Spirit, through Peter, drove these nails and clinched them on the other side till there is not the shadow of a loophole for you to thrust the wedge of doubt into.

CIRCLE I. THE USHERING IN OF THE DISPENSATION OF THE HOLY SPIRIT ACCOMPANIED BY MIGHTY SIGNS AND WONDERS

On the day of Pentecost some three thousand souls were saved. Then we see Peter and John, going up to the temple to pray, pass a lame man at the beautiful gate, who asks alms of them.

Peter answers:

"Silver and gold have I none "(I do not think the Pentecostal people ever were or ever will be overly blessed with silver or gold) "but such as I have I give unto thee; in the Name of Jesus Christ rise up and walk." The lame man was healed instantaneously, and whether the priests in the Temple believed in manifestations or not I know not, but at any rate the man went into that Temple walking, leaping and praising God.

In Acts 5:16 we see the multitudes out of the cities round about Jerusalem bringing sick folks and those that were vexed with unclean spirits, and they were healed every one. Sick were brought forth into the streets and laid on beds and couches that at least the shadow of Peter passing by might overshadow some of them. Signs and wonders were wrought everywhere by the hands of the Apostles, true to the word of Him who had said:

"Greater works than these shall ye do because I go to My Father."

While the tree seen in Circle One stood in its perfection, the Church stood blazing with the full Pentecostal Power and Glory of the Holy Spirit. Jesus' words were fulfilled, and in deed and

187

in truth they were endued with power from on high.

Timid Peter, who had once feared a little girl who asked him if he knew Jesus, was timid no longer. Illiterate men and women were turned into flaming evangels.

The outpouring of the Holy Spirit was not unto the Jews alone, but also unto the Gentiles. In Acts 10 we see Peter answering the voice of the Lord, who spoke to him through a vision, going down to preach Jesus unto the Gentiles. "While Peter yet spake the Holy Ghost fell on all them which heard the Word;" the Jews who came with Peter were astonished that on the Gentiles also was poured out the gift of the Holy Ghost, "for they heard them speak with tongues and magnify God."

Again in these wonderful days of the former rain outpouring of the Holy Spirit, we see Saul, on his way to Damascus to persecute the Christians, slain and prostrated in the road by the power of the Spirit, hearing the voice of Jesus saying:

"Saul, Saul, why persecutest thou Me?" Later we find Paul not only converted and baptized with the Holy Spirit, with the Bible evidence of speaking with other tongues (I Cor. 4:18), but himself preaching salvation and the Baptism of the Holy Spirit. In Acts 19, Paul, finding certain disciples at Ephesus, asks them they have received the Holy Ghost since they believed. They tell him "No." They have not even heard whether there was any Holy Ghost. "And when Paul had laid his hands upon them the Holy Ghost came on them and they spake in tongues" and magnified God. This marvelous manifestation of speaking in other tongues accompanied the infilling of believers with the Holy Spirit everywhere. Simon offered money for the power to bestow that which he saw and heard.

THE TREE WITH ITS PERFECT FRUIT

Every gift and fruit of the Spirit was manifested in the Church till the nine gifts and the nine fruits of the Spirit hung as eighteen perfect apples upon the perfect tree. "For to one was given by the Spirit the Word of Wisdom, to another the Word of Knowledge, by the same Spirit, to another Faith, by the same Spirit, to another the gift of Healing, by the same Spirit, to another the working of Miracles, to another Prophecy, to another Discerning of Spirits, to another divers kinds of Tongues, to another Interpretation of Tongues"

The sick were healed, miracles wrought, and when messages were given in other tongues in the assembly, someone gave the interpretation. (I Cor., 14:37.) Each of the nine fruits were in the Church Love, Joy, Peace, Gentleness, Goodness, Faith, Meekness, Temperance, Longsuffering, thus we have the perfect picture visualized in "Circle I" of the Chart.

Thus ends the first chapter of the early Church History, leaving the tree rooted and grounded in the faith of Jesus, every limb, branch, leaf and fruit in perfect power and strength.

CIRCLE II. THE PALMER WORM AT WORK

O glorious days of harmonious love and unity, days when none called aught that he had his own, days when the children of the Lord had all things in common, days when prison bonds were broken, signs and wonders were wrought, how we have often wished they might have continued!

These puny minds of ours only feebly grasp events of the past, and are utterly unable to probe the depths of mystery shrouding the future. Unlike us, however, the great mind and eye of the Almighty God beholds the future as clearly as the past. Before His burning eyes of Fire, and the Glory of His presence, darkness turns to day, and the deepest mists are rolled away. Looking thus ahead with clear, unerring eye, God saw, and moreover prophesied through the prophet Joel, that the Church would not always retain this glorious state of Power, saw that the palmerworm, the locust, the cankerworm and the caterpillar were going to rob and strip and mutilate and destroy this perfect tree with its gifts and fruits. He saw that the Church, or tree, was going to lose gradually more and more, till it would be left desolate, barren and despairing. The falling away and destruction of the perfect tree did not occur in one day. It was a gradual deterioration accomplished day by day and stage by stage.

One day the palmerworm appeared, eating and destroying as it went, until as the years went by the gifts and fruits of the Spirit began to disappear from view. Not so many sick were healed as of yore, not so many miracles were performed, faith was on the wane, when someone in the assembly had a message in tongues there was no one who had the gift of interpretation, messages in prophecy were not so frequent as of yore. The fruits of unselfish love and joy and peace were also attacked by the palmerworm, who grew bolder and bolder day by day. Gradually the eighteen apples began to disappear from the staunch and upright tree which had stood so gloriously heavy laden for many years after the day of Pentecost.

This state of fruitlessness was indeed a condition worthy of lamentation, but the pity of it all is that the devastation did not stop with the havoc wrought by the palmerworm. Other years, and other worms took up the work of destruction where the palmerworm had left off, and "that which the palmerworm hath left hath the locust eaten."

CIRCLE III. THE LOCUST AT WORK

The work of the locust is, of course, wrought upon the leaves sweeping over vast territories of country he strips and lays barren all that he touches. Thus not only were the gifts and fruits of the Spirit lost sight of by the vast majority of believers, but the personal incoming and indwelling of the Holy Spirit, accompanied by speaking in other tongues, was also in a great measure lost sight of. The oldtime seeker's meetings, the earnest prayer and praise meetings were disappearing; formality and sectarianism were taking their places.

As humility, godliness, and the manifestations of the Holy Spirit vanished persecution and reproach vanished also. As meetings of the older order were converted into dignified services of a more orthodox form, the Holy Spirit, as a gentle dove, was quenched and grieved and stifled till He silently withdrew His wonder-working manifestations, and joy and gladness were withheld from the sons of men.

Because it meant too great a sacrifice, too much emptying out and humbling in the dust before God, too much seeking and waiting, the Baptism of the Holy Spirit was not received as of old.

Then came men who professed to have the Holy Spirit in a new way, i. e., without the Bible seal or evidence of speaking with other tongues as the Spirit gives utterance. This simplified matters greatly, and the professor no longer needed to be a possessor. Thus the Baptism of the Holy Spirit was lost sight of by many, though there always was a remnant of a faithful few Spirit-filled saints through whom God manifested Himself in a real and supernatural way.

It was a sad day when the leaves were thus stripped from the tree, and the locust had done its work, but days that were still more sad were to follow, for we read "that which the locust hath left hath the cankerworm eaten."

CIRCLE IV. THE WORK OF THE CANKERWORM

After the fruit and the leaves had been destroyed, the cankerworm immediately made his appearance and began his work upon the branches and tender shoots of the tree, making cankerous and unsound that God-fearing walk of Holiness above the world and sin, so long enjoyed by the children of the Lord. As the sap, the life of the tree, was consumed and the branches became more and more cankerous, and unsound things that used to seem sinful appeared sinful no longer, the world that used to be barred outside the doors of the Church now leaned back in contented languor in the cushioned pews, or sang in the choir.

Christians let down more and more the high standard of Holiness unto the Lord, which they had been holding aloft, and now it trailed bedraggled and unnoticed in the dust. Quickly upon the trail of the cankerworm followed the caterpillar, and we read that "that which the cankerworm hath left hath the caterpillar eaten."

CIRCLE V. THE WORK OF THE CATERPILLAR

We are now nearing the bottom of the large circle. The perfect tree is perfect no longer, stripped of her fruits, denuded of her leaves, her branches made white, laid clean bare, it was not long till the trunk and the roots began to decay and the caterpillar made his nest in the decayed and rotted hollows of the tree.

No tree can eke out its existence long without leaves through which to breathe, and branches and limbs through which the sap of life courses through its veins. For a believer to live without the Holy Spirit, the breath of life, or the Holy life of Jesus as revealed by the Spirit, coursing through his veins, is to eke out a meager, barren existence nowhere recorded in the Word of God.

And now, in circle five, we see the tree in the most lamentable condition yet described, fruit gone, leaves gone, branches bare, trunk decayed and rotten, a nest for the caterpillar. In other words, the gifts and fruits of the Spirit gone, the Baptism of the Holy Spirit gone, separation and Holiness gone, justification by Faith gone. Well might the Angels lean over the battlements of Heaven and weep; of the noble Church, the perfect tree, which had once stood clad with the Power and Glory of the Holy Ghost, there remained now naught but a -name, not even a remnant of its former splendor, as she entered into the DARK AGES.

CIRCLE VI. THE DARK AGES

No wonder they are called the dark ages. Ah! dark indeed is the night without Jesus. He is the Light of the world, and when the Church lost sight of justification by Faith, lost sight of the atonement, the blood of Jesus, there was a total eclipse and the face of the Sun of Righteousness was obscured, and the succeeding years that followed are known as the dark ages.

Men and Women groping in this gross darkness tried to win their way to Heaven by doing penance, by locking themselves up in dungeons, walking over red hot plowshares in their bare feet, and by inflicting unnameable tortures upon themselves and upon one another, blindly trying by some work or deed of theirs to pay the debt that had already been paid on Calvary's rugged cross. They had lost sight utterly of the fact that

"Jesus paid it all,
All to Him we owe;
Sin had left a crimson stain,
He washed it white as snow."

The great arrow you see in the chart had been steadily going down and down, pitilessly and relentlessly going down, as I saw it in the vision, till it seemed as though it would never reach the bottom. And now it had struck the bottom, the church had lost all, the tree was dead.

Angels might have wept, mortals might have wrung their hands, and their souls have failed within them in utter despair, but GOD, Hallelujah, looking on ahead into the future still, had spoken through the prophet Joel (Joel 2:25), saying:

"I will restore to you the years that the locust hath eaten, the cankerworm, the caterpillar, and the palmerworm, My great army -which I sent among you" O beloved, do you see it? Then shout aloud and praise Him. Why that was all. ALL, think of it, All that had been lost was to be restored. Hallelujah! What is impossible with man is possible with God.

Now the Church had not lost this "all" at one time. The restoration came as "meat in due season as line upon line, precept upon precept, here a little and there a little, till today we are nearing the completion of this Restoration, and Jesus is coming soon to take His perfect Church, His Bride, His fruit-laden tree, unto Himself, where, transplanted from earth to Heaven, the tree will bloom and yield her fruit by the great River of Life, forever.

No, God did not restore to the Church all at once what she had lost. He was willing to do so to be sure, but they did not have the light at that time. Therefore the last thing that had been lost was the first to be restored. They had a name that they did live, but were dead, and therefore must

190

needs repent and do their first works over again before taking any higher step.

CIRCLE VII. THE YEARS OF THE CATERPILLAR RESTORED

Just before the arrow began to ascend, and the work of Restoration began, we see the scene of ruin depicted by Joel in all its awfulness, in the first chapter of Joel, the meat offering and the drink offering cut off, the field wasted, the corn wasted, the new wine dried up, garner laid desolate, barns broken down, the beasts groan, the herds of cattle are perplexed, the sheep are made desolate, the rivers of water are dried up, and the fire has devoured the pastures of the wilderness.

Then one day amidst all this desolation God began to move, the treading of His footsteps was heard, and in Circle VII we see the roots of the tree again sinking deep into the earth, and Justification by Faith restored. This is the way it all came about:

MARTIN LUTHER

Martin Luther one day was walking up the steps of the cathedral on his hands and knees over broken glass, endeavoring to do penance, thereby seeking to atone for his sins. As he was toiling painfully and laboriously up the steps in this manner, blood trickling from his hands and knees, cut by the broken glass, he heard a voice from Heaven saying:

"Martin Luther, the Just shall live by Faith."

At the words, a great light fell from Heaven. It banished the darkness and doubts, it illuminated the soul of Martin Luther, and revealed the finished work of Calvary and the blood that alone can atone for sin.

"For nothing good have I,
Whereby Thy grace to claim,
I'll wash my garments white
In the blood of Calvary's Lamb."

The days that followed were eventful days, epoch-making days, fraught with self-sacrifice and suffering. The Lord had spoken, and promised that all the years that had been eaten should be restored, and out of the seas of travail and suffering that followed the preaching of Justification by Faith there was born a little body of blood- washed, fire-tried pilgrims, willing to suffer persecution for His Name's sake.

You have read, perhaps, how Martin Luther and his followers were turned out of the churches, spoken against falsely, and accused of all manner of evil. As Martin Luther, Calvin, Knox, Fletcher and many other blessed children of the Lord, stood firm for the truths of salvation and a sinless life, they suffered all manner of persecution. God's Word says, "They that will live Godly shall suffer persecution." (If you or your church profess to live Godly and yet never suffer persecution, if you have become popular and the shame and reproach of the cross is gone, there is something radically wrong somewhere, for those who live Godly still suffer persecution.)

As the noble tree again put down her roots of justification into the fertile soil faith, as life again began to surge through the trunk and the limbs of the tree, every demon in Hell seemed to be raging and howling against those who saw and accepted the light of salvation. Martyrs were burned at the stake, stoned to death, swung from public scaffolds, suffered the tortures of the inquisition, their eyes were put out with hot irons, they were beaten till great gashes were cut in their backs, salt was rubbed into the wounds and they were cast into the dark dungeons, still true and unflinching for Jesus. They were tortured in unspeakable ways, beheaded, sent to the guillotine, the covenanters were driven from hill to hill and often had to hide themselves in caves in order to pray or sing the praises of the Lord, hunted and harassed at every turn.

But God had said; "I will restore the years that have been eaten" and in spite of the burning stake, in spite of the blood and fire and the deep waters of tribulation in spite of the raging of the demons in hell, the great arrow that had so long been going down had at last started upward and was never to stop till it reached the top and the tree was again restored to its perfection.

Persecutions cannot stop God. Floods cannot stay His step. Fire cannot delay His

191

progress.

So line upon line, precept upon precept, here a little and there a little, the work of restoration has been going on. Not only did the Lord restore the years the caterpillar had eaten but

CIRCLE VIII. THE YEARS OF THE CANKEEWORM ARE RESTORED

An entire consecration, and holiness unto the Lord were preached; God called out a still more separated people, with a deeper realization of what it meant to live a life wholly given up and consecrated to the Lord. The people a step lower always seem to fight the people a step higher.

Nevertheless as the work of sifting and separation went on, God led His people forth to higher heights.

As one church grew cold, lost their first love, or fought higher truths, they lost out spiritually.

As soon as one creed would refuse to walk in the light, as given by the Lord, or begin to organize and set up man rule, the Lord simply stepped over their walls and left them to their forms and ceremonies, and took with Him the little "called out, out of a called out" flock. In many instances the recording angel had to write upon the door of the fashionable churches:

"Thou hast a name that thou livest, and art dead," or "You have a form of godliness, but deny the power thereof." But the work was not stopped; somewhere people were praying, somewhere hungry hearts were meeting in little cottage prayer-meetings, or on the street corners, and the tender shoots and branches were being thrust forth on the tree. Consecration and holiness were being preached and the years of the canker worm being restored.

JOHN WESLEY

Was a man with a message. He, too, suffered persecution. Preaching on the street-corners in those days, faithful followers were stoned, and rotten-egged. They were fought but not defeated.

The power of God was manifested in the dear old Methodist Church, also in Charles Finney's meetings, in a wonderful manner. Men and women were slain under the power of God. At times the floors were strewn with the slain of the Lord.

Signs and wonders accompanied those who preached the "meat in due season."

While these churches lived godly, prayerful, mighty lives in Jesus, they suffered persecution.

But when they too began to drift into the same cold, formal state as the others before them, the power and manifestation of the Spirit began to lift from their presence. When supper rooms take the place of upper rooms, and concerts the place of prayer meetings, the Spirit is grieved away.

As each body began to organize and throw up walls of difference, God simply stepped over them again and called out another separated people, willing to suffer and sacrifice for Him.

Then came the day when William Booth was called upon to decide whether he would compromise or would follow the greater light God gave him. As he hesitated a moment his wife called from the balcony of that thronged church: "Say No! William."

And William Booth said "NO," and refused to compromise, went forth preaching the message that had been given him. In the early days of the Salvation Army they were unpopular, suffered persecution, were a peculiar people, just as the others before mentioned had been in the beginning.

They too were stoned and imprisoned. Some were even martyred, but neither the devil nor his angels could stop God and His work of restoration. In these early days of the Army it was nothing uncommon to see men and women slain under the power of God. Some of their number received the Holy Ghost and spake with other tongues.

All night prayer meetings, dancing before the Lord, and mighty power was manifested in their midst. True to prophecy, while they lived this separated, holy life, they were persecuted and unpopular with the world. Then came the Holiness churches, wonderfully blessed of God, and the

Lord moved in their midst in a mighty manner.

These dear people, many of them, thought that the Lord had now restored all He was going to restore to the Church, and believed that they had all the Lord had for them. But not so! God had said,

"I will restore the years that the locust, the cankerworm, the caterpillar and the palmerworm hath eaten" This necessarily meant A-L-L. Now so far, only the years eaten by the caterpillar and the cankerworm had been restored. What about the years eaten by the locust and the palmerworm?

When God says "ALL" does He mean all or only half? Why, He means all, to be sure. Therefore next

CIRCLE IX. THE YEARS OF THE LOCUST ARE RESTORED

Although in previous years several saints had received the Holy Spirit and spoken in tongues as in Bible years, yet upon the church at large the years which the locust had eaten (in Circle III), the baptism of the Holy Spirit, in other words, had not been restored in any great measure. Therefore this was the next to be restored. Peter in quoting from the prophet Joel says:

"In the last days, I will pour out my Spirit upon all flesh." Joel says that He who gave us the

"former rain" moderately, will cause to come down for us the rain, both the former and the "Latter Rain" in the first month.

LATTER RAIN

It was just a few years ago that this latter rain began to fall. Perhaps you recollect the great Welch Revival, where, under the preaching of Evan Roberts, the fire fell. Many were saved, and baptized with the Holy Spirit, those who received the Comforter, the Holy Spirit, spoke with other tongues.

Over in Mukti, India, a missionary, Pandita Ramabai, was praying with a band of Hindoo girls. They had spent days and nights in prayer, when suddenly the Spirit was poured out in their midst, as He had been on the day of Pentecost.

Visible fire is said to have been seen upon one girl's bed, and when the other girls went for water to extinguish the fire it was discovered that this was the fire of the Holy Spirit, such as Moses saw in the burning bush that was not consumed. These dear Hindoo girls who received the Holy Spirit spake with other tongues as the Spirit gave them utterance, when they received the Holy Spirit.

One girl spoke in the English language (which she had never learned) and this is the message which was spoken through her:

"Jesus is coming soon, get ready to meet Him."

And the great revival spread on and on. Almost simultaneously the Spirit was poured out in our own United States of America, in England, in Canada, in Africa, upon missionaries in China, and in the islands of the sea. Never was such a world-wide revival known to spread so quickly and simultaneously. The Spirit was poured out upon praying bands in numberless places, who had never heard before of the incoming of the Holy Spirit. In every instance, without exception, those who received the Holy Spirit spake in other tongues, exactly as those who had received in Bible days had done. The latter rain was falling on the earth.

In order to receive the Holy Spirit one had to be empty, and humble. Poor and rich, black and white, the mistress and the maid alike received the Holy Spirit when they humbled themselves, and sought with all their hearts. Those who received, praised the Lord and magnified His name, as no one but Spirit-filled saints can do. Waves of glory, floods of praise saved over assemblies who had received the Holy Spirit. There was no way of stopping this great revival, it seemed.

LATTER RAIN TRUTHS FOUGHT

Just as demons and men had fought the restoration of the years eaten by the caterpillar and cankerworm, so now they fought with renewed vigor the restoration of the years that had been eaten by the locust. Again history repeated itself, and the saints a step lower, unwilling to humble themselves, fought those who had gone a step higher, and many refused to walk in the light.

They failed to realize that God really meant what He said when He promised to restore "ALL" that had been lost. They lost sight of the fact that the Lord was coming for a perfect church clad with all power and the glory of the Spirit. Some even declared that the baptism of the Holy Spirit was not for these days, and did not understand that we are still living in the dispensation of the Holy Spirit, and will be till Jesus comes.

Preachers jumped to their pulpits and began to condemn those who had received the Holy Spirit in the Bible way; they cried "Wildfire! Excitement!! Hypnotism! False Teaching!" etc. All sorts of names were flung at them, and O the blindness of these dear prosecutors' eyes. They who themselves had been persecuted for the light of a few years previous, were now themselves persecuting those who were moving on into greater light.

Papers were printed to condemn the outpouring of the Spirit, great preachers mounted their platforms and denounced it, but they could no more stop God from restoring the Baptism of the Holy Spirit and pouring out the latter rain than the former persecutors had been able to stop the restoration of Salvation and Holiness unto the Lord.

THOSE WHO FIGHT THE HOLY SPIRIT LOSE OUT

Those who fought the Holy Spirit, barred their doors, or put up umbrellas of unbelief, began to dry up spiritually, immediately. Assemblies and churches who once were on fire for God, and preaching Holiness, without which no man shall see the Lord, the moment they rejected the Holy Spirit they began to lose their power. O why could they not see that this latter rain outpouring of the Spirit was just what they needed and had been pining for! Why could they not just have humbled themselves and let the Spirit, who had been "with them" now come "In" them, making them the Temple of the Holy Ghost? All the fighting and persecution, however, was unable to quench the outpouring of the Spirit, upon those who sought earnestly with pure and humble hearts.

To fight the outpouring of the Holy Spirit, accompanied by the Bible evidence, speaking with other tongues, according to Acts 2:4, was just like a man with a broom in his hand, endeavoring to sweep back the tidal waves of the Atlantic Ocean.

While he is sweeping it back in one place it rolls in   countless others; moreover, if he remains long where the full tides are rolling in and does not withdraw, the waves will soon flow over him, and he will be "one of them." Hallelujah!

A broom cannot stop the tide of the ocean, neither can fighting stay the falling of the latter rain, for God hath spoken it. "In the last days I will pour out My Spirit upon all flesh." O stop fighting God and open up your heart to receive and welcome His gift, the Holy Spirit.

During the past twelve years hundreds of thousands of hungry seekers have received the Holy Spirit, and when and wherever He came in, those who received Him spoke with tongues and glorified God.

Thus, in Circle IX on the chart, I saw in my vision the leaves which had been eaten by the locust were again restored to the tree. Just as many in Circle 7 and 8 had believed that when the Lord had restored full Salvation and Holiness they had all there was for them, so now many who had received the baptism of the Spirit believed that they had all the Lord had for them. They conscientiously believed that once they had been filled with the Spirit and had spoken with other tongues, they really had all the Lord had for them, and stopped seeking for more.

This, however, had not been all the church had lost, and was therefore not all that was to be restored.

CIKCLE X. THE YEARS OF THE PALMER WORM RESTORED

Just as the Father bestowed the gift of His only Son Jesus to the world, and just as Jesus bestows the gift of the Holy Spirit, the promise of the Father upon the believer, so now in turn, the Holy Spirit has gifts to bestow upon those who receive Him. The nine gifts and fruits of the Spirit seen in Circle one are again being restored to the tree. Many blessed children of the Lord stop short at salvation and consecration and fail to receive the Holy Spirit, also many who have received the Holy Spirit stop short and fail to covet earnestly the best gifts.

In seeking more of God's will to be wrought in our lives, after having received the Holy Spirit, do not ask for more of the Holy Spirit, because if you have received Him you have received all of Him. He is not divisible. Either you have, or have not received the Holy Spirit. Therefore if He has come in and taken up His abode and spoken through you with other tongues, as in Acts 2:4, pray that you may be more yielded to the Spirit who dwells within.

Someone says "O do not seek the gifts, seek the giver." But, beloved, if you have received the Spirit you have received the giver, and Paul says:

"Covet earnestly the best gifts. Seek that you may excel to the edifying of the church. Let him who speaketh in an unknown tongue pray that he way interpret, that the church may be edified; covet to prophesy "etc. There is a real genuine gift of prophecy even though the enemy has tried to imitate it. Discerning of spirits is needed; gifts of healing, etc., should be in our midst. The gift of tongues is also given. All who receive the baptism of the Holy Spirit speak with tongues as the Spirit gives utterance, but very few receive the real GIFT of tongues so that they are enabled to speak at will to foreigners. This gift, however, has been bestowed upon some, and we have met people who have received it and speak languages to foreigners and are understood though they never studied the language in their lives. In such instances the message is of Jesus and His soon coming.

THE GIFTS AND FRUITS ARE AGAIN APPEARING UPON THE TREE

In Circle 10 we see the fruit not yet fully mature, perhaps, but as we pray and yield ourselves to the Spirit, He will divide to every man severally as He will, and cause the gifts and fruits of the Spirit to be visible in our midst.

JESUS IS COMING SOON

Coming for a perfect church, clad in power and glory, for the perfect tree with every gift and fruit hanging in luscious, mellow, developed perfection upon her branches. O let us wake up and press on to perfection. The winter is over and gone, the spring with its former rain has passed, the summer is passing, and the latter rain has long been falling. The harvest is at hand and the Master is searching for ripened, developed fruit. Praise God for the roots and trunk of salvation. Praise God for the firm, strong limbs and branches of holiness and consecration. Praise God for the green leaves, for the Holy Spirit, but the Master demands fruit from His tree these last days before His coming. Not green, immature fruit, but perfect fruit. He is whispering just now:

I Will Restore All the Years That have Been Eaten.

Dear ones, there is land ahead to be possessed.

Let the fruit of Love be wrought out in your life, with Joy, Peace, Longsuffering, Gentleness, Goodness, Faith, Meekness, and Temperance. Let us get back to Pentecost, and on to the fulness of Pentecostal power and glory recorded in God's Word, for Jesus is coming soon, very soon, for His perfect waiting church, His bride, unspotted with the world; His tree with its unblemished and perfect fruit. Soon He will lift us up and transplant us to the Heavenly garden where our leaves shall not wither, neither shall the fruit decay.

The arrow is almost to the top now, the hour when Jesus will burst the starry floor of Heaven and descend for His beloved is at hand. The great clock of time has almost reached the appointed hour. Let nothing hinder the work of preparation in your life. Let us beware that we quench not the Spirit.

Watch that we do not fall into the same snare which other people formerly used of God have fallen into; snares of formality, of coldness and organization, building walls about ourselves

195

and failing to recognize the other members of our body (for by one Spirit are we all baptized into ONE BODY). If ever we put up walls and fall into these snares of formality God will step over our walls and choose another people as surely as He did in days of yore. He will not give His glory to another, but will take the foolish to confound the mighty, the weak to confound the strong.

Press on therefore to perfection, do not stop short of God's best. If you lay down your crown another will take it up, the number will be complete, none will be missing, only those who have pressed on all the way to His standard will be caught up. If you have been doubting God doubt no longer. He is waiting to restore all the years that have been eaten, and cause you to stand forth in that glorious perfect tree company ready and waiting for Jesus. AMEN.

YOU NEED THE HOLY SPIRIT

LIVING as we are today in the closing hours of the dispensation of the Holy Spirit, it is of utmost importance that the work and incoming of the Comforter should not only be preached, but understood and received.

Is it necessary for the saints of today to receive the baptism of the Holy Spirit, you ask?

Is it necessary for the roses to receive rain as well as sunshine?

What the SUN is to the flowers, Jesus the Son of Righteousness is to His blood- washed children.

As the RAIN to the thirsty, parched gardens, so is the Holy Spirit to the growing child of God.

Salvation is not the baptism of the Holy Spirit.

Sanctification is not the baptism of the Holy Spirit.

Salvation and sanctification (whether you have been taught holiness as one or two definite experiences or not), all must agree, are wrought through Jesus and His precious, atoning blood.

The baptism spoken of by John the Baptist, (Matt. 3:11) and by Peter (Acts 2:38), is the coming of the Comforter into the cleansed, empty vessel which makes the body of the recipient the temple of the Holy Ghost. He comes to exalt and glorify Jesus, to equip the soul for service, to endue with power from on high, power to testify, power to pray, power to overcome as never before, and to prepare that soul for the coming of the Lord. It is the blood of Jesus that cleanseth from all sin; the Holy Spirit longs to enter the cleansed and waiting heart.

Some have thoughtlessly declared "I have Jesus, and I do not need the Holy Spirit." But you do need Him, dear one. Jesus Himself said:

"Receive ye the Holy Ghost," and "If you love Me keep My commandments and I will pray the Father and He shall give you another Comforter that He may abide with you forever."

For you to start out independently to meet the Lord, denying your need of the indwelling Spirit, is like a child insisting that it has wisdom and education enough, and needs no tutor to teach it to read or write; or like boarding a vessel bound for Liverpool, and insisting on steering the ship yourself, with no need of the captain's experienced hand or chart.

Without a doubt, dear Christian, this literal, tangible, incoming of the Holy Spirit is just what you need and have been longing for years.

Thank the Lord for salvation, for Jesus who shed His precious blood, but remember that just as it took three stories to complete the ark which lifted Noah and his family above the waves, just so it has taken the combined efforts of the Triune God, Father, Son and Holy Spirit, to form the ark that shall catch up His people above the waves of tribulation that shall soon sweep o'er this earth.

The dispensation of the Father, as recorded in the Old Testament, from Genesis to Malachi, is past; the dispensation of the Son and His walk upon this earth, as recorded in the four Gospels, ended; the dispensation of the Holy Spirit, which opened on the day of Pentecost, Acts 2, and will not close until the church and the members of the body have been sealed and caught up to meet the Lord, is nearing its completion. This age of the Holy Spirit was promised by the Father through the prophets in the Old Testament. Isaiah 28:11 declares that with stammering lips and another tongue will He speak to this people.

Speaking through the prophet Joel, our God promised the baptism of the Holy Spirit, saying:

"In the last days I will pour out My Spirit upon all flesh. Your sons and your daughters shall prophesy. . . . Upon My servants and My handmaidens I will pour out My Spirit. He will cause to come down for you the rain, both the former and the latter rain in the first month."

"Ask ye of the Lord rain in the time of the latter rain" another prophet writes, "and He will send bright clouds and give to everyone grass in the field."

John the Baptist caught the vision and prophesied to the multitude that flocked to him on Jordan's bank.

"I indeed baptize you with water unto repentance but He that cometh after me . . . He shall baptize you with the Holy Ghost and with fire."

How significant that John should select this particular prophecy concerning that which our Lord should do. He might have said,

"He, when He is come, will heal the sick; He will raise the dead; He will feed the multitude, or He will be smitten and nailed to the tree."

But though all these were wonderful and worthy of being declared by such a remarkable preacher, the thing which God spoke of Jesus through his inspired lips, was:

"He, when He is come,
HE SHALL BAPTIZE YOU WITH THE HOLY GHOST AND WITH FIRE."

Then came Jesus, who had been conceived of the Holy Spirit, and whose life was tenderly wrapped up and associated from birth to resurrection with the Spirit, and was baptized of John in the Jordan. Then it was that the Spirit in bodily form as of a dove came down and abode upon Him.

If Jesus needed this enduement of power before He began His ministry, how much more do you and I need the Spirit today. Many have asked the question:

"Why did Jesus not speak in tongues when He received the Holy Spirit?" We do not know whether He did or not. All power was given unto Him in Heaven and in earth, but we do know that we have no record of any person ever having spoken in tongues until the curtain rolled up on the dispensation of the Holy Spirit on the day of Pentecost as recorded in Acts 2. Then the very instant that the Holy Spirit came, those who received Him "began to speak with other tongues as He gave them utterance."

Have you ever been impressed, in reading the four Gospels, to notice the ever-increasing emphasis that the Lord placed upon the necessity for receiving the Holy Ghost? In fact the last words that He spoke, before His feet lifted from this earth and He was taken up from them into Heaven, were of the Holy Spirit, as recorded by Luke:

"Behold, I send the promise of My Father upon you, but tarry ye in the city of Jerusalem until ye be endued with power from on high" As recorded by Mark:

"These signs shall follow them that believe. In My name they shall cast out devils; they shall speak with new tongues" etc. As recorded in the first chapter of Acts:

"John truly baptised with water, but you shall be baptized with the Holy Ghost not many days hence. Ye shall receive power after that the Holy Ghost is come upon you, and ye shall be witnesses of Me both in Jerusalem and in Judea and Samaria and unto the uttermost parts of the earth." The next verse tells us that when He had spoken these things, while they beheld, He was taken up.

'Tis as though the last thing that had been upon the mind of the Lord, and that which He sought to impress upon His disciples, was the necessity of receiving the Holy Spirit. Oh, dear Christian, how can you hesitate any longer? Go quickly unto the Lord today, and under the precious blood, lift up your heart in praise and thanksgiving unto Him; ask, and you shall receive, seek, and you shall find, knock, and it shall be opened unto you, for He is truly more willing to give the Holy Spirit to them that ask Him than are our earthly parents to give good gifts to their children.

197

ALTHOUGH there were but twelve apostles, the Lord whilst here on earth had many disciples and followers. These disciples He commanded to go into all the world and preach the Gospel, but bade them tarry first in Jerusalem until they should be endued with power from on high.

Appearing to many after His resurrection, and He reiterated His command:

"Go, but tarry until you receive the Holy Spirit whom I shall send you from My Father above."

Just how many heard His command we know not. There were at least five hundred, but we do know that out of even that five hundred, three hundred and eighty knew a better way. Had they not walked with Jesus? Had they not seen the sick healed and miracles wrought? Their experience was good enough for them why should they go up to Jerusalem and tarry ten days for this promised power?

There were a faithful few, however, about one hundred and twenty in number, who were simple enough to believe the Lord implicitly, take Him at His word, and make haste into Jerusalem, there to tarry until the Comforter should come.

Have you ever tried to picture that little company hurrying along the streets toward the upper room, looking neither to the right nor the left; filled with but one idea, one longing to receive the Holy Spirit as their Lord had commanded.

Can you not close your eyes and picture Peter hurrying around the corner, a light of expectancy and hope in his eyes. Someone may have stopped him and said:

"Peter, where are you going in such a hurry?"

"I am on my way to the upper room, to tarry until I receive the gift of the Holy Spirit."

"Why Peter, you don't mean to say that you need the Holy Spirit?" Have not great miracles been wrought at your hands. Did you not preach throughout the land for Jesus? Were not the sick brought unto you, and did not demons go forth at your command? Surely you are mistaken.

You do not need the Holy Spirit. Then, too, you might lose your standing if people see you down seeking some new experience; they will think you are backslidden." But I can seem to hear Peter reply:

"Oh yes, I do, I do need the power of the Holy Ghost. There is such a lack in my life. Did you not hear how I denied the Lord? Failed in the most crucial testing hour. Hinder me not; I must be on my way. I need the Holy Spirit." And up the stairs He goes to "Tarry Until"

Before long other footsteps are heard, and round the corner comes -Thomas.

"Thomas, where are you going in such a hurry this morning?"

"Going to the upper room, there to receive the Holy Spirit. My Lord has ascended unto His Father that He might pour Him out upon us."

"But, Thomas, surely you do not think that an old doubter like you could ever receive such an experience."

"Yes, Glory to Jesus. The promise is unto me. The past is all under the blood. This is just the power that I need to banish doubts forever from my heart and mind," and on he hurries, down the street until he turns in at the upper room stairway.

Before he has more than vanished from sight, two soft, earnest voices are heard, and round the corner in their long, flowing robes, come Mary and Martha. By the light in their eyes and the tenderness of their voices it is easy to know they are talking about their beloved Jesus.

"Pardon me a moment, Sisters, Mary and Martha, but where are you going this morning?"

"We have come to Jerusalem, there to meet and wait with other hungry hearts in obedience to our Lord's command, until we have received the Comforter whom He shall surely send from on high."

"Oh, Mary," someone expostulates, "surely you do not mean to admit that you have lived so close to Jesus, you who have sat at His feet and learned of Him, need to tarry for another experience.

Now if it was Martha, I might understand, but you, Mary!"

"Ah, yes, Brother, every fiber of my being cries out the need of this promised gift of the

Father.

'Tis more than an experience, it is the incoming of the Holy Spirit who shall lead and guide into all truth, who shall pray through us with groanings that cannot be uttered, who shall take the things of Jesus and reveal them unto us, show us things to come and endue us with power from on high.

"Kindly pardon our haste, but we have no time to lose. Come, Martha, we must away."

What a procession they must have made, that little hundred and twenty. Yonder goes Mary Magdalene. From the other direction come James and John. There is Andrew and Philip, Bartholomew and Matthew, James and Judas but hark! Again I hear voices and the tread of feet upon the pavement, and round the corner comes Mary the Mother of Jesus, leaning upon the arms of His brethren. Though her head is bent a little and the lines in her pale face reveal the suffering and the sword which had lately pierced her heart, there is a new light and glorious hope shining in her eyes.

"Be not downcast, nor discouraged, my sons, for Jesus, your brother and my Son, hath plainly declared that lie would not leave us comfortless but that if He went away He would send another, even the Holy Ghost and that when He was come He would lead us into all truth."

"Why, Mary, thou pure virgin, surely Y-O-U do not need the Holy Spirit, you who were so consecrated and abandoned to the will of God that you could look up into the face of the angel in the face of misunderstanding, reproach, persecution, and the likelihood of being taken into the market square and stoned to death, as was the custom, and say:

"'Behold the handmaiden of the Lord. Be it done unto me even according to thy word'"

"You who have been sanctified through suffering and the death of your Lord, Mary, do you really mean to say that you feel the need of this baptism of the Holy Spirit?"

"Ah, yes, never did I feel the need of the Comforter as now that Jesus is gone unto His Father.

But even outside of my feeling the need of the Spirit, the command of my Lord would be enough for me. He said that I needed the Spirit. He commanded us to tarry until He came, and surely Jesus knew best." With a gracious bow they move on and e'er long lift their voices with those of the others in prayer and supplication in the upper room. (Acts 1:14.)

Who can describe or picture the heart-searching, the humbling, the crying out to be made conformable to the will of God's dear Son, that took place in the ten days that followed His ascension? We read that they continued with one accord, Peter not pointing to the failures of Thomas, nor do we read that any pointed the finger of accusation at Peter, saying:

"You have no business up here, you denied the Lord."

The past is all under the blood; past failures have been acknowledged, confessed and forgiven; earthly cares and the duties and the stress of the busy world outside have been shut out. With open hearts they simply and humbly wait before the Lord with prayers' and supplications, knowing that His Word cannot fail and that they that ask shall surely receive.

"And when the day of Pentecost was fully come, they were all with one accord in one place.

"And suddenly there came a sound from Heaven as of a rushing, mighty wind, and it filled all the house where they were sitting. And there appeared unto them cloven tongues like as of fire, and it sat upon each of them.

"And they were all filled with the Holy Ghost, and began to speak with other tongues, as 'the Spirit gave them utterance." (Acts 2:1-4.) They had met the conditions the Lord had kept His Word the Comforter had come.

Believer, are you tarrying before the Lord for the promise of Father today? Have you come to the end of yourself, empty, cleansed, humble, low under the precious blood of Jesus? Are you waiting with prayer and supplication as did those Bible saints of old? If so, the Lord will meet you quickly. God's time is now. It is not His will that you should wait until some vague tomorrow for His Spirit. In the day you seek Him with your whole heart He will be found of you.

Have you failed in the past? Have you at times denied your Lord just when you should

199

have stood most true? Have you been a doubting-Thomas? And do you feel your need of strength and power? Does your soul cry out for a greater revelation of Jesus and His Word, for a greater vision and a broader horizon? Then TARRY UNTIL you are endued with power from on high.

Believer, have you been used mightily in the past in soul- winning? Have the sick been healed and demons cast out in answer to your prayer?

Have you, like Mary of old, sat learning at the feet of Jesus? Has the joy of salvation and the presence of the Spirit abiding with you, and at times anointing with gladness until your soul overflowed with joy, seemed precious?

If so, thank God, but you, too, like Peter and John, Thomas and Bartholomew, with all the other apostles, and with Mary the Mother of Jesus, and the other women with their brethren, need the Holy Spirit. Oh, how you need Him! Doors are opening just before you. The land of Canaan a new land, a land of power and glory, lies just beyond. Jesus is coming soon. The message must be spread broadcast, and souls gathered in before His appearing.

He is calling you to go, preach the Gospel, witness to all about you GO, BUT TARRY UNTIL the Holy Spirit has come in to abide go, but tarry first in Jerusalem until you have been endued with power from on high.

THE BAPTISM OF THE HOLY SPIRIT

THE curtains of the clouds which angelic hands had saved together when, the redemptive work of Jesus on earth completed, His ascending form disappeared from view, had again been parted, and the Holy Spirit, of whom Jesus had said

"He will abide with you forever" had been sent forth from the presence of the Father. No sooner were they filled with the Holy Spirit than they began to speak with other tongues as the Spirit gave them utterance.

And they were all filled with the Spirit.

What was the immediate result and the outward evidence of that filling? They began to speak with other tongues.

Is there any record of anyone ever having spoken in other tongues (languages which they had never learned and were unknown to themselves; see I Cor. 14:2), previous to the day of Pentecost and the opening of the dispensation of the Holy Spirit? NO.

The devout Jews who were gathered into Jerusalem at this time, for the religious feasts and ceremonies, came running together in multitudes, and, upon hearing the languages of the countries in which they had been born, spoken by these simple, unlearned Galileans, they were amazed, astonished, and in doubt.

At what were the people astonished? At what did they marvel? At the rushing mighty wind?

No.

The tongues of fire? No; they are not again mentioned, and it is doubtful whether those who came together after the one hundred and twenty had been filled even saw them.

What then? They were amazed and marveled at the supernatural power that rested upon these men and women, causing them to reel and stagger, Acts 2:13, as though drunken with wine, and to speak with tongues unknown to themselves.

The spectators who looked upon the out-pouring of the Holy Ghost on the day of Pentecost were divided into two classes just as they are today.

One class were the mockers, who said in derision, "These men are full of new wine. Come on, let's have nothing to do with these people. They are fanatics. This is all excitement.? Tis ridiculous to create so much noise and excitement over religion; the whole city is in an uproar; nothing but wildfire. They ought to be arrested" etc.

The other class were the thinkers the thoughtful, intelligent men and women, who said:

"Wait a moment. There must surely be something behind all this. The ring in these people's voices the shout in their souls the joy and love, worship and adoration reflected in their faces there must be some specific reason for it. They are certainly not reeling and staggering about like that for nothing. They must surely realize that the people who look on will make fun of them and think they have lost their senses.

If they are not doing it for money nor for popularity, then why are they doing it? They are certainly not all fools. If there were only one or two we might think they were, but here are about one hundred and twenty; surely they cannot all be mad. I am going to investigate this matter and see what there is behind it all.

Tell us, Oh tell us, some of you good, happy people in there stop your shouting and your rejoicing for a little space, and answer
WHAT MEANETH THIS?"

Then Peter, standing up
"Peter, what are you rising up for? Are you frightened, Peter? Are you going to run away and seek to escape from this big, excited, questioning multitude as you did from the little girl that night you denied the Lord?"

"Burn away? Oh no! I will never run away any more now. I have been baptized with the Holy Ghost and fire. He has endued me with power from on high. He has taken fear away and put a holy boldness within my heart and words within my mouth, insomuch that out of my innermost being flow forth rivers of living water." Acts 4:13.

And Peter, standing up (ah, the Holy Spirit puts a real "stand up for Jesus" in the timid soul) with the eleven, lifted up his voice and said:

"Ye men of Judea, and all ye that dwell at Jerusalem, be this known unto you, and hearken to my words; for these are not drunken, as ye suppose, seeing it is but the third hour of the day, but this is that which was spoken of the prophet Joel. It shall come to pass in the last days, saith God, I will pour out My Spirit upon all flesh. Your sons and your daughters shall prophesy ... on My servants and My handmaidens I will pour out in those days of My Spirit, and they shall prophesy. I will show wonders in the Heavens above, signs in the earth beneath . . . and it shall come to pass that whosoever shall call on the name of the Lord shall be saved.

"Ye men of Israel, hear these words; Jesus of Nazareth ... ye have taken, and by wicked hands have crucified and slain."

"Why, Peter, aren't you afraid to talk like that to this great mob of people? Do you not know that they gnash their teeth and hiss at the very name of Jesus? Are you not aware that you are laying yourself open to the danger of being seized upon, carried to the whipping post, stripped, beaten and stoned to death? I thought that you were a timid man who was ashamed to be known as one of them?"

"Oh no, I will never be ashamed to be called one of the despised, persecuted, peculiar few any more.
The Holy Ghost has come to abide in this life of mine, and the words that I speak I speak not of myself; the works that I do I do not of myself, but the Holy Spirit who has come to dwell within, He speaks the words; He does the works.

This Jesus hath God raised up, whereof we are witnesses. Therefore being by the right hand of God exalted and having received of the Father the promise of the Holy Ghost, He hath shed forth this which you see (in the reeling bodies of those who appear to be drunken), and hear (in the speaking in other tongues)."

So boldly did this transformed man speak under the mighty power of the Holy Spirit that his hearers were pricked to their hearts and said unto Peter and the rest of the apostles:

"Men and brethren, what shall we do?"

"Then Peter said unto them Repent, and be baptized, every one of you, in the name of Jesus Christ for the remission of sins, and ye shall receive the gift of the Holy Ghost.

For the promise is unto you, and to your children, and to all that are afar off, even as many as the Lord our God shall call."

What promise is unto all that are afar off, even as many as the Lord God shall call, Peter? The promise of the Holy Ghost that which you see and hear.

But how much of the promise is unto us, Peter? Surely not all this mighty power accompanied with the speaking in tongues. Was this not only the opening of the dispensation and for the Jews?

But no, says Peter, "The promise is unto them that are afar off, even as many as the Lord shall call, for now in Christ Jesus there is neither Jew nor Gentile; there is neither bond nor free. In Him we are one and are baptized into the one body."

Acts 10:44, eight years after the day of Pentecost, the door of salvation and the baptism of the Holy Spirit is opened unto the Gentiles. Walking into the home of Cornelius, in the 44th verse, we find a meeting in progress. Cornelius has gathered his household, his servants, and his neighbors together to hear the words which Peter is to speak, words whereby they may be saved.

"And while Peter yet spake these words, the Holy Ghost fell on all them which heard the Word.

"And they of the circumcision which believed were astonished, as many as came with Peter, because that on the Gentiles also was poured out the gift of the Holy Ghost.

"For they heard them speak with tongues, and magnify God."

In all these eight years the manner in which the Holy Spirit came in had not been changed the same Bible evidence speaking in tongues, remained. Even though there were no foreigners who came from other countries and spoke other languages, present to be benefited by the speaking in tongues, the Spirit spoke through them just the same, as He had on the day of Pentecost, In Acts 19 a new voice is heard preaching Jesus Christ and the baptism of the Holy Spirit.

"have you received the Holy Ghost since you believed?"

Why, that voice and face seems familiar. have we seen or heard this man before?

Excuse me, brother, but is your name not Saul of Tarsus? Is this really you preaching the necessity of receiving the baptism of the Holy Spirit! I thought you condemned all this, thought it to be folly and not to be permitted. Did you not say that you were going to put an end to all this nonsense, when, after you had looked on approvingly at the stoning of Stephen, you rode away to Damascus with the intention of still further persecuting these Pentecostal Holy Ghost people?"

"Yes, I used to persecute these Christians. I thought that they were all wrong and should be wiped out of existence, but that was before my eyes were opened.

Did you not hear how that, when riding on my way to do them greater hurt, the light of the Lord shone round about me and I was stricken from my horse and fell as one dead in the dust of the road, and how Jesus, whose face was brighter than the sun, and whose raiment was whiter than the light, came and spoke to me, saying:

'Saul, Saul, why persecutest thou Me?'

Three days was I blind from the vision of His brightness. Then was I converted and my name was changed from Saul to Paul.

Yes, I am one of them today. I will talk with you later, but now I must go on with my meeting."

After the baptismal service wherein the disciples are buried in the watery grave, in verse six, we see Paul laying his hands upon them, and read that the Holy Ghost came on them and they spoke with tongues and prophesied. Here, as in Jerusalem and in the house of Cornelius, the first thing that was mentioned of the souls that received the Holy Spirit was that they spoke with tongues.

In Acts 8:17, 18, we find sinful and wicked Simon the sorcerer, so impressed with the mighty power displayed when the believers received the Holy Ghost upon the laying on of the apostles' hands, that he offered money to the apostles in the hopes of being able to purchase the same power, saying:

"Give me also this power, that on whomsoever I lay my hands, he may receive the Holy Ghost."

Without a doubt Simon saw and heard the same things that the onlookers saw and heard on the day of Pentecost. But Oh, this power could not be bought. All the money in the world could not have purchased it, but to those who humble themselves in lowliness and in sincerity before the Lord shall the Spirit be given freely without money and without price.

Oh, tell me, Peter and Paul, tell me John and James, and all you who received this mighty incoming of the Holy Ghost with its attendant power and glory, may we, in this 20th century, receive .this like precious gift, or did the Holy Spirit empty Himself of all His power in the apostolic days? Did you consume all of these supernatural wondrous blessings, or did you leave enough to spare for us today?

"Yes, indeed" they answer in unison. "Heaven has not gone bankrupt. Heaven's storehouse still is full. The Holy Spirit has never lost His power, the promise is unto them that are afar off, even as many as the Lord our God shall call. Did not our Lord say: 'When He is come, He will abide with you forever'?

"Doubt no longer, but with open heart ask ye of the Lord rain in the time of the latter rain. Remember the words of Joel the prophet: 'It shall come to pass in the LAST days,' saith God, 'I will pour out My Spirit upon all flesh.' Remember, too, that when the high priest went in to the Holy of Holies the bells rang, and when the high priest came out the bells rang again.

"When Jesus ascended up on high the bells rang and the people spoke with tongues and magnified God. Now this same Jesus, our high priest, is coming forth again for His waiting church, and on earth the bells are ringing, the latter rain is falling, and again those who have received the oldtime power speak with other tongues."

WORK OF THE HOLY SPIRIT

JUST as God the Father promised, with ever increasing emphasis in the Old Testament the coming time in which His Son should be manifested, so during the latter months of Jesus' ministry He promised when He went away He also would bestow a gift upon the world, even the Holy Ghost.

As the hour of his departure approached, and Calvary's cross cast its shadow over the fearful hearts of His disciples, Jesus more and more sought to impress upon the minds of His people the necessity and importance of receiving His gift the Comforter.

So many times did the Lord promise the Spirit and explain the importance of His coming and His office work in our lives from conviction to baptism, and on to perfection, that time and space will permit our giving only a few quotations at this time.

In the 16th chapter of John, Jesus said: "It is expedient for you that I go away; for if I go not away the Comforter will not come unto you, but if I depart I will send Him unto you." Here and in other places He begins to enumerate the different reasons why we should receive the Holy Ghost, and to explain still more fully His office work in this world:

(1) When He is come He will reprove the world of sin, and of righteousness, and of judgment. John 16:8.

(2) Howbeit when He, the Spirit of truth is come, He will guide you into all truth. John 16:13.

(3) He will not speak of himself; but whatsoever he shall hear, that shall he speak. John 16:13.

(4) He will show you things to come. John 16:13.

(5) He shall glorify ME. John 16:14.

(6) He shall receive of mine, and show it unto you. John 16:14.

(7) But when the Comforter is come, whom I w4ll send you from the Father, even the Spirit of truth, which proceedeth from the Father, He shall testify of me. John 15:26.

(8) But the Comforter, which is the Holy Ghost, whom the Father will send in my name, He shall teach you all things and bring all things to your remembrance, whatsoever I have said unto you. John 14:26.

(9) But ye shall receive power after that the Holy Ghost is come upon you. Acts 1:8.

Jesus' parting words to His little flock after His death and resurrection, as His pierced feet were rising from earth as He ascended to His Father, rang out clear and plain: "Behold I send the promise of my Father upon you: but tarry in Jerusalem until ye be endued with power from on high." Luke 24:49.

True to His commission, Acts 1:12 shows the little band of faithful followers (one hundred and twenty in number) wending their way to Jerusalem, to tarry until they should receive the promised gift. "And when they were come in, they went up into an upper room, where abode both Peter and James and John, and Andrew and Philip and Thomas, Bartholomew and Matthew, James the son of Alphaeus, and Simon Zelotes, and Judas the brother of James. These all continued with one accord in prayer and supplication with the women and Mary the mother of Jesus, and with His brethren. Acts 1:13, 14.

PENTECOST

Then just as the Father, true to His word gave Jesus, His promised gift to redeem the world, so Jesus at the close of His dispensation fulfilled His word, and bestowed the gift of the Holy Ghost to abide with us forever. "And when the day of Pentecost was fully come they were all with one accord in one place; and suddenly there came a sound from Heaven as of a rushing mighty wind, and it filled all the house where they were sitting. And there appeared unto them cloven tongues like as of fire and it sat upon each of them; and they WERE ALL FILLED WITH THE HOLY GHOST, AND BEGAN TO SPEAK IN

OTHER TONGUES, AS THE SPIRIT GAVE THEM UTTERANCE. Acts 2:4.
CAESAREA

The same Bible evidence, speaking in other tongues (that is; languages they had never learned), accompanied the incoming of the Holy Ghost at Caesarea, for we read that while Peter was preaching Jesus to them and telling them of His death, burial and resurrection . . . "while Peter yet spoke these words, the Holy Ghost fell on all of them which heard the word. . . .

FOR THEY HEARD THEM SPEAK WITH TONGUES AND MAGNIFY GOD." Acts 10: 44-46.
EPHESUS

This same sign accompanied the incoming of the Holy Spirit during Paul's ministry at Ephesus, for we read: "And it came to pass that while Apollos was at Corinth, Paul having passed through the upper coasts came to Ephesus: and finding certain disciples he said unto them:

"'have ye received the Holy Spirit since ye believed?' And they said unto him: 'We have not so much as heard whether there be any Holy Ghost

AND WHEN PAUL HAD LAID HIS HANDS ON THEM, THE HOLY GHOST GAME UPON THEM, AND THEY SPAKE WITH TONGUES AND PROPHESIED" Acts 19:l-6.

Simon the sorcerer, seeing the gift of the Holy Ghost bestowed through the laying on of the apostles' hands, was willing to pay money for the power that he saw manifested through the apostles.

Just as God the Father and Jesus Christ His Son gave gifts unto the world, so in turn the Holy Spirit bestows His gifts upon all who receive him and yield themselves wholly unto Him.

The gifts of the Spirit are found in 1st Corinthians 12:8-10.

(1) Wisdom,
(2) Knowledge,
(3) Faith,
(4) Healing,
(5) Miracles,
(6) Prophecy,
(7) Discernment of Spirits,
(8) Divers kinds of Tongues,
(9) Interpretation of Tongues;

all of which were manifested in their midst, even as we see them manifested in our midst today.

We are still in the dispensation of the Holy Ghost; have been ever since the day of Pentecost; and will be until the coming of the Lord.

He is still here to convict the sinner of his sin, for no man can come to the Father, except the Spirit draw him. He is here to lead the repentant soul to Jesus, to apply the blood to his heart, to bear witness with his spirit that he is now a child of God, and has passed from darkness unto light, from bondage unto liberty, from death unto life and to rejoice with him in the finished work of Calvary.

Just as the Spirit was with the sinner to condemn him and convict him of unrighteousness, so He is now with the regenerated heart to lead him on in righteousness and to baptize him with the Holy Ghost, and witness that the work of perfection has begun. Jesus said: He who is with you shall be in you, and Peter said: "Repent and be baptized every one of you in the name of Jesus Christ for the remission of sins, and ye shall receive the gift of the Holy Ghost; for the promise is unto you, and to your children; and

TO ALL THAT ARE AFAR OFF, EVEN AS MANY AS THE LORD OUR GOD SHALL CALL. Acts 2:38, 39.

The blood washed heart with whom the Spirit is bearing witness is now a clean, empty

205

temple for the third person of the Trinity to enter. When we seek with all our heart, humbly, prayerfully, praisefully, He will come in to abide, and seal us unto the day of redemption, giving us today the same Bible evidence speaking in other tongues, as the Spirit gives utterance as He did in the days of old.

When the Holy Ghost comes in to abide He takes control of body, soul and spirit; out of our innermost being there flows forth rivers of living water. Even the vocal organ the unruly member, the tongue He takes hold of and controls. Jesus is made so real, and our souls so overflow with praise as the Spirit reveals the King in His beauty that here, it seems, our language fails, and we cry out: "Where, my soul, shall I begin to praise the name of Jesus!" Then the Holy Spirit himself rises up within and glorifies Jesus in a language that we know not, and as we hear Him speaking for Himself floods of joy, and billows of glory sweep over our whole being and we realize that the Holy Spirit is praising our Bridegroom with more beautiful praise than we ever could have thought of.

Oh, glory to Jesus, for wells and rivers of praise that do not have to be pumped up nor primed, but gush forth in uncontrollable, ecstatic glory and thanksgiving!

The baptism of the Holy Ghost is the incoming of the Spirit as the great leader who is to guide us from earth to Heaven; who is never to leave us until we meet the Lord in the air. As we yield ourselves to Him He leads us to higher heights and deeper depths, and causes us to be

"Changed from glory to glory,
'Till in Heaven we take our place,
'Till we cast our crowns before Him,
Lost in wonder, love and praise."

Oh, dear one, if you have not yet received the Holy Spirit in His fullness, seek Him with all your heart, and when He comes in you will have the same Biblical evidence that they had in Bible times, speaking in other tongues

AS THE SPIRIT GIVES UTTERANCE. THE LORD HAS NO TWENTIETH CENTURY MODE OF BAPTIZING PEOPLE IN THE HOLY GHOST, BUT STILL FILLS AND SEALS IN THE SAME WAY HE DID IN THE EARLY DAYS.

The latter rain is falling on the earth.

"And I say unto you, ask and it shall be given unto you, seek and ye shall find, knock and it shall be opened unto you. For every one that asketh receiveth, and he that seeketh findeth, and to him that knocketh it shall be opened. If a son shall ask bread of any of you that is a father, will he give him a stone? or if he ask a fish give him a serpent? or if he shall ask an egg, will he offer him a scorpion? If ye then, being evil, know how to give good gifts to your children, how much more shall your Heavenly Father give the Holy Spirit to them that ask Him."

A PLAIN TALK TO SEEKERS

"Ask, and it shall be given you; Seek, and ye shall find; Knock, and it shall be opened unto you. For every one that asketh receiveth; and he that seeketh findeth; and to him that knocketh it shall be opened. If a son shall ask bread of any of you that is a father will he give him a stone? Or, if he ask a fish, will he for a fish give him a serpent? Or, if he shall ask an egg, will he offer him a scorpion? If ye then, being evil, know how to give good gifts unto your children; how much more shall your Heavenly Father give the Holy Spirit to them that ask Him?" Luke 11:9-13.

FROM AN AFTERNOON TALK GIVEN AT THE NATION-WIDE CAMP MEETING

IF THERE is any humble little ministry that the Lord has given me, it has been mainly that of praying for those seeking the baptism of the Holy Spirit. Each member of the body should have its own particular ministry. Some are definitely led out along the line of praying for the sick, and when the message comes that someone is ill and suffering in body, there is that within the child of God which leaps up with great desire to pray for the sick one. Others are led out definitely along the line of casting out demons, and the Spirit rises up within them, using them with great unction and power.

As for myself, whenever I hear of someone seeking the baptism of the Holy Spirit with all his heart, I feel such great drawing power within that I can scarcely resist leaping over all the others to get to that person 'to pray for him that he may receive. Ofttimes I have been invited to go to meetings far and near without feeling any particular interest in the call until word would come saying:

"O, we have so many here that are just starving and crying for the baptism of the Holy Ghost; do come and pray for them." And immediately a great urging would rise within me to go and pray for those precious seekers. When God gives us this longing to see seekers filled with the Spirit, how much more does the Father Himself long to pour out the Spirit on all those who wait upon Him.

My heart goes out to all the dear seekers who are tarrying for the baptism of the Holy Spirit.

How I long to bring you a message from the Lord, a message of encouragement and instruction that will help to lift up the hands that hang down and strengthen the feeble knees, that will cause you to press on into this glorious realm, this life filled and controlled by the Holy Spirit!

First of all let us make it plain that God is on the giving hand, and is more willing GOD'S TIME to give than you are to receive. Let is NOW us remember that God's time is now, not tomorrow, but NOW.

Many people say: "Well, when God is ready, when my time comes, He will baptize me with the Holy Spirit." Dear ones, the WAITING Lord has been ready for many years; GOD'S TIME it is YOU who have not been ready.

He is waiting above you just now, longing to pour into your soul great floods of glory, and to make you the Temple of the Holy Spirit. If the devil can make you believe that you are waiting for the Lord to fill you, if he can persuade you to put off definite seeking day after day, day after day. Till Jesus comes and vou will be found still waiting unfilled with the Spirit, he will have fulfilled his purpose.

O, dear heart, stop forever making this excuse.

If you are not filled with the Holy Spirit today it will be your own fault, not the fault of the Lord, for He is more willing to give than you are to receive.

Others say, "I would like to receive the Holy Spirit, but I am afraid I am not ready." Well, beloved, how long would it take God NOT READY to get you ready? Just one moment, as long as it takes you to get under the blood. I have seen sinners come to the altars in our tent just laden with sin and iniquity. I have seen them fall on their knees, and throwing up their hands, cry aloud to God

207

for mercy; I have seen the light breaking over their faces and the glory sweeping over their souls as they passed from death unto life, and their sins were washed away. Inside of fifteen minutes from the time that they came to the altar seeking salvation I have seen such penitents fall prostrate under the power of the Spirit, receive the Holy Ghost, and burst forth speaking in other tongues as the Spirit gave utterance. I have watched such lives through the following years, and know that they are standing today declaring the whole Word of God, and living a holy life before Him. God has no favorites, He is no respecter of persons, we are all on one common footing before Him. What He has done for others He will do for you.

If you feel that you are unworthy, that is a splendid, humble place from which to start seeking. Come empty and be filled. Just tell Father all about it; ask Him to cover you with the precious blood afresh today, and under the covering of that blood ask Him to fill you with the Holy Spirit, that He may lead and direct and fill your whole life for His honor and glory.

Someone else says: "Well, I have been seeking for years, and I have never received." But O, as I look over the long altar benches with seekers in our tabernacle, I find so many that think they are seeking who are in reality just sitting down at ease, resting their heads in their hands, elbow propped on the altar bench, hardly open their mouths to praise God. No desperate earnestness or hundred-fold praises, and they call that seeking. Look up all good gifts come from above.

I have in my hand a glass, an empty glass. In my other hand I have a pitcher, filled with cool, refreshing water. Let us say you are the glass, and that Jesus is holding the pitcher filled with water, which is a type of the Holy Spirit. We want to fill the tumbler with water, but it is turned bottom side up, the mouth is down, just as many of you seekers put your heads down instead of up. We can pour all the water we like on the bottom of the tumbler, but it will never be filled. It will come out from under the downpour just as empty as ever, wondering why all the other tumblers were filled and it left empty.

But now let us turn the tumbler right side up.

Pour the water out from the pitcher and the glass begins to fill and fill and fill, till the water is overflowing on the dry ground all about it. Dear ones, do just like this glass, look up. Lift your face up toward the Heavens, lift up your hands, begin to praise God with all your soul, and He will fill you to overflowing.

Another seeker says, "Ah! but I fear I will not run over or be demonstrative; I am deep, I am such a quiet sort of a person; I believe in praising the Lord in my heart."

Dear ones, there is not one of you so deep but what God can fill you. You may feel that you are big and deep, but God is bigger and deeper than you, and when He fills you just so full, you have to run over and speak, as the Spirit gives utterance, the glorious praises of Jesus.

Take, for instance, this pitcher filled with water: it is larger than the glass the tumbler cannot

possibly contain all the water held in the pitcher it must overflow. Just so, God is bigger than you, and when He pours the Holy Spirit into your heart you must overflow with His praises.

Now we will suppose that we have a glass which was marred in the making. There is no way of filling it, but the glass with the wide open mouth can be readily filled.

Then we will take a bottle with a small mouth; it takes a great deal longer to fill than it does the tumbler. Seekers, "Open your mouth wide and I will fill it, saith the Lord."

We open our mouths wide as for the latter rain. O, Hallelujah! Open up every avenue of your being, every channel of your soul, open your lips in praise, "be ye lifted up, ye everlasting doors, and the King of Glory shall come in."

ASK, AND YE SHALL RECEIVE

Ask, and you shall receive. Here is a definite promise from God. If you ask, He has promised that it shall be given you. Remember the widow who went to the unjust judge; at first he refused her, but morning after morning we can picture her putting on her hat, walking down the road to the judge's office, knocking on the door, and waiting her turn till she could cry out: "O, Judge, please avenge me of mine adversary." When she was refused she was still undaunted, and the next morning found her pressing and pinning on her hat, walking down the road and up to the judge's office, waiting her turn again, and saying: "O, Judge, please avenge me of mine adversary."

Refused again, she was still undismayed, and the next morning found her again in the ante-room. No doubt the judge said: "Is that woman here again to weary me?" But again she pled her cause.

Oh, I believe that when the unjust judge granted her request, he seized his pen and paper quickly, and wrote off the order, and said: "Here, woman, take it quick, and get out of my sight. You weary me with your oft coming."

Ah! dear ones, if the unjust judge heard the widow's plea, how much more will our just Father hear your cry. If you ask, you shall surely receive, yes, and receive quickly, for in such an hour as ye think not he shall come suddenly and fill His temple.

SEEK, AND YE SHALL FIND

Here is another definite promise. Do you remember the woman who saved the floor, lighted a candle and saved on until she found her lost money? Oh, dear hearts, be willing to rise early in the morning to seek, and to seek by the lighted candle if necessary. Seek till you forget your meals, till you forget your bed; forget all else till His gift is received.

KNOCK, AND IT SHALL BE OPENED UNTO YOU

If the door has not been opened unto you, the fault is not with God. Perhaps there has been something amiss with your knocking. Do you remember the man who went to knock at his friend's door for bread, and he said: "Friend, rise and give me three loaves; a friend of mine in his journey has come, and I have nothing to set before him"?

But the man from within answered him:

"Trouble me not. My children are with me in bed; the hour is late."

Perhaps the enemy has whispered to you: "Come now, it is eleven o'clock; time you were in bed.

You know you have to get up early in the morning."

How often have you reasoned like this, and gone to your rest, but not so with the man who knocked in the Bible. "Knock, and it shall be opened unto you." Oh, I love these definite assurances of our God. "Heaven and earth shall pass away, but not one jot or title shall fail until all be fulfilled."

"Rap! Rap! Rap!" I can hear that man knocking at the door.

"Trouble me not," says the voice from above.

"Rap! Rap! Rap!" "O, friend, arise and give me three loaves."

"The hour is late; surely you can come back another time for bread."

"Rap! Rap! Rap!" "A friend in his journey has come and I have nothing to set before him. Rise and give me the three loaves."

And so the man knocked and knocked, and rapped, and called and pled, till at last the man from above swung his feet out of bed, lighted his candle, went to the pantry shelf, jerked out three loaves of bread, and thrust them into his neighbor's hand, and said: "Here, man, here are your three loaves not because you are my friend, but because of your importunity. Take them, and go your way."

How much more then shall Jesus, who is our friend, the friend above every other friend, rise and give us the blessed, promised Holy Ghost.

Do you feel ashamed before God this afternoon for the feeble pretense of your asking and seeking and knocking? Rise, beloved, and seek Him with all your heart, for here is a promise that you can stand on flat-footed, without wavering or doubting.

"In the day that ye seek Me with your whole heart, I will be found of you" If you seek

Him, then with your W-H-O-L-E H-E-A-R-T, your whole mind and strength and voice, He shall be found of you, for "Every one that asketh receiveth."

We have heard many people say, "Oh, Sister, I fear the Holy Spirit is not for me." Now, dear ones, look at God's Word. Can you not believe Him? "Every NOT FOR ME one that asketh receiveth." God is no respecter of persons. You are just as dear to Him as any other child.

"Every one." Yes, that means you, dear, discouraged soul. "He that seeketh findeth, and to him that knocketh it shall be opened."

Then someone says, "Yes, I would like to receive the Holy Spirit, but I am so afraid when the power of God falls upon me that it might be my own mind, or the flesh, or the devil." "I am so afraid that I might receive something that was counterfeit and not of God." Here is a promise for you, dear, timid soul. "If a son ask bread of any of you that is a father, will ye give him a stone, or if he ask fish, will he for fish give a serpent, or if he ask an egg will he offer him a scorpion?" In the Eastern countries the loaves of brown bread resembled very much a stone. The eel, which is a member of the fish family, resembles very much the serpent. The egg of the scorpion resembles very much the eggs which are used in domestic cooking. Now, we do not deny that there is the counterfeit. The devil is always trying to counterfeit God's work. We do not deny that there is the stone, the serpent and the scorpion. But we do deny that our Heavenly Father gives stones, scorpions and serpents to His blood-washed children.

Oh, how the Father's heart must be grieved when you go to Him under the precious blood and say, "I would like the Holy Spirit, but am so afraid that if I get down on my knees here at the altar with these Pentecostal folks and ask for it, You might give me a serpent, or a demon, or a counterfeit spirit." Are you, then, afraid of your Father? If this is the kind of father you have, a father that you are afraid to trust, a father who would give you a serpent instead of a fish, a scorpion instead of an egg, you had better change your father and accept God as your parent? for He gives good gifts to His children.

If you had ten dollars in your hand, and you found that one of them was a counterfeit, would you throw away the other nine dollars and say you were never going to handle another dollar again?

Why, of course, you would not. If you happen to have been so unfortunate as to have seen someone who was not genuine, will you then discountenance all that God has done, and say, because this one had a wrong spirit, which had never been received from God, that you would henceforth cease seeking for the genuine gift of the Holy Ghost?

Just suppose you invited me to come to your house for dinner. You had read my writings, you had heard people speak of me, and now you were writing me a letter of invitation to dine and spend a few days of rest. I accept your invitation and take my suitcase and travel many miles to get to your home. I rap at your door and you open to me, and ask:

"Who are you?" I reply, "Why, I am Sister McPherson. You invited me to come to spend a few days with you for rest and quiet;" and you look at me with a doubtful air, and say:

"Well, you do not look just as I thought Sister McPherson would. I thought she would be a much older woman. I had pictured her differently. You are not dressed as I thought Sister McPherson would be dressed. Your voice is not just the same as I imagined it would be, and I fear you are not the woman you claim to be."

I reply: "Why, yes, dear sister, I really am the one you have invited here." But you still hold the door almost closed, and peer out through the aperture and say:

"No, I really cannot let you in; I am so fearful. I am afraid that you are not the one that I invited here. Perhaps I just imagine you are.

Perhaps it might be myself, that just thinks it is you, or you may be the devil, himself, for all I know."

How grieved, and hurt, and surprised I should be. I should probably take up my suitcase, walk slowly down the steps, and the next time an invitation came to go to your house, I should be just a little hesitant, perhaps, in moving in that direction.

Now, how many of you have done just this with the Holy Spirit? You have read about Him. You have heard about Him from some who have described His glorious presence to you, and you have invited Him to come into your house and make you His Temple. But when He came to your door, when you began to tremble under His power, you drew back and said:

"Oh, perhaps this is only myself" When He began to knock gently at the door of your lips, to stammer with His power, or you were prostrated to the floor, you straightway permitted the devil to whisper doubts into your ear, and said: "Why, this is not just as I imagined the Holy Spirit was to come. I thought He would come as a still, small dove, or vice versa,, I expected Him to come as a mighty, rushing wind. Perhaps this is not the Holy Spirit. Perhaps this is the devil, himself."

Oh, you grieve and wound the dear Holy Spirit, and He spreads his pinions and passes on to others kneeling beside you, and fills them instead, and you wonder why they are filled and you are left unfilled.

So many people I find have got it all fixed up in their minds just how the Holy Spirit is going to come to them. Some feel that He is to come to them as a still, small dove, in a gentle way as they sit in their seats, or as they kneel in a dignified manner at the altar. To such He usually comes as a mighty, rushing wind, slaying them under the power and giving mighty manifestations.

Others have it all figured out that the Holy Spirit is to come to them as a great dynamic, explosive power, accompanied with a mighty, rushing wind and tongues of flame and great manifestations.

To these He sometimes comes as the still, small dove, and quietly fills them, speaking through them in other tongues softly and tenderly, the glorious praises of Jesus and the message of His coming. But in whatsoever form He comes, do not doubt Him. You have invited Him to come, now just receive Him.

When you come to the altar, come determined to praise God. Come not to seek, but to receive.

Do not look miles and miles away for the Holy Ghost to come to you, for He is right near you. Praise and glorify the name of Jesus with ALL your heart, and He will pour His Spirit upon you.

Some say: "Well, I am not going to praise the Lord when I do not feel like it, I do not want to put anything on." I do not believe there is a person in the world that dislikes seeing anybody put anything on more than I do myself, but bless the Lord, there is one thing that God's Word authorizes us to put on, and that is to put on praise as a garment. "Well, but," you say, "I cannot praise Him unless I feel like it."

Is that the way your spiritual life is ruled, by feeling? Praise Him because He is worthy; because He has washed your sins away. Praise Him because he deserves all the praise in Heaven and in earth forever and forever, and you soon will feel like praising Him. Bless His Holy Name! Do not attempt to go by feeling. Isaac was the only man in the Bible that went by feeling. Just see how much he was deceived. He got hold of the wrong son through feeling the hairy covering that was upon his son's arm. Do not go by feeling, but go by faith.

Oftentimes when our altars are filled with hungry seekers, I stand on the platform for a moment looking over the people, and wondering to myself, "Where shall I begin? Whom shall I pray for first?" And passing by the ones who are sitting down resting their heads on their hands, in a half-hearted way, I look for that one who acts as though he were desperately in earnest, who, with uplifted hands and face, is praising God from the depths of His heart and seeking with all his might; and we workers say to ourselves: "There is someone who is desperately in earnest. Let us go and pray for that one." And do you know, I believe that is almost the way the Lord looks down upon it. And He stands there this afternoon at this altar, ready and willing to pour out His Spirit; He is looking for someone who is seeking with all his heart. This one He will surely fill. Praise the Lord until you feel his power taking control of you, until your lips begin to move and tremble under the power, then stop talking in your own language and let the Holy Spirit do the rest. You have nothing to do at all but yield and He will speak.

In my experience of seeking the Holy Spirit, there was day after day when He came upon

211

me with stammering lips before He spoke in other tongues. Since I have received the baptism, I can see where I hindered Him from speaking in other tongues a great deal. Every time that my lips would begin to tremble and my chin to quiver, I would begin to praise the Lord with redoubled force, feeling that if ever I praised Him I must praise Him then, or He would leave me. This was perhaps a mistake, as two could not talk at once, and while I was doing the talking the Holy Spirit could not speak.

We are all too courteous to interrupt another while he is speaking, and the Holy Spirit is just as courteous as we are. When I got all through talking and just yielded my lips, my tongue, and all my vocal organs, the stammering increased, and the first thing I knew my chin began to quiver and jerk sideways and up and down, my tongue began to move about in my mouth, and as I gave Him my voice He began to make strange sounds, syllables, words, fragments of sentences, and then like a mighty torrent there flowed forth from my innermost being rivers of praise, as the Spirit gave utterance in other tongues. Praise Him, dear ones, until you feel His power upon your lips, your vocal organs, then as you have talked all your life, be still and let the Holy Spirit do the talking. He can praise Jesus in so much more excellent a way than you can. He has glorious words that our human minds can never fathom.

Rivers of praise will flow forth, rising and rising until they ascend to the Father's throne in glorious tributes of thanksgiving.

Falling, falling, 'tis the latter rain.

Coming, coming, Pentecost again.

Hasten, hasten, 'tis the day of power.

Come beneath the Holy Spirit's shower.

WHAT a glorious privilege it is to live in these last days, the days of the latter rain.

The Holy Spirit is being poured out in a wonderful manner. Showers of blessing are falling.

Times of refreshing have come from the presence of the Lord refreshing for the dry and parched ground, the barren fields, the trees, the grain, everything and everybody, in fact, that comes beneath its downpour.

There is no excuse or reason for any hungry, blood-washed child of God to remain in a barren, fruitless condition, pining for the Holy Spirit. He is being outpoured as the rain from Heaven, and is willing to baptize, fill, and come in to abide wherever an empty, hungry, upturned vessel is found. Turn your cup right side up, and if you are out in the open where the rain is falling, He will surely fill you now.

The Lord is no respecter of persons. Old and young, black or white, yellow or brown, the servant and the maid, irrespective of race or creed, are invited to ask, that they may receive. "Every one that asketh receiveth; and he that seeketh findeth."

Latter Rain for the asking. The precious Holy Spirit for the seeking. Hallelujah!

As Peter stood, filled to overflowing under the downpour of the moderate former rain lifting up his eyes and, with the "clairvoyance of the Spirit, looking away ahead and seeing the latter rain falling upon our generation, he cried aloud: "This is that which was spoken by the prophet Joel" - and declared that "the promise is unto you, and to your children, and to all that are afar off, even as many as the Lord our God shall call."

Ask ye of the Lord rain in the time of the latter rain; so the Lord shall make bright clouds, and give them showers of rain, to everyone grass in the field. Poor, drooping, struggling soul, thirsting and wilting in your spirit, look up what you need is the Holy Spirit, His incoming is as necessary to your spiritual growth and health, as is rain to the grass and flowers of the field. The Spirit is being outpoured upon all who come beneath His downpour. If you are not filled it is because you are under cover of some sort, or else your cup is wrong side up or filled with something else.

If you are in a house of theology, forms, ceremonies, preconceived ideas or teachings, the roof is too thick; it is rain proof; you will never be filled in that house. Open the door, poor thirsty soul, and come out into the freedom of the big outdoors of God's fullness. Can't you hear the patter

212

of the rain upon the roof? Can you not see it beating against your window-panes? Rise up from your seats and pews of prejudice and slothfulness, and get out into the open where the rain is falling. Do not stop to put up your umbrella over your head either, but just lift up your hands in praise, to Heaven; lift up your face to the falling of this blessed latter rain; lift up your voice aloud in adoration and glorifying the Lord; lift up the everlasting doors; open wide the floodgates of praise, and let Him fill you.

O what you have been missing all this time! What an incomparable loss! Because you have been taking shelter beneath the wails of doubtings and questions, instead of taking out God's Word, and searching whether these things be so.

Instead of asking and receiving, you have been slowly withering and drying up spiritually.

"It shall come to pass, in the last days, saith God, that I will pour out of My Spirit upon all flesh. Be glad, then, ye children of Zion, and rejoice, for He hath given you the former rain moderately, and He will cause to come down for you the rain, both the former and the latter rain in the first month." Glory to Jesus! Dear ones, we are in these last days. The latter rain, which is falling upon the earth today, is just as much a fulfillment of Bible prophecy, and a sign of the soon coming of Jesus, as the world war, the plagues and the pestilences now ravaging our nations.

If you have not yet received your portion, if your cup has not yet been filled to overflowing, do not blame God, do not blame your pastor, do not say: "Perhaps God's time has not yet come."

God's time is always now. There is no one to blame but yourself. Look up, and be sure there is no roof over your head, no umbrella of doubts or unbelief or criticism. Be sure you are empty and your cup right side up. Lift up your whole being in praises to the King. Ask rain in the time of the latter rain, and you will be filled to overflowing.

When the Holy Spirit has filled you, and taken up His abode, you will speak with other tongues and magnify God today, just as in the days of the former rain. The Lord did not have one way of filling people and manifesting that filling in Bible days, and another way today. No! this is the same kind of rain, the same shower of refreshing, the same Holy Spirit. The Lord has not invented a twentieth century outpouring of the Holy Spirit, but still pours out His Spirit without measure, in the Bible way, with Bible evidence, as in Acts 2:4. "This old-time religion is good enough for me" you have been singing that, but do you believe it? Then get out into freedom, and be filled with the Spirit.

Stop complaining that the rain is not falling today as it was ten years ago it is because you have gotten under some rain-proof shelter of carelessness, or lack of prayer and confidence. It is falling today, dear ones. Do not be satisfied with dried-up, stale pastures. See! The pastures of the wilderness do spring, for the tree beareth her fruit, the fig tree and the vine do yield their strength. Ask, and ye shall receive. Every one that asketh receiveth!

"And you'll get your portion yet, praise the Lord; In His storehouse there is plenty, More than enough for the hundred and twenty, And you'll get your portion yet, praise the Lord."

SHEPHERDS, "FALSE AND TRUE"

"I will feed them in a good pasture, and upon the high mountains of Israel shall their fold be; there shall they lie in a good fold, and in a fat pasture shall they feed. I will feed my flock, and I will cause them to lie down, saith the Lord." Ezekiel 34:14, 15.

THROUGHOUT the entire word of God there is not a more beautiful picture presented to the reader than that of the good Shepherd caring for and feeding His sheep. He has always been the good Shepherd; and as we, His sheep, get to know Him and His voice, we cannot turn a page of the Bible without seeing Him as the tender Shepherd of the sheep, leading, guiding, feeding, seeking, chastising, healing the sheep of His fold.

From the day that this Shepherd first led His sheep to pasture in the fruitful Garden of Eden, he has been feeding and pasturing richly all who followed Him closely.

From the day that sin entered that first pasture field and the good Shepherd walked amongst the trees of the garden calling:

"WHERE ART THOU?"

He has been calling and seeking wandering sheep. As the pages turn before us we see Him walking, leading His sheep through each experience. We hear His stately steppings as He leads His flock from Egyptian bondage to Canaan's land. His hand is revealed as He feeds them in the wilderness, His voice echoes from every page, reproving, comforting, correcting, encouraging. We hear His voice speaking from the mount of Sinai, we hear the voice of the good Shepherd speaking from Calvary's hill as "the good Shepherd giveth His life for the sheep." We hear His voice today, wooing, calling, interceding, and soon, yes, very soon, we hope to hear that dear, beloved voice calling to His sheep to come up higher to the eternal fold He has gone to prepare for us. Hallelujah!

The good Shepherd has prepared a wonderful pasture field for His sheep, a pasture so great and wide that its supply is inexhaustible and its boundaries have never been reached. He maketh the pastures of the wilderness to spring, and the desert to blossom, as a rose. The green grass and the clover have not grown stale, nor have they withered away; the clear, crystal streams of water still flow direct from the throne of God, fresh and sparkling as ever. His pasture fields afford full salvation from all sin, deliverance from the ravenous beasts of prey, holiness without which no man shall see the Lord, the Baptism of the Holy Spirit in the Bible way, with the evidence of speaking in other tongues, according to Acts 2:4. Even this is not the end of the richness of His pasture, for as His sheep press on, the land of Canaan lies; before flowing with milk and honey. There are the fruits and the gifts of the Spirit, healing for the body yes, the human mind and pen fail to describe the glories that He hath prepared and laid up for them that love Him and will follow where He leadeth.

In the employ of the great and good Shepherd are many under shepherds, shepherds false and shepherds true, shepherds who have volunteered to feed the sheep through ulterior motives and hope for earthly gain, and shepherds who have just for pure love of the good Shepherd and His sheep, left all to do the bidding of Him who said:

"Lovest thou Me? then feed My sheep"

The TRUE under shepherd leads forth his flock into pastures ever new. He declares that Jesus is "the same yesterday, today and forever." He preaches that the Lord still saves His people from all sin, fills them with the blessed Holy Spirit, speaks through them in tongues, bestows the gifts and graces of the Spirit, and heals the sick in answer to prayer. He says:

"Is any sick among you, let him call for the elders of the church; let them lay hands upon him, anoint him with oil, and the Lord shall raise him up." He urges his sheep ever to press on and on till they are changed into the likeness of the good Shepherd.

The FALSE shepherd leads his sheep forth no further than he himself has gone. It is a difficult problem to lead another into an experience you have not yourself had or understood. Therefore he declares that it is foolish and preposterous to expect the same green pastures, the same

214

clear water, the same grapes and pomegranates today that they had in Bible times. He declares wisely that the baptism of the Holy Spirit, with the evidence of speaking with other tongues, is not for today is absolutely unnecessary. In other words, the disciples and other sheep of that day ate all of that pasture up and exhausted God's supply in that line. We must be content with the leftovers, and not blame God for running out of stock.

As for Divine healing: "Tut! Tut! Child! That is not for today. God has given us good common sense and expects us to use it. Get the doctor if you are sick. What were medicines made for if not to be taken? The days of miracles are past, the early church sheep ate all that clover up, and drank the last of that miraculous healing power.

Is any sick amongst you, let him run for the doctor, get a bottle of good tonic and a box of pills, and the doctor will raise him up. You sheep must not murmur at the little, stale pasture that is left over or the muddy waters trampled by so many feet learn with what things ye have, there-with to be content."

"Now as for dancing, shouting, falling under the power, and such like, that is all excitement" say the false shepherds; "things should be done decently and in order; the amen corner is out of date, it is undignified to shout today (unless it is for some ball game or something for the devil); and this falling under the power is all hypnotism.

You sheep had better keep away from that pasture, for the grass is surely poisoned." And because joy and gladness have withered away, and the power of God not preached, the sheep are scattered on every high hill and become a prey to the beasts of the fields, such as the card-parties, dance-halls, theatres, church entertainments, oyster suppers, in fact any poor painted bauble that can try to conceal the real, pitiful absence of the golden hours of long ago when all-night prayer meetings used to take the place of suppers and entertainments, when the genuine took the place of the sham, when men and women used to dance and shout for the Lord instead of for the devil.

You wonder why so many of your members are at the different places of amusement rather than in your prayer meetings? It is because of the false shepherds who have fed themselves rather than feeding the flock. It is because the sheep long for something to satisfy, and if they cannot find the old-time joy in the church they will go to the world for happiness and take the devil's substitute, fun.

But God's pasture field has never withered away.

Those who claim that the day of His visitation and miraculous power is ended have made a hideous and grievous mistake, they have been robbed themselves, and are robbing their flock, for in His storehouse there's a plenty, more than enough for the hundred and twenty. Hundreds of thousands of His sheep are today feeding in luxuriant pastures not only knee-deep but over their heads.

Glory! They enjoy the fulness of salvation; the Holy Spirit abides within, speaking forth the praises of the Master Shepherd; they enjoy healing for their body as in days of old. Cancers, tuberculosis, broken bones, even leprosy have been healed right in our present day in answer to prayer, according to the Word.

THE RAIL FENCE DIVIDING THE TWO PASTURES

A great rail fence divides the two pasture fields.

On the one side where the pasture is waving green and inviting, and the clover heads are nodding under the bright sunlight of God's love, there the sheep are fat and flourishing, their faces radiate their happiness; they kick up their heels, and skip and leap and bleat for joy. (Really, you can't blame a person for dancing and leaping and shouting when we have so much to dance and shout for. Glory!)

But at the sight of the joy manifested in the sheep abiding in the good pasture, the false shepherd, standing on his side of the rail fence, with a club of unbelief and theological training in his hand, warns his poor, thin, starved flock to keep clear of those Pentecostal sheep, and warns them, too, that the grass over there is all poisoned, and that if ever they should leap the fence and eat of that grass, they, too, would soon be just as crazy, kicking up their heels and shouting, Glory! But in spite of all the solemn warnings, hundreds of thin sheep, so thin you never hear them say "Amen" or "Hallelujah," never saw them leap or dance in their lives for God (poor things, they have little to dance or shout over), are coming up to the fence in curiosity to see those "foolish" Pentecostal sheep dance and bleat for joy, and as they stand there looking through the rails of doubt and pride, unbelief, former teaching, preconceived ideas and public opinion, someway even what they can see through the fence looks so green and fresh and inviting, the water looks so cool and clear and sparkling, the sheep over there seem so happy, that they long to leap the fence and be "one of them." Surely that preacher must have been mistaken, surely that grass can't be all poisoned, to make such fat, happy sheep.

Then once in a while, a poor, thin, starved sheep takes a leap, and over the fence it goes into the green pastures. Ah! He buries his nose in the clear water of salvation, and just drinks and drinks as though he could never get enough. (What a change from the muddied pools where you just "hope so" and try in your own strength to be a Christian. Then he buries his head in the green pastures, lies down under a shady tree with great delight; then eats and eats again, and would you believe it, it is not long till that sheep has grown fat like his neighbors, not long till he, too, begins to kick up his heels and dance and bleat for love and praise of the good Shepherd who provides such a satisfying pasture.

Standing on the other side of the fence the false shepherd points to the now joyful sheep and says to the remainder of his hungry flock:

"There now, what did I tell you? Didn't I tell you the grass was poisoned over there, and that those sheep would soon act as crazy as the others if they went over there?"

But brother, sister, just you go to "one of them" who have once tasted of the fulness of the Spirit, eaten of the good pasture, drunk from the living waters, received the Holy Spirit with the Bible evidence, speaking in tongues as the Spirit gives utterance, been healed in answer to prayer, one whose head has been anointed with oil and whose cup "runneth over" and see whether you can persuade that sheep to go back to the stale pastures and the muddied pools of a lukewarm, haphazard, make-believe experience. They will tell you NO! a thousand times NO! for "Before it is a garden of Eden, behind a desolate wilderness?"

O, poor, tried, hungry, longing sheep everywhere peering through the fence today, don't hesitate a moment longer, but leap the fence, get over into the good pasture, into the fold of the Good Shepherd. He will satisfy your every longing. And as for you, false shepherd, you who are declaring that God has no more of the old-time pastures left, you are standing in a most deplorable and perilous position; for thus saith the Lord God:

"I am against the shepherds, I mill require my flock at their hand."

There was once a miner, who had made a "lucky strike" after long months of toil in the gold mines. having lived many weary months on canned goods he longed for a real "square meal" and started, with his pockets filled with gold nuggets, for a big city where he could find a good restaurant and the good meal anticipated. Walking along the street he saw a big sign that read "RESTAURANT." Hastening toward it he opened the door and seated himself at the snowy white table; the waiter brought a fine china plate and an elegant silver knife, fork and spoons, and presented him with an elaborate bill of fare.

"Roast Turkey, Roast Duck, Roast Goose," read the hungry man, and his mouth watered at the prospects.

"I believe I'll have some of the Roast Turkey," said he.

"Why, I'm sorry, sir," but the fowl are out of season here now, sir, and we have none of that," apologized the waiter.

"Then I'll have some of your roast beef," said the man. "Sorry, sir, but it is near the end of the day now, and we are just out of all our regular meat orders, as regular dinner hour is passed."

"Well, then, what have you got left, anyway?" cried the exasperated man.

"Well, to tell the real truth, sir, we have not got much of anything left at this late hour unless it is some canned goods we can open for you."

216

At the mention of canned goods the poor miner pushed back his chair, and laying down the big, elaborate menu card, hastily left the place in search of a better service.

How much like the way many preachers preach the Word. The sign still hangs in front of the building, hungry travelers on life's journey still swing the doors wide and seat themselves at the table, hungry to hear the message of salvation and the Holy Spirit, and a deeper walk with God; the snowy linen, and the fine silver, the stained glass windows and the pipe organ may be there, the imposing, appetizing bill of fare, the Word of God, may be presented, and as the traveler reads of the wonderful feast of good things his soul longs for its fulness. So he says to the waiter, the preacher:

"Please, I'd like some of that, I'd like the baptism of the Holy Spirit in the Bible way, with the Bible joy, I would like to dance like David of old with all my might; I would like to have divine healing for the body." But ah! the false shepherd cannot fill the bill, for he teaches that these things are not for today.

"I am very sorry, my dear man, but the disciples ate the last of that. These things you are asking for are now out of season, the day too far spent; there is not much stock left on hand now, but a make-believe salvation. Do the best you can; live a moral life; sign your name on our roll, and by way of pleasure you can enjoy the canned goods, the oyster suppers and socials."

Oh, the shame of it all! Hungry soul, the good Shepherd is calling you, saying:

"I will FEED them (not starve them) in a good pasture, and upon the high mountains of Israel shall their fold be; they shall lie in a good fold." Hallelujah! "They shall eat in plenty and be satisfied" then over there in that bright tomorrow, the good Shepherd will come walking to meet us in the clouds of Heaven, will come to call His sheep and His faithful under shepherds home to the eternal fold He has gone to prepare.

Saul, Saul, why persecutest thou me?" . .

"It is hard to kick against the pricks."

SAUL was filled with indignation and ire as he hastened along the road that led to Damascus.

Saul, a Pharisee of the Pharisees Saul who had been taught at the feet of Gamaliel Saul, who walked uprightly and kept the law in all points-Saul, the holiness man, who endeavored to walk holy before God Saul, who believed in having things done decently and in order, was all wrought up and stirred to the innermost depths. He breathed out threatenings every time he thought of those peculiar people called Christians, who taught salvation through the blood of Jesus, and had the baptism of the Holy Ghost and spoke in other tongues.

As Saul hastened on down the long road, riding upon his high horse accompanied by his attendants his pockets bulged with papers and accusations against these people whom he was threatening.

How persistent, audacious, foolish and erroneous those Pentecostal people were, those so-called Christians, who claimed to be filled with the Holy Ghost and spoke with other tongues, those people who on the day of Pentecost had acted like drunkards and stirred up the whole city into a tumult.

Saul set his face like a flint with, a grim determination to persecute those fanatics, to warn his people against them, to put an end to them if that should be possible. Had he not witnessed the death of Stephen? While he had not thrown the stones, yet he had stood by and had believed that he was doing God a favor and his church a justice to denounce and crush such heresy.

News had doubtless reached the dignified, proper Saul of the unheard-of and shameful doings of those people on the day of Pentecost in Jerusalem.

Exaggerated reports in all probability poured into his ears concerning the great stir and seeming confusion caused in that city when the one hundred and twenty in a little upper room had suddenly seemed to go mad, from a natural point of view, shouting, talking in languages they had never learned, speaking in tongues as the Spirit gave them utterance, reeling and staggering under the power of the Spirit till the mockers had cried out in derision.

"These are filled with new wine." True, Peter had stood up and denied the charge that they were drunken and had declared it boldly, saying:

"These are not drunken as ye suppose, seeing it is but the third hour of the day, but this is that which was spoken of by the Prophet Joel." But surely evidence had been against them, they had certainly acted like drunken men and women and had talked in tongues and glorified the Lord until when this was noised abroad the multitude came running together confounded, amazed, and in doubt as they marveled at the manifestations of the Spirit upon those peculiar people.

All this was most disgusting and distasteful to the order-loving Saul, who liked to see religious services conducted quietly, decently and in order, in a dignified and ceremonious fashion. Surely such actions were a disgrace to religion, and nothing was too hard to say or do against those erroneous Pentecostal people. He spurred his horse on as he remembered the many who had been converted under Peter's preaching and, as it seemed to Saul, deceived and led astray. Therefore Saul was going down to Damascus that day, in all his power, yearning to do God the favor and his church the justice of persecuting and putting an end to all such error and false teaching.

Whether these early Christians were called Pentecostal fanatics, tongues people, holy rollers, or any of the other present-day names flung at them by their opposers and modern Sauls of Tarsus I know not; but at any rate they were people who had been filled with the Holy Ghost with the Bible evidence of speaking in other tongues they had never learned. Acts 2:4, 10:46.

All this was seemingly not only unnecessary, but foolish and sacrilegious to the wise and mighty Saul, for the wisdom of God is foolishness to man. Were there not churches enough or synagogues enough to worship in without getting out and separating themselves in these cottage

218

meetings, etc.?

The whole affair was a seemingly fanatical and erroneous movement to Saul and he had been making havoc of the church, entering every house and haling men and women, committing them to prison. And yet breathing out threatenings and slaughter against the disciples of the Lord, he had gone to the high priest and desired of him letters to the synagogues of Damascus, that if he found any of this way, he might bring them bound, whether they were men or women, to Jerusalem.

But as he journeyed, he came near Damascus, when suddenly there shined round him a light from Heaven, and he fell to the earth, and heard a voice saying,

"SAUL, SAUL, WHY PERSECUTEST THOU ME?

He said, "Who art thou Lord?" and the Lord said, "I am Jesus whom thou persecutest; it is hard for thee to kick against the pricks." And he trembling and astonished said, "Lord, what wilt thou have me to do?"

O, Saul! Saul! What has happened? Man never could have convinced him that all this which he had been so industriously fighting, and self-righteously opposing was of God. Man might have reasoned and argued forever without wailing anything. But suddenly, O how I love those words!

God does do things suddenly. On the day of Pentecost suddenly there came a sound from Heaven, as of a rushing mighty wind; and now here to doubting Saul suddenly there shined round about him a light from Heaven.

O! dear reader, I am just praying as I write, that suddenly a light may shine upon some fighting, persecuting Saul, riding upon his high horse of theology, learning and wisdom, as he reads these words, and that he too may fall to the earth and hear the voice of Jesus saying "Saul, Saul, why persecutest thou me?"

Saul, lying on his back in the middle of the dusty road! Could such a thing be possible? Saul who thought it unnecessary and shameful to see people lying prostrate under the power of the Holy Ghost, himself slain full length, crying, trembling and astonished, "What wilt thou have me to do?"

Hallelujah! I can hardly keep from shouting as I write, for dear, present day Sauls, as you read this, the very same power will fall on you if you let God have His way. O how Saul must have trembled 'and repented when he found to his amazement that it was Jesus, not the people, he was persecuting! and indeed "It is hard to kick against the pricks."

Ah! what a change took place in the heart of the proud, stiff, self-righteous Saul in those few moments he lay prostrate under the power of God!

What a mellow, broken, humble Paul arose from the earth, blinded by the glory of God till he saw no man. He was led by the hand and after three days of blindness and fasting he received his sight and was baptized and meekly abode with the disciples, and was soon himself preaching Jesus and the Word; but all that heard him were amazed, saying:

"Is not this he who destroyed them which called on this name in Jerusalem?" We read that he increased in strength, and know that he was not only converted but received the Holy Ghost, and was one of the despised people who spoke with other tongues, for he himself writes in I Cor. 14:18: "I thank my God I speak with tongues more than .ye all." Without a doubt Paul became "one of them" forever.

PRESENT DAY SAULS

Since that day there have been many other Sauls: Sauls that fought Martin Luther and all the Christians of the dark ages; Sauls that burned believers at the stake, put out their eyes, tortured them in unspeakable ways and manners. There were the Sauls that persecuted Calvin and Knox, Fletcher, Finney, Wesley and Booth; Sauls that put martyrs upon the rack and the guillotine, and thought they were doing right; Sauls that have thrown stones and bitter words at each new step forward toward the restoration of the church to her full power and Pentecostal glory. There have been Sauls that fought the Adventist people when first they preached the soon coming of Jesus. Sauls who fought the holiness people when they preached whole-hearted surrender and holiness unto the Lord. EVEN NOW we have present day Sauls, and will have till Jesus comes.

These present day Sauls are fighting present day truths just as industriously and just as conscientiously as did Saul of Tarsus of old. Our Sauls of today feel as Saul of old that the manifestations of the Spirit, such as being slain under the power of God, speaking in tongues, etc. are not at all necessary or proper. They stride along on their high horses of earthly knowledge, theology, formality, and ceremonial and clerical dignity, breathing out threatening against the despised Pentecostal people who still preach Salvation, holiness, and the baptism of the Holy Ghost with the Bible evidence of speaking with other tongues as the Spirit gives utterance, exactly as did the disciples in the early church, with signs and wonders following.

Many present-day Sauls, feeling that they are doing their duty, ignorantly pace up and down their pulpits, breathing out threatenings, and warning their people to shun these same Holy Ghost people who are receiving the Holy Spirit today as in the days of old. Many of them have papers against them in their pockets, too, I fear, as did Saul of old. Many of them have their pockets bulging with tracts and literature condemning these peculiar people, and feel they are serving God and doing him a kindness to persecute and try to crush them.

To see believers lie prostrate under the power of the Holy Ghost, or to hear them speak in tongues, or to see the mighty manifestations of the Spirit resting upon them, seems just as foolish to the natural man, seems just as much confusion and unnecessary to the wise Sauls of today as to the Sauls of old.

The wisdom of God is indeed foolishness to man, and God still takes the things that are naught to confound the mighty, still takes the foolish to confound the wise, and a worm to thrash a mountain. But God's arm is not shortened, and we are still in the same dispensation, the dispensation of the Holy Ghost. God is restoring His church step by step, through the ages to her full power and Pentecostal glory. He is again manifesting Himself in mighty power upon and through humble, yielded vessels of clay.

Many present-day Sauls, who at first fought bitterly against the Lord, for it is the Lord Jesus and not the individuals they fight, have fallen to the earth and seen the light shine suddenly from Heaven. They too have received the Holy Ghost and with the Bible evidence have begun to preach the word with power and boldness. Many Sauls whom man could never have convinced that "this is that" have felt God's mighty power, and themselves have fallen to the earth, crying "Lord what wilt thou have me to do?" He would have all stiff necks and stubborn knees to bend and bow. He would have you dismount your horse and get down in humility low in the dust before Him; He would fill you as He did Saul of old till your name shall be no more known as Saul but as Paul, the least of all.

O what a glorious picture to see Paul in the nineteenth chapter of Acts laying his hands upon the disciples at Ephesus and saying "Receive ye the Holy Ghost" and then to see the Holy Ghost come upon them and hear them speak with tongues and prophesy.

Dear ones, He would do for you what He did for Saul of Tarsus. Why resist him longer? How can you resist in the face of such overwhelming light from Heaven and from the Word?

"Saul! Saul! why persecutest thou me? It is hard for thee to kick against the pricks; "for those who kick against God's work and His people, and the outpouring of the Holy Ghost, dry up spiritually, and find it indeed hard to kick against the pricks.

Never yet has there been a church or preacher who fought the little flock of Holy Ghost baptized people, and persecuted them as did Saul of old, but soon came into a dry and barren place. No matter how their fields may have been blooming and bearing before, as soon as they refused the latter rain outpouring of the Holy Ghost, and cast those out of their midst who had received, and unknowingly barred their doors against the Holy Ghost who longed to come in the Bible way, at once their fields began gradually to dry up and wither, their power began to wane and disappear.

The light has shone from Heaven now, dear ones.

Read the Word of God on your knees concerning the coming of the Spirit, and His manifestations and power upon the people, and then cry out, Lord, what wilt thou have me to do? He will fill you till, like Paul of old, you will have to teach this glad story to others, you will be so full you cannot keep from shouting His praises aloud, for out of your innermost being will flow rivers of living water. Do not resist longer.

WHAT ABOUT THOSE MANIFESTATIONS?

DANCING, SHOUTING, SHAKING, FALLING PROSTRATEUNDER THE POWER, SPEAKING IN TONGUES, INTERPRETATION

INTRODUCTION

THE power was falling everywhere in the tent, sinners being saved, believers baptized in the Holy Spirit (with Bible evidence, speaking in tongues), sick bodies had been healed, many were leaping, dancing and praising God, the slain of the Lord were many; my heart felt full to the bursting with joy at the sight, and with uplifted hands I was walking up and down the aisles amongst the audience, praising my wonderful Redeemer for the way in which He was working.

Suddenly I felt a restraining, kid-gloved hand laid upon my arm, and a dignified, silk-gowned lady drew me down beside her. Her husband, a fine, dignified type of man, was seated beside her.

They had snow-white hair, both of them, and every well-tailored line of their faultless apparel bespoke refinement and culture. This dear lady seemed so sweet, and I was so filled with joy, that I remember I could hardly resist throwing my arms around her and kissing her and shouting "Glory to Jesus."

Her troubled, agitated look checked this impulse, however, and as she began to talk to me in her rapid way, her breast was rising and falling, with her quick breathing and (I was going to say, "Indignation," but hardly think that would be the word to apply to such a sweet and proper person-age.)

As she spoke, she alternately gazed through her lorgnette, which hung on a slender thread of gold from her gown, and pointed with it to some manifestations (for the saints wore dancing, shouting, and praising God), or tapped it lightly upon her book for emphasis:

"Of course, I believe in the power of God," she said, "but O, the noise, these awful manifestations!

What is the good of them, anyway? Did not Paul say that all things are to be done decently and in order? Now, take, for instance, that dancing and shaking, it seems like confusion, and is not at all necessary. And that falling on the floor and lying for an hour. Do you think that looks dignified or proper?" she demanded. "As for this leaping and shouting, why cannot these people praise God in a quiet, orderly way in their heart and give expression to their worship soberly in a quiet hymn of thanksgiving? You know the world would think far more of them," she added, "and stop criticising and persecuting if only they would put down these awful manifestations. Oh! Oh! I am so disturbed. Do tell me, what about these manifestations?"

Knowing that many honest Christians are asking the same question, might it not be well to look at this important matter from the standpoint of God's Word today? Let us begin with the seventh verse in the twelfth chapter of I Corinthians, which says:

"THE MANIFESTATION OF THE SPIRIT IS TO PROFIT WITHAL"

Quoting the whole context we read as follows: "Now there are diversities of gifts, but the same Spirit. And there are differences of administrations, but the same Lord. And there are diversities of operations; but it is the same God that worketh all in all. But the manifestation of the Spirit is given to every man to profit withal." "Yes, but what is the good of these manifestations?" you ask. Why, "to profit withal" answers Paul.

"Well, but what can be the profit resulting from manifestations such as shouting, dancing, shaking, falling under the power, etc.? you ask.

Just a moment, and we will take these things up one by one, but first let me say that when the power of the Holy Spirit is upon ,a person or an assembly, you can no more stifle the manifestations without quenching the power of the Spirit than you can shut off all air from a fire without extinguishing it, or turn off the water- faucet without stopping the flow of water, or turn off the electric light switch without putting out the lights, or cut the telephone wire without breaking the connection.

WHEREVER THERE IS LIVING, VITAL, TANGIBLE POWER, THERE IS BOUND TO BE A MANIFESTATION

Turn on the gas-jet of your stove, apply a match to it and there will be a hot flame. The greater the gas pressure the greater the flame.

THE KETTLE

Then take down your shining teakettle that has stood so long, filled with cold water, on the shelf, quiet, cold and orderly enough to please any church member; put it over the hot flame, keep it there a few moments, and the first thing you know it will just be obliged to break forth into singing (if the fire burns low, singing may be as far as your kettle will get), but keep it on the hot fire and soon steam and vapor will rise like praise from a heart that is warmed by His love. The hotter it gets, the more manifestations there are in the kettle, till at last it is bubbling and dancing and boiling all over.

If you do not like manifestations, dear preacher, turn the gas or power off and you will not be bothered with the manifestations very long, your particular kettle will soon sit still enough and cold enough to suit even your most rigid ideas of propriety and order.

We repeat that where there is power there is a manifestation of that power. Put your church or your assembly or self on the hot flame of Jesus' love and the Spirit's power, and you, like yonder kettle, will soon break forth into singing, and the vapor of praise will rise, not from outside sources, but from within the innermost depths of your being, and as the fire burns brighter there will be a bubbling and dancing in your soul. Amen. Try to put the lid on tightly if you will, but 'twill only boil over through the spout. Stop up that and keep it on the fire, and there will be an explosion (hat will blow the cover off, and the bubbling and dancing will go on as long as the kettle stays on the fire. Hallelujah!

The wind is invisible, but there is a power there, and when it blows through the trees there is a manifestation, the leaves begin to shake. The harder the wind, the more the power, the greater the manifestation; the branches, the limbs, and even the trunk sway. I have known greater trees than you to be slain prostrate beneath this visible power of the invisible wind.

We might mention many more instances wherein the workings of nature are analogous to the workings of the Spirit. Let us turn, however, from these comparisons in nature to the Word of God. Let us ascertain what saith the Scriptures pertaining to the subject of manifestations, and let them be the authority on the subject.

DANCING

Is dancing in the Spirit Scriptural in the light of God's Word? Yes, the Word is full of it.

Dancing belongs to the Lord. The devil has simply tried to imitate it and has made as poor an imitation of this as of most of the other things he has tried to counterfeit. If you read carefully what the Scripture says about dancing you will find that singing, music and dancing have their place in the Lord's church. I am wondering if you who disapprove of dancing in the Spirit today disapprove also of Exodus 15:20, 21, where: "Miriam, the prophetess, took a timbrel in her hand, and all the women went out after her with timbrels and with dances. And Miriam answered them, Sing ye to the Lord a new song, for He hath triumphed gloriously." The whole multitude of women and Miriam, the prophetess and leader, went forth praising the Lord with dancing, shouting and music.

I am wandering if you approve of Moses, who also led the hosts in the same way, with music and dancing; whether you approve of David in II Sam. 6:14, where "David danced before the

Lord with all his might" His wife disapproved, you remember, as she stood behind her window. I have always believed, however, that if she could only have been outside where the full tides of praise were flowing, could she but have heard the music, she, too, would have wanted to dance and praise the Lord. Oh, come outside of the window of self and formality and remember that David's wife was stricken with barrenness to the day of her death because she disapproved of and fought manifestations. Did you ever know of an individual or an assembly who fought the manifestations of the power of God without being stricken with barrenness and leanness? I never did. Remember, too, they who laid their hands upon the Ark to steady it were consumed immediately by the indignation of God.

Psalms 149:3 says: "Let them praise His name in the dance; let them sing praises unto Him until the timbrel and harp." Psalms 150:4, "Praise Him with the timbrel and dances." Jeremiah 31:13. "Then shall the virgins rejoice in the dance, both young and old together." Acts 3:8 tells us that when the lame man was healed, "He, leaping up, stood, and walked, and entered into the temple, walking and leaping and praising God."

This same Redeemer which was theirs is ours today. He heals in the same way. How can we keep from dancing and praising such a Savior?

SHOUTING

It seems almost impossible that any Bible student should question for a moment the right of, the children of the Lord to shout His praises, the Word is so filled with it. You recall that "When the Ark came into the camp, all Israel shouted with a great shout so that the earth rang again, and when the Philistines heard the noise of the shout they said, What meaneth the noise of this great shout in the camp of the Hebrews?" I Sam. 4:5. Again we read that "David, and all the house of Israel brought up the Ark of the Lord with shouting and with the sound of the trumpet."

II Sam. 6:15. Psalms tell us, "O clap your hands, all ye people, shout unto God with a voice of triumph!"

"There's a shout in the Camp. Hallelujah!

Glory to God!

There's an echo in Heaven. Hallelujah!

Glory to God!

Truly, "the children of the Lord have a right to shout and sing." We are in the same battle today as that we read of in Joshua 6:5, where it came to pass that "When they made a long Hast with the ram's horn, and heard the sound of the trumpet, that all the people shouted with a great shout and the wall of the city fell down flat."

There will be a wonderful shout some of these days, for we read that "The Lord Himself shall descend from Heaven with a shout, with the voice of the archangel, and with the trump of God."

Why, even the Lord shouts, and He is our great example.

Truly, we have something worth shouting over.

Joy always manifests itself. The shouts at ball games, races, political celebrations, etc., are accepted as a usual and expected thing. The day would be considered tame and with something radically wrong and missing without it. Remember how the announcement of peace was met right here in our own country, how they tied down the horns and the whistles, how every conceivable noise-making device was brought forth to swell the sound of jubilee. Now we have heard the proclamation of everlasting peace, from the King who has won the greatest battle ever fought. How can we keep from shouting? There are so many shouting for the devil with none to hinder, that we thank God for those who shout for Jesus.

When shouting is in the Spirit it comes from such depth and rings so true and genuine that none can mistake it. The devil will try to imitate the shout in the camp of the Hebrews, but there will be a hollow, forced sound that does not ring true. There are many who do not like the noise of the shouting, but we advise all such to let Jesus fill them with the same power and glory, to out a shout in their soul, for this is by far the quietest world they will ever live in. In Heaven John heard the shouting and praising of the multitude as they cried, "Holy, holy, holy, salvation and honor and dominion belongeth unto Him till the voice and shouting of the people was as the sound of many waters, and as the voice of great thunder." Surely those who dislike shouting would dislike Heaven, or must learn to join the song. O, how can you look upon such a wonderful Savior without shouting His praise? And as for those who are cast into hell, "there shall be weeping and wailing and gnashing of teeth.-' That will surely be a noisy place, and I would much rather hear the noise of shouts and rejoicing than weeping. Wouldn't you?

O, Beloved, thank God for the shout and the dance and the sound of joy. Let us never be ashamed of it. How many denominations once had God's power resting on them in this same way, and became too proud and haughty and dignified to remain yielded to His will. Soon the power left, the Amen corner left, and, as Joel 1:12 put it, "The vine becomes dried up, the fig tree languisheth; the pomegranate tree, the palm tree also, and the apple tree, even all the trees of the field are withered because joy is withholden from the house of your God". Each of the churches that once had the power and glory of God resting upon it, and later fought this power, is barren today. The enemy would like Pentecost to do the same as those who have gone before, but if we ever do this thing God will cause the cloud of glory to lift from us, and mil call another people who will be willing to go on and who are not ashamed to let Him have His way. We will be left to our creeds and ceremonies and forms as surely as were our predecessors.

The outpouring of the Holy Ghost on the day of Pentecost, Acts 2:4, stood for a mighty manifestation of the power of God; men and women reeled, staggered, talked in tongues, were accused of being drunken. Did it turn the people away? No. Three thousand souls were added to the church that day. If we call ourselves Pentecostal, if we have the sign "Pentecostal" over our assembly door, let us stand behind all that it means, or else change our name, take the sign 'Pentecostal" from our door, and go back to church forms and ceremonies. The Holy Spirit never intrudes nor forces His way and manifestations where he is not wanted. Many flourishing assemblies once filled and swayed by the power of God, have quenched the Spirit, criticised and checked the manifestations, until today they have no manifestations to quench or to bring reproach upon them.

It is not difficult to rid an assembly of this outward working of the supernatural power of God. Just a little criticism and disapproval, and the gentle dove will spread His wings and pass on to some other abode where He can find a people humble enough to let Him have His way, and not ashamed of the manifestations.

Thank God we have not come to the place where we have to try to be popular or pleasing to the world. Even if we are a gazing-stock, or a spectacle, let God and His Spirit have the right of way, whatever the cost may be.

SHAKING AND TREMBLING UNDER THE POWER

As for the shaking and trembling under the power, very often when the great power of the Eternal, Omnipotent, Almighty God comes in direct contact with, or moves upon a weak, earthly frame, there is quaking and trembling, not of fear as men count fear, but of power. Moses said, "I do exceedingly quake and tremble." In Acts we read of one place where the house wherein they sat was shaken.

Heb. 12:26 says: "His voice then shook the earth, but now . . . once more shall I shake, not the earth only, but also Heaven." See Acts 9:9, how Paul trembled in the presence of the Lord. Daniel tells us that he did exceedingly quake and tremble, and in speaking of those who were with him, says that a great quaking fell upon them. Sacred history tells us that this manifestation has not been uncommon all down through the ages, and coming to modern days we note that the Quakers came by their name because of the way they shook and quaked under the power of God. We might mention the shaking Methodists, etc. This is the same power which we see in our midst today.

BEING PROSTRATED UNDER THE POWER

225

"What about this being slain, prostrated, lying under the power?" You do not think it looks at all dignified or proper, you say. I wonder whether Peter looked dignified or proper when he lay in the trance on his housetop and saw the vision of the sheet let down, etc. (Acts 10:9 to 16), or John, on the isle of Patmos, when he lay at His (Jesus') feet as one dead, or Daniel, as he lay in a vision, or Saul, when he fell from his horse in the dust of the road as Jesus revealed Himself to him. It was as though Jesus, when He conquered, got both of Saul's shoulders to the ground, and he surrendered there and then. 'Twas not at all dignified or anything for the "Flesh" or "Pride" to boast over, I agree; in fact they were so ashamed and mortified they gave up in despair and died there and then; but O, the Spirit Life of Humility and Knowledge of God's power that took their place!

We might go on to mention Isaiah, Jeremiah, and others who fell prostrate before Him. We might mention the prostrations in the early Methodist church, the Salvation Army, the Welch Revival, and today, throughout the world, wherever God is pouring out His Spirit, and when I get to Heaven I expect to see angels and men before Him prostrate fall as they "bring forth the royal diadem and crown Him Lord of all."

SPEAKING IN TONGUES AND INTERPRETATION IS SCRIPTURAL

In Isaiah 28:11 we read, "With stammering lips and another tongue will He speak to this people." Jesus Himself said, "These signs shall follow them that believe . . . they shall speak with new tongues" Mark 16:17. In Acts 2:4 those who were filled with the Holy Ghost began to speak with other tongues as the Spirit gave them utterance. Likewise Acts 10:46, Acts 19:6.

WHAT ABOUT THOSE MANIFESTATIONS?

And Paul tells us (the 14th chapter of I Cor.) "Let him that speaketh with an unknown tongue pray that he may interpret" and that, in the assembly, "If any man speak with an unknown tongue, let it be by two, or at most by three, and that by course, and let one interpret."

GENUINE AND COUNTERFEIT

Are manifestations of the Spirit scriptural? Y-E-S. Are ALL manifestations scriptural? N-O.

How can we tell the difference? It is easy to discern, in the Spirit, between the real and the counterfeit. There is a different shine on the face, a different ring in the voice, a majesty and holiness. There will be that which edifies and builds up (but just here remember that your conception of edifying manifestations and that of God may vary. Had you seen the hundred and twenty reeling and staggering like drunken men Acts 2:13, 15 you might not have thought it edifying, yet God was in it, and Peter said they were filled with the Spirit, and three thousand souls were added to the church that day).

But do we claim that all manifestations are in the Spirit? you ask. We answer, No, for the devil has tried to imitate manifestations as he has everything else. There are also some manifestations in the flesh by those who are anxious for God to manifest Himself and use them, who run before the Lord.

BUT WHAT SHALL WE DO IN OUR ASSEMBLY WHEN WE FIND MANIFESTATIONS THAT ARE NOT OF GOD?

Shall we quench the Holy Spirit for fear of that which is not of the Spirit? Not at all. Do as Aaron did when the enemy sought to counterfeit; you remember, he threw down his rod and it became a serpent. Straightway the magicians threw down their rods and immediately they became serpents. Did Moses and Aaron begin to wail and regret that they had obeyed God, thus giving the enemy an opportunity to manifest himself? Why, no, their God was bigger than the devil. Their serpent opened up his mouth and swallowed up all the other serpents until they were out of sight.

226

completely. So will the true Holy Spirit, if we let Him have His way, swallow up and spoil every trick and tactic of the enemy, If you let Him have His way YOU will have no need to fight in this battle, HE will do it all, and get greater glory to Himself than as though there had been no struggle. The counterfeit makes the genuine to shine the brighter. When the Ark is in the midst all earthly goods must fall and be broken before it. Hallelujah!

MORE THAN A MATCH FOR THE ENEMY

Many leaders seem to fear the enemy so much that they almost act as if they had to protect " poor little God" from the onslaughts of the "Great, Big D-E-V-I-L" but Oh, dear ones, our God is Great and Big and High and Wide. He sitteth in the Heavens, the earth is his footstool, the seas are in the palm of His hand, the mountains are but as the small dust in His balances.

He is more than a match for the enemy. Let Him have His way when He will, where He will, how He will y and the earth will quake and His enemies be scattered before Him as clouds before the whirlwind.

He is getting a "sign and wonder" people today, a people who are a gazing-stock to the world.

The Holy Spirit is His own advertising agent today as He was on the day of Pentecost when the multitude came running together crying, "What meaneth this?"

STUPENDOUS MANIFESTATION COMING SOON

There is going to be a great manifestation some of these days, dear ones, a greater shaking, a greater leaping and shouting than ever you have heard or imagined before. The graves of those who died in the Lord are going to be shaken open wide and with them the liberated souls of those who remain are going to leap so high that they will not return to this earth again for a long, long time, and shouting! Oh, what a triumphant, victorious, joyful shout will rend the sky as our eyes behold the Bridegroom descending out of Heaven, clad in power and might. What a manifestation there will be that day! Every band, every stringed instrument in Heaven will be there. Every mouth will be filled with the shouts of His praises, as the saints are saved into His presence. They will come with songs of everlasting joy upon their heads.

In the meantime, dear heart, let Him have His way with thee, quench not the Spirit, but let Him move upon the waters as He will, for from Genesis, the first chapter, when He moved upon the waters, saying, "Let there be light, and there was light" there was a manifestation. From the moment that at His Word the moon and the stars sprang into being, down into the present day on into eternity, where God is, where God moves, where God speaks, there will be a manifestation of His presence and of His power.

227

RECEIVE YE THE HOLY GHOST

JESUS says "If you love me, keep my commandments." It is one of his commandments that we "receive the Holy Ghost." The Word of God repeatedly tells us of the importance of the work done in the life of the believer by the Holy Ghost.

John the Baptist preached this in the wilderness, saying: "There cometh one after me, the latchet of whose shoes I am unworthy to unloose. I indeed baptize you with water, but He shall baptize you with the Holy Ghost."

Once it is fully understood that we are still living in the dispensation of the Holy Ghost and will be until Jesus comes again, the importance of the work of the Holy Spirit is at once realized.

Jesus the Savior, who shed His blood to redeem a world of lost sinners, has ascended into the Heavens and sat down upon his Father's throne, until the day when His waiting bride will be ready to rise to meet Him in the air. But during this long interval He has not left us comfortless, but has sent us another Comforter, even the Holy Ghost, that He might lead us into all truth. How important it is therefore that we understand the office work of the Holy Spirit in our lives, and are led by Him, who has come to take the things of Jesus and reveal them unto us.

The first work of the Spirit is begun in our lives while we are yet sinners, for no man can come unto the Father except the Spirit draw him. The Holy Spirit is with the sinner, therefore, to convict or convince him of sin, to show him his helpless and lost condition without Jesus, and when he is willing to repent, he leads that penitent one to the feet of Jesus, the sinner's best friend.

Now the Holy Spirit cannot cleanse away his sin nor save him, for Jesus paid it all, all to him we owe, and by faith we cry to Jesus the Lamb of God who taketh away the sin of the world. The blood is applied to the sinner's heart, and the Spirit Himself bears witness with his spirit that he is now the child of God. It is the precious blood of Jesus that cleanseth, and the Spirit that bears witness to our hearts that the cleansing is done.

The same Holy Spirit, who was with the sinner, to convict of sin, is still with the newly converted soul, to witness of righteousness and lead him on to perfection. Moreover He seeks to come within the cleansed soul and make it the temple of the Holy Ghost.

Right here let me emphasize the difference between having the Spirit "WITH" you and having the Spirit "IN" you. Jesus told His disciples that He that is with you shall be in you, then He breathed upon them and said, "Receive ye the Holy Ghost."

Someone says, "O, but I know I received the Holy Ghost when I was saved, for I had such joy and peace, and such a witness in my soul." No, dear one, that was Jesus you received as your Savior, not the Holy Ghost, Do not underestimate the great work of salvation, for Jesus brings joy and peace, and the Spirit with you gives you this witness, but now after salvation and consecration, the Holy Ghost seeks to come in. When He comes in to abide, you will know it. He will fill every bit of your being and flood your soul to overflowing until out of your innermost being there flow rivers of living waters and you speak in other tongues (languages you never learned) as the Spirit gives utterance.

There will be no "think so" about it when yon receive the Holy Ghost, but you will have the same Bible evidence Paul, Peter, Matthew, Mark, Luke, John and all the other disciples had, the same evidence that Mary the Mother of Jesus had, that they had at Ephesus and Caesarea speaking in other tongues will follow your infilling with the Holy Ghost, This incoming of the Spirit will be so real that never to the longest day you live will any one be able to make you doubt for the fraction of a second that you have received the Holy Ghost, for you can put your finger on the chapter and verse, Acts 2:4, and say, "I received the Holy Ghost just like the hundred and twenty," or on Acts 10:46, and say, "I received just as the believers did in the house of Cornelius," or, again, upon Acts 19:6, and boldly affirm that without a doubt you received the Holy Ghost as did the disciples at Ephesus, for you had the same Bible evidence and spake in other tongues. When the Spirit comes in you will have this evidence today just as in the days of old.

Now being made the temple of the Holy Ghost ever let Him have His way. He will take the things of the Father and reveal them unto you if you will close your eyes to all else. You will be endued with power from on high if you remain humbly submissive to His dealings. He will pray through you with groanings that cannot be uttered.

He will rejoice through you with joy unspeakable and full of glory if you let Him have His way.

O dear ones, you need the Holy Ghost so much in your lives. If He is with you today, open up your hearts and let Him come in. Seek and you shall find, but never stop short of the real Bible experience in the Bible way, accompanied with the Bible evidence.

ACCORDING TO THY WORD

"And Mary said, Behold the handmaid of the Lord; be it unto me according to thy Word." Luke 1: 38.

IT was the Virgin Mary (who later became the mother of Jesus) that spoke the above words: The angel of the Lord had spoken to her concerning God's will for her, namely that she, a virgin, should bring forth the Christ Child. No doubt many thoughts flashed like lightning across the mind of Mary, the reproach, the misunderstanding that this would bring to her. Mother would not understand, Father would misunderstand, Joseph, her espoused husband would think evil of her, neighbors would falsely accuse her, and worse still, flashed a vision of herself, perhaps standing in the public square, as was the custom of the day, degraded, hissed at and stoned to death in the most ignominious manner. Yet, in the face of the future, Mary, knowing that it was the Spirit of God who spoke through the angel, looked up unflinchingly into His face and said submissively:

"Behold the handmaid of the Lord; be it unto me ACCORDING TO THY WORD."

Ah! There was the secret, A-C-C-O-R-D-I-N-G T-O T-H-Y W-O-R-D. As long as whatever happens to us is according to the Word of God, all will be well. Can you say "Yes" to the will of God today, in spite of what Husband or Wife, Father or Mother, children, neighbors or pastor will say?

"No matter what misrepresentation it will bring, no matter if I am so situated that my name will be cast out as evil, Behold, here I am Lord! Be it unto me according to Thy Word."

Mary did not need to go about forever explaining her position or seeking to vindicate herself; all she had to do was to say an eternal "Yes" to God's will and God vindicated His own so wonderfully that her reproach was turned into glory.

It is God's highest purpose for each of us today that we, like the Virgin of old, should bring forth the Christ life to those round about us. We have been made virgins, clean and pure in heart through the atoning blood of Jesus Christ our Lord, but in order truly to bring forth and reveal the Christ to the world about us, we must be overshadowed with the Holy Spirit, and so yielded in His hands whatever the cost, that His dear will may be fully wrought out in our lives.

The four words, "A-OOO-R-D-I-N-G T-O T-H-Y W-O-R-D" strike the keynote of each new Christian experience; God will never work in any other way than ACCORD ING TO HIS WORD. When the sinner comes to Jesus, he must needs come according to His Word, repenting of his sins, forsaking the world, being born again through the precious blood, without which there is no remission of sins.

He must leave unrighteousness behind, and according to the Word, He, Jesus Christ, is faithful and just to forgive us our sins and to cleanse us from all unrighteousness on one simple condition, namely, that we confess our sins.

According to the Word, He not only forgives but cleanses us from all unrighteousness. Indeed, a sinner who has not yet been cleansed from all unrighteousness is not yet saved. For all unrighteousness is sin, and he that committeth sin is of the devil. Again he says, without holiness no man shall see the Lord; therefore, unless we have been cleansed and made holy through the blood of Jesus we shall not enter Heaven nor see God. Therefore, according to the Word, nothing short of holiness constitutes a born again experience. Either we are righteous or else we are unrighteous, there is no middle ground; and it is the blood of Jesus which cleanseth white as snow. Sin is sin, whether it is inbred sin, Adamic sin, actual sin, or whatever name you may give it, sin is sin, and NO sin shall enter there. The blood of Jesus Christ, God's Son, cleanseth us from ALL sin.

Having been cleansed and made holy according to His Word, the believer should press on crying: "O, Lord, fill me with the Holy Spirit according to Thy Word; not according to how my minister or church ordinance says I should receive, but ACCORDING TO THY WORD, LORD."

Do not be satisfied with any other kind of an experience than is according to His Word and bears the Bible label upon it. According to His Word, those who were filled with the Holy Spirit in the Bible days spoke with tongues and magnified God (See Acts 2:4, Acts 10:46, Acts

19:6, I Cor. 14:18 and 39, etc.) , and according to the same Word, God the Father has made the statement that "I am the Lord God, I change not." Jesus says: "I am the same yesterday, today and forever." And we are told that Heaven and earth may pass away, but His Word shall never pass away.

O Beloved, do you not long for an experience that is according to His Word, not some new twentieth century brand marked "Just as Good," but the real, genuine, Bible experience, received in the Bible way, with the Bible evidence mentioned in the previous paragraph. Of course you do.

Then as God's angel is hovering about you as you read these words, just as he hovered over Mary of old, look up into His face, and in spite of the visions of reproach, misunderstanding and misrepresentations the devil may bring before you to frighten you into refusal, say:

"Yes, Lord, here I am. Behold the handmaid of the Lord; be it unto me according to THY WORD." And never stop seeking till you receive an experience that really is according to the Word, and measures up to like experiences recorded there. Thus will the Christ life be brought forth to the world and His star be seen afar off.

Then, according to His Word, there is a full overcoming life, there is divine healing, there is power and glory, and untold riches in store for those who live and pray and submit themselves, A-C-C-O-R-D-I-N-G T-O T-H-Y W-O-R-D.

TWENTY-FOUR QUESTIONS A YOUNG WORKER IS APT TO MEET, AND ANSWERS FROM THE WORD HE SHOULD BE ABLE TO GIVE.

*Note: The Baptism of the Holy Spirit, with the Bible evidence, speaking with other tongues, is absolutely scriptural and founded upon the Word of God. Nothing could be plainer than the Word upon this subject; and as you study the scriptures with your Bible helps and concordance, you will find that all through the Bible the scriptures fit and dovetail together, and none is left wanting for a mate.

Q. 1. WHO OR WHAT IS THE HOLY SPIRIT?

He is the third spoken of in the Godhead. See I. John 5:7.

A. "For there are three that hear record in Heaven, the Father, the Word and the Holy Ghost"

Q. 2. HOW DO YOU KNOW THAT THE HOLY SPIRIT IS A PERSON AND NOT AN INFLUENCE?

A. Jesus Himself spoke repeatedly of the Holy Spirit as a person, for instance in John 14th, 15th and 16th chapters, not once did He ever refer to the Spirit as "IT," but always as "HE"

"HE will abide with you forever; even the Spirit of Truth, whom the world cannot receive, because it seeth HIM not, neither knoweth HIM, but ye know HIM, for HE dwelleth in you.

HE shall teach you all things and He shall testify of me. When HE is come HE will reprove the world of sin, of righteousness, and of judgment.

HE will guide you into all truth.

HE will not speak of Himself.

He will show you things to come and

HE will glorify Me.

Moreover, we know that the Holy Spirit Appoints and commissions His servants Acts 13: (24), Acts 20:28. He directs where to preach, Acts 8:29. He suffers Paul not to go to Bithynia, Acts 16: (6-7). He instructs Paul what to preach, I Cor. 2:13. He comforts, Acts 9:31.

Q. 3. WHY IS IT VERY NECESSARY TO BE ABLE TO PROVE, WHEN PREACHING THE BAPTISM OF THE HOLY SPIRIT THAT THE HOLY SPIRIT IS A PERSON AND NOT AN INFLUENCE?

A. Because if the Holy Spirit were merely an influence, He could be received in portions, and professors would be justified in excusing themselves from seeking and receiving the "ONE baptism" spoken of in Eph. 4:5, by saying, "Well, I have received a measure of the Holy Spirit," and would confuse the many anointings of the Spirit with the "ONE Baptism," and the Holy Spirit would be considered, for instance as a vessel of water which could be received measure by measure, little by little. This, we at once realize, is un-scriptural when compared with the Baptism of the Holy Spirit as recorded in the Word, Acts 2:4, Acts 8:17, Acts 10:46, Acts 19:6.

Immediately, however, when one recognizes the fact that the Holy Spirit is a person, one realizes that when He comes in, making the body His temple, He comes in altogether (not a portion at one time and a portion at another), and that one has either received all of the Holy Spirit, or has received none of Him, i.e., in the sense of His personal, literal incoming. There may be many anointings, but only "ONE Baptism".

Q. 4. WAS THE COMING OF THE HOLY SPIRIT, WITH THE ACCOMPANYING OUTPOURING OF POWER PROMISED IN EITHER THE OLD TESTAMENT OR THE FOUR GOSPELS OF THE NEW?

A. Yes, His coming was promised in both the Old Testament and the New promised by both the Father and the Son.

Q. 5. WILL YOU PLEASE SHOW ME WHERE I CAN FIND A FEW OF THESE SCRIPTURES WHICH REFER TO THE DEFINITE AND LITERAL COMING OF THE HOLY SPIRIT IN THE LAST DAYS?

A. There are many portions of scripture referring to the dispensation of the Holy Spirit but we have space for only a few of them here. In speaking of his age, GOD said, through the prophet Isaiah:

"For with stammering lips, and another tongue will He speak to this people, to whom He hath said, This is the rest wherewith ye may cause the weary to rest, and this is the refreshing; yet they would not hear. Isa. 28: (11-12). Isa. 28: (11-12).

Through the prophet Joel:

"Be glad, then, ye children of Zion, and rejoice in the Lord your God; for He hath given you the former rain moderately, and He will cause to come down for you .the rain, the former rain and the latter rain in the first month.

And the floors shall be full of wheat, and the fats shall overflow with wine and oil." Joel 2: (23-24).

"And it shall come to pass afterward, that I will pour out my Spirit upon all flesh, and your sons and your daughters shall prophesy, your old men shall dream dreams, your young men shall see visions. And also upon the servants and upon the handmaids in those days will I pour out My Spirit." Joel 2: (28-29).

Through Zechariah:

"Ask ye of the Lord rain in the time of the latter rain; so the Lord shall make bright clouds, and give them showers of rain, to every one grass in the field." Zech. 10:1.

Through John the Baptist:

"I indeed baptize you with the water unto repentance; but He that cometh after me is mightier than I, whose shoes I am not worthy to bear: He shall baptize you with the Holy Ghost, and with fire." Mat. 3:11.

The promises in the Gospels concerning the coming of the Holy Spirit are plentiful JESUS said:

"Nevertheless, I tell you the truth; it is expedient for you that I go away: for if I go not away, the Comforter will not come unto you; but if I depart, I will send Him unto you.

And when He is come, He will reprove, the world of t sin, and of righteousness, and of judgment." John 16: (7-8). "And I will pray the Father, and He shall give you another Comforter that He may abide with you forever;

Even the Spirit of truth; whom the world cannot receive, because it seeth Him not, neither knoweth him: but ye know Him; for He dwelleth WITH you, and shall be IN

you." But the Comforter, which is the Holy Ghost, whom the Father will send in My name, He shall teach you all things, and bring all things to your remembrance, whatsoever I have said unto you." John 14: 26

"But when the Comforter is come, whom I will send unto you from the Father, even the Spirit of truth, which proceedeth from the Father, He shall testify of Me: And ye also shall bear witness, because ye have been with Me from the beginning." John 15: (26-27).

"If ye then, being evil, know how to give good gifts unto your children; how much more shall your Heavenly Father give the Holy Spirit to them that ask Him?" Luke 11:13.

"And these signs shall follow them that believe: In My name shall they cast out devils; they shall speak with new tongues; They shall take up serpents; and if they drink any deadly thing, it shall not hurt them; they shall lay hands on the sick, and they shall recover." Mark 16: (17-18). "For John truly baptized with water; but ye shall be baptized with the Holy Ghost, not many days hence.

But ye shall receive power, after that the Holy Ghost is come upon you; and ye shall be witnesses unto Me, both in Jerusalem, and in all Judaea, and in Samaria, and unto the uttermost part of the earth." Acts 1:(5-8).

"And behold, I send the promise of My Father upon you: but tarry ye in the city of Jerusalem, until ye be endued with power from on high." Luke 24:49.

Q. 6. HOW CAN YOU POSITIVELY KNOW THAT ISAIAH WAS REFERRING TO THIS BAPTISM OF THE HOLY SPIRIT AND THE SPEAKING IN TONGUES IN ISAIAH 28:11? WHEN HE REFERS TO STAMMERING LIPS AND ANOTHER TONGUE?

A. Because Paul plainly tells us so in I Cor. 14: (21-22): "In the law it is written, With men of other tongues and other lips will I speak unto this people; and yet for all that will they not hear Me, saith the Lord.

Wherefore tongues are for a sign, not to them that believe, but to them that believe not; but prophesying serveth not for them that believe not, but for them which believe."

Q. 7. HOW DO YOU KNOW THAT THIS BAPTISM OF THE HOLY SPIRIT, AS RECORDED IN THE BOOK OF ACTS IS THE ONE JOHN THE BAPTIST REFERRED TO? (Mat. 3:11).

A. Because Jesus Himself makes this plain by His words recorded in Acts 1:5.

Q. 8. HOW DO YOU KNOW THAT THE DISCIPLES DID NOT RECEIVE THE HOLY SPIRIT WHEN JESUS BREATHED UPON THEM? (John 20:22.)

A. Because the Holy Spirit was not yet given; Jesus Himself plainly states that before the Holy Spirit could be sent He (Jesus) must ascend on high and pray the Father that He would send the Comforter (John 16:7); also the last words Jesus spoke before the clouds received Him out of their sight prove this statement beyond a doubt, for the Word reads:

"And being assembled together with them, commanded them that they should not depart from Jerusalem, but wait for the promise of the Father, which, saith He, ye have heard of me:"

"But ye shall receive power, after that the Holy Ghost is come upon you: and ye shall be witnesses unto me, both in Jerusalem, and in all Judaea, and in Samaria, and unto the uttermost part of the earth." Acts 1:8

Q. 9. WHAT DID JESUS MEAN, THEN, WHEN HE BREATHED UPON THEM AND SAID: "RECEIVE YE THE HOLY GHOST"?

A. He was merely commanding them, as He had in many other places, such as Luke 24:49, Acts 1:4, etc., to receive the Holy Spirit, for whom they were to tarry until He was sent from the Father.

Q. 10. WHAT IS THE OFFICE WORK OF THE HOLY SPIRIT?

A. His office work is three-fold (I) to the sinner; (II) to the new born -again soul; (III) to the baptized believer.

(I)   His office work to the sinner is

a. to convict and reprove him of his sin. (John 16:8.)

b. To show him his true condition as described in Isaiah 1:6.

c. To prick the sinner to his heart, as He did in Acts 2:37.

d. To draw him to Jesus. (John 6:44.)

(II). His office work to the newly born again soul is

a. To bear witness when the work is done. (The Spirit itself beareth witness with our spirit, that we are the children of God. Rom. 8:16.)

(He that believeth on the Son of God hath the witness in himself: he that believeth not God hath made Him a liar; because he believeth not the record that God gave of His Son." I. John 5:10.) In other words, He who was with the sinner to convict him of sin, is now still with the young Christian rejoicing with him that the work is done, and endeavoring to lead him on to the place where he may receive the promise of the Lord which said: "He dwelleth WITH you, and shall be IN you." John 14:17.

b. To baptize him with the Holy Spirit according to Acts 2:4.

(Ill) His office work in the baptized believer

a. He is a teacher. John 14:26.

b. He testifies of Christ. John 15:26.

c. He guides. John 16:13.

d. He glorifies Christ. John 16:14.

e. He comforts. Acts 9:31.

f . He searches deep things. 1 Cor. 2:10.

g. Our helper in prayer. Read Romans 8:26, also I. Cor. 14:2.

Q. 11. IS IT THE PRIVILEGE OF EVERY BELIEVER OF TODAY TO RECEIVE THE HOLY SPIRIT?

A. Yes, Acts 2: (38-39), "Then Peter said unto them, Repent, and be baptized, every one of you, in the name of Jesus Christ, for the remission of sins, and ye shall receive the gift of the Holy Ghost.

"For the promise is unto you, and to your children, and to all that are afar off, even as many as the Lord our God shall call."

The gifts of God are without repentance; Jesus said: "And I will pray the Father, and He shall give you another Comforter, that He may abide with you forever." John 14:16.

Q. 12. IS IT NECESSARY FOR EVERY CHILD OF GOD TO RECEIVE THE BAPTISM OF THE HOLY SPIRIT, EVEN THOUGH GREATLY USED OF GOD IN THE PAST IN SOUL-WINNING, HEALING, CASTING OUT OF DEMONS, ETC.?

A. Yes, Peter and other disciples, though greatly used in this way, still needed the Holy Spirit and enduement of power that should not be as an anointing that should lift, but a baptism that should abide.

Q. 13. CAN ONE RECEIVE THIS BAPTISM MORE THAN ONCE?

A. No, there is but one Lord, one faith, and ONE BAPTISM. There are many anointings, but ONE Baptism.

Q. 14. IS THERE ANY WAY BY WHICH THE SEEKER MAY KNOW WHEN THE HOLY SPIRIT COMES IN TO TAKE UP His ABODE? IF SO, HOW?

A. Yes, this ONE BAPTISM, which comes but ONCE to a person, is far too precious and wonderful to be left without a mark or seal by which it may be known without the possibility of a doubt, and sought for until consciously received.

It will be made known by the speaking in OTHER TONGUES (languages), as the Spirit gives utterance.

Q. 15. WILL ALL WHO RECEIVE THE HOLY SPIRIT SPEAK IN OTHER TONGUES TODAY AS IN THE BIBLE DAYS?

A. Yes, there is but ONE BAPTISM. The pattern for this Baptism has not changed, but is the same today as when first outpoured in apostolic days.

Q. 16. DID ALL WHO RECEIVED THE HOLY SPIRIT IN THE BIBLE DAYS SPEAK WITH TONGUES? IF SO, WHERE WILL I FIND THE SCRIPTURES RELATING TO THE EXPERIENCE?

A. Yes, Scriptures can be found as follows: Acts 2:4: "And they were all filled with the Holy Ghost, and began to speak with other tongues, as the Spirit gave them utterance."

Acts 8: (17-18): "Then laid they their hands on them, and they received the Holy Ghost.

And when Simon saw that through laying on of the apostles' hands the Holy Ghost was given, he offered them money."

Acts 19:46: "For they heard them speak with tongues and magnify God."

Acts 19:6: "And when Paul had laid his hands upon them, the Holy Ghost came on them; and they spake with tongues, and prophesied."

Q. 17. TAKING THE STAND THAT YOU DO, HOW DO YOU EXPLAIN THAT IN ONE INSTANCE OUT OF THE FOUR, viz. ACTS 8:17, IT DOES NOT STATE IN SO MANY WORDS THAT THE PEOPLE OF SAMARIA SPOKE WITH TONGUES WHEN THEY RECEIVED THE HOLY SPIRIT?

A. Because if the believers during the eight years between the 2nd and 8th chapters of Acts all spoke in tongues when they received the Holy Spirit, it would be superfluous to mention the speaking in tongues in every case.

For instance, today we write a report or make a statement that, say, "ten received the Baptism of the Holy Spirit last Sunday night." We do not deem it necessary to add "And they all spoke in tongues," because this is taken for granted.

Or, in announcing that Mr. B. and Miss D. were married last week, we do not consider it necessary to add that a minister performed the ceremony and a license was granted. If the fact of the believers having received the Holy Spirit is questioned or doubted, however, as it was in the 10th chapter of Acts, where during the preaching of Peter the Holy Ghost fell upon the Gentiles, it is mentioned as convincing evidence:

"For they heard them speak with tongues and magnify God" just as if the legality of a wedding ceremony is questioned, the marriage certificate and the name of the minister are brought forth as convincing proof.

Besides, we may settle it that the incoming of the Holy Spirit was attended by unmistakable, miraculous, outward evidence, or this old Jew, Simon the Sorcerer, who was "In the gall of bitterness and the bond of iniquity" would not have wondered at it and offered money for the power to bestow this gift.

Then, too, we know that the Bible does not in so many words state that Paul spoke with tongues when he received the Holy Spirit, yet we have unmistakable evidence that he did, for in I. Cor. 14:18, he said: "I thank my God I speak with tongues more than you all."

Q. 18. WHAT DID PAUL MEAN WHEN, IN I. COR. 12:30, HE SAID: "DO ALL SPEAK WITH TONGUES?"

A. Paul is referring throughout this entire chapter to the gifts of the Spirit, and is here referring directly, amongst other gifts, to the gift of tongues, which is subject to the prophets, as proven by the 14th chapter, 27th and 28th verses, and not to the Bible evidence (speaking with tongues), which bursts forth as the Spirit gives utterance, as in Acts 2:4.

Q. IS THERE ANY DIFFERENCE, THEN, BETWEEN THE SPEAKING WITH TONGUES AS THE BIBLE EVIDENCE OF THE INCOMING OF THE HOLY SPIRIT, AND THE GIFT OF TONGUES?

A. Yes, all who receive the Holy Spirit speak with tongues, but not all receive the gift of tongues (or power to speak at will). It is of this latter gift Paul is speaking when he says:

"For if I pray in an unknown tongue, my spirit prayeth, but my understanding is unfruitful. What is it then?

I WILL pray with the Spirit and

I WILL pray with the understanding also;

I WILL sing with the spirit, and

I WILL sing with the understanding also.

I. Cor. 14: (14-15).

This means he will sing and pray in tongues (in the Spirit), which he does not understand, and also in his understanding, (that is with his own language). And when he says:

"If any man speak in an unknown tongue, let it be by two, or at the most by three, and

235

that by course; and let one interpret.

"But if there be no interpreter, let him keep silence in the church; and let him speak to himself (softly), and to God, "(I. Cor. 14: 27-28), he is speaking to saints who have already received the Spirit and spoken in tongues.

Q. 20. WAS PAUL DISCREDITING OR BELITTLING THE SPEAKING IN TONGUES IN ANY WAY WHEN, SETTING THE CHURCH IN ORDER (I. COR. 14:19), HE SAYS: "IN THE CHURCH I HAD RATHER SPEAK FIVE WORDS WITH MY UNDERSTANDING THAN TEN THOUSAND WORDS IN AN UNKNOWN TONGUE"?

A. Not at all, for he has just stated that he speaks in tongues more than they all, and has said:

"I would that ye all spoke with tongues (verse 5). He commands the brethren to "Forbid not to speak with tongues "(verse 38). He is exhorting the people, rather, to covet to prophesy, and bids them "Let he who speaketh in an unknown tongue pray that he may interpret" explaining that the one who speaks in prophecy and the one who interprets are on an equal footing of edification to the church (verse 5). Were a whole sermon preached in tongues, and did no interpretation follow, it would be uninstructive and unedifying.

Q. 21. IF IT IS LEARNED THAT THERE IS NO INTERPRETER IN THE CHURCH, SHOULD THE SPEAKER, IF HE FEELS THE POWER UPON HIM, CONTINUE TO SPEAK ON AND ON ALOUD IN TONGUES?

A. No. "If there be no interpreter let him keep silence in the church, and speak to himself (that is softly, under his breath, so as not to interrupt the preacher), "and to God."

Q. 22. DOES THIS MEAN THAT NO ONE SHOULD EVER SPEAK ALOUD IN TONGUES IN AN ASSEMBLY WHERE THERE IS No ONE UPON WHOM THE GIFT OF INTERPRETATION HAS BEEN BESTOWED?

A. No, because in the 22nd verse of the chapter Paul declares that tongues (not interpretation alone, but tongues) are a sign ... to them that believe not, Paul, in setting the Corinthian church in order, merely instructs those who speak much in tongues to speak (softly) to themselves and to God, so as not to disturb the exhorter, when they find the message is not being interpreted, and further, Paul advises such an one to pray that he may interpret, that the church may receive edifying, explaining that greater is he that prophesieth than he who speaketh with tongues, except he interpret, that the church may receive edifying.

Q. 23. IS THE SPEAKING IN TONGUES GIVEN TO THE CHURCH FOR THE PURPOSE OF ENABLING THEM TO PREACH TO FOREIGNERS, USING THESE OTHER TONGUES INSTEAD OF LEARNING THE LANGUAGE?

A. No. There is no record in the Bible of tongues being used to preach in other languages after the day of Pentecost. We are told that the apostle Paul spoke with tongues more than all the others, yet it is nowhere hinted that he ever used the gift to preach in another language at will. He may have done so, however, even as many have been enabled to speak to foreigners in this day under a mighty enduement of the Spirit, The Scripture, however, plainly states that it is an unknown tongue, and that he who speaketh in an unknown tongue speaketh not unto men, but unto God, for no man understandeth him, howbeit in the Spirit he speaketh mysteries.

Q. 24. JUST WHAT SHOULD BE THE ATTITUDE OF THE SEEKER AS HE TARRIES FOR THE HOLY SPIRIT?

A. His attitude should be one of: Prayerful waiting upon God, and of Praiseful expectancy that believes the Lord implicitly and takes Him at His word.

When the amazed onlookers, on the day of Pentecost, pricked to their hearts as they SAW (in the staggering bodies, Acts 2:13) and HEARD (in the speaking in tongues, Acts 2:4-6) cried out to Peter and the rest of the apostles: "What shall we do?" Peter, in simple words, said unto them:

"Repent, and be baptized, every one of you in the name of Jesus Christ, for the remission of sins, and ye shall receive the gift of the Holy Ghost."

First of all make sure you are washed in the precious blood of Jesus; make a whole-hearted, unconditional surrender and consecration to Him who gave Himself for you. Then, as you praise Him with a pure heart, lifting up holy hands, claiming the Promise, He will come into His temple to abide.

"Be ye lifted up, ye everlasting doors, and the King of Glory shall come in."

"Open your mouth wide and I will fill it," saith the Lord. Remember, the promise is unto you, even as many as the Lord our God shall call, and every one that asketh receiveth.

This filling may be at meeting when amongst the saints, or in your own home as you wait upon Him in secret communion, or as you go about your work. The land of Canaan is before you and Jesus is coming soon for his Spirit-filled Bride. Amen.

THE COMING OF THE CHRIST

IF I GO AWAY I WILL COME AGAIN

ALL down through the long centuries there had been a faithful few who believed God's word implicitly, and looked forward to the hope of the soon coming of the Lord Jesus Christ from Heaven. With longing hearts and unassuaged zeal did they look for Him, knowing that He who was to come would come and would not tarry, for this God had spoken by the mouth of His holy prophets since the world began. Many indeed cried out:

"Where is the hope of His coming? All through our lives, and the lives of our forefathers have we heard His soon coming prophesied, till now they slumber in the dust, and still He is not come. Surely you wait in vain. Strain your eyes no longer in searching the Heavens for the sign of His coming; come eat, drink and be merry in this world with us."

But through all the stream of unbelief and silent years, their faith neither waned nor faltered. Their eyes of faith were still undimmed, and they looked toward the Heavens with untiring hope for the coming of the Christ, their Messiah.

Then to His faithful few, God began to reveal that the time was at hand, and that the Lord was near, even at the door. In Jerusalem there was a man whose name was Simeon, who was just and devout, waiting for the coming of the Christ. It was revealed to him, by the Holy Ghost, that he should not see death before he had seen the Lord.

Anna, the prophetess, and many others whose eyes were anointed, began to rejoice with great joy as the signs were fulfilled all about them, and the Holy Spirit witnessed, not the day nor the hour, but that the coming of the Lord was at hand.

"And there were in the same country, shepherds abiding in the fields, keeping watch over their flock by night. And, the angel of the Lord came upon them, and the glory of the Lord shone round about them, and they were sore afraid.

And the angel said unto them, Fear not; for, behold, I bring you good tidings of great joy . . Unto you is born this day ... a Savior, which is Christ, the Lord

. . . Ye shall find the babe wrapped in swaddling clothes, lying in a manger. And suddenly there was with the angel, a multitude of the Heavenly host, praising God, and saying, Glory to God in the highest, and on earth peace, good will toward men.

And it came to pass, as the angels were gone away from them into Heaven, the shepherds said one to another, Let us go ... and see this thing which the Lord hath made known to us. And they went with haste, and found Mary and Joseph, and the babe lying in a manger." Luke 2: (8-16).

And behold, there came wise men from the east, saying, where is He that is born King of the Jews? For we have seen His star in the east, and are come to worship Him. And lo, the star which they saw in the east went before them till it came and stood over where the young child was. When they saw the star they rejoiced with exceeding great joy. Matt. 2:1, 2, 9, 10.

On and on they trudged, all unmindful of their footsore and weary condition; the long years of waiting seemed but as a day now. On they hastened, over the hills and through the valleys, bringing with them their treasures and gifts, gold, frankincense and myrrh. Still on they hastened spreading the joyful news and bearing witness in their eager search in the country and in the city, till at last they found Him, and fell down and worshipped Him, opened their treasures and presenting to Him their gifts. God had fulfilled his promise and the weary ones were rewarded, for THE CHRIST HAD COME.

All this happened over nineteen hundred years ago, and now the hands on the great clock of time have revolved until they point to the hour of the second coming of the Christ foretold by His Word.

As the angel spoke unto the shepherds of old of the first coming of the Lord; and as the angels spoke to the watching multitude of His second coming saying, "This same Jesus, which is taken up from you into Heaven, shall so come in like manner as ye have seen him go into Heaven"

(Acts 1:17) they are again appearing today to announce the soon coming of the Christ.

Ever since that day Jesus Himself told the disciples that He would return and that wars and rumors of wars, plagues, pestilences, blood, fire and vapors of smoke; nation rising against nation, famines and earthquakes would be the sign of His coming (Matt. 24) eager longing hearts of a faithful few have looked and yearned for His appearance. To be sure, many have cried in derision:

"Where is the sign of His coming? For years we have heard it foretold that His coming was nigh, our forefathers who preached His second coming-no w slumber in their graves, and still He is not come. Let us eat, drink and give in marriage; His coming is not near."

But today as in the days of old, the Lord is revealing to His faithful few that His coming is near even at the doors. "For the Lord himself shall descend from Heaven with a shout, with the voice of the archangel and with the trump of God The dead in Christ shall rise first, then we which are alive and remain, shall be caught up together with them to meet the Lord in the air and so shall we be ever with the Lord." Again today anointed eyes see the signs of His coming fulfilled with unmistakable vividness on every hand.

Shepherds abiding in the field, keeping -watch over their flock through the long night while the light of the world is absent, have looked long and earnestly with unutterable desire towards the east for the rising of the sun of righteousness who would dispel all darkness. At His first coming a star had appeared, but now they look for the sun of righteousness to arise and as the sun outshines the star, so shall His second coming outshine his first appearing, for this time He will not appear wrapped in swaddling clothes and in a manger, but will march forth triumphant, his kingly robes upon Him, His scepter in His hand a king victorious the hope and reward of His people.

Already the hearts of the shepherds are flooding with joy, for the Heavens are filling with the first rays of morning dawn. The long night of silent waiting and longing is almost over, and again they see His sign in the East.

Wise men, wise not as this world counts wisdom, but wise with the wisdom that cometh down from above are looking for and hastening unto the coming of the Lord. Even as the wise men of old left their flocks and ran to meet the Lord with treasures of gold, frankincense and myrrh; so the wise virgins today leave the foolish virgins behind and go out quickly to meet him, carrying the treasures of gold, the divine nature of Jesus, and the frankincense of acceptability to God and praises, and myrrh with its fragrance, and bitterness of suffering with Him that they might also reign with Him that having known Him in the fellowship of His sufferings they may now know Him in the power of His resurrection.

Beloved, awake and see His light from afar off.

Rise and go out to meet the coming Christ, for He is near even at the doors. He is coming, and is even now approaching the portals of this world.

He shall sweep back the Heavens as a scroll and those who are ready shall rise to meet Him in the air. Already the whole earth is being taxed even as it was at the birth of Christ when Joseph and Mary went up to Jerusalem to pay taxes. Every sign is fulfilled, history is repeating itself and as soon as He is come and taken his waiting ones away, tribulation will sweep over this world, as it did after His first coming. Even now the voice of Rachel is heard lamenting and wailing for her dead children, slain by the sword of evil rulers.

Awake! Arise! go ye out to meet the coming Lord Jesus Christ.

"If ye will enquire, enquire ye." Isa. 21:12.

INQUIRER: I have heard it said that you have made many statements and contain much teaching regarding the literal return of our Lord to this earth again. Is this report true?

-THE WORD. Absolutely true. Within the 260 chapters of my New Testament alone there are 318 references to the coming of the Lord, i. e. practically one out of every twenty-five verses.

INQ. Speak to my heart, O Word of God, some simple word of the Master, whereby I may know that He is really coming.

THE WORD. "If I go away ... I will come again." These were the words of Jesus to His disciples. (John 14:3). Did He go away?

INQ. Yes. "While they beheld He was taken up and a cloud received Him out of their sight.

(Acts. 1:9.)

THE WORD. Then He is coming again.

INQ. But does this not mean that Jesus is here now first in our hearts as revealed by the Holy Spirit? Second in our midst wherever two or three are gathered together in His name? and thirdly, refer to His coming for us at death?

THE WORD. No, Jesus, who is soon to come in the clouds of glory, is now at the right hand of the Father. (Rom. 8:34.) 'Tis the Holy Spirit who has come to reveal Jesus during His absence and prepare us for His coming. He reveals Jesus in the heart (Jn. 14:23), in the midst of the congregation (I Cor. 14), and lifts us, when life and death are over, into His presence (Rom. 8:11).

Speaking of the Holy Spirit, Jesus said: "I will not leave you comfortless." (Jn. 14:16.) "But when the Comforter is come, whom I will send you from the Father . . . He shall testify of Me." (Jn. 15:26.) Then, too, He plainly said: "It is expedient for you that I go away, for if I go not away the Comforter will not come to you, but if I depart I will send Him unto you." (Jn. 16:7.)

These scriptures make it plain that it is the Spirit who is with us today, while if you will turn my pages to I Thess., the 4th chapter, 16th and 17th verses, you will plainly see that "the Lord Himself shall descend from Heaven with a shout and with the voice of an archangel, and with the trump of God: and the dead in Christ shall rise first: then we which are alive and remain shall be caught up together with them in the clouds, to meet the Lord in the air." We read also (Mat. 24:30) that we "shall see the Son of man coming in the clouds of Heaven with power and great glory."

INQ. Yes, yes. Your teachings have made it plain to me that this Jesus who ascended to the Father and poured out the Holy Spirit (the Comforter who was to abide during His absence) is to come again. But what will be the manner of His coming? You surely do not mean, as some have understood you to say that He will come back in the body the same, real, tangible Jesus who went away?

THE WORD. Yes, I mean just that. This same Jesus who was taken up from you into Heaven shall so come, in like manner as ye have seen Him go into Heaven. (Acts 1:11.)

THIS SAME JESUS who was taken up not another Jesus whose body was destroyed, and who is naught but spirit, as many suppose, but the same Jesus, the one who, after His resurrection, said: "Handle me and see" (Lu. 24:39) , who talked and walked with His disciples, and who did take a piece of a broiled fish and an honey comb and did eat before them. (Lu. 24:15, 42, 43.) This same Jesus, who shall drink anew with us the wine in His Father's Kingdom, the real, literal Jesus who was taken up from you into Heaven, SHALL SO COME. He who said, "I am the Lord, I change not, will be seen by His ready, waiting people just as He was when He went away.

IN LIKE MANNER When the company of faithful disciples who watched His ascension into Heaven, hear the trump of God and rise from their tombs (I Thess. 4:16) their eyes shall behold the same Lord descending in the same form as that in which they did see Him go.

INQ. Will His feet touch the earth again at this next coming?

THE WORD. No, not at this time. Those who are ready shall rise to meet Him in the clouds.

(I Thess. 4:17.) He shall return later bringing His saints with Him. (Jude 14.) Then shall appear the sign of the Son of man in Heaven, and then shall all the tribes of the earth mourn, and they shall see the Son of man coming in the clouds of Heaven with power and great glory. Then shall His feet touch upon the top of the Mount of Olives (Zech. 14:4) and it "shall cleave in the midst thereof toward the east and toward the west, and there shall be a very great valley."

INQ. What of the sinful people of the earth and those who are unprepared, will they see Jesus at His next coming when He appears in the clouds of glory?

THE WORD. No, only those who die ready and watching. He shall come as a thief in the night. (Mat. 24:43.) "Two women shall be grinding at the mill, one shall be taken and the other left, two shall be sleeping in one bed, one shall be taken and the other left." (Mat. 24:40, 41.) It is at His final return, when He Comes to set up His kingdom and reign a thousand years (Rev. 20:4) that every eye shall see Him. (Rev. 1:7.)

INQ. Is it possible to know the day and the hour of His return?

THE WORD. Of that day and hour knoweth no man, no not the angels of Heaven, but the Father only. For as in the days that were before the flood, they were eating and drinking, and marrying and giving in marriage, until the day that Noah took them all away, so shall also the coming of the Son of man be (Mat. 24:38, 39.)

INQ. You see that we will not know the day nor the hour, but is it not given to us to know the seasons?

THE WORD. Yes. "Of the times and the seasons ... ye have no need that I write unto you," for "ye are not in darkness, that that day should overtake you as a thief." (I Thess. 5:1,4.) There are manifold signs given through my pages, whereby ye may know when the season is nigh.

INQ. Tell me, Oh thou light unto my path, thou blest lamp unto my feet, when shall these things be and what shall be the sign of thy coming?

THE WORD. Many shall come, saying, I am Christ, and shall deceive many. Ye shall hear of wars and rumors of wars. Nation shall rise against nation, kingdom against kingdom; there shall be blood and fire and vapor of smoke. (Joel 2:30, 31.)

There shall be famines and pestilences and earthquakes in divers places. When they cry peace and safety, then shall sudden destruction come upon them.

Iniquity shall abound, the love of many shall wax cold. Then shall arise false Christs and false prophets, and shall show great signs and wonders in so much that if it were possible they should deceive the very elect.

Then, too, when the fig tree putteth forth her leaves ye know that summer is nigh, so likewise, when ye see these things come to pass, ye know that the kingdom of God is now nigh at hand (Lu. 21:31). In the last days, saith God, I will pour out My Spirit upon all flesh! your sons and your daughters shall prophesy.

INQ. Why! these are the very things that are taking place today wars and rumors of wars, blood, fire, vapors of smoke, are covering the earth as the fog covers a ship at sea. Six million have been saved into their graves during the past few years of warfare, and plague. Almost every home has been entered by death. Never so many homes in America in all its history have been entered by the death angel as in the past five years.

Cries of peace and safety, sudden destruction, coming plagues, pestilences at home and abroad the fig tree putteth forth her leaf, and the Jews are today, for the first time in centuries, free to return to Jerusalem and rebuild their temple. Chariots, automobiles and ears run like the lightnings and jostle each other, because of their very numbers, in the broad ways. (Nah. 2:4.)

All about me I see the love of many waxing cold. Forms and ceremonies are taking the place of power. So-called Christian Science and Spiritualism has flooded the land with false Christs and false prophets. Then, too, in these days the Holy Spirit is being poured out upon all flesh, and in every land a spiritual company are preparing for the rapture. Surely, surely, according to your words, and the signs of the times, the coming of the Lord must be near at hand, yea, even at our very doors.

241

With all these signs being fulfilled and thy word so plain, why is it that the people of today are so stupid and dull that they do not realize this truth?

THE WORD. For the same reason that the Jews did not recognize the signs attending His first coming or discover that the Slain Lamb of Isa. 53 and their crucified Lord were one and the same. Their eyes are holden by sin. They slumber and are drunken with the intoxication of the world.

INQ. I thank you for making it plain to me that the Lord Jesus Christ is soon to come, and in view of this truth I see that we should quit ourselves like men and stand with our loins girded about with truth, our sandals upon our feet, with oil in our vessels with our lamps, ourselves filled with love and robed with praise, transformed daily by the Spirit's power into the likeness of God's dear Son, watching earnestly unto the coming of our Lord, insomuch that I shall be enabled to pray the last prayer recorded in the Bible: "Even so, Lord Jesus, come quickly."

SIGNS OF THE TIMES

"WHAT SHALL BE THE SIGN OF THY COMING?"

MATT. 24:3

IN reading the Bible prophecies concerning the last days, have you not been struck forcibly with the astounding similarity of conditions as recorded by the news of the day, and the Word of God?

I want to take you back in memory just a few years ago to the great world-wide talk of peace you doubtless recall the great Hague convention, where peace was the theme. And universal peace was talked of continually. Then true to Bible prophecy when they cried peace, peace, suddenly came gloom and destruction. If you have not recently read the 24th chapter of Matthew, read it now and compare it with this present day.

"What shall be the sign of thy coming, and the end of the world?" In answer to this query the Lord tells us of many signs whereby we may recognize the season, amongst others He tells us there will be WARS and rumors of wars, that nation shall rise against nation, kingdom against kingdom. We see this prophecy fulfilled in a startling literal manner. There shall be

FAMINES we are told. Glance over your paper again, and run back over the past few months'

famines. Note the prices of food and clothing in Europe. Consider Belgium, Bulgaria, parts of Russia, Armenia, Serbia, the high prices and potato famine in Germany; read of the small rations dealt out to starving women and children, the shell-torn, blood-soaked fields that used to bear grain and vegetables and feed the flocks and you will not fail to agree this sign is fulfilled, in a ghastly real way.

As for the PESTILENCES he tells of, I have just looked up Noah Webster and he defines the word as an infectious or contagious disease, noxious to health and morals. Pestilences and PLAGUES go hand in hand today. Recall the accounts of sickness caused from the unburied bodies on the battle fields, the smallpox epidemic, the black death, the infantile paralysis, right at our doors. I suppose you have been reading of the plague of sharks that are infesting our shores, of the ships lost at sea, of the thousands of fires, explosions and accidents, with their train of silent victims; of the wrecking of homes in Europe, of the terrible fate and destruction of innocent women and children, too horrible to even record or contemplate. No one can help admitting that the time of famines, pestilences and plagues is up-on us, as are the earthquakes in divers places.

FALSE PROPHETS are arising on every hand, also those who have claimed to be the Christ have been mentioned at different times in the newspapers. We are told that the false prophets will have power to do many wonderful things, and show forth signs and wonders that would deceive the very elect if that were possible; today we see Christian Science, Spiritualists and other organizations (which we recognize as false because they deny the power of the blood of Jesus)

242

working miracles and healings, seeking to deceive the elect.

True to prophecy, we are told not to marvel at all these things because they must all come to pass before the end.

The second chapter of Nahum, in speaking of this day, says that THE CHARIOTS SHALL RAGE IN THE STREETS; they shall jostle one against the other in the broad ways; they shall seem like torches, they shall run like lightnings. Today this has been true not only of the automobiles in the streets of our own land, but of the armored cars on European battlefields, and in Jerusalem, as they dashed through the streets with the speed of lightning, bearing their swift messengers of death, doing their part to fulfill their share in the prophecies of the coming of the Lord.

We are told also that there are to be signs in the Heaven and in the earth.

BLOOD God knows there has been enough of that shed today;

FIRE See accounts of the huge fires on the battlefield composed of the corpses of the slain, burning of towns and cities.

VAPOR OF SMOKE The air has been filled and permeated with it; smoke from the mouths of cannon, smoke from burning homes, vapors of poisonous gases.

The prophet Joel makes some wonderful prophecies, concerning these last days, that are intensely interesting to Christians. You remember that after aptly describing the DARK AND CLOUDY DAY he told of the outpouring of the Holy Spirit, describing it as the former and latter rain. The former rain, you will recall, began to fall at the day of Pentecost; today you will observe the LATTER RAIN is falling on the earth. The same identical signs which followed the preaching of the word in the former rain, accompany the present outpouring. On the day of Pentecost, also at Ephesus and Caesarea, and throughout the Word of God, when the Holy Spirit fell upon them as in the former rain they all spoke in tongues.

Today in every land the latter rain is falling, and the people are speaking in other tongues, the sick are again being healed through the power in Jesus' Name, demons are being cast out, signs and wonders being wrought by the Holy Spirit, who gives all the glory to Jesus. In the law it is written, "with men of stammering lips and another tongue will I speak to this people and yet for all that, will they not believe."

As for the Jews returning to Jerusalem, many said this could never be yet one breath from God and it is accomplished. The Fig Tree today is putting forth her leaves. Yes every sign is being fulfilled that indicates His coming, men are marrying and giving in marriage, as in the days when Noah predicted the flood.

The cry, Behold the Bridegroom cometh; go ye forth to meet him, is sounding through our land.

Remember the 25th chapter of Matthew. Wake up and examine your lamp. See that it is lighted by the fire of the Holy Ghost; be filled with the Spirit. Consider these things carefully; compare the Word of God with the rapid history-making events of today, and I am sure you will readily agree with me that we are living under the shadow of His near approach, of which He spoke, saying,

"In the morning ye say it will be foul leather today, for the sky is red and lowering. ye fools and hypocrites, ye can discern the face of the sky: but can ye not discern the signs of the times?" Matt 16. Likewise when ye shall see all these things, know that It is near, even at the doors.

THE MARRIAGE OF THE LAMB

A VISION MONTWAIT CAMP RELATED UNDER THE POWER

"To whom shall I my Love compare? Fairest of the fair. Soon I His glory'll share, In the meeting in the air.

"What are these that are arrayed in white robes? and whence came they?" Rev. 7-13.

"Who are these that fly as a cloud, like doves to their windows?" Isaiah 60:8.

THERE is a mighty stir going on in the earth in these days; not only in the earth, but in the Heavens also; a mighty preparation for a swiftly approaching and mighty event. Continuous tremors of excitement are thrilling the Bride and her friends, as with loving hands, all tremble with haste, she is donning her finely embroidered wedding gown, and minutely inspecting her trousseau. Her sandals are upon her feet; she is hastening her final preparations, as the mighty event approaches an event so mighty and near that, as it looms and towers above her, the shadow of its near .approach excludes all else from her view.

There is a mighty examining of lamps. Vessels of oil are being investigated, and those whose oil has either leaked out or been consumed are rushing breathlessly to those who have to sell. Matt, 25. People who intend to be present at the meeting in the air are leaving business, cares of this life, and earthly duties, and with hasty feet, rushing on trains, in cars, everywhere, to Camp Meetings and tarrying meetings in search of oil for their lamps. There is a great washing of robes in the blood of the Lamb. Clear, clarion calls are penetrating the night, commanding sleeping virgins everywhere to awaken, saying:

"BEHOLD THE BRIDEGROOM COMETH"

The Bride is yearning for the Bridegroom. The Bridegroom is yearning for the Bride. The wife is making herself ready. A great longing is filling her soul that naught but He can satisfy. Her eyes are lifted to the clouds, with an unspeakable yearning. Her eyes have caught the vision. She has caught one glimpse of His face; and she is on tip toe, with upturned face, watching, waiting, longing to behold Him whom her soul loveth. Her ears have caught one strain of the Heavenly anthem; she has heard His voice. There are many faces and voices about her, but they cannot win even a fleeting glance. She is waiting, looking, searching the sky, through the darkness and gloom of the long night, with expectant, tear-dimmed eye and up-stretched hands.

The messenger whom God has sent, even the Holy Spirit, to seek and bring the bride for His Son, the Heavenly Isaac, is gathering together those who have said: "I will go with this Man" (Gen. 24:58), and is getting them upon the Holy Ghost elevator, which is to lift them up to Him, and will never leave the Bride till she is safe in the arms of her Lover.

In Heaven also a mighty preparation is going on. The angelic hosts are assembling. There is a great tuning of harps, and stringed instruments; the Heavenly orchestras are learning the Bridal Song for the grand occasion; the greatest day ever known in Heaven, when the Son is to clasp the wife of His bosom in His arms. All the eyes of Heaven are gazing upon the Bride. The Bridegroom is overcome of love for her. Sol. Song 6:5.

The very air is tense with expectancy, as the day approaches.

Suddenly the starry floors of Heaven are split in twain. The faith of the bride has not been in vain.

He that has promised has fulfilled His word; He has kept His promise. The Heavens are opened, and suddenly the rays of light from the throne penetrate and illuminate the gloom of earth. Her enraptured, upturned face is transfigured with His radiance, as she beholds His pierced feet appearing, descending; and then His whole form in wondrous, resplendent robes of light. The whole Heavens are filled with clouds of angels, myriads of angelic hosts. And with leaping, bounding heart, her eyes at last behold His face.

Every harp, every stringed instrument, every trumpet in the orchestra of all Heaven strikes and holds one long, sweet note, that shivers the silence, and explodes with rapturous melody. At the sound a mighty quaking and trembling stirs the earth. The graves burst open. The same Spirit that raised Jesus from the dead, quickens their mortal bodies; and at the call of that rapturous music, they rise, clad in white robes of His righteousness, and with upturned faces and outstretched hands, they bound forth and upward through the air, towards that glorious Form that is radiating the Heavens and filling them with splendor.

Another strain of melody bursts forth in such power that all Heaven trembles with its majestic splendor. At the sound, those waiting upon the earth are transformed. The laws "of gravity lose all control and power to hold them from Him who waits with outstretched arms, as He descends with a shout: "Arise, My Love, My Fair One! and come away" Sol. Songs 2:13. The mortal puts on immortality; the corruptible puts on incorruption.

Her eyes have seen her Lord. She is sweeping through the air to meet Him, and He towards her; with outstretched arms they meet. O, that meeting the air! At last He clasps her in His arms; she for whom He died, and has waited so long.

At last she lays her queenly head upon the bosom of Him for whom she lived, and has pictured so often in her dreams. He wipes away her tears.

Their lips meet as they embrace. All Heaven rocks and sways and trembles as every harp and musical instrument bursts forth with the might and majestic splendor of the wedding song, that rises and falls, echoes and reechoes, through the air.

All Heaven has come forth to behold the meeting in the air, and to welcome the Bride, saying:

"Let us be glad and rejoice, and give honor to Him, for the marriage of the Lamb hath come, and the wife hath made herself ready" Rev. 19:7. They rise together; the Heavens roll together again.

Deeper darkness settles on the earth; but beyond the starry floors of Heaven is great jubilation.

Myriad hosts of angels are banked, tier upon tier, as far as the eye can see, on either side of the long path that leads to the throne, upon which rests a cloud of radiant glory. To the strain of that wondrous wedding march, which beats and pulsates in indescribable grandeur, He leads her, leaning upon His arm, towards the throne, and presents her unto His Father, spotless, blameless, in radiant purity, clad in His righteousness and power.

Then follows a wondrous ceremony, so wonderful that it is unlawful for man to describe; and then the marriage supper of the Lamb, where the Bride and the friends of the Bride are served with joy unspeakable, by angelic hosts in robes of white.

They drink together the wine of the kingdom. She has eyes but for one, her Lord, her Savior, her King, her Husband.

All tears are dried forever. Rev. 21:4. Darkness has vanished away. Rev. 21:23. Naught from her Lord shall ever sever. She will dwell in his presence for aye and aye.

Who is this clad in the splendor of the Sun?

It is Jesus, the Holy One.

The rainbow of peace is under His feet, And in Him the Godhead power complete.

THAT WONDERFUL DAY

JESUS, the Son of God, is soon coming back to this earth again, and the Holy Spirit is sending forth the last call to the Bride to be ready to meet Him in the air. There is a mighty stir going on in the earth today, not only among the sinful nations but amongst the righteous saints who are preparing for the great day of His appearing.

"For the Lord, Himself, shall descend from Heaven with a shout, with the voice of an archangel and the trump of God. The dead in Christ shall rise first, then we who are alive and remain shall be caught up together with them to meet the Lord in the air, and so shall we be ever with the Lord."

What a wonderful day that will be! The most eloquent tongue, the most inspired pen cannot begin to tell of the glory of that great triumphal day.

There have been some wonderful days since the beginning of time, but this day will outshine them all. It was a wonderful day when God spoke the world into being a wonderful day when He set the sun, the moon and stars in the Heavens.

It was a wonderful day when He created man in His own image a wonderful day when man.

having fallen into sin, had been doomed to die and God so loved the world that He promised to send His Son Jesus to suffer and die that He might lift him up from the depths of sin to the highest heights of Glory. It was a wonderful day when the wise men saw His star in the East and Jesus was born a babe in the manger.

There were many wonderful days in Jesus' ministry when He healed the sick, cleansed the lepers, raised the dead, cast out demons, performed miracles and fed the multitudes.

It was a wonderful day when Jesus was tried before Pilate and as a lamb before his shearers is dumb, so He opened not His mouth.

It was a wonderful day when He was nailed to the cross and when He took our place and paid our debt and bore our punishment in His own body on the tree. It was a wonderful day when they laid Him in the tomb and a still more wonderful day when He was resurrected and came forth in triumphant glory and power.

It was a wonderful day when He left the wondering disciples and ascended to His Father in Heaven and a cloud received Him out of sight.

Ah! there is a still more wonderful day coming, the crowning day of all other days, when Jesus shall come back to earth again, when He shall part the clouds and we shall see Him descending from Heaven clad in robes of splendor. This time He is not coming to be spurned and rejected and spit upon and beaten. This time He is coming back a King, victorious, to awaken the overcomers, those who are saved unto the end, who awaken to the Bridal Call. You, too, are called to be in Thai bridal procession. Make restitution, get under the blood, for Jesus is coming soon.

TOWARD MORNING

IT is always darkest just before the dawn. Today the world is enveloped with the darkest shroud of midnight sorrow that has ever been known. Death and misery, slaughter and despair, destruction and devastation are rampant. In hundreds of thousands of homes mothers and wives are weeping and mourning as one who refuses to be comforted, even as I write these words. Plagues and pestilences have been loosed upon the earth today, even as in Egypt's darkness of old. And now, just before morning, the firstborn are being slain, blood is flowing forth like a river, and few indeed are the homes and hearths that have not been touched.

Exodus 12:29 says: "And it came to pass, that at midnight the Lord smote all the firstborn in the land of Egypt, from the firstborn of Pharaoh that sat on his throne, unto the firstborn of the captive that sat in the dungeon. And there was a great cry in Egypt, for there was not a house where there was not one dead." Then came deliverance, and the children of Israel were led forth with singing.

Dear tired, troubled, grief-torn heart, look up, the night is far spent, the long, weary way is almost ended. Weeping may endure for the night but JOY cometh in the morning. And just as sure as yonder sun rose over the hills this morning, banishing the shades of night, just so sure will Jesus, the Sun of righteousness, rise over the hills in immortal glory to take His people, His overcoming children, to that land where tears never flow.

Today, the powers of darkness are closing on every hand. Wickedness is waxing worse and worse, till sometimes, as we read of the staggering condition of affairs, the slaughter of our bravest and best, the shot-torn fields, the stricken homes, the crying of fatherless children, the burning of homes, as we look into the faces blackened and pinched with hunger, as the photographer sends the pictures from over there, as we see the pitiful sight of little children, walking skeletons, perishing horribly for want of bread, our heads reel before the appalling spectacle and it all seems like some hideous nightmare. But no, it is too, too true, darkness has fallen, fallen also in many churches where men have become lovers of pleasure more than lovers of God, fallen where lukewarm professors have a form of godliness but deny the power thereof. But look up, beloved, 'tis almost morning. Hallelujah!

"Strengthen ye the weak hands, and confirm the feeble knees. Say unto them that are of a fearful heart, be strong, fear not: behold your God will come with vengeance, even God with a recompense; He will come and save you. And the ransomed of the Lord will return, and come to Zion with songs and everlasting joy upon their heads; they shall obtain, joy and gladness, and sorrow and sighing shell flee away."

Sometimes in your daily life, amidst the heartaches, the pressure brought to bear against you, the weight of the cross, the thorns along the path, you have almost fainted by the way, but stand fast a little longer, dear one, press on a little further. See! Just over yonder hill tops the gray dawn is breaking, Jesus is coming soon. He is coming to wipe all tears from all faces wherefore comfort ye one another width these words.

Were ever words of comfort so sweet to weary pilgrims? If "Jesus is coming soon" the wondrous words lift the drooping head. "Jesus is coming soon." At that glorious hope the weak hands are lifted high with renewed strength and hope.

"Jesus is coming soon." The words bring with them such a vision of glory that even in this vale of tears eyes are lightened and suffused with rapture because of that glorious morning.

"For the Lord Himself shall descend from Heaven with a shout, with the voice of the archangel, and with the trump of God, and the dead in Christ shall rise first, then we which are alive and remain shall be caught up together with them in the clouds, to meet the Lord in the air; and so shall we ever be with the Lord. I. Thess. 4:16, 17.

Let nothing hinder your progress; though discouragements rise overwhelmingly as an impassable barrier in your path, press on in Jesus' name and that barrier will melt away as shadows before the summer's sunshine. Have you ever walked along a lonely country road at night, and seemed to "see men as trees walking"? Do you remember how yonder crooked stump looked like some giant ready to spring upon you as you passed, how yonder innocent fence-post appeared like some grim spectre of the night, crouching in readiness for some dire, unspeakable deed even the sounds of the night seemed different and at the lowing of the cow or its nibbling at the grass your heart pounded as you cried, "What's that!" You laughed at your fears when morning's light drove away the shadows and revealed the source of the sounds; so it is with us, dear ones, if we press on through the gloom all our fears will prove but folly, for in Him we are safely hidden from all danger.

The lions that roar are in reality chained and unable to harm you while you walk close to him.

Fear not the grim spectres of the night, no matter how the enemy may seek to intimidate you. Press on, 'twill not be long now till all the shades of night are rolled away and we see Jesus face to face.

All that we have sacrificed and suffered down in this old world will be forgotten, yea, will fade into insignificance before just one look into the eyes of our beloved who cometh quickly. Go through, though it means losing every friend on earth, though it means standing alone, persecution, reproach, death to self, and a daily reckoning ourselves crucified with Him. For He that endureth to the end, the same shall be saved. Keep low under the blood; be filled with the Spirit; let your robes be kept spotless, your sandals upon your feet, your vessels filled with oil, in readiness until the day break and the shadows flee away.

THE PLAN OF REDEMPTION

IN order to make the great Plan of Redemption simple and plain to a certain audience, and that the eye might assist the ear and the understanding of many who knew little or nothing about God's Word, or of the combined efforts of the Triune God to save a sinful race, I conceived the idea of drawing "The Plan of Redemption" chart. It sets forth in a simple, panoramic form the chain of events from creation and the fall to the final restoration of all things.

The first three divisions in this chain, as you will see, represent the dispensation of the Father, the dispensation of the Son, and the dispensation of the Holy Ghost, as linked together in their combined efforts to redeem sinful humanity.

FATHER

Over the first circle is placed a coffin, representing the sin and death that reigned from the time of Adam to Moses, and from Moses on to Christ.

Satan, who had been cast out of Heaven, tempted our forefathers (the first inhabitants of the earth), led them into disobedience and sin, thus causing the downfall of the whole human race. God, in His holiness, could not look upon sin with the least degree of allowance, "wherefore, as by one man, sin entered into the world, and death by sin, death passed upon all men for that all have sinned."

The first chapter of Genesis opens with life and creation pulsing everywhere; the last verse of the last chapter of Genesis ends with a dead-man embalmed and buried in a coffin in Egypt. "The soul that sinneth, it shall die" was the verdict that God had given, and His word could not be broken; thus the whole human family had gotten themselves into a box, a coffin that they could not get out of.

The human race began with a perfect man and woman, fashioned in the likeness of God's own self, walking together with Him in life and purity beneath the fruitful trees of the garden of Eden and ended in a coffin, the sentence of death passed upon the seed of woman.

God, in His plan of Redemption, reversed the whole order of things.

He began with a man (Jesus Christ whose blood was shed for sinners) lying in a tomb, still and cold in death, and ends with a perfect man and woman (Christ and His bride) walking with God beneath the never-fading trees of the New Jerusalem in eternal life and purity.

Just as Eve was deceived by the fair words of the serpent, and just as Adam was not deceived, but took willingly and knowingly of the forbidden fruit, so it was that when the whole human race was deluded and deceived by the tempter and condemned to death, Jesus, our second Adam, willingly and knowingly came down and partook of the fruits of death and stood by the sinner's side that he might take the sinner's place, bear the sinner's banishment, die the sinner's death, and lift him from the fall.

In that fall from grace, mankind fell so low and descended to such depths, that nothing short of the combined efforts of the Triune God could lift him up or reinstate him in the presence of the Father blameless, without spot or wrinkle or any such thing. During the dispensation of the Father, as recorded from Genesis to Malachi, God had repeatedly promised that in the fulness of time He would bestow a love gift upon this sinful world that gift was to be Jesus, His only begotten Son.

He, Jesus, was to bruise the serpent's head, and by His own precious blood on the cross bridge the gulf 'twixt man and God, rend the veil, and open a new and a living way into the Holy of Holies.

Through the centuries recorded in the Old Testament, and divided into periods Creation and Adam sin enters flood Moses leads the children of Israel forth Canaan land minor prophets a faithful people had been looking forward to the cross and the day when Jesus would shed His blood see types and shadows shedding of blood of bulls, goats and lambs), just as we who live in the dispensation of the Holy Ghost today look back to the cross and the blood shed thereupon.

249

True to His promise, in the fulness of time, "God so loved the world that He gave His only begotten Son, that whosoever believeth in Him should not perish, but have everlasting life."

SON

The second dispensation (that of the Son), is recorded in the four Gospels of the New Testament.

It is overshadowed on the chart by the cross, even as the old dispensation had been overshadowed by the coffin (sin and death), and is joined to the first dispensation by the small preparatory link the preaching of John the Baptist.

In delivering his two great messages "Repent" and "Behold the Lamb of God," John the Baptist prophesies the coming of the dispensation of the Holy Ghost. "There cometh One after me the latchet of whose shoe I am not worthy to unloose.

He, when He is come, will baptize you with the Holy Ghost and fire." It is as though John looked right straight through this circle upon the chart the work of the Son and saw the end from the beginning. There are many things he might have said about Jesus.

He, when He is come, will heal the sick; He, when He is come, will raise the dead, feed the hungry multitudes, cleanse the lepers, shed His blood, and be resurrected the third day; but looking through all of these things, wonderful as they were, with the clear vision of the Spirit, John looks ahead and cries:

"He, when He is come, will baptize you with the Holy Ghost and fire."

The second dispensation, the life of Jesus, taking in the birth of Christ boyhood baptism in Jordan ministry last supper and garden crucifixion and burial and the resurrection of our Lord while completely spanning the gulf between God and man, and bringing salvation from sin through His precious blood, still needed the work and dispensation of the Holy Spirit, third person of the Trinity, to complete the plan of redemption in its fullest sense. Jesus plainly declares:

"It is expedient for you that I go away; for if I go not away, the Comforter will not come."

There must needs be a third story to the ark, in which the sin-cursed multitude might take refuge to escape the flood of judgment which must fall upon the iniquities of earth.

HOLY GHOST

Just as the Father bestowed the gift of Jesus Christ, His Son, as a love gift to the sinner so now in turn, Jesus bestowed the Holy Ghost, the promise of the Father, His love gift to the believer.

The link which joins the dispensation of the Spirit to that of the Son is the ten days between the ascension of the Lord and the outpouring of the Holy Spirit, wherein the one hundred and twenty tarried for the promised Comforter. 'Tis as though the Father joined hands with the Son and the Son with the Holy Spirit, that by their unity and oneness of purpose, the plan of redemption might be wrought out.

Just as sin and death overshadowed circle one and the work of the cross rises high aloft above any other event in circle two, so now the Holy Spirit, as a dove, broods over and overshadows the dispensation of the Holy Ghost.

The dispensation of the Holy Ghost, which began on the day of Pentecost, we are still living in, and will be living in, in fact, until Jesus sweeps back the billowy clouds which curtain earth from Heaven, and takes His bride unto Himself.

Today we live in the closing hours of the dispensation of the Holy Spirit. Looking back through the centuries which it embraces, since the day of Pentecost, we see first, the church filled with power signs and wonders wrought under the downpour of the former rain which accompanied the first seed-sowing days loss of the gifts and power-loss of the teaching of the Holy Ghost the days when the curtains of the dark ages obscured the light of justification by faith then restoration begins, and the teaching of the Holy Ghost and latter rain is flung broadcast.

We stand today on the verge of the coming of the Lord. Through the power of the Spirit the church is being restored to the full standard of Pentecostal power and perfection. A little band of despised overcomers is coming through blood and fire, triumphant, purged and made white through the blood of the Lamb. With uplifted faces and stretched-out arms, its members are yearning for the coming of the Lord the bright and morning star the Son of righteousness who shall arise with healing in His wings.

"For the Lord Himself shall descend from Heaven with a shout..the dead in Christ shall be raised first; then those that are alive and remain shall be caught up together with them to, meet the Lord in the air, and so shall we ever be with the Lord."

SON

While the resurrected and translated saints are caught up in the rapture to the wedding and marriage supper of the Lamb, link three, the tribulation, sorrow and punishment such as was never known, leads on to the day in which the Lord shall descend with His saints, and the government shall be upon His shoulders. "For He must reign till He hath put all enemies under His feet."

The dragon, that old serpent, which is the Devil and Satan, shall be bound a thousand years and cast into the bottomless pit, where an angel shall shut him up and set a seal upon him that he deceive the nations no more till the thousand years shall be fulfilled, and after that he must be loosed for a little season.

Then shall be fulfilled the prayer of our Lord "Thy kingdom come; Thy mil be done on earth as it is in Heaven." The saints, who have overcome, who have neither worshipped the beast nor His image, who have refused to receive his mark upon their forehead, or in their hand, shall "live and reign with Christ a thousand years." Rev. 20:4.

Read Rev. 20 (1 to 15). When the thousand years have expired Satan shall be loosed out of his prison for a little season, and shall go out to deceive the nations, inasmuch that they shall gather round the beloved city and compass the camp of the saints, but fire shall come down from God out of Heaven and devour them. The devil that deceived them shall be cast, not into the bottomless pit again, but this time into the lake of fire and brimstone, where the beast and the false prophet are, and shall be tormented day and night forever and ever.

FATHER

Then comes the great white throne judgment, when the dead, both small and great, shall be called to stand before God, before the face of whom earth and Heaven flee away.

The book of life shall be opened and the dead shall be judged out of those things which are written in the books, according to their works.

The sea shall give up the dead which are in it; death and hell shall deliver up their dead and they shall be judged, every man according to his works.

Then it is that Jesus "shall have delivered up the kingdom to God, even the Father" and "shall be subject unto Him that put all things under Him, that God may be all in all" I Cor. 24, 28.

Thus the Lord, having subdued His enemies, places the reins again in the hands of the Father, the plan of redemption completed.

Read the chart from left to right Father, Son, Holy Ghost, Son, Father. Now read it from right to left it is the same.

The circle has been closed, but the work of redemption is not complete until the vision seen by John on the Isle of Patmos has materialized and again the perfect man and the perfect woman Christ and His bride walk beneath the ever-verdant trees, whose leaves shall not fade, and whose fruit shall not decay. The final overthrow of the devil and his power shall be brought about: sin shall never enter there.

Oh, the infinite love and patience the sweat drops of blood the thought the labors the toils of the Triune God to redeem a fallen world and bring back unbroken communion with Father, Son and Holy Ghost!

251

THE BRIDE IN HER VEIL OF TYPES AND SHADOWS

AN AFTERNOON TALK GIVEN AT VICTORIA HALL, LOS ANGELES, CAL, FEB. 9, 1919

"Come hither, I will show thee the Bride, the Lamb's Wife." Rev. 21:9.

THE great Wedding of the King of Kings is soon to take place. The most colossal preparations are being made, both in Heaven and in earth. In the angelic hosts above, and in the Bridal Company on earth, harps are being tuned and the first superb strains of the New Song the Wedding Song are flowing forth from love-filled hearts in liquid streams of praise.

Every Spirit-filled child of God each member of the Bridal Body, is wide awake and on tip-toe now, looking for the coming forth of the Bridegroom who is soon to appear in the clouds of glory.

Mortal mind cannot picture nor conceive the stupendous glory and beauty that will flood the Heavens at His appearance.

Have you ever stood, spell-bound, in the rosy glow of early morning, as the rising sun threw back the shades of night, touching and illuminating each snowy cloud and transforming them into flaming, livid beauty, until the whole sky seemed filled with angels' wings of gold and fire and crimson?

Have you ever wondered, if the earthly sun could rise with such attendant glory, what the coming of the Son of Righteousness, who shall rise with healing in His wings, will be?

Yes, the Marriage of the Lamb is at hand. The Bridegroom, who has gone to prepare a place for His Bride, is soon to appear.

On earth the Bride is making the final preparations: the last finishing touch is being put upon her trousseau. The days of her purification with oil of myrrh and with sweet odors are almost accomplished; the day when she shall be brought forth unto the King has come.

Even in the natural, a bride is ever an object of interest and a whispered

"Here comes the bride" is enough to arouse the instant attention and smiling interest of an hundred pair of eyes.

In the spiritual the interest in the Bride is intensified a thousand fold, and surely this interest is begotten by the Spirit, for just as the angel spoke unto the beloved disciple on the Isle of Patmos, saying:

"Come hither, I will show thee the Bride, the Lamb's wife" and caught him away in the Spirit to a great and high mountain, there to reveal her glories to him, so the Holy Spirit today speaks to the children of God, saying:

"Come hither (to the Word of God) and I will show thee the Bride, the Lamb's wife."

Once He has caught us up unto the mountain, and has begun to unfold the Word before our wondering eyes, we gaze into its pages and see the Bride in almost every picture.

We see her in the PAST, wrapped in a mist of types and shadows.

We see her in the PRESENT, emerging from the types and shadows, coming forth a living, visible, Spirit-filled, Spirit-led people, humble and lowly, yet walking with the dignity and majesty of her coming Lord.

We see her in the FUTURE, reigning with her Bridegroom upon the everlasting throne, in that glorious City, where the streets are all pure gold, the gates are a solid pearl, and where joy and praises forever echo through His courts.

THE BRIDE - A RIB COMPANY - BROUGHT FORTH FROM THE WOUNDED SIDE OF THE BRIDEGROOM

Gen. 2:21.

Looking into the past where the Word is filled with types and shadows of the Bride and her coming forth to meet the Bridegroom, one of the first types that the Spirit shows us is that of Adam and Eve.

It was a man and a woman (Adam and Eve) who first brought sin and death into the world, and It will be a man and a woman (Christ and His Church) who will go forth together, hand in hand, ruling and reigning, when the last grim foe of sin and death is conquered. Bless the Lord.

For the FIRST ADAM "there was not found an help meet" (Gen. 2:20), in all the beautiful garden of Eden wherein he dwelt. "And the Lord God caused a deep sleep to fall upon Adam "(Gen. 2:21), and while he slept He took out one of his ribs, and of the "ribs which He had taken from man made He a woman and brought her unto the man." (Gen. 2:22.) Here immediately we see a beautiful type of The SECOND ADAM for whom, amongst all the seraphic hosts of Heaven there was not found an help meet. Then came the deep sleep of death which the Lord God allowed to come upon Him, and as He slept, there on the cross, His side was opened wide and Hallelujah! From the wounded side of Jesus, our Second Adam, a rib company is being formed today and will soon be brought to the man Christ Jesus, to be His wife and His help meet forever.

THE CLOTHING OF THE BRIDE MUST BE BLOOD-BOUGHT

Gen. 3:21

Then comes the day when Adam and Eve realized their need of clothing. By their own efforts an apron of fig-leaves was made but not approved of by God. Man by his own works and by garments of his own self-righteous making, can never please the Father. His covering must needs be bought at the price of blood, therefore was the blood of an innocent creature shed and the Lord God did make coats of skins (skins typifying the covering and righteousness of Jesus), and clothed them.

THE OFFERING OF THE BRIDE MUST BE MADE BY BLOOD

Gen. 4:4, 5

Though CAIN brought the best fruits of the ground the best results his own works and labors could make unto his offering the Lord had no respect.

But when ABEL brought the firstlings of his flock, the slain lamb, and God saw the blood, He had respect unto this offering.

Good works and man-made efforts can never win the respect of God, but when the humblest saint, upon his knees, comes with an offering made through the blood of Calvary's Lamb, he, through that blood, commands the respect and approval of all Heaven.

PREPARATION OF ARK SEPARATION AND OBEDIENCE OF BRIDE

Gen. 6, 7, 8

"Come hither and I will show thee the Bride, the Lamb's wife" cries the living Word, as we turn our eyes upon the Ark, the Noahic Covenant, and the flood of waters that covered the earth.

The Holy Spirit catches up the searchlight of Mat. 27:37-39, and turns its blazing light full upon the mists and shadows that before so shrouded this Genesis 6th, 7th and 8th chapters as to make it seem nothing more than a history of bygone days.

The illuminating words of Jesus:

"As IT WAS, in the days of Noah So SHALL IT BE" reach out and draw aside the outer veil and reveal the inner depths, until the pages seem alive again, peopled with the surging, sinful masses of today. Again the wickedness of man is great the earth filled with corruption and violence.

Again through raging storm, through war and plague and pestilence, we hear the warning voice of God:

"My Spirit shall not always strive with man . . . I will destroy them with the earth" Again we see God's little remnant, His infinitely precious few His Noahs, the just and perfect ones, who, with their households, walk with God. Again we see the faithful, whose ears are open to the call of God, whose eyes have discerned the darkening sky, overcast with threatening clouds. Then in their midst there looms the three-storied Ark, with its one door set within the side, and the one window, in the top. At the words:

"As IT WAS ... so SHALL IT BE" the three-storied Ark blazes forth throughout obscurity, and we perceive that its three stories are composed of none other material than the combined, united, three-fold efforts of a loving, Triune God. The dispensation of the SON was builded upon the sure foundation of the Father's love (John 3:16); the dispensation of the Holy Spirit was built upon that of the Son (John 16:7).

The OPEN DOOR within the side that seemed but common-place before, now fills our hearts with love our eyes with tears, for the Spirit whispers:

"The Door? Who could it be but Jesus, through whose wounded side a new and living way was opened, leading through Himself unto the depths of the Father's love and the heights of the Spirit's power?"

Again we hear the call ring in our ears:

"Come, thon, and all thy house, into the Ark"- we see the Bridal Company passing through the Door separated and shut away from the outside world, within the staunch and storm-proof vessel of the Triune God that will weather every gale.

In the CLOSING OF THE DOOR we see the closing of the day of mercy.

In the FALLING OF THE RAIN the raging of the seas the rising of the floods that envelop the earth and all that therein is (Rev. 16), we see the coming tribulation and dire sorrow soon to burst upon this world.

The RISING OF THE ARK, surmounting every wave, shielding the little, chosen, faithful few from wind and rain, is Father, Son and Holy Spirit, enveloping, catching up the Bride, and holding her on high above the turmoil of coming tribulation's waves.

THE WARNING, HASTY FLIGHT AND ESCAPE OF THE BRIDE

Gen. 19:17-30

The Bride small in number (Math. 7:14) despised of men beloved of God how she rises from each Spirit-filled page, as the Spirit takes the things of Christ and reveals them unto us.

We turn our eyes upon the destruction of Sodom and Gomorrah, and again, as the Spirit's hand sweeps back the curtain, we find ourselves gazing into the living, surging throngs of today the vain, sin-filled earth the coming tribulation the escape of the obedient few and the falling of God's fiery wrath.

In that wicked city, Sodom, we see our lands today, wherein wickedness has waxed worse and worse.

In the humble, obedient Lot, we see the Bride dwelling in the midst of a perverse and crooked generation, in the world and yet not of it.

In the coming of the two angels at even, and their warning cry at midnight, we recognize the " SPIRIT AND THE WORD" warning of the coming tribulation and urging instant flight. As soon as the two angels had warned Lot, he, in turn, hastening to warn his sons-in-law, crying:

"Up, get you out of this place, for the Lord will destroy this city "This is the cry of the CHURCH" today as she prepares to leave this earth.

In the mocking and unbelief of the sons-in-law we see mirrored the attitude of the world at large today when warned of the impending of God.

As they lingered, the two angels laid hold upon the hands of Lot, his wife and his two laughters, and brought them forth and set them without the city. The Spirit and the Word are today aying hold upon the hands of God's little children and bringing them forth and setting them without the city in a life of real separation unto the Lord.

The cry "Escape for thy life, look not behind thee, neither stay thee in all the plain escape to the mountain lest thou be consumed," is the cry of the Spirit and the Word to God's little family today. "Escape for thy life, destruction is coming, no time to look back now; neither stay thou in all the plain" for the Lord is calling a called-out, out of a called-out, out of a called-out people who will escape to the mountains (rise up into the heights of God).

At the hesitation of Lot, the cry of "Haste thee, for I cannot do anything until thou be come hither," we find mingled with the cry of the angel ascending from the east in Rev. 7:2-3, "hurt not the earth, neither the sea, nor the trees, until we have sealed the servants of our God in their foreheads."

In the looking back and the turning to a pillar of salt of Lot's wife, we see the condition of backsliding churches and individuals today, standing, stiff and frozen, at the very point where they first looked back. This is no time for looking back, 'tis a time to go forth quickly, Bless the Lord.

In the raining upon Sodom and Gomorrah of brimstone and fire from the Lord out of Heaven the overthrow of the cities and all the inhabitants of the cities, and that which grew upon the ground" we recognize the fiery wrath and indignation and judgment of God, the great tribulation foretold in Revelation.

Lot and his daughters took refuge in a cave in the mountain. The Cave in which we hide is Christ; the Cave is in the Mountain God (Dan. 2:45.)

In the safe refuge of Lot and his daughters in the cave in the mountain we see the faithful children of the Lord whose lives are hidden away with Christ in God, far above the fiery indignation poured upon the earth.

THE SPIRIT ABIDES WITH AND GUIDES THE BRIDE

FROM THE WELL OF SALVATION TO THE ARMS OF THE BRIDEGROOM

Gen. 24

Turning the pages we open at the story of Rebecca, the bride chosen for Isaac by Eliezer, the servant of Abraham.

Again the Spirit holds aloft the light of Revelation, and again the printed page, with its history of what seemed at first glance but an interesting account of the romance and love of an earthly Isaac and Rebecca, fades away.

We find ourselves gazing into the mirror of yesterday, which throws back the reflection of today.

REBECCA RISES with a new dignity the dignity of the Bride of Christ
AND COMING OUT (separation)
To THE WELL (salvation)
GOES DOWN (humility)
AND FILLS HER PITCHER (with joy shall ye draw waters from the wells of salvation)
AND COMES UP (the way down is the way up "he who humbleth himself shall be exalted.")

As the servant runs to meet her; tells her of the glorious Bridegroom far away, and opens the door to bridehood, the light of understanding falls upon him, and we recognize at once the blessed Holy Spirit sent to guide us into all truth.
(John 16:13.)
RUNNING to meet the pure in heart at salvation's well
REVEALING the beauties and attributes of the Heavenly Bridegroom, and

INVITING all who are willing to bid farewell to earth's dearest relations and ties, to mount the bumpy camel of daily tests and trials (knowing that when we are tried we shall come forth as pure gold)

LED BY the Spirit, and go forth to meet the Bridegroom. (Mat. 25:6.)

In Isaac's walking forth in the field to meet Rebecca at eventide, we see in type our Bridegroom Jesus coming forth in the clouds to meet His Bride at the end of her pilgrim journey.

And when Rebecca, lifting up her eyes, beholds Isaac, and alights from off her camel, our hearts leap within us at the vision of the day when the Bride's lifted eyes shall behold her Redeemer.

Then shall she alight forever from the camel of tests and trials and hardships, and all her tears shall be wiped away.

In the veil with which she covered herself we behold the Bride at His coming, completely shut off and obscured from the sight of the world.

The closing words: "And SHE BECAME HIS WIFE," set the chiming wedding bells of Revelation 19:7 ringing in our hearts.

The words: "And HE LOVED HER" flood our souls and overwhelm us with holy joy and rapture.

If, when we were yet sinners, He loved us enough to shed His blood for us; if He loved us at the cross enough to wash our sins away; if He loved us enough to fill us with His Spirit and put the finely embroidered wedding gown upon us, what mortal pen can be enough inspired the boundaries of what human mind can be enough enlarged to depict the LOVE that will be wished upon the Bride when she becomes (O, holy, sacred word) His wife!

CONSECRATION UNTO LIFE OR DEATH GLEANING HUMILITY, AND REWARD OF THE BRIDE

Ruth 1,2,3,4

Turning to the book of Ruth we again behold the Bride.

Chapter One, Leaving HER NATIVE COUNTRY, following the God of Naomi, and making her consecration, which was to be unto life or death.

Chapter Two, GLEANING in the fields, from the beginning to the end of the harvest gathering sheaves watched over and fed by the Bridegroom, Boaz.

In Chapter Three, we behold her LOVE FOR THE BRIDEGROOM,, and her desire to be his bride, and the deeper consecration that caused her (verse 3) to WASH HERSELF (from all her works and labors) ANOINT HERSELF WITH OIL (the anointing that abides the oil of the Spirit)

PUT HER RAIMENT UPON HER (the fine linen, clean and white, which is the righteousness of the saints, Rev. 19:8, embroidered with the fine needlework and wrought gold of Psalms 45:13-14),

AND GET HER DOWN TO THE FLOOR (in lowliness and humility to lie at the feet and mercy of the Bridegroom, covered with the skirt of his garment (verse 13) "till the morning" breaks and the shadows flee away.)

In Chapter Four we behold RUTH THE BRIDE, who, though shut out by her nearest kin the Law who was unable to redeem her (Deut. 23:3) , was admitted by Grace when wedded to Boaz, who became at once her Redeemer and her Bridegroom.

What a picture! Bless the Lord!

THE BRIDE, TRUE IN THE MIDST OF FIERY TRIAL

PROTECTED FROM ITS BLAST

Dan. 3:21

The pages turn again. This time we gaze upon the three Hebrew children, Shadrach, Meshach and Abednego.

Firmly do they refuse to bend the knee in worship or in compromise to the gods of this world.

Fearlessly, their words ring out, declaring unsaverving faith and allegiance to Jehovah, the one true God.

Breathlessly, we watch them bound in their coats, hosen, hats and other garments; cast into the midst of the burning, fiery furnace, protected, preserved, and delivered from the heat of the flame.

Then, all at once, we opened our eyes in amazed recognition and look again to find, as the burning flame penetrates the mists of types and shadows, that these THREE (with the Son of God in their midst) are none other than the BRIDE herself, BODY, SOUL and SPIRIT, protected and preserved amidst the raging flames. (Pray God your whole spirit and soul and body be preserved blameless unto the coming of our Lord, Jesus Christ I Thess. 5:23.)

Walking unharmed in the midst of temptation and fiery trial, without the smell of scorching, we catch a glimpse of the glorious Bride who is being prepared by the Spirit to abide the "day of His coming" (Mal. 3:2), and to dwell with our God, who is a consuming fire.

Suddenly the furnace door swings wide, and the voice of the King is heard crying:

"Ye servants of the Most High God, 'COME FORTH' and 'COME HITHER' and with eyes of faith and hope we see a doorway opening in the Heavens, leading from the furnace of this world into the presence of the King, and hear the voice of the Kingly Bridegroom saying:

"Well done, good and faithful servants, 'COME 'UP, higher 'OUT OF' the 'FIERY FURNACE' and 'TRIALS OF EARTH' and be thou promoted in My provinces, even to My throne to reign with Me."

THE PRAYING BRIDE DWELLS THROUGH THE NIGHT WITH LOCK- JAWED LIONS, AND IS LIFTED AT BREAK OF DAY

Dan. 6:10-23

Next we catch a glimpse of the praying bride as revealed through the prophet Daniel.

His eyes of discernment are open wide (Dan. 5:25-28.)

The windows of his chamber (the eyes of his soul) are open toward Jerusalem (the coming of the Lord Rev. 21:2).

Neither threat nor cunning of the enemy could stop this valiant, earnest soul who, down in the depths of the lions' den, watched and prayed while the angel of the Lord held and locked the lions' jaws.

At break of day the stone was rolled away from the mouth of the den, and the voice of the King was heard saying:

"It is enough, come up unto me," and was lifted from the lions' den, and stood upon his feet beside the King.

The BRIDE of King Jesus, though shut in by the dark night of this world, and surrounded by raging lions demons and men, who would gladly gnash upon her and rend her with their teeth is protected by the Holy Spirit (the angel of the Lord), who shuts the mouths of all who would destroy her.

Watchfully, trustfully, she lifts her eyes, clear, undimmed, luminous with the light of faith, and fixes them upon the door in momentary expectancy.

Well does she know that He who will come, will come and not tarry. Well does she know that the long night will soon be over and that at break of day the King's voice will be heard calling her from above, as He rolls back the clouds and opens a door in Heaven through which He will lift her forever from the lions' den of this world into His own glorious presence, in that land where no ravenous beast can come.

In verse 24 we behold the wicked ones who had cast her into the den of trials and persecutions, themselves cast into the midst of the furious, ravenous beasts. No angel's hand will be there to stay their fury; all their bones shall be broken and they shall be utterly consumed.

Here again is the tribulation which immediately follows the catching up of the Bride into the presence of the King.

THE SLAIN LAMB MUST HAVE A SLAIN BRIDE THE RESURRECTED BRIDEGROOM A RESURRECTED BRIDE

On and on through the long, Heaven-canopied corridors of the Word, the Spirit leads, until at last a hush enwraps our souls, as we are brought to a manger, and our reverent eyes, looking down into its depths, behold the Christ-child cradled in its soft embrace.

The Holy Spirit Christ-revealing Guide softly whispers in our ear:

"As He was in the world, so shall you be . . .

that when He shall appear ye shall be like Him and see Him as He is."

Looking still upon the tiny form, the Christ-child fades from our vision; and in its place we see the Christ-life of the Bride, conceived and brought forth from a pure and virgin life, o'ershadowed by the Holy Spirit's power. (Luke 1:35.) As the child in stature grows (Eph. 4:15) from milk to meat (Heb. 5:13-14), we see him walking ever in the shadow and the glory of the Cross. (Mat. 16:24.)

Knowing Him in the fellowship of His sufferings, the Bride dies out to earth and self, until she cries aloud with Paul:

"I am crucified with Christ; nevertheless I live, yet not I, but Christ liveth in me; and the life that I now live in the flesh, I live by the faith of the Son of God; who loved me, and gave Himself for me." (Gal. 2:20.)

Thus we behold the Bride the Lamb's wife, knowing Him not only in the fellowship of His sufferings, but also in the power of His resurrection; yielding herself as one who is alive from the dead one who is risen with Him and shall, therefore, reign with Him forevermore. Just as resurrection power preceded the translation of our Lord, so the Bride, now rising up and coming forth in resurrected glory, shall soon receive the translation power of Acts 1:9, I Thess. 4:17, and rise mid-air, to meet her Lord.

These are but a few of the many mist-wrapt types unveiled before our eyes a few of the erstwhile concealing shadows now dispersed by the illumination of the Spirit as He reveals the Bride before our wondering eyes. (John 14:26, John 16:13-14.)

We might continue our search of the hidden treasures revealed through Esther, the Songs of Solomon, the ten virgins with their lamps, and many others.

We might press on and gaze through the eyes of "John the Beloved" from Patmos, the blest and sea-bound isle, at the glorious, REIGNING BRIDE, seated with her royal Bridegroom upon His throne.

We might gaze upon the regal power and splendor with which the King hath clothed her upon the Heavenly Jerusalem in which she dwells, with its streets of gold, its jeweled walls, its gates of pearl, its flowers that never fade, and the fruits that ne'er decay, its sea of glass, its ransomed throng with harps of gold, and its light that never shall grow dim.

The time for this afternoon talk is gone, however, before our subject is well begun. But get your Bibles down when you go home, open wide its pages, take the lighted lamp of Psalms 119:105 in your one hand, place the other in the hand of the Holy "Spirit, and let Him guide you through the long, begemmed, Heaven-lit corridors of God's eternal Word, that stretch in an unbroken line from the first verse of Genesis to the last verse of Revelation.

Then quicken your step, beloved, fasten your girdle tightly about you; bind your sandals securely upon your feet; and with spotless robes and glowing heart, go quickly forth to meet your Lord, for He is coming soon.

258

ISAAC AND REBECCA

A REMARKABLE TYPE OF CHRIST AND HIS BRIDE

(From a sermon, Bethel Temple, Chicago, 111)

THERE are many beautiful types of Christ and His Bride in the Old Testament. One of the most precious and striking of these types is that of Isaac and Rebecca.

Just as in the Word of God, the whole story and plan of Redemption circles around a company of four namely, the Father, the Son, the Holy Spirit and the Bride so, in this type, the story is woven around the four central figures of Abraham, who is a type of God, the Father, Isaac, who is a type of Jesus, the Son, Eliezer, the servant, who is a type of the Holy Spirit, sent from God to search for and bring the Bride, and

Rebecca, who is a type of the Bridal Body being called forth to meet the Bridegroom.

ISAAC AND JESUS, BOTH LONG LOOKED FOR, COME AS A FULFILLMENT OF PROMISE

For many long years Sarah had looked forward with intense longing for the coming of Isaac, the birth of the man-child who was to take away her shame. Sometimes hoping, sometimes despairing, she waited 'till finally God spoke out of the long silence, and Isaac came as a fulfillment of promise.

For centuries humanity had waited and looked for the coming of Jesus the Son, who was to redeem and bear away the shame of each sinner w r ho put his trust in Him. Then God spoke, by His Spirit, to Mary, and Jesus came as a fulfillment of the promise of the Father, and a sacrificial offering to everyone that believes.

Who can describe or fathom the flood of love that must have filled the heart of Abraham, as he looked upon his son, his only son, Isaac, the son of promise. As the lad grew, he was the pride of Abraham's heart; he was the treasure of his house. But much as Abraham loved Isaac, he loved God more.

The greatest test of Love is Sacrifice, and to sound the depths of Abraham's love God put him to the test, by saying to him:

"Take now thy son, thine only son, Isaac, whom thou lovest, and get thee unto the land of Moriah; and offer him there for a burnt offering "(Gen. 22:2.) How similar is this verse to John 3:16, which says: "God so loved the world that He gave His only begotten Son."

Abraham stood the test, and rising up early in the morning, he saddled his ass, and taking with him two young men and his son, he clave the wood for the burnt offering, and rose up, and went to the place God had told him. Then came the long journey, but though his heart was bleeding with love for his only son, the steps of the father never faltered, but he went on and on, surmounting every hill of difficulty, till he saw the place afar off.

Bless His dear Name. How far God our Father journeyed to offer His Son Jesus! He surmounted every hill; He climbed the mount of Sinai; He never faltered; but though it meant giving the richest treasure of Heaven, the Son of His bosom, He came on and on till at last He saw the place, and Calvary's hill came into view. Still, without a moment's hesitation, He journeyed on. "For God so loved the world that He gave His only begotten Son, that whosoever believeth in Him should not perish, but have everlasting life."

ISAAC BEARS THE WOOD TO HILL OF MORIAH, JESUS BEARS CROSS TO TOP OF CALVARY'S HILL.

"And Abraham took the wood for the burnt offering, and laid it upon Isaac his son; and he took the fire in his hand, and the knife; and they went, both of them together." It was Abraham's own hand that placed the wood upon him whom he was to have offered, upon the shoulders of Isaac, as he ascended Mount Moriah. It was God's own hand which willingly suffered the cross of wood to be laid upon the bleeding back of Jesus, as He bore it up Calvary's hill.

"Then Isaac spake unto Abraham his father, and said, 'MY FATHER'" (O, the great heartfelt cry of Jesus "MY FATHER, My God, why hast Thou forsaken Me?" Isaac said:

"My father, here is the fire; here is the wood; but where is the lamb for the offering?" And Abraham said:

"My son, God will provide Himself a Lamb." Ah! What a Lamb, what a bleeding, spotless Lamb God did provide when He gave Jesus as a propitiation for our sins!

A RAM TAKES THE PLACE OF ISAAC, NONE COULD TAKE THE PLACE OF JESUS

At last the top of the hill had been reached; the altar was completed; the wood had been laid in order, and Abraham had bound Isaac his son, and laid him on the wood on the altar. Then, just as Abraham stretched forth his hand and took the knife to slay his son, the angel of the Lord called to him out of Heaven (Why, I believe every angel in Heaven was looking down to see this wonderful exhibition of faith and obedient love to God), and the angel said:

"Lay not thine hand upon the child, for now I know that thou fearest God, seeing that thou hast not withheld thy son, thine only son, from me" (Gen. 22:12.)

And Abraham lifted up his eyes, and behold, behind him was a ram, caught in a thicket by his horns. And Abraham took the ram and offered him up for a burnt offering INSTEAD OF HIS SON.

A ram was able to substitute for Isaac, but none could ever substitute or fill the place of Jesus. He was led up Calvary's hill, bearing His cross of wood. He was laid like Isaac upon the wood, the hand with the knife (the hand with the spear, in Jesus' case) was raised for the blow, but even though the Father Himself had to turn away His face, no angel cried from Heaven to stay the blow. It fell, and the blood of Jesus flowed forth with the healing of the nations in its crimson flood. Jesus, the Lamb of God, slain from the foundation of the world, had paid the price; by His sacrifice brought redemption to all who should come beneath the cleansing blood forever.

ABRAHAM SENDS HIS ELDEST SERVANT BACK INTO HIS COUNTRY TO SEARCH OUT A BRIDE FOR HIS SON ISAAC. GOD SENDS THE HOLY SPIRIT BACK TO THIS WORLD TO SEARCH OUT AND BRING A BRIDE FOR HIS SON JESUS

Skipping lightly over the intervening years, we come, in the 24th Chapter of Genesis, to the day when Abraham called his eldest servant to him and commissioned him solemnly to go back into his own country to choose a wife for his son Isaac. Abraham made the servant swear he would not choose a wife from amongst the Canaanites, where he then dwelt, but commanded him thus:

"Go unto my country, and to my kindred, and take a wife unto my son Isaac."

How far beyond our feeble minds is this great love of God! How the magnitude of His abounding grace o'er whelms us when we remember that He did not permit a bride to be chosen from amongst any of the angelic hosts of the Heavenly Canaan, but sent the Comforter, the Holy Spirit, back into this world, which indeed is His country, to His kindred brought nigh through the blood of His Son to call out a people who would follow Him to the great marriage of the Lamb, not only as a guest, but as the Bride, without spot or blemish. Hallelujah!

ISAAC AND REBECCA

"And the servant said unto him: 'Per adventure the woman will not be willing to follow me unto this land: must I needs briny thy son again into the land from whence thou earnest?"

"And Abraham said unto him: ' Beware that thou bring not my son thither again. If the woman will not be willing to follow thee, then thou shalt be clear of this my oath; only briny not my son thither again'."

I can never read those words of the servant, "Peradventure the woman wilt not be willing to follow me," without tears springing to my eyes. O the gentle, pleading, wooing drawings of the Holy Spirit, as He walks up and down these aisles tonight, enquiring: "Will you go?" There is no conscription in this Bridal procession only free-will enlistment. But whether the woman says yes or no; whether she is willing to go to meet the Heavenly Isaac who shall soon appear, or chooses to remain where she now abides, the Son of God will never be brought here again to plead with her, or plead His cause other than by the Spirit sent down by the Father. Jesus has made the sacrifice; His dear feet trod this earth to be rewarded only by unbelief and spittings and death.

He will never come again to be beaten, rejected, and nailed to the tree; the next time He comes it will be with power and great glory. His kingly robes will be upon Him; His sceptre will be in His hand. Whether you will be willing to follow the leadings of the Spirit who has come to guide you into all truth, or not, must rest with you tonight. What have you decided to reply to this invitation?

Each man, woman and child in the world, irrespective of earthly standing, color or creed, is invited to accept the leadings of the Spirit and follow Him to meet Jesus, the Heavenly Bridegroom. If you would find this Heavenly guide I will tell you where to find Him at the well of salvation.

ELEIZER WAITS FOR REBECCA AT THE WELL OF WATER. THE HOLY SPIRIT MEETS AND CHOOSES THE BRIDE AT THE WELL OF SALVATION

As Abraham's servant journeys he comes to the well, where the daughters were wont to bring their pitchers for water. There he prays, and waits for the coming of the bride, saying:

"Behold, I stand here by the well of water."

Dear child of God, you who have drawn with joy from the wells of Salvation, lift up your eyes tonight and behold the Spirit, open your ears and hear Him say:

"Behold, here I stand, waiting to baptize you and lead you on to meet your Jesus."

"And it came to pass, before He had done speaking, that behold Rebecca came out."

HOW similar is this instance to that recorded in Acts 10:44. "While Peter yet spake these words, the Holy Spirit fell on all them which heard the Word!" He is speaking to you now; will you receive Him?

"Behold Rebecca came out "(He is calling a come out people these days, a called-out, separated people) "with her pitcher upon her shoulder. And the damsel was very fair to look upon, a virgin, neither had any man known her; and she went down to the well, and filled her pitcher and came up."

As I look over your faces it seems I can almost pick out the Rebeccas who have come here tonight with their pitchers on their shoulders, empty pitchers, clean pitchers, ready to go down in humility to draw from this inexhaustible well of Salvation. If your pitchers or heads are filled with learning or earthly wisdom, you must empty them out in order to be filled at this well. No matter how big or great you may be you must all alike get down in humility to draw with joy from these waters. Rebecca went down and filled her pitcher, and came up! The way up is down, bless God.

We read that the servant ran to meet her, just as the Spirit is running to meet you tonight. At his invitation she gave him to drink, and all his camels did she draw for also. The Word says:

"She hasted, and emptied her pitcher into the trough, and ran again unto the well to draw water for his camels." Dear ones, is your pitcher empty enough, are you down low enough, to have this abundant supply that not only satisfies the demand of your own soul, but hastens to draw and empty for others about you, knowing, with unbroken confidence, that you can run again to the well and draw again and again from the hidden source that never runs dry?

She was fair to look upon. Can the Lord look down into the depths of your soul and say: "Thou art fair, My love, there is no spot in thee?" Are you a virgin, pure in heart, that knows not the old man of sin and worldliness? Then the Spirit is calling you to be a member of the Bridal Body.

261

Earrings, and bracelets and precious gifts were given to Rebecca, and she returned with the servant to her parents' house, and there the servant brought forth jewels of silver (which represents Atonement), jewels of gold (or the Divine nature of Jesus), and raiment (which typifies the Righteousness of Jesus), and the marriage robe. These he gave to Rebecca. Then to the brother and the mother he also gave precious things. But though there are precious things to be given to those who do not go all the way through to the perfection of full sacrifice, the Bride receives the best and most beautiful gifts. There is no comparison to be made between the two.

Then before eating or drinking, the servant told his message, and of the wonderful master, Isaac, and his beautiful home, far away, and of his desire to take Rebecca to this home to be the son's Bride.

"And they said, 'We will call the damsel and enquire at her mouth' and they called Rebecca, and said unto her:

"'Wilt thou go with this man?" and she said:

"'I will go."

This is the great question of today, the question now facing each one of you, "Wilt thou go with this man?" Each individual must answer it for himself and herself. Oh, can you say, as Rebecca of old, "'I will go!' Where He leads me I will follow"?

Trust yourself in His hands, and He will never leave you till you are safe in the arms of Jesus.

As Rebecca journeyed through the wilderness she did not lose her way; she did not have to run about enquiring of every passer-by which road to take; the Servant had come to guide, lead, yea, and carry her, all the way to Isaac's house. What tales he told her by the way, how her heart was gladdened and lifted above all earthly things, as she listened to his glowing description of her Bridegroom and his home awaiting her. I am sure she forgot the bumpy camels, and the dusty road and the blazing sun, as she pressed on toward the longed-for moment when she should see him face to face.

Just so is the Holy Spirit leading and guiding all who will receive Him and follow Him over every obstacle, surmounting every hill of difficulty, taking the things of Jesus and revealing them unto us as we journey, till we cry out in longing:

"O Lord Jesus, how long till we shall see Your blessed face?" Our hearts swell with love and gratitude, and unutterable longing, as the Spirit speaks, "not of Himself but of Jesus, our Bridegroom, and lover divine.

At last, after long days of traveling we read of that wonderful meeting.

ISAAC MET REBECCA IN THE FIELD. JESUS TO MEET HIS BRIDE IN THE AIR

As Isaac went out to meditate in the field at eventide, he lifted up his eyes, and behold the camels were coming! O Jesus! Jesus! He is lifting up His eyes just now, this very eventide, and He sees, and beholds the camels are coming. Are you amongst that little company that is swiftly coming up the road to meet Him? Steadily, surely, we are drawing near the glorious day, dear pilgrims, when the consummation of our journey will arrive and we, as Rebecca, will lift up our eyes and see our Bridegroom; and even now, as we see in faith our Bridegroom from afar, we should take the vail of greater separation, and cover ourselves, that we shall indeed be a separate people unto Him.

We read of Isaac that he brought her into his mother's tent and took Rebecca, and she became his wife, and He loved her. Soon our Savior shall come for His Bride who has set out to meet Him, come for those who have heard and answered the call:

"Behold, the Bridegroom cometh, go ye out to meet Him" Soon the great song will resound.

"Let us be glad and rejoice, for the marriage of the Lamb hath come, and the wife has made herself ready." The tables are being spread, the marriage is at hand. Beloved, will you go, will you receive the Holy Spirit and let Him guide you to the wedding of the Lamb?

If you have not yet found the well of Salvation, empty that pitcher you carry upon your shoulder, and get you down in haste to the wells of Salvation, for it is there you will meet and receive the Holy Spirit, who, if you will follow Him, will lead you on over the hills and through the valleys till you meet your Bridegroom in the air.

THE LIFE AND GROWTH OF PETER

IT is not only God's will, but it is absolutely necessary and essential that every child of God should grow in grace and enlarge in love daily.

When I was a little girl my Mother used to stand me up at the door once in so often and take a pencil and make a little mark just at the top of my head on the frame of the door. After a few more weeks she would again put another mark above the last one to measure and see how much I had grown since the last mark was made. It is a good thing for Christians to measure themselves carefully and frequently, not by one another, but by the Word of God. God's Word is a true measuring rod, also the life of Paul, of Peter, and many others. Let us take the latter, the life and growth of Peter, today, and see whether we have grown as quickly and as much as he; if not, let us press on, for God is no respecter of persons, and what He has done for Peter He is not only able but anxious to do for us.

Peter's first sight of Jesus came unexpectedly, one day as he was about to cast his net into the sea. Jesus saw Peter, and went and spoke to him, saying:

"Follow me and I will make you a fisher of men." Peter straightway left his net and followed Jesus. Dear one, do you remember the day when first your eyes were opened to the lovely form of Jesus walking along the shores of time to your heart, when first you heard that dear voice, sweet as the sound of rushing water, bidding you to leave your nets of worldly cares and your sinful life and follow Him? Praise His name, just one sight of that lovely face and all other faces lost their attraction and power to satisfy; just one cadence of His voice, and earthly voices lost their charm. Hallelujah! No wonder Peter left his old, worn-out fishing nets and followed; no wonder we left our unrighteousness and accepted His righteousness.

Straightway Peter left his nets and followed Him. How eagerly he promised to follow, and how little he understood just where the following would lead him. No shadow of the cross did he see, no whisperings of a dark night when he would deny his Lord, the future with its train of joys and sorrows, its victories and defeats, its honor and dishonor; no visions of a cross where he himself should hang, were foreseen as he eagerly and joyfully promised to follow all the way.

How little did we realize the mountain tops of transfiguration and the valleys of trial we should pass when our hearts said yes to Jesus and promised to follow all the way. The main and most important thing is to say an eternal Yes to Jesus, and whether it is weal or whether it is woe, the Jesus who took Peter through will bring us forth triumphant if we trust and follow all the Array.

Through the many days that followed, wonderful days lived in the presence of Jesus, precious days of submitting to His leadings and dealings, Peter learned the meaning of faith and trust. He had seen his wife's mother instantly healed of the fever; he had witnessed the healings of many sick, and the raising of the dead; he had beheld and assisted in the feeding of the multitudes; and now in the 14th chapter of Matthew, we find him in the ship with the other disciples, tossed and driven by the tempestuous waves of the sea.

Dimly through the darkness of the night, then clearer and more distinctly, they saw a calm figure in white raiment walking to meet them on the waves, and in fear they cried out: "It is a spirit."

O, faint heart, tempest-tossed in your frail craft of faith, have you ever found your Lord walking to meet you over the roughest wave of trial, surmounting the highest crest of difficulty and tests?

Did you, like Peter, fail to recognize Jesus as you were passing through the storm? Or have you learned to see Jesus in every test walking forth to reveal Himself to you in some new attribute, in greater beauty and power than you have yet known Him? And when all around you seemed turmoil and strife, and you saw nothing but circumstances and trials, did you ever hear His voice saying: "It is I; be not afraid"? Cease seeing waves and tests and turmoil, and recognize the Jesus that walks to meet us on their billows.

Have you ever, like dear Peter, had your faith inspired and encouraged by that word, "Come," till you swung your feet over the side of your small craft, and yourself began to walk in naked faith, with all material and earthly foundations removed from beneath your feet, to meet the Lord on top of the waves that so lately threatened to engulf you?

Perhaps you, too, got your eyes on the wind and the waves, saw people and conditions and circumstances instead of Jesus, and began to sink. Put Jesus' ear was open to Peter's cry, and is open to the cry of every follower. "Lord, save me." Peter cried, and immediately Jesus put out His hand and caught him, chiding him for his lack of faith.

More blessed days of growing and learning passed and Peter is found still following Jesus.

He is called blessed by the Lord, for recognizing the divinity of the Son of God. We find him rebuked in the same chapter for trying to persuade Jesus from going to suffer that shameful and ignominious death upon the cross. Dear Jesus, how quick He has been with Peter and with each one of us to praise and encourage that which sworeth of faith and sacrifice, and to rebuke and chasten that which sworeth of the human and selfishness.

"And after six days, Jesus taketh Peter and James and John and bringeth them up into an high mountain apart, and was transfigured before them, and His face did shine as the sun, and His raiment was white as the light." Beloved, how about that measuring rod? Are you measuring up so far to Peter's experience? Have you been upon the Mount of Transfiguration, and seen Jesus revealed and transfigured in His beauty and loveliness before your amazed and adoring eyes?

Soon after we find Peter receiving another lesson in faith, when he was sent to the sea to take the first fish he caught, and in its mouth to find the needed money to pay the tribute or tax, for himself and his Lord.

Through the many, but swiftly passing days of Peter's walk with Jesus, he grows in faith and wisdom, he hears the preaching and sees the life of his Master, he sees miracles wrought, sick healed, demons cast out, and even sees the sick healed and demons depart through his own prayer and faith. But now, with ever increasing emphasis Jesus informs and seeks to impress upon the minds of His little flock, that soon He is to lay down His life, to be resurrected again and ascend unto His Father. Moreover, He tells them again and again that although He departs He will not leave them comfortless, but will send another Comforter, even the Holy Ghost to lead them into all truth, and endue them with power from on high.

Again we find Peter seated with his Lord at the last supper, declaring that though all men should be offended because of Jesus, yet would he never be offended. Upon hearing the warning of the Lord that he would deny Him, we hear his impassioned denial:

"Though I should die with Thee, yet will I not deny Thee" How we, too, have promised the Lord in those precious hours of feasting and communion, that we would never again deny Him in any way! Truly the Spirit was willing, and the flesh weak.

Then Jesus took His disciples, and went forth to the garden of Gethsemane to pray through the great depression and sorrowful heaviness He felt pressing down upon Him. Leaving the rest behind with the injunction to "sit here while I go and pray yonder - Jesus took with Him Peter and the two sons of Zebedee, and said to them: "My soul is exceeding sorrowful, even unto death: tarry ye here and watch with me." Jesus went a little further, and falling down upon His face, travailed in prayer. O, the yearning of His soul to have someone to watch and pray with Him, but coming to His disciples and finding them asleep, He did not address the others, but said unto Peter: "! Could ye not watch with me one hour?" Again He prayed, and upon returning a second and a third time, found them sleeping.

O? Beloved, have you, too, failed Jesus miserably on this same line of prayer? Now, in this last short hour before the door of mercy is forever closed, and intercessors are needed as never before, have we, too, been guilty of sleeping at our post?

Have we also been overcome with the slothfulness that has wrapped us in slumbering blindness to the face of Jesus bending over us, beseeching us to rise and pray, not only for others but that we ourselves enter riot into temptation? Jesus knew that Peter was going to be specially tempted and singled him out with a command to pray. What dismay it would bring us to hear Him say:

"Sleep on now, and take your rest. The souls you might have prayed through to salvation are lost forever, the brand you might have plucked from the burning is now in hell. Your opportunity for prayer and intercession is past. Sleep on.

Peter sprang to his feet, wide awake now. His Lord was grieved, his beloved Lord. What could he do to show his love? With zeal he smote off the ear of the high priest's servant. He would just prove his love and zeal. But, ah! Peter, obedience is better than sacrifice, and to hearken than the fat of rams. The ear was restored by Jesus, and the little procession of captors and captive moved on to the judgment hall. Jesus was taken inside to be tried, but Peter remained outside and began to warm his hands by the fire. Ah! it is a dangerous place to go to warm your hands by the fire of this world; and as Peter sat there a damsel declared that Peter had been with Jesus. But Peter indignantly denied it before them all, and was ashamed of Jesus.

Peter moved off to the porch, but could not escape the notice of the people, for if we have been with Jesus and walked with Him the world will know it. Another maid asked him if he had not been with Jesus, and soon yet more standers by asked him if he were not "one of them ". But Peter began to curse and swear, saying, "I know not the man."

O Peter, how our hearts have ached for you and the shameful thing you did in denying your Lord!

Yet, dear ones, how many of us have denied Him?

Just the time we should have been true and witnessed from the house tops that He was our Savior, how many times we sat silent just too long.

We must either deny ourselves or deny our Lord, deny the flesh or deny the Spirit. Surely some thing was radically wrong with Peter, something was missing that was much needed. O, it was surely the Holy Ghost that Jesus said would endue them with power.

Then followed those agonized hours and days of suffering for Peter, reproach and conviction over his failure, the crucifixion of his Lord, the burial, and days of utter loneliness and despair. His Lord was gone, the tender voice was hushed, the face he loved was still in death. And there was a great, big empty void everywhere that none could fill. Then out of that black, vacant void, came the swift, breathless messenger, Mary, with the message that Jesus was risen. Jesus' first words and thought were of Peter, and now we see him arising, running, out-stripping the others, stooping down before the sepulchre, looking, wondering in himself.

Again we find Peter fishing, still discouraged, for he knew not where his Lord had gone, leaping from the boat and rushing to the shore at the first glimpse of Jesus. Ye see him eating of the bread and fish upon the fire, hear him declaring his love for Jesus, hear His commission, "Feed My sheep, feed My lambs." Then came the day of departure, when Jesus was to leave for His Father's throne, and we hear Him still impressing upon the disciples the necessity of obeying His command to tarry in Jerusalem until they were filled with the Holy Ghost, saying: "You shall receive power after that the Holy Ghost is come upon you."

After Jesus had been caught up, we find Peter hastening to the upper room, tarrying until the Holy Ghost was poured out on the day of Pentecost. We picture him filled with the Holy Ghost, Acts 2:4, speaking with other tongues as the Spirit gave him utterance, so filled with the Spirit that onlookers thought him drunken with wine. Hear the shouts and praises of the hundred and twenty, see the multitude come running together, astonished, amazed, in doubt, crying, "What meaneth this?" O, it meant that the Holy Ghost had come. That the hundred and twenty, and Peter, had been endued with power from on high, and were now able to stand up and witness with holy boldness of Jesus the crucified. It meant that out of their innermost being now flowed rivers of the Spirit that none could check nor gainsay.

"What meaneth this? cried some. "Others, mocking said: ' These are filled with new wine. But Peter, standing up, said, of these are not drunk with wine, but this is that, which was spoken by the prophet Joel'."

Peter standing up! O, what a change from the cringing, cowardly, denying Peter! This new Peter had received the Holy Ghost and now, instead of fearing a little maid, he stood boldly before this scoffing, doubting multitude of Jews, and boldly preached in the Holy Ghost, of Jesus, while multitudes turned to the Lord and accepted Him as their Savior.

Are you measuring yourself by the measuring rod as we go on, dear ones? If you have left all to follow Jesus, have you received the Holy Ghost since you believed, with the Bible evidence? Have you felt your lack of power to testify and your heart has been dismayed when you denied Him or failed in prayer, or lacked in power? Then what you need is the Holy Ghost. Or have you perhaps been on the mountain top, and beheld Him transfigured before you? Have you been as Peter, used in praying for the sick and casting out demons?

Have you mistaken these experiences for the baptism of the Holy Ghost? Then measure up today; compare your experience with the Bible evidence of the incoming of the Spirit.

If you have measured up so far and have received the Holy Ghost evidenced by the speaking in tongues, as Peter of old, don't stop there. This is just the beginning, the preparation for further advancement and growth, for when He, the Spirit of truth is come, He will lead you on into all truth.

Behold Peter's life after Pentecost, where he received the Holy Ghost. See him at the beautiful gate saying to the lame man, "Silver and gold have I none, but such as I hare, give I thee. Rise up and walk" See the sick being brought out from all the villages and towns round about, as recorded in the 5th chapter of Acts, and when even the shadow of Peter fell upon them they were healed, every one.

Behold Peter at Samaria, and at Caesarea, laying hands upon the believers in the one instance and while he was yet preaching, in the other, they received the Holy Ghost as had the hundred and twenty in the beginning. Follow Peter through his imprisonments, his beatings and scourgings, his shame and reproach. Follow him through his courage and faith, his love and life of power.

Follow him to his death on the cross, crucified head downward because he felt unworthy to be crucified as his Lord. O, dear ones, I fear that e'er now the measuring rod, upon being applied to our lives, will find us all far short. But God is no respecter of persons, and He who took Peter through from his first eternal "WILL" at the sea of Galilee to the cross where he laid down his life, will take us through if we will follow Him.

"Follow thou Me." The future all unknown and trusted in His hands. Dear Peters, weak in ourselves, He will make you strong in Him. Follow Him to the cross, to the grave, through the resurrection, to the upper room and the reception of the Holy Ghost, on to the gifts and fruits of the Spirit, perfect development and identification with Him in His death on the cross, and on to meet Him in the air.

Let us then press on and follow all the way. Do not stop short of God's best and perfection.

"Following Jesus day by day, Nothing can harm while He leads the way, Sunshine or darkness, what e'er befall, Jesus, my Savior, is my all in all."

THE TEMPLE

"Ye also, as lively stones, are built up a spiritual house."
I. Pet. 2:5.

Visions and Revelations of the Temple - As Revealed to Isaiah - As Seen by John on the Isle of Patmos - The Structure as Revealed by Paul The Temple as Described by Peter - The Marvelous Mystery of the Transformation Wrought in the Stones from Quarry to Temple - Chris. Seeking and Preparing the Stones Digging, Separating, and Excavating - "Be Still and Know That I am God" - Heaving and Shaping Then Comes the Polishing - The Refiner's Fire, the Crucible - The Majesty and Grandeur of the Completed Temple.

THE wondrous Temple great and grand which has been under construction for almost six thousand years, is now rapidly taking shape and nearing perfected completion.

Of such vast proportions is this temple that there can be no end of the universe where God is to which this great temple does not reach.

Of such grandeur is it this temple (with God for its Architect, Christ for its High Priest made up of living stones composed of blood- washed souls its domes and arches of divine love and adoration with saints and teachers for its pillars, and worshippers for its pavement) that it hath need of neither the sun nor the moon to shine in it, for the glory of God doth lighten it, and the Lamb is the light thereof.

So firm and indestructible, so infinitely precious, so thoroughly tested by fire and by flood, by hammer and chisel, is each stone that is built into the great structure, that deterioration and decay will forever be unknown within its walls, and it will abide the temple of the great God forever and forever.

Here it is that they which are arrayed in white robes they which have come up out of great tribulation, having washed their robes, and made them white in the blood of the Lamb, stand before the throne of God, and "serve Him day and night in His temple: and He that sitteth upon the throne dwelleth among them." Here it is that His people know neither hunger nor thirst, neither does the sun light upon them nor any heat, "for the Lamb, which is in the midst of the throne," doth feed them, and "leadeth them unto living fountains of waters" and here it is that God wipeth away all tears from their eyes. Rev. 7:13-17

VISIONS AND REVELATIONS OF THE TEMPLE

We lift our eyes in the Spirit and are transfixed with wonder as we behold the grandeur of the great completed structure rising before us with its belfries and turrets, its gold-crowned towers and domes gleaming through the thick mist of our mortal conception of the great plan of the Eternal God.

Our hearts are caught up on the wings of Heavenly rapture, as we catch the great swelling waves of melody bursting forth from a thousand windows as the singers and players become as one, making one sound to be heard, praising and glorifying God, and the glory of God so fills the temple that the priests and the Lord's ministers cannot minister.

Isaiah catches us up and carries us to the very temple, when he declares: "I saw also the Lord sitting upon a throne, high and lifted up, and His train filled the temple.

Above it stood the seraphims and one cried unto another: 'Holy, holy, holy is the Lord of hosts; the whole earth is filled with His glory And the posts of the door moved at the voice of him that cried, and the house was filled with smoke." Isa. 6:1-4.

John, on the isle of Patmos, brings us right into the midst of the thunderous praises and the grandeur and the glory of God within the temple, when the Lord God Almighty taketh unto Himself His great power and doth reign. He tells us that: "The temple of God was opened in Heaven, and there was seen in His temple the ark of His testament: and there were lightnings, and voices, and thunderings, and an earthquake, and great hail." Rev. 11:19.

Paul brings us right up to a literal and tangible examination of the structure and the foundation itself, and our own part in the building, by the words: "Know ye not that ye are the temple of God, and that the Spirit of God dwelleth in you?" I. Cor. 3:16.

Why, 'tis as though the great temple were comprised of myriads of smaller temples, for "to whatever worlds He carries our souls when they shall pass out of these imprisoning bodies, in these worlds these souls of ours (if we have submitted ourselves to His dealings) shall find themselves part of the same great temple, for it belongeth not to this world alone" but shall stand through the ages of eternity.

Peter walks round the temple with us and points out to those who "have tasted that the Lord is gracious" that our Lord is Himself the chief cornerstone, elect, precious, disallowed indeed of men, but chosen of God. Then, suddenly, Peter points his finger at each saint individually, and says: "Ye also, as lively stones, are built up a spiritual house, an holy priesthood, to offer up spiritual sacrifices, acceptable to God by Jesus Christ" and "ye are a chosen generation, a royal priesthood, an holy nation, a peculiar people, that ye should show forth the praises of Him who hath called you out of darkness into His marvelous light," I. Pet. 2:3, 5, 9.

THE MARVELOUS MYSTERY OF THE TRANSFORMATION WROUGHT IN THE STONE FROM QUARRY TO TEMPLE

Lively stones, living stones, chosen, peculiar stones, stones called from the depths of the dark quarries of sin and despair into the marvelous light of the Lamb which doth lighten the temple-Stones once all unshapen and rough, and unlovely, now perfect in shape and size, with smooth corners and mirror-like, polished surfaces Once piled in confusion, one upon another, disrupted, without unit, or promise of ever fitting together in any semblance of a building, Now, chiselled, shaped and fashioned under the skilled hands of the mighty Master- workman, until each perfect, polished stone slips noiselessly into place beside its neighbor, there to remain forever, held fast by the cement of unchanging, Heaven-born love.

What a transformation is bespoken in every stone! What patience, what love, what skill of Master- workmanship, what dicing- and blasting, what lifting and carrying-, what chiselling and polishing, what beauty and praise! Is it any wonder the stone cries aloud and says: "What I am, I am by the grace of God"?

"How marvelous!" we exclaim, "Is the boundless love of God. How unfathomable is the great, immeasurable grace and mercy that has called each one of us (no matter how deeply buried in the dark quarries of sin), to fill our place in the great and glorious temple which is being built without hands, eternal in the Heavens." Is it any wonder that tears of gratitude and unworthiness fill our eyes when we remember that He does not ask us to help ourselves, does not ask us to do any of the blasting or lifting, or hammering, or chiselling, or polishing or building of the temple. One thing, and one alone He asks:

"Be still and know that I am God. Be pliable, be yielded and submissive in My hands." Accept all things (every blow of the hammer, every gouge of the chisel) as working together for good to them that lore the Lord and are called according to His purpose.

SEEKING AND PREPARING STONES FOR THE TEMPLE

His eye runneth to and fro through the whole earth: "He discovereth deep things out of darkness, and bringeth out to light the shadow of death," as He searches for material with which to build His temple. No depths are too deep for Him to descend into, no trouble or labor too intricate or great for Him to undertake, if only the object of His love be it gold, silver or precious stone be willing and submissive under the dealings of His hands. His voice can be heard as He walks through the earth, searching material for His temple, saying:

"Surely there is a vein for the silver, and a place for gold where they find it. He setteth an end to darkness, and searcheth out all perfection: the stones of darkness, and the shadow of death...As for the earth, out of it cometh bread; and under it is turned up as it were fire. . . . The stones of it are the place of sapphires; and it hath dust of gold. . . . He putteth forth His hand upon the rock; He overturneth the mountains by the roots. He cutteth out rivers among the rocks; and His eye seeth every precious thing. . . . He bindeth the floods from overflowing; and the thing that is hid bringeth He forth to light. Job 28:1-11.

The great, rough, unlovely stones, hard-hearted as granite, lying in the bottom of the quarry, buried deep beneath the earth and mire of sin and self, have but to express the desire and willingness to be digged for and removed and shaped into His likeness, and the Lord is at the place, ready to begin the work of excavation. No stone is too far distant, too unworthy, too insignificant, too un-promising, too great or too small for Him to see the longing to be made worthy for a place in His temple.

From the moment the stone cries to Him, and the Lord thrusts the spade of conviction into the earth of sin which covers the stone, He presses it ever deeper and deeper, with the strong foot of His Word till the stone lies clean and bare before Him.

The stone is entirely too large and too attached to its surroundings and environment, however, and in order to dislodge and detach it, great quantities of explosives oft have to be imbedded in the midst of our heretofore comfortable surroundings.

Blast may follow blast. Huge cracks and splits may run out in every direction. The trials may be hard, the separation keen and vitally near our heart. We may not understand, friends may criticise, misjudge, or offer advice, but one thing only is required of us by the Lord:
"BE STILL AND KNOW THAT I AM GOD"

He will do all the blasting, all the separating. Our part is but to be willing and pliable and yielded submissive to His will.

The stone need not worry itself with planning and foreseeing, but needs only to give itself up to God's Holy Spirit within, and His dealings and providence without. Once thoroughly separated from surroundings, no matter how unshapely and rugged we be, one has but to look upward to see that the great Master-builder has brought the huge derrick of His love and power to the place, has fitted the cords of grace and mercy about the boulder or rock, and is lifting it from the depths of darkness into His own marvelous light.

Then the shaping process Oh, those great, jagged, rough, sharp corners that gash the feet and wound each passer-by one by one they disappear beneath the daily, hourly, ring, ring of the hammer of love as it falls with steady blows upon the chisel of daily tests and circumstances.

That unkind word, the undeserved reproach, that unmerited rebuke, the hasty tear, that hour you fled to your room and fell, face-downward, at His feet in seeming defeat, the opportunity for doing good, the call for sacrifice, unapplauded, unobserved all these were but hammer and chisel blows that made rough corners disappear.

Oh, to see the will of God wrought out in blows and buffetings, in tears and smiles, and in encouragements and discouragements, in wilderness wastes and Eden's bloom, in fire and water, in heat and cold, on mountain top and in valley depths, in lion's den or plains of freedom, in battle front or isolated dungeon! Oh, but to recognize His hand in the dealings of .today, is sweetest balm of Gilead.

Hardness and self-centered aims disappear mellow tenderness, solicituousness and brotherly love take their place as we weep with those that weep and rejoice with those that do rejoice.

Then comes the polishing, the pressure brought to bear, the continuous rubbing and friction, the eternal passing to and fro of the same POLISHING trials and circumstances, of daily grind and routine. Each day of yielding hastens the work of shaping and polishing.

Each day of murmuring and repining hinders and stays the hand, mars the work and inflicts deep scars and scratches that only time and labor can efface.

In the quarry, in the blasting and in the chiseling process, there is much noise and action, but when at last the stone is carried to the spot and slipped into its appointed place in the great temple, there will not be the sound of a hammer to be heard (that will all have been gone through before) "Work on in me, Oh, Lord, let not Thy hand be stayed."

From beginning to end it is God. From the quarry of sin to the beauty of the temple it is God, GOD, G-O-D. We can do nothing to help but to yield, submissive and passive to His dealings, as wrought out hourly, daily in the circumstances with which He surrounds our lives.

The gold and the silver which adorn His temple must be refined in the crucible until all dross is melted away. Only that which can THE REFINER'S stand in the fire and not be burned FIRE, AND can abide in His tabernacle, for CRUCIBLE "Our God is a consuming fire," and no wood, hay nor stubble can dwell in His presence, for when the Lord whom we seek suddenly comes to His temple we find that "He is like a refiner's fire, and like fuller's soap" that He purges us as gold and silver that we "may offer unto the Lord an offering in righteousness." Mal. 3:1-3.

Each stone must be set and fitted into place by God man's efforts on this line have ever been but a failure. Each pillar and support, each decoration, overlaid with gold and silver, each golden tower and dome, encrusted with precious stones each gold-embroidered hanging each section of the building from threshold to the throne, must be set into its place by the God who has fitted it for its particular place.

Today the building is well-nigh completion Softly and quickly, yet firmly and with utmost precision and perfection the last finishing touches are being added to the temple, the last sections are being slipped into place. Holy calling You are called to fill your place in the temple. . Are you letting Him work His will in your life, that great or small, you may perfectly fill and adorn the little space He has selected for you?

MAJESTY AND GRANDEUR OF COMPLETED TEMPLE

No matter where He shall place us in the house of the Lord (wherein we are to dwell forevermore), we will be able to inquire in His temple; and behold the Ancient of Days in His beauty, as He shall sit upon His throne, whose garment is white as snow, and whose hair is like the pure wool,, whose throne is like the fiery flame and His wheels as burning fire, to see the fiery stream that issues forth before Him, to see the thousand thousands who minister unto Him and the ten thousand who stand before Him (Dan. 7:9, 10.) to hear the thunders of His praises, see the lightnings of His power, and to hear His voice, sweet as the rushing of many waters surely one such moment is worth a millionfold more blasting and chiselling and polishing. So deal on, O Lord, deal on.

GETTING DOWN

"For thus saith the High and Lofty One that inhabiteth eternity, whose name is Holy, I dwell in the high and holy place, with him also that is of a contrite and humble spirit; to revive the spirit of the humble, and to revive the heart of the contrite ones."
Isa. 57:15

SO much has been said through the Spirit these last days about the necessity of "getting down" before the Lord in humility and adoration, that it is well for us to find out "what saith the Scriptures?" on the subject.

ZACCHAEUS CAME DOWN

There are many different ways of getting down recorded in the Word; there was Zacchaeus, you remember, who ran and climbed up into a sycamore tree, and when Jesus came to the place He looked up and saw him, and said unto him:

"Zacchaeus, make haste and come down; for today I must abide at thy house. And he made haste, and came down; and received Him joyfully."

There are many today who, like Zacchaeus of old, just literally have to come down from their preconceived ideas and notions of themselves; down from their exalted opinion of their own righteousness; down from old forms and ceremonies, to humble themselves under the mighty hand of God. Jesus walked so humbly that those who walk with Him must get down. Zacchaeus had put himself higher than Jesus Himself, for we read that when Jesus came to the place He looked up. Truly He is still looking up today, and crying:

"Make haste and come down; for today I must abide at thy house." Make haste and come down and receive Him today joyfully; He is waiting to bless thee. Get down! Get down!! Get down!!!

THE LEPER KNEELED DOWN

Then we remember the leper whom Jesus healed, and we read, with an understanding and sympathetic tug at our hearts, how he kneeled down.

How well we remember the day when we came to Jesus, full of uncleanness, filled with the leprosy of sin, and how as we kneeled down at His feet, our sin was cleansed away and we were made whole. First of all, dear ones, you must come down from your own righteousness, which is as "filthy rags," and secondly you must kneel down at His feet, humbly crying:

"Be merciful to me a sinner," and He will wash your sins away, and so fill you with joy that the tears of love and gratitude will stream down your face, and your heart will pulsate with the knowledge that you are His child, and passed from darkness into His own clear light. "Old things will have passed away, and all things become new," a new world, a new life, a new light, the Son of Righteousness.

PETER FELL DOWN

Then there was Peter. Have you ever ascended to the top of the mountain of Transfiguration and beheld Jesus so clearly revealed to your enraptured vision that you, like Peter of old, have fallen prostrate at His feet? John on the Isle of Patmos, writes:

"I, John, fell at His feet as one dead." So did Ezekiel, and many others that walked with Jesus in the days of old. These frail bodies of ours are no stronger than were those of the prophets of those days; and when we come in direct contact with Jesus or His mighty power, we, like them, fall down and proclaim Him King and Lord of all. O, it is when we fall down helplessly at His feet that we see our own helpless condition, and our utter insufficiency and dependence upon Him.

Then He takes us by the hand and lifts us up.

But He says:

"I will resist the proud and the haughty, but be gracious to the humble." Humble thyself to walk with God. O, never be ashamed to fall at His precious feet, for around the throne myriads of angels fall before Him, and the twenty Elders are crying:

"Holy, holy, holy, Lord God Almighty."

Then we come to Mary, the sister of Martha. We are told that

- MARY SAT DOWN

O! the clear vision of sweet communion that is opened up by these simple words: "Mary sat down."

"Sitting at the feet of Jesus, what words I hear Him say. Happy place; so near, so precious! May it find me there each day; "Sitting at the feet of Jesus, I would look upon the past;

For His love has been so gracious. It has won my heart at last."

It is there, while busy Marthas are hurrying all about us Marthas who seldom find time to pray or read the Word, Marthas have floors to sweep and dishes to wash that we steal away, like Mary of old, and, closeted with Him, take time to "sit down" and learn of Him. How He talks to us and communes with our souls. How He brings forth the treasures of the golden divinity of His nature, fills us with the frankincense of praise, and entrusts us with the fellowship of His sufferings, and reveals the power of His resurrection to us. It is to those who find time to sit at His feet, like Mary of old, that He reveals His perfect will.

Beloved, take time to sit at Jesus' feet.

Then, coming to our precious Lord, we remember that JESUS LAID DOWN His life for the brethren, and seek to echo His word: "Greater love hath no man than this, that lie lay down his life for his friends."

O, beloved, He is calling a people this day who will get down before Him. Down! down! down! has been my cry since mine eyes have beheld the King.

O that it might be no more I, but Christ that liveth in me for "I must decrease and He must increase" Down, down till we follow Him all the way to the cross, and lay down our lives gladly at His feet for 'He that exalteth himself shall he abased, and he that humbleth himself shall be exalted'." We shall be exalted even up to His right hand upon the throne, lifted from the depth of the mire to the glory of the cross of Jesus Christ, washed in the blood, furnished with the white robes of the wedding garment, and filled with His Spirit. We are lifted up to Heavenly places to talk and walk with Him forever and forever.

JUST as God the Father gave Jesus, His only begotten Son, as His love gift to the sinner and as Jesus gave the Holy Ghost as a gift to the believer, so in turn, the Holy Ghost has gifts to bestow upon those who receive Him and yield themselves to His control.

Many baptized believers have made the grave mistake of believing that when they had received God's gift, Jesus as their Savior and had received the Holy Ghost, His gift to the believer that they had received all there was for them.

They lost sight of the fact entirely that the Spirit had gifts and fruits to bestow upon all those who covet earnestly the best gifts.

After being made recipients of full salvation, and the baptism of the Holy Ghost they settled down in contentment, with folded hands, forgetting that the incoming of the Spirit to lead us into all truth is just the beginning, just the entrance to the land of Canaan. The Red Sea has been left far behind, the desert has been safely crossed, the gates of Canaan's land have been entered, but now if having gone thus far we sit down just inside the gates, will we not miss the grapes and pomegranates? Will we not miss the land that flows with milk and honey?

When He the Spirit of truth is come, He will lead you into all truth. Now the incoming of the Holy Ghost is just the coming of the leader, who can only lead us on, and bestow His gifts upon us as we submit ourselves to His leading and press forward. Just as the Father longed to give us Jesus, and Jesus longed to bestow upon us the gift of the Holy Ghost, so now the Holy Spirit longs to bestow His gifts upon the baptized believer.

There are nine gifts of the Spirit spoken of in the 12th chapter of I. Cor which reads:

"Now concerning spiritual gifts brethren, I would not have yon ignorant. For to one is given by the Spirit the Word of Wisdom to another Knowledge by the same Spirit to another Faith to another Gifts of Healing to another Working of Miracles; to another Prophecy to another

Discerning of Spirits to another Divers Kinds of Tongues to another Interpretation of Tongues;

"But all these worketh that one and the self-same Spirit, dividing to every man severally as He will:"

Surely it is God's plan that each of these gifts should be manifested in each assembly, and we are told to covet earnestly the best gifts, and to seek that we may excel to the edifying of the church.

To one is given THE WORD OF WISDOM

If ever there was a time that the church needed wisdom, it is now. It is not our own wisdom or understanding that we need but the wisdom that cometh down from above. "Wisdom is the principal thing" says Solomon, "therefore get wisdom."

He also tells us to cease from our own wisdom.

The wisdom of man is foolishness to God, therefore if any man lack wisdom let him ask of God who giveth to all men liberally and upbraid eth not and it shall be given him.

The Holy Spirit has a real literal gift of wisdom, for those who seek. Wisdom to speak or not to speak, wisdom to give or to withhold, wisdom to understand God's word, and to understand His leadings, wisdom to discern between the flesh and the Spirit, wisdom to look above earthly things and circumstances and see no man save Jesus only, and wisdom to use the gifts the Spirit has given us.

To another is given THE WORD OF KNOWLEDGE

Just as the reins of a spirited horse are held in the hands of a competent driver, so is wisdom to knowledge, for many have knowledge without wisdom. Hosea 4:6 says, "My people are destroyed for lack of knowledge." Zeal without knowledge is a hindrance instead of a help. Each child of God should cry to the Lord for the work of knowledge to be buried deep in his or her heart. Knowledge to know God, whom to know is life eternal, knowledge to understand and rightly divide the Word of truth, is needed today as never before.

Paul cried aloud from the depths of his being for knowledge, saying: "O that I may know Him and the power of His resurrection, and the fellowship of His sufferings, being made conformable unto His death."

There is a real gift of knowledge, which is not gained from earthly sources but which is taught us from God, for all who covet earnestly to know Him, and His word. There is a God-taught knowledge that will cause us to study to show ourselves approved unto God, a workman that need not be ashamed, rightly dividing the word of truth.

In the garden of Eden in the midst of life God gave a commandment, forbidding man to eat of the tree of knowledge of good and evil, but now we are in the midst of death and God commands us to eat of the tree of knowledge, which is Christ, in whom are hid all the treasures of wisdom and knowledge.

To another is given FAITH

Without faith it is impossible to please God. Faith is the substance of things hoped for, the evidence of things not seen. It is one thing to have faith in God, and another thing to have the gift of faith that can move mountains small or great.

Faith believes God, takes Him absolutely at His word, and through faith sees the promises of God materialize and that for which it prays brought to pass. Faith believes and can appropriate the promises of God today as in the days of old.

Faith prays the prayer of faith, and sick are healed, miracles wrought, and indeed it is impossible to receive any of the gifts of the Spirit without faith. Faith comes by hearing, and hearing by the Word of God. He that believeth shall be, saved, he that believeth not shall be damned.

Jesus says, these signs shall follow them that believe, in my name they shall cast out demons, they shall speak with new tongues . . . they shall lay hands on the sick and they shall recover, etc.

O beloved, if the children of the Lord would ask for Faith as earnestly as they sought salvation, and the baptism of the Holy Ghost, sought by hearing and believing the Word of God, signs and wonders would be worked in our midst, and the arm of Jehovah laid bare, and His glory break forth in a way that would be exceeding and abundant, above all we could ask or think.

To another is given the GIFTS OF HEALING

Still today as in the days of old the gift of healing is bestowed and operated through yielded vessels by the Holy Spirit. Jas. 5 says, the prayer of faith shall save the sick, but there is also the gift of healing that says: "In the name of Jesus, rise up and walk." This gift of healing was manifested through Peter when in the 5th chapter of Acts a multitude of sick folks were brought from the towns and villages round about, and laid in the streets on beds and couches, that even the shadow of Peter overshadowing them they should be healed, and they were healed every one.

This same gift of healing is manifested today, cancers, tumors, tuberculosis, all manner of sickness has been healed instantaneously in answer to prayer right in our meetings, and we give Him all the glory. For it is Jesus who heals. This gift of healing should be in every assembly, that the name of the Lord should be glorified.

To another is given the WORKING OF MIRACLES

Miracles that keep oil in the cruse and meal in the barrel are still witnessed in the lives of those who live the life of faith. We see broken bones instantaneously and miraculously set and healed in answer to prayer, and why not for Jesus is the same yesterday, today and forever.

To another is given the gift of PROPHECY

In Joel 2:28 God says: "It shall come to pass in the last days, that I will pour out my Spirit up-on all flesh, and your sons and your daughters shall prophesy." I. Cor. 14:39 Paul tells us to COVET TO PROPHESY. He tells us to desire spiritual gifts but rather that we may prophesy, for lie that prophesieth speaketh unto men to edification, exhortation and comfort.

In speaking to the Corinthian church, which had received the baptism of the Holy Ghost accompanied with the Bible evidence of speaking in other tongues, he urges them not to stop there but to go on and covet to prophesy, saying: "Greater is he that prophesieth than he that speaketh

275

with tongues, except he interpret, that the church may receive edifying." Therefore the prophet and the interpreter are placed on the same level.

In prophecy the Spirit takes control of the vocal organs, just the same as when speaking in tongues, except that in prophecy the words come out in English. Out of your innermost being shall flow rivers of living water, not out of your head, but out of your innermost being. This gift is being restored to the church, and in these days the sons and daughters prophesy under the power and inspiration of the Spirit as in the days of old.

To another is given DISCERNING OF SPIRITS

There was never a time in the history of the church that the gift of discernment was needed as it is today. And bless the Lord, the Spirit still bestows this gift upon yielded, seeking hearts, and gives power to discern between the flesh and the Spirit, power to discern the difference between the spirits, and to see hidden things as did Peter in the case of Ananias and Sapphira. Power to discern between the voice of the Lord and the voice of the enemy, power to discern between the genuine and the counterfeit is surely needed in these last days when the devil would deceive the very elect if that were possible. But praise God it is not possible, for His sheep know His voice and a stranger will they not follow. With the gift of discernment, surely the Spirit of wisdom is needed, to speak and reveal when the Lord leads, or to keep silent, when the Lord so wills.

To another is given DIVERS KINDS OF TONGUES

Although everyone who received the baptism of the Holy Ghost speaks in other tongues as the Spirit gives utterance, yet not everyone, in fact comparatively few, receive the Gift of Tongues, i.e. power to speak at will in foreign languages.

This gift, however, is still given today, and many whom we know personally have spoken in tongues to foreigners in their own language, and have told them of Jesus the might to save.

One dear washerwoman that has never learned a word of another language in her life speaks to the Greek fruit store man, to the Chinese laundry man, etc., in their own tongues, of Jesus, and God sends His truth home. Another young lady we know preached to the Chinese in Chinatown in the Chinese language, which she never studied, and many were saved.

To another is given the INTERPRETATION OF TONGUES

Cor. 14:13 says: "Let him that speaketh in an unknown tongue pray that he may interpret."

Also verse 5 of the same chapter says: "Greater is he that prophesieth than he that speaketh with tongues EXCEPT HE INTERPRET, that the church may receive edifying. Verse 27 tells us that when we come together if any man speak in an unknown tongue let it be by two or at most by three and that by course and let one interpret.

But if there be no interpreter let him keep silence in the church, and let him speak to himself and to God. So at once we see the necessity of having the gift of interpretation in our assemblies. Let us take Paul's advice, and pray that we may interpret.

When all these gifts are in the church, and the Spirit has divided to each man severally as He wills, they (when coupled with the fruits of the Spirit) form a perfect organism not an organization but an organism, each member is incomplete without the other, and the hand cannot say to the foot I have no need of you. But each member must recognize the ministry of the other, and all work together as a perfect body, in perfect unity, for while there are many members there is just one body. While we are made up of many members we must all be controlled by Christ who is the head of the body.

Dear, sleeping, baptized believers wake up and let us press on into the land of Canaan and possess our heritage, and accept the gifts and the fruits of the Spirit which God is waiting to bestow upon those who covet earnestly the best gifts.

THE VALLEY OF DRY BONES

Ezekiel 37: (1:14).

LET us begin this wonderful chapter with the first words of the first verse and go down into this valley and its experiences step by step with the Prophet Ezekiel.

THE HAND OF THE LORD WAS UPON ME:

What a wonderful thing it is for an individual to know that the hand of the Lord is upon him!

Away down in Florida, when we were preaching to the dear colored people, they used to love to sing this verse:

"Chil'en, Ah knows de Lawd,
　Chil'en, Ah knows de Lawd,
Ah knows de Lawd,
Dun got His hand on me."

And O, this afternoon I am so conscious of the hand of the Lord resting upon me. Praise His name.

THE HAND OF THE LORD WAS UPON ME, AND CARRIED ME OUT IN THE SPIRIT OF THE LORD:

This was by no means the first time the hand of the Lord had been upon Ezekiel. Had he not been caught up unto mountain tops of Revelation?

Had he not seen the four living creatures, the cherubims and the Ark? Had he not beheld the glory of the Lord? And the mighty movings of His power? Ezek. 1:28 and 10:4.

Doubtless, when the hand of the Lord came down upon him and carried him out in the Spirit, Ezekiel longed to be lifted again to some ethereal height of glory. The Lord was moving him out; what wonders was the Lord about to show him now? Have you ever wondered what Ezekiel's feelings must have been when he opened his eyes and discovered that the Lord had Being wet suddenly down in a valley after a hill-top experience is bad enough, but that was not the worst of it, this was a valley

WHICH WAS FULL OF BONES

I think that perhaps some of us know in a little measure how to appreciate and understand what the feelings of Ezekiel were. We, too, have felt the hand of the Lord upon us. We, too, have, at many times, beheld His glory and dwelt in the midst of life and power. We, too, have had the Spirit of the Lord set us down in a certain assembly, home, neighborhood or city, wherein we have opened our eyes to discover, with a start, that we have been deposited right in the "midst" of a valley which is literally "full" of bones.

AND HE CAUSED ME TO PASS BY THEM ROUND ABOUT: AND BEHOLD THERE WERE VERY MANY IN THE OPEN VALLEY, AND THEY WERE VERY DRY

Behold, there were very many. Oh, the pity of it! Were there only a few it would not seem so terrible, but the multitudity of these dry bones is staggering. There are so many precious Christians in so many churches, in so many climes, that are down in the valley, no spiritual strength or meat to cover their frames of profession, nothing but bones bones bones.

IN THE OPEN VALLEY

You need neither a spade nor a pickaxe to find the kind of bones that I am speaking of. They are in the open valley. Why, I would not be surprised if you could turn round and find some of them sitting right in the seat beside you at this moment.

AND THEY WERE VERY DRY

So dry they cannot say "Amen" or "Hallelujah" so dry they have not said "Praise the Lord"

since they entered this building so dry that they can neither shout nor clap their hands themselves, and would like to stop everybody else shouting and rejoicing if they could. (They are almost like the dog in the manger who could not eat the hay himself and would not allow the horse to eat it) so dry that there is no real victory in their lives or ring to their testimony, or sterling worth to their profession. Dry! Dry! Dry! You can almost hear the bones rattle beneath their cloak of profession whenever they preach or testify or move.

AND HE SAID UNTO ME, SON OF MAN, CAN THESE BONES LIVE?

What a staggering question it was with which the Lord confronted Ezekiel a question which would at once stop his murmuring over the dried-up condition of affairs in the bone-yard, and require unlimited hope and faith in the resurrected, life-giving power of the Lord.

Have you been placed in a valley (be it home or assembly or neighborhood or workshop) that is full of dry bones? Is your minister dry? Your congregation, etc.? Then God is confronting you today with the same question that faced Ezekiel away back yonder.

"Son of man, have you a faith that can cause these dry bones to live?" It is one thing to find fault with and lament over deplorable conditions of dearth and barrenness; it is quite another thing to have the prayer and faith and confidence in God which will bring life and strength and better conditions round about you.

If you have discovered that you are in the midst of a valley of dry bones, stop lamenting and complaining because you are there and wishing you had been placed in a different environment on the hilltop where revival fires are burning and live armies are marching. Thank God that YOU are alive and that GOD is alive, and that as you believe and pray life will vanquish death in those round about you today as surely as it did in the day of Ezekiel.

Your being placed in that hard, dry, difficult place was not an accident, not an oversight or a mistake on the part of God. Just as surely as the hand of the Lord set Ezekiel down in that valley of dryness and death, so surely has the hand of your loving Father set you down in that valley, or position, or home or parish.

"All things work together for good to them that love God, to them who are the called according to His purpose"

And now, having placed you there, He has confronted you with the same question with which He confronted Ezekiel:

"Have you faith to believe and to lay hold upon Me, the Life Giver, and claim that life for these dry bones?"

AND EZEKIEL ANSWERED, OH, LORD, THOU KNOWEST

Here again many can heartily sympathize with the hesitancy of Ezekiel, for many children of the Lord, I fear, have often answered the challenge to faith in the same way:

"Oh, Lord God, Thou knowest! They are a pretty dried-up lot of people. There does not seem to be a spark of life, or even a longing for it. It hardly seems possible that this church or these people ever could be brought to a real live spiritual place. But, Oh, Jesus, increase my faith. Help mine unbelief, for I long to see them live, Oh, Lord."

THEN HE SAID UNTO ME, PROPHESY UPON THESE BONES AND SAY UNTO THEM: OH YOU DRY BONES, HEAR THE WORD OF THE LORD GOD, BEHOLD, I WILL CAUSE BREATH TO ENTER INTO YOU, AND YOU SHALL LIVE:

Poor, dried-up lifeless professor, there is hope for even you. You dear ones that do not believe in noise and shouting, you who do not believe in so much earnest prayer and praise to the Lamb, He will cause breath to enter into even you (and you know that Psalm 150 says "Let everything that hath breath praise the Lord"), and you shall live.

SO I PROPHESIED AS I WAS COMMANDED

Ah! There was the secret of the power and success of Ezekiel's prophecy in the valley. Do you see it. A-s I w-a-s c-o-m-m-a-n-d-e-d, not with enticing words of man's wisdom, which seemed wise and plausible to himself not words to please and lull his audience into a false security, not yet a self-righteous tirade of condemnation that merely showed them their condition and dryness; but a prophecy that was according to the commandment of the Lord.

Hallelujah! "The entrance of His Word giveth light" and life and liberty. Oh, for more Ezekiels today who would prophesy according to the commandment of the Lord instead of bringing in side issues and divisions and strifes then would we see more shaking in the valleys of dry bones, and the wind of the Spirit should blow, bringing life to those that sleep.

AND AS I PROPHESIED THERE WAS A NOISE

God grant that even as, whilst Ezekiel prophesied, there was a noise, and as whilst Peter yet spake the Holy Ghost fell (Acts 10), that while I am yet speaking, the power may fall upon you just now. Oh that our words may be so in accord with the commandments of God that whilst we are yet speaking we, too, will hear a "noise" of men and women crying out:

"What shall I do to inherit eternal life, and to receive the Holy Spirit?" the noise of praise and intercession, the sound of an abundance of rain, the sound of His chariot wheels upon the mountains, and the stirring in the tops of the mulberry trees.

AND AS I PROPHESIED THERE WAS A NOISE, AND BEHOLD, A SHAKING, AND THE BONES CAME TOGETHER, BONE TO HIS BONE

You notice that as Ezekiel prophesied there were three distinct things that took place in the valley of dry bones three periods that they passed through. Firstly, the noise: Secondly, the shaking: Thirdly, the bones came together.

When the latter rain began to fall in copious showers in 1907, the Spirit moved mightily in answer to prayer the whole world.

FIRST, over, awakening and bringing to life THE NOISE innumerable valleys of dry bones there was a noise. Sinners wept their way to Jesus and cried aloud:

"What shall I do to be saved?" Believers were filled with the Spirit, shouted, and often talked for hours at a time in other tongues (Acts 2:4) as the Spirit gave utterance. The noise of their joyous praises filled the sky. The glimpse which believers caught of the body and of the plan of God to restore the church to her full Pentecostal power and life caused them to shout aloud before the glorious vision, and well, it is putting it very moderately to say:

"There was a noise."

But stop! Listen! What is this remarkable shaking as of an earthquake, which immediately follows surely and inevitably everywhere behind the first noise of the Spirit's outpouring? If you but open your eyes and look about you throughout this movement the world over, you too will see, "and behold a shaking."

Has your assembly or the company with which you have been wont to worship, been going through a shaking? Have you personally been subjected to a severe shaking? Has your heart ached? And have you, too, asked a continual Why?

Why? And wherefore? When you have seen brothers, that were bosom friends and comrades in the battle, separate and drift apart, assemblies split in two, or half a dozen factions, as the case may be. Have you wondered why this one doesn't come back, and that one compromised, and those two couldn't agree and were so widely divided? I will tell you why it was. It was because of the shaking which followed the noise. It is following in the life of every assembly. It is following in the life of every believer. A mighty shaking-time is on.

Just as God shook out of Gideon's army until there were but three hundred left that could not be shaken (Judges 7) so the Holy Spirit is today sifting, purging and shaking, for He "whose

279

voice then shook the earth . . . hath promised saying, yet once more I shake not the earth only, but also Heaven, and this word 'yet once more' signifieth the removing of those things that are shaken. that those things which cannot be shaken may remain. Wherefore, we, receiving a kingdom which cannot be moved . . . may serve God acceptably." Heb. 12:26-28.

When first one sees the shaking, the splits and divisions amongst those whom we know should be bound together in love, it is heart-rending, but when we begin to see the plan of God as revealed in His Word, we enter into a place of rest, and when we read the next clause: AND THE BONES CAME TOGETHER, BONE TO HIS BONE, we lift our hands and shout for joy.

There is going to be a coming together after the shaking, some of these days, dear hearts and those that come together will be bound by such cords of unity and love that nothing can separate them again, and moreover when the body comes together it will be "BONE TO HIS BONE."

This is no patched-up affair, no man-made peace, no temporary armistice, but a unity that shall remain.

"Bone to his bone" When man in his own wisdom tries to fix the body up by choosing and ordaining, pastors, teachers, evangelists, prophets, helps, governments, etc., he is almost sure to pick the wrong bones or else put the right bones in the wrong places. That is why so many man made organizations have the ear where the eye ought to be, or the foot where the hand ought to be.

Aren't you glad that God sets His own church in order and that sets some in the church first apostles, secondly prophets, thirdly, teachers, etc. (I Cor. 12:28), and that when He has shaken out all that can-be shaken and tossed about by every wind that blows, and has

gathered together the firm, true, uncompromising, unshakable bones, He will Himself put them in their appointed places in the body, bone to his bone. "For as the body is one, and hath many members, and all the members of that one body, being many, are one body, so also is Christ, for by one Spirit are we all baptized into one body". . .and "now hath God set the members every one of them in the body as it hath pleased Him now ye are the body of Christ and members in particular."

We will not see the body come together in an entirety which will be apparent to the human eye, before the coming of the Lord. This movement, please God, will never be one great organization, but rather an Organism. We are expecting, however, a unity amongst the different members of the body (such as we have never seen before) to develop right down here in this old world.

One member of the body is made up of many joints which are in one accord and work harmoniously, one in connection with the other, joined together by the cords of love. The members of the body (that is the assemblies or communities) are moved and controlled not by their own wisdom or the orders of one another, but by the Head, which is Christ. And as each member, moved by the Head, obeys His will, there will be unity and harmony and a coming together. Each member is made up of many smaller members. In the arm there are the fingers, the hand, the bones of the wrist, of the forearm, and the shoulder. Today is the day that the smaller bones and joints are taking their place in forming the members. When Jesus shall appear the many members of the body shall be gathered, and the final great coming together will take place in the air. Hallelujah!

AND WHEN I BEHELD, LO, THE SINEWS AND THE FLESH CAME UP UPON THEM, AND THE SKIN COVERED THEM ABOVE; BUT THERE WAS NO BREATH IN THEM THEN SAID HE UNTO ME, PROPHESY UNTO THE WIND, PROPHESY, SON OF MAN, AND SAY TO THE WIND, THUS SAITH THE LORD GOD, COME FROM THE FOUR WINDS, O BREATH, AND BREATHE UPON THESE SLAIN, THAT THEY MAY LIVE. SO PROPHESIED AS HE COMMANDED ME, AND THE BREATH CAME INTO THEM, AND THEY LIVED, AND STOOD UPON THEIR FEET, AN EXCEEDING GREAT ARMY

Oh, if there is a soul here tonight who was once as a dried-up skeleton, has now been redeemed and has been covered with the sinews and flesh and skin (the covering of grace and salvation), and you have been slain by the mighty sword of His power, what you need now is the baptism of the Holy Spirit. The same Holy Spirit that filled the house with the sound as of a rushing, mighty wind on the day of Pentecost, shall come upon you, endue you with power, stand you upon your feet, and join you to this exceeding great army. (Rev. 7:9.)

Sinner, backslider, lukewarm professor, whosoever and wherever you are, you do not need to remain in the grave or the valley of dry bones any longer. The Lord is waiting to bring you up out of your graves of coldness and death, and cause you to know Him in salvation, to fill you with His Spirit and lead you to Canaan's land. Read the 12th, 13th and 14th verses of this 37th chapter of Ezekiel.

"Behold My people, I will open your graves and cause you to come up out of your graves" (sin), "and bring you into the land of Israel "(salvation)." And ye shall KNOW that I am the Lord when I have opened your graves, Oh, My people, and brought you up out of your graves." (Notice He says you will KNOW there will be no "think so" about your salvation. You will have a definite knowledge that you have passed from death unto life.)

The 13th verse is glorious. Do not stop there, however, but go on into the 14th, "and shall put My Spirit in you and ye shall live; and I shall place you in your OWN land; then shall ye know that I, the Lord, have spoken it and proclaimed it, saith the Lord"

(Here is another definite experience you will know about. He does not say you will guess I have performed it My promise to fill you with the Spirit or you will take it by faith, but you will KNOW I have performed it. Then praise the Lord. When He saves you, you know it, for He has brought you into the Land of Israel, and when He baptizes you in the Holy Spirit and speaks through you with other tongues you will know it, and He will bring you into your own land, the land of fruitfulness and victory which He has made as a promised land to those who will obey Him.

And you, dear child of God, no matter how dead and dry the bones in your particular valley may be, do not be discouraged or question the divine wisdom that set you down, just where you are, but respond to the call of faith the Lord is sending you, and prophesy as His Word commands, and if you, hidden behind the cross, lift Jesus up, He will shine down into the cold, benighted hearts round about you, bringing healing and life and filling with His Spirit until from that valley of dry bones a transformed, triumphant army shall rise and inarch forth to join the great body (for now are they many members, yet but one body. I Cor. 12:20).

The great, final coming-together day when the many members of the same body shall be united, and when the body shall be united to the Head, is at hand. What a wonderful day it will be when Jesus speaks from the Heavens the NOISE of His triumphant shout shall be heard (I Thess. 4.16); the graves shall be SHAKEN wide, fetters of mortality shall be shaken loose; and from the four quarters of the earth, from the dead and from the living, each bone, each member of the body SHALL COME TOGETHER and rise to fill its allotted place in that body, bone to his bone.

The time is short now, dear ones. Each setting sun brings us just one day nearer the catching-up of this triumphant body who shall rise to meet the Lord in the air. 'Twill be a body of overcomers, a band of people who have been tested, shaken, and proved who have washed their robes in the blood of the Lamb and come up out of great tribulation.

Will you yield yourselves as never before to the dealings of the Lord, and instead of murmuring at His shakings in your life, cry unto Him:

"Strip me, Lord, of everything,
Of this world and self, and sin,
That I may see the coming King,
And a crown of glory win."

"DEATH IN THE POT."

"And Elisha came again to Gilgal: and there was a dearth in the land; and the sons of the prophets were sitting before him: and he said unto his servant, Set on the great pot, and see the pottage for the sons of the prophets.

And one went out into the field to gather herbs, and found a wild vine, and gathered thereof wild gourds his lap full, and came and shred them into the pot of pottage: for they knew them not.

So they poured out for the men to eat: and it came to pass, as they were eating of the pottage, that they cried out, and said, O thou man of God, there is DEATH IN THE POT. And they could not eat thereof.

But he said, Then bring meal. And he cast it into the pot; and he said, Pour out for the -people, that they may eat. And there was no harm in the pot." II. Kings 4:38-41.

"ELISHA came to Gilgal and there was a dearth in the land" - There had not always been a dearth in Gilgal: Gilgal had once been wondrously blessed of God. Blessing and bounty had walked its streets hand in hand. Had they not echoed and resounded with shouting and rejoicing and the marching feet of four thousand men of war, as the priests, led by Joshua, had borne the ark of the covenant of the Lord thither?

After they had pitched camp and set up their twelve stones as a monument of Jordan's parted waters (Jos. 4:3 and 20), and kept the Passover, had they not eaten of the old corn of the land and the fruit of the land of Canaan? The long-looked-for Promised Land had been reached. No more need for wilderness wanderings, "and the manna ceased on the morrow after they had eaten of the old corn of the land; neither had the children of Israel manna any more, but they did eat the fruit of the land of Canaan that year " (Jos. 5:11, 12.) Was it not at Gilgal that, after the Lord had appeared as Captain of the host (Jos. 5:14), and Joshua had fallen on his face to the earth, the Lord said unto him:

"Loose thy shoe from off thy foot; for the place whereon thou standest is holy?"

And after Samuel had anointed Saul, did he not send him unto Gilgal to "tarry until" the

"Spirit of the Lord "should "come upon" him with "signs" following, that should give him "another heart" and turn him "Into a new man? "(Read I Sam. 10:6-9.) What a wonderful type of Pentecost! Later Samuel said to the people:

"Come, let us go to GILGAL and renew the kingdom there" even as the early apostles had returned to Jerusalem for fresh anointings of the Spirit.

"A DEARTH IN THE LAND"

But behold, now, something has happened. The children of the Lord have become cold, lukewarm, backslidden. Such a great dearth has come to Gilgal and the surrounding countries that they have "cleanness of teeth and want of bread" (Amos 4:6.) "Transgressions have been multiplied " but in Hosea 4:16, the Lord promises Israel (who, in her iniquity, He has likened to a backsliding heifer and forbidden to enter Gilgal), that if they will follow Him He will feed them as a lamb in a large place.

During the former rain outpouring of the Holy Spirit, which began on the day of Pentecost (Acts 2:4), the ark containing the glory of the Lord (spiritually speaking), rested in Jerusalem as in Gilgal of old. Even as Saul had been sent to Gilgal to tarry till the Spirit of the Lord was come upon him and till the signs came to pass, so the hundred and twenty had been commanded to tarry in Jerusalem until the Holy Spirit should come upon them with signs following.

The long-looked-for, long-prophesied (Isaiah 28: 11, 2:13; Joel 2:23 and 28; Zech. 10:1; Mat. 3:11; Luke 24:49; John 14, 15, 16; Acts 1:5 and 8) promised land had been reached. True, God had kept them whilst in the wilderness, and manna had come upon them, as the inspired words fell from the mouths of the holy prophets of old as they were moved by the Holy Spirit true, the words of Jesus had been as manna from Heaven, whilst He walked this earth in the fleshly body, but now the Holy Spirit had come N-O-W they had entered Canaan's land, and instead of the manna which had been taken away, and fell no more upon them (Jesus being returned to the Father and His voice being heard no more), they had corn and oil and wine (Joel 2:19), as the Spirit spoke through them of Jesus and His coming kingdom. "And they did eat the old CORN of the land' (Jos. 5: 11, 12) "neither had they manna any more, but they did eat the fruit of the land of Canaan." (See fruits of the Spirit, Gal. 5:22.)

Jerusalem (as Gilgal of old) rang with the praises of the Lord, and with the marching feet of new converts, new men of war, who went forth to follow the Captain of the host. On the day of Pentecost three thousand souls were added to the church; with pure hearts overflowing with joy, and with unshod feet, His people walked softly before Him and fell upon their faces in adoration. Just as the twelve tribes erected their monument of twelve stones, so the twelve disciples stood as a monument of the mighty power of the great and holy One who had parted the waters of the Red Sea "Salvation" and parted the waters of Jordan to bring them to Canaan's land "The Baptism of the Holy Ghost." Each time did the Lord Himself have to part the waters before His children could cross over into the new experience.

Humanity could neither swim nor ford the Red Sea the Lord Himself miraculously opened, through His blood, a path salvation which meant at once deliverance and Life to repentant believers and Death to unrepentant unbelievers.

Mankind could not cross the judgment of old Jordan's waves, nor make themselves worthy to enter Canaan and, again through parted waters (His GRACE and His WORTHINESS, which towered on either side) He led His people forth to the promised land, and filled them with the Spirit.

Here are two experiences Salvation and the Baptism of the Holy Spirit which we could not have brought ourselves into, therefore did He part the waters each time. Bless His name.

"ELISHA CAME AGAIN TO GILGAL"

After the disciples and apostles had fallen asleep in the Lord, and the many years of blessing wherein the power and glory of the Holy Spirit had been manifested, came the gradual falling away of the spirituality of the church. The apostacy and dark ages followed, but holy, inspired prophecy had said:

"He who sent the former rain moderately shall send you the rain, both the former and the latter rain together in one month," and "It shall come to pass in the last days, saith God, I will pour out My Spirit upon all flesh," etc.

"AND ELISHA CAME AGAIN TO GILGAL," Hallelujah! The time for the latter rain outpouring of the Spirit which was to take place in the last days had come, and Elisha (who stands for the visual manifestation of the power of God in signs and wonders) came A-G-A-I-N to Gilgal.

And when he came he found that "THERE WAS A GREAT DEARTH IN THE LAND." Ah, yes! What a dearth there was in the land!

What a crying out for food, and pottage, and bread and lentils in and just prior to the years 1905 and 1906. How many churches and saints cried to Heaven: "Oh, for the old-time power! Oh for another Pentecost!" The Methodist church, the Salvation Army, the Holiness church, and many others sang and prayed these words over and over (but Oh, how few really recognized the answer when it came, "wrapped in swaddling clothes and in a manger") . Nevertheless the word of God said: When you call upon Me I will answer, and in the day that you seek Me with your whole heart I will be found of you; turn unto the Lord with weeping and mourning, and . . . "He will return and repent and leave a blessing behind Him, even a meat offering and a drink offering."

"SET ON THE GREAT POT"

Therefore, when Elisha came again to Gilgal, that is when the Holy Spirit, at the specified time for the latter rain, found the hungry saints sitting before Him with one accord and one desire, even as the hundred and twenty had sat in waiting expectation of old, "He said unto his servant:

"Set on the great pot and seethe the pottage for the sons of the prophets." "Blessed are they that do hunger and thirst, for they shall be filled."

Oh, glory to Jesus! I can just close my eyes as I write, here before my open Bible tonight, and see the great Pentecostal pot (the entire Pentecostal movement), being brought out and set upon the fire the Holy Spirit is, of course, the fire our prayer, and praises are the WOOD (and Oh, it takes good dry wood, full of pitch, to make a real red hot fire water-soaked, rotten wood of worldliness and unbelief will only smoke and smudge and hinder).

283

Once suspended over the fire of the Holy Spirit, the Pentecostal pot soon began to boil and simmer, as hungry saints came together, each bringing a contribution of carefully tilled vegetables in their hands as an offering.

What a mixture, what a conglomeration came together in that pot!

Perhaps there is not another movement on earth made up of such a varied assortment of teachings, creeds and organizations, yet all melt and blend into one when put into the WATER of the Word, and boiled over the fire of the Holy Spirit.

It was as though myriad streams, corning from myriad fountain-heads, had met and mingled together, and NOW flowed on in ONE great stream as though they had never been divided.

Its fire was as that of a great burning pile of WOOD, hewn and gathered from many sources from varied kinds of trees from widely separated forests, now leaping Heavenward in one great flame of love and devotion.

It was as many VEGETABLES, planted, watered, cultivated, tilled and brought from many fields, put into one pot, and now forming, with the strong meat of the Word, and the water of the Spirit of life, a rich, nourishing food, whose appetizing and inviting fragrance was wafted to all about upon the vapor of praise and testimony which arises from the dancing, joyful mixture within.

With lightning rapidity the Pentecostal revival has encircled the world; thousands and thousands of hungry souls have been filled with the Spirit.

Wait a moment! You who are investigating, or gazing curiously into the lively, bubbling, dancing Pentecostal pot. Let us halt and examine some of, the people the endless procession of people who are coming to contribute some edible to the movement. Let us begin with this man hurrying along toward the pot, laden with vegetables and bread of the first fruits, and see what he has to say.

THE METHODIST

Q. "Halt! Who goes there? From whence do you come?"

A. "I am a METHODIST. I come from a church founded upon the sound doctrines of Justification and Faith in the present Power of God, as revealed to John Wesley a church where the power of the Holy Spirit used to fall in bygone years, until saints shouted, and sinners wept, and the joyful danced before the Lord."

Q. "O? And what bring you in your hand?"

A. "I bring with me carefully tilled vegetables and bread of the first fruits, from a grand old field a little sparsely 'sprinkled,' and well a little 'short of water' nevertheless, diligently cultivated by watchfulness and the Word of God."

"Our harvests come from various gardens and are tilled by different gardeners, some of which are known as 'The Epworth League', 'The Free Methodists', 'The Ranters,' 'The Shaking Methodists' etc., yet 'tis the same sun of righteousness which, from the lofty Heavens, shines upon one and all."

"Coming out from the parent field I bring with me an appetite whetted by the cherished memories of how God once did work in the old-time Methodist church; for, alas! Dearth and formality came into our field, and many therein were anhungered."

"Kindly excuse me, and allow me to pass, for in these last days (Acts 2:17) the great pot of blessing has been set upon the fire of the Spirit, and thither do I hasten that I may find this old-time power increased an hundred fold."

(There! He is gone! I would that I could have detained and conversed with him a little longer.

Let not our hearts be troubled, however, for lo, one goeth, and behold, another cometh.)

THE BAPTIST

Q. "Halt! Who goes there? And whence come you?"

A. "I am a BAPTIST. I come from a garden whose original plan of gardening (as recorded in our book of instructions) was patterned by the Word of God, the planting and springing up of the seeds required Justification and a Change of Heart.

The young plants were well watered, too in fact 'completely immersed' in the beginning of their growth, but as the plants grew and developed, and had need of the wind of the Spirit and the falling .of the latter rain for developing the harvest.

Alas! Between the high, well-guarded fence of 'close communion- and the heavy overhead trellis of theology and forms and ceremonies, neither wind nor rain could reach the garden."

"Consequently, many of our gardeners, realizing that the fruit of their labors was exceedingly 'hard shelled' and that some life and breaking of the dry stiffness was needed, tried an artificial irrigation process of worldiness and structural magnificence. Lectures, concerts and amusements were 'recommended' and tried as fertilizers. The spiritual life of the plants, however, did not thrive well under this method, and many withered and pined away, and there was a dearth in the land."

"Coming forth from behind our 'close communion' fence, I am hastening toward yonder brightly burning fire, for I do both 'see and hear' that the great pot has been set upon the flame. Hark! Can you not hear its dancing and bubbling, and see the vapors of praise rising, even from here?"

Q. "And what bring you in your hand to contribute to the Pentecostal pot?"

A. "I bring with me, as bread of the first fruits, the knowledge of the scriptures, sound doctrine, and a firm stand on Water Baptism as set forth by our forefathers. I bring with me a hunger for the real, tangible power of God."

"But, Ah! I catch the fragrant odors rising from yonder steaming caldron."

"Please allow me to pass, that I may receive my portion from the great pot."

THE SALVATIONIST

Q. "Halt! Who goes there? From whence come you, and why do you come?"

A. I come from the SALVATION ARMY, that   obedience to the call of God, marched fearlessly beneath their banner of 'Blood and Fire' into the very heart of the enemy's territory, taking captives and making love-prisoners for King Jesus."

"I come from a people who in their extensive gardening found labor for both the 'servant and the maid' a body of people who were once deeply spiritual and prayerful, and entirely separated from the world and its earthly lore."

"True, amidst persecution and trial, they sowed the seed and gathered the harvest not behind fenced enclosures, but in the streets and market-place, the slums and the hovels."

"I come from a people that used to stand for the manifestation of the Spirit, and many there were among them who shouted and danced, and fell prostrate under the power, and saw visions of the glory of God."

"Why do I leave? Why, because there is a dearth in our land the old-time power is sadly lacking today, times and business are so pressing, pressing, popularity our war work in the great world contest never-ending financial needs new barns for the extended harvest fields have been as quick-growing weeds that have sadly choked and crowded out the old spirituality and whole-hearted abandonment and humble dependence upon God."

"Seeking and hungry for the old-time power, I come for food to the great pot which has been set over the fire of this Holy Ghost movement."

Q. "And what bring you in your hand?"

A. "I bring with me the first fruits of our labors. Our field of vegetables had a wonderful beginning; the planting was beyond criticism, and if our field had been watered according to the instructions of Chief Gardener Jesus, none should have excelled it. Our under gardeners, however, felt neither the prescribed water baptism nor the latter rain outpouring (The Baptism of the Holy Spirit, as recorded in Acts 2:4) to be necessary.

"Our vegetables were not even sprinkled, Nevertheless they contain a real zeal for souls and a courage to go after them. I bring in my hands the old 'Amen Corner' and the ringing Hallelujahs, singing and music, and a faith and perseverance that sow beside all waters."

On and on they come!

285

They are flocking in from every direction, each bringing some contribution to the Pentecostal Pot.

Here comes the staunch PRESBYTERIAN the old Scotch COVENANTER the HUGENOT, and the staid EPISCOPALIAN follows after pride and formality forgotten.

One breath from the fragrant, boiling Revival on the fire brings back a rush of memories that recall the Faith and Power which rested in their midst in days of yore, when steadfast persecuted forefathers fell upon their knees in caves and dens and dungeons, where plush and padded prayer-cushions were unknown memories of old-time power and glorious blessing that followed in the days w T hen "they who lived godly suffered persecution" memories of long nights spent in prayer the sincere unaffected heart's devotion of the Savior and His love.

Ah, no! Neither gilded dome, nor frescoed arch, nor rolling tones that throb and thunder in the organ loft, nor surpliced choir, nor e'en the college-moulded, eloquent 'divine' (?) who speaks in modulated tones from flower-embowered canopy, can still the longing for the old-time power that glorified the sacrifice, surrender, prayer and faith of the Pilgrim Fathers' day.

Devoted saints come from the HOLINESS church, bringing the message of Heart-Purity and the Coming of the Lord, and wonderfully blessed of God, as fruitage needing but one thing the latter rain.

The ADVENTIST adds his teachings on the Coming of the Lord, deep study of the Prophetic Wordy teachings of Holiness and Freedom from Worldiness.

The QUAKER hastens up deep wells of joyous recollections rising in his soul eyes alight beneath his broad-brimmed hat, with the memories of how HIS church, once shaken and controlled by the Spirit's power (before the dearth), had walked so close to God. Glowing coals within his heart, long banked and smouldering, now burst forth in flames again as he hastens to the Holy Spirit's fire and the great Pentecostal pot suspended thereupon. He adds the fruitage from his field 'sterling qualities of truth,' 'unsaverving faith' and 'yieldedness to the in or ings of the Spirit.'

And, would you believe it, here comes the ROMAN CATHOLIC not one, but many of them, leaving the old church, many have come to the Savior, have been redeemed, filled with the Spirit, and bring with them a Holy Reverence and Obedience and deep appreciation of this new found reality and life in Jesus to add to the happy mixture bubbling in the pot,

So many come from every quarter that it is impossible to halt and question them all. There comes THE SINNER Yes, what lines and lines of them. Attracted by the reality and the mighty moving of the Spirit, they bring with them the Fruits of Repentance and First Love.

"And Elisha said: SET ON THE GREAT POT, AND SEE THE POTTAGE FOR THE SONS OF THE PROPHETS."

Oh, what a glorious feast we are going to have! What wonderful pottage!

Lift up the cover and peep in at the dancing, joyous mixture. See how, when boiled over the great FIRE OR THE SPIRIT and with the WATER OF LIFE, with the MEAT OF THE WORD and the SALT which has never lost its savor, a great, change comes to all the viands within the pot; the fruits of the fields, the vegetables and the barley, lose their "hard shells," slip out of their wails of differences,, creeds and forms forget they came from widely separated gardens and were tilled by gardeners who never could agree as to methods, and soon they burst with praise as their innermost hearts flow forth in love.

Then, as the fire burns on, they melt and melt and M-E-L-T until the pottage is but one united, savory mixture. Outside walls crumble and fall away, for vegetables must be peeled before entering the pot (that is barriers of organizations and differences must be left outside; peelings do not make good pottage). Then, as the fire still continues to burn and the pot to boil, each vegetable and fruit, in melting, has lost its own identity and has so united and merged itself into the other broken, melting hearts round about it, that 'tis hard to realize they ever were divided.

THE MAN WITH THE LAPFUL OF GOURDS

Many eyes and many footsteps were turned eagerly toward this Pentecostal movement brethren patted each other on the back and said:

"No more need of hunger or separation or dearth. Here is unity everlasting with nothing to mar". Hungrily, servants and handmaidens alike drew near with clean plates and shining spoons. "What a wonderful feast we are going to have," they said.

But stop! Who is that man, slipping in so stealthily behind the others, carrying something in his garment? Let us question him.

Q. Halt! Who goes there? From whence do Y-O-U come?

A. "Me? Oh I come from no particular garden. I am the 'ONE WHO WENT OUT IN THE FIELD TO GATHER HERBS.' "

Q. "And what sort of vegetables do you bring in your lap?"

A. "Why er that is, I It is not vegetables I bring. Vegetables must be most carefully planted in prepared ground, tilled and cultivated (study to show thyself approved unto God, a workman that needeth not to be ashamed). Whilst wandering yonder I found a wild vine full of nice, fat gourds, no trouble to till them at all. They were there already, and all I had to do was to pluck the wild gourds in passing. "See? I have a good big lapful here. Fine looking specimens, are they not?"

Q. "Good specimens of 'gourds,' yes, but I am not so sure of their being good to eat, or being a desirable addition to yonder feast. I fear that they are poisonous?"

A. "Oh, no, they are not poisonous, I assure you."

Q. "Well, what are the names of these different gourds?"

A. "Why a This one is called 'False Teaching:' this one is called 'Error': whilst this prickly one is known as 'Doctrinal Issues.' This puffy fat one is 'Lover of Power and Recognition.'

Then there is 'Self -Righteousness', 'Formality' 'Preconceived Ideas and Teaching', 'Fear of Manifestations', 'Flesh' and 'Fanaticism.' There are many other gourds, and amongst their number are 'Lack of Brotherly Love', 'False Reports', 'Harsh Criticism' and 'Tale Bearing.'

Q. "Why, Man! You would never think of bringing such things into the midst of a Pentecostal gathering!

You are wrong, and the gourds are poisonous. They will destroy unity and curdle love and make endless confusion and trouble. Surely you do not realize what you are doing?"

A. "Oh, yes I do. The Lord (?) revealed this thing to me and I know this new idea is the only right one. I know these gourds are perfectly all right and you can't teach me anything about them. Kindly allow me to pass."

Q. "Wait, wait, come back. There, he is gone' he worms his way into the inner circle, gets close to the pot, lifts his lapful of gourds, and in they go, the whole lot of them, into the pottage. On-lookers innocently allowed the gourds at first to pass them, and even Shred them into the pot of pottage, "for they knew them not." So they poured out for men to eat; and it came to pass as they were eating of the pottage that they cried out and said:

OH, THOU MAN OF GOD, THERE IS DEATH IN THE POT, and they could not eat thereof."

Amidst the many who come with good contributions to the pot, here and there steals up a man or woman with a lapful of gourds, which they have plucked from some wild vine as they journeyed, and they are thrown, sometimes ignorantly, sometimes knowingly, into the great pot upon the fire.

"Oh, what a distressingly large lapful of poisonous gourds!" exclaims the onlooker who had been approaching with his empty dish and spoon, ready to dine, and who now draws back in fear.

"Horrors the whole thing is spoiled!"

There is false teaching and error in that movement, and I am afraid to have anything to do with it.

There is "So and So, "who did "such and such" a thing and if that's Pentecost, or if that's the Baptism of the Holy Ghost, I for one, don't want it.

There's Mr. "So and So" in our assembly, and there's that one who professed to be a Holy

Ghost preacher did you hear what he did?

Did you hear of the gourd that he brought and dumped into Pentecost?

No, Sir! The whole pot is contaminated and poisoned. I tell you there's DEATH in the pot," and they are in a straight between two, whether to try to overturn the whole pot or to walk away and leave it, warning others as they go.

Some say, "Come on, let's fight this movement. Let's write some tracts against it and do what we can to overturn the whole thing." Others who walk away, warn everyone they meet by saying:

"Did you hear the news about that Pentecostal movement down there? Why, 'So and So' has just brought the most distressing lapful of gourds and dropped them into Pentecost; unity is disrupted; love is curdled, the people are made sick at their very hearts. Don't you go near that place."

Perplexity and confusion falls upon many an onlooker, some stay to criticise; others to wring their hands and weep.

What shall YOU and I do? We know that the movement is ninety-nine per cent pure, but Oh that lapful of gourds has brought so much trouble!

Of course we know that "WHEN THE SONS OF GOD CAME TOGETHER THE DEVIL CAME ALSO" and that there never was a movement but where someone came in to bring reproach, and that even amongst the twelve disciples one was a Judas. We also know how one who does not measure up to the standard is singled out from the ninety-nine others and enlarged upon until the "ninety and nine just ones" are forgotten in pointing to and discussing him who went astray.

"Well, we know the thing is not right anyway, as it is, and I guess we better go away. Too bad, isn't it?"

"But wait a moment: Who is this so swiftly approaching with a well-filled sack clasped tightly in his arms?"

Q. "Who goes there, and what do you bring in your hands?"

A. "I am the man with the sack of meal. The meal is the Word of God. I go to cast it into the pot. This meal will simmer down to the bottom of the whole affair and settle all disturbances. It shall cry aloud:

"'What saith the scriptures? Bring forth the plumb line. Let God be true and every man a liar. Prove all things. Abhor that which is evil; cleave to that which is good. Be not overcome of evil, but overcome evil with good."

This word is quick and powerful and shall not fail, if cast into the pot, to purify and bring order out of confusion.

BRING THE MEAL THE WORD OF GOD

"And Elisha said, bring meal, and he cast it into the pot; and he said, pour out for the people that they may eat, and there was no harm in the pot."

Oh hallelujah! The Word of God is being poured into this movement and His Word is accomplishing that whereunto it has been sent. The Holy Spirit today is calling as did Elisha of old:

"POUR OUT FOR THE PEOPLE THAT THEY MAY EAT"

I can seem to see the surrounding circle of empty plates and see the hungry faces of the dear ones as they are partaking themselves and calling to others to come, "taste and see that the Lord is good."

"POUR OUT TO THE PEOPLE THAT THEY MAY EAT"

Oh, yes, that is the greatest mission of the hour. Give unto the people that they may eat.

If you have discovered something somewhere in your vicinity or in the movement at large, which looks to you like a gourd, instead of turning your back and your judgment and

288

wholesale condemnation upon the whole thing, go bring the meal (II Kings 4:41), get the Word of God and find out what saith the scriptures. "If this work be of men it will come to naught; but if it be of God, ye cannot overthrow it, lest haply ye be found even to fight against God." - (Acts 5:38-39.) Get out the meal if you see this Baptism of the Holy Spirit with the Bible evidence, speaking in tongues, in the WORD, with the accompanying gifts and fruits of the Spirit, believe God and come boldly to receive this Bible experience even though every one round about you seems to be in error or falls below the standard.

INSTEAD OF BEING THE ONE WHO CRIES "THERE IS DEATH IN THE POT" BE AN ELISHA WITH A SACK OF MEAL; receive YE the Holy Ghost; let God make YOU to measure up to the Word. All your criticising or scolding or telling where the trouble is or even trying to fix it, can never help. The Meal of the Word will alone avail.

Pour out for the people that they may eat.

Dear worker, what are you feeding your hungry people on? Are you telling them and repeating over, meeting after meeting, every story and incident that has come to your knowledge where gourds have been put into the pot? If so you are guilty and putting gourds of doubts and discouragement in the pot yourself.

When you set the table for your guests that hunger all about you, do not frighten people away by bringing up from your cellar the poorest potatoes or the mouldy preserves, or the mildewed bread from your larder THEY DO NOT WANT TO HEAR ABOUT MAN'S WORST; THEY WANT TO HEAR ABOUT GOD'S BEST. What are you feeding your people on? Relating the worst things you ever heard of man doing or the best things you ever heard of God doing? The former makes poor fighting food the latter makes firm spiritual muscles and makes strong, developed, matured men and women who grow quickly under such teaching "unto a perfect man, unto the measure of the stature of the fulness of Christ." (Eph. 4:13.)

Remember that by relating past wrongs, etc., you are as guilty as those who committed them, and are only frightening people away by crying:

"There's death in the pot." Go bring the meal: preach the Word. Lift up the pure standard and God will vindicate and honor His Word.

Does it seem sometimes that you have very little to set before the people and do you feel your own lack and insufficiency? Remember that the servant felt it that day, too, when he said: (II. Kings 4:43) "What, should I set this before an hundred men?" And Elisha said: "Give the people that they may eat; for thus saith the Lord, they shall eat, and shall leave thereof. So he set it before them, and they did eat, and left thereof, according to the word of the Lord."

The Word of God rights every wrong, dispels all darkness, removes all impurities, settles all misunderstandings, and it dissolves or eliminates all the gourds or just what becomes of them I cannot exactly say, but at any rate I know that after the meal was cast into the midst " THERE WAS NO HARM IN THE POT."

If you have been standing afar off in doubt and are an hungered, hesitate no longer but bring your meal with you and come and dine, for there is no harm in the pot.

With all the gourds (and indeed they are comparatively few in number, considering that this movement has enveloped the entire globe, and into it have come streams of people from every creed and clime and color), this great pot set upon the fire, this Holy Spirit movement is the best thing in the world and contains the best food on earth.

REJOICE IN THE LORD

"Rejoice in the Lord alway: and again I say, Rejoice."
Phil. 4:4.

IT is the will of the Lord that His people should praise Him and rejoice in Him at all times, in all places and under all circumstances, rejoice in Him with a joy so deep, and springing from such an inexhaustible fountain-head, that it is as an artesian well that rises upward day and night unceasingly, unchanged, by summer's heat or winter's cold, sunshine or clouds.

"Rejoice in the Lord alway: and again I say, Rejoice. Pray without ceasing, and in everything give thanks. Let His praise be continually in your mouth" This does not mean a spasmodic praise, here today and gone tomorrow, that shouts with joyous gladness when all goes well and the sea is calm, only to fret and pine and murmur when the sky is o'ercast with darkness and the surrounding seas are lashed to foam. It is not a joy that flows only when showers of blessing are falling, but which flows even-tempered, unhindered, with a stream of just as great volume, its quantity and quality unchanged, when drought and barrenness is all about it,

WHY is this stream unchanged by circumstances and outward change in the elements?

Why, because of its source, of course, because of the fountain-head from which it flows. Rejoice IN THE LORD not in circumstances, not in blessings past or present, not in money, not in popularity, not in numbers, not in good or evil report, but rejoice IN THE LORD.

"Although the fig tree shall not blossom, neither shall -fruit be in the vines; the labor of the olive shall fail, and the fields shall yield no meat; the flocks shall be cut off from the fold, and there shall be no head in the stall: yet I will rejoice in the Lord, I will joy in the God of my salvation." Hab. 3:17, 18.

'Tis here, in this land of continual, unmolested joy, 'tis here by the rivers and streams of God-inspired praises, that the Christian finds deepest peace, peace that passeth all understanding, peace immeasurable and fathomless as the billows of the sea, peace that emanates from the Prince of Peace Himself.

ABOVE CIRCUMSTANCES

Rejoice IN THE LORD. You will no longer deal out your joy or praise in the stinted little measuring-cup of your own feelings or circumstances. The words, "I do not feel like it," will be eliminated from your vocabulary. You will no longer say: "I could rejoice if such and such a thing had not happened," or "I could have rejoiced had not 'so and so' said such and such a thing." "So and So" and "Such and Such" will have nothing more to do with your rejoicing, for your eyes have been lifted above circumstances and surroundings and been riveted upon the Lord.

He will hold your eyes with adoration when He stands revealed in His power and beauty before you. When there is nothing else to rejoice in you cannot rejoice in circumstances, nor in earthly gain, and there seems to be nothing in yourself or life to cause rejoicing, and when you see your efforts, strivings and plans crumbling about you, when you have seen the King and caught a vision of your own nothingness and insufficiency, and have abhorred yourself if your eyes are fixed unwaveringly upon the Lord and His righteousness, holiness and mercy, you will still be able to lift your head and rejoice IN THE LORD.

Joy in the night, joy in the hard places, joy in misunderstandings, when you did your best and seemed to fail, such joy gives "beauty for ashes, the oil of joy for mourning, the garment of praise for the spirit of heaviness." Well did David know the security of this hiding place when he said:

"In the shadow of Thy icings will I rejoice"

From such a retreat one can look out through His feathers and laugh at the futile attempts . of the enemy, and rejoice that his life is "hid with Christ in God."

CHASTENING, HARD PLACES, AND OVERCOMERS

Has the chastening rod fallen upon you? Then rejoice IN THE LORD, for he whom He loveth He doth rebuke and chasten. Have you been going through testings and hard places in your home life, and does it seem that no shoulders but they of the Master Himself e'er bore a cross so heavy as that which has been given you? Then rejoice in the Lord, for He has put you in a place wherein you may be more than conqueror, and win an overcomer's crown. If you had nothing to overcome, then how could you ever be an overcomer?

Never hath He allowed a temptation but what He hath provided a way of escape. And have you failed in that home, in that appointed place, again and again until the tears of discouragement have filled your eyes and you have felt that it was of no wail? Have sharp been spoken, of which you have instantly repented with bitter tears?

Then arise, Oh captive daughter of Jerusalem, shake thy garments from the dust, lift up your head and your hands, and rejoice IN THE LORD who hath bidden you, "forgetting those things which are behind" to press on "toward the mark for the prize of the high calling of God in Christ Jesus."

Put your hand in His, plead the blood, and He will undoubtedly bring you up again and again to that same testing place, that same peculiar set of circumstances, until you shall emerge a triumphant victor and just such a conqueror as He seeks to reign with Him on His throne.

When you have conquered, after many failures, you will not rejoice in yourself, your own strength or prowess, but will rejoice IN THE LORD, without whom you could have done nothing. The harder- the battle the greater the victory, the harder the home life or environment, the brighter the victor's crown. When reading of the victor, the overcomer, and the conquering warrior in his armor of steel, one naturally calls to mind an army with flying banners waving in the breeze, music and cheering. We have longed and asked the Lord to make us overcomers, but when He has taken us at our word and in order to answer our prayer has placed us just where we are, in just these circumstances, how many times we have failed to see God and realize that the conflict in which we are now engaged is but a living answer to that prayer, is just the place and just the conflict where God has put us and where He wants us to overcome and keep rejoicing in the Lord.

Have you suffered earthly losses and bereavements? Have you been stripped of that which life held most dear, in a way that you could not understand? Then rejoice IN THE LORD, for "the Lord gave and the Lord taketh away, and blessed is the name of the Lord."

"Yes, Oh yes, He understands,
All His ways are best,
Hear, Oh hear, He calls to you,
'Come to Me and rest.'
"Leave the unknown future,
In the Master's hands,
Whether sad or joyful,
Jesus understands."
BOAST NOT OF THYSELF

Has God been blessing your labors and the fruit of your vine? Has He permitted you to be a soul-winner for Him, and given great results and numbers from the sowing of the seed with which He has entrusted you? Then rejoice I-N T-H-E L-O-R-D, not in your own works (for man's works shall be burned up as by fire), not in your own strength (for without Him we can do nothing), not in your own power (for the Lord will not give His glory to another, and all flesh, even good flesh, is but as the grass of the field that withereth away), not in your own righteousness (for all our righteousnesses are as filthy rags), but rejoice in the Lord. He is the Alpha and Omega, the beginning and the end; in Him is all righteousness and power, honor and glory.

Have you been used in your assembly in teaching, in admonition, in leading souls to Christ, in praying for the sick, in casting out of demons, in interpretation or prophecy, or discerning of spirits? Do men and women look up to you and speak well of you? Rejoice IN THE LORD. Take heed rejoice in the Lord alone, be careful to give Him all the glory, as did Peter when he cried:

"Why look ye so earnestly on us, as though by our own power or holiness we had mad this man to walk?" Acts 3:12.

Look to the Lamb of God, who said, "The words that I speak unto you I speak not o myself; but' the Father that dwelleth in Me, He doeth the works." John 14:10. Many, O so pitifull many, have lost out with God and man, have lost their gifts, lost their usefulness, because the rejoiced in themselves and in the approbation of people rather than in the Lord. The joy of the Lor is your strength; take away this joy and, like Sampson of old, you will be shorn of your locks, you eyes put out so that you can no longer see His face, and you will soon be bound with fetters of brass (bondage), grinding in the prison house, round and round, round and round, the same ol grinding machine, all you will have to tell, or testify of will be the same old story of healings, tha used to be and the victories that once were yours.

SEEKING WITH REJOICING

Would you receive aught from the Lord? Then rejoice in Him. "Let the heart of then rejoice that seek the Lord" I. Chron. 16:10. Are you seeking healing? Do not look at symptoms, o rejoice even in the prayers of the saints alone, but fix your eyes upon Him who hath borne all you sicknesses in His own body on the tree, and by whose stripes ye are healed, and rejoice in the Lor until His life and strength and joy flow through every avenue and enter into every fibre of you being.

Are you seeking The Baptism of the Holy Spirit?

Then rejoice in the Lord who hath said: "Everyone that asketh receiveth; and he tha seeketh findeth; and to him that knocketh it shall be opened." Mat. 7:8, and who is more willing t give the Holy Spirit to them that ask Him than earthly parents are to give good gifts to thei children.

Yes, dear seeker, enter in through the gates of praise, rejoice in the Lord. Let your prais fill every corner of the room and echo out into the surrounding atmosphere until it rings in th highest Heavens. Open your mouth wide and He will fill it. And when the Comforter has come, you will let Him, He will teach you to rejoice in the Lord in a way of which you have neve dreamed.

And this joy is the privilege of every child of God, the joy of the Lord. Enter into you joy, and into this kingdom which the Lord wants you to possess, where shadows and obscurin clouds are unknown, and the sun is never dimmed. Fix your eyes upon Jesus, dig deep in humilit till you reach the fountain-head, the inexhaustible source of supply, then through the golden pipe o your life, every day, every hour, shall leap up a deep, ne'er-changing stream of joy, a joy that neithe adversities nor trying circumstances can suppress or keep down, because it is a JOY IN TH LORD.

PRAISING THE LORD the Lord has ever been to me one the most inspiring and exaltin of themes. Oh! how I love to praise Him and hear Him praised.

It has been my privilege, on several occasions, to witness, the never-to-be-forgotten scen of one thousand saints standing on their feet with uplifted hands, and tears streaming down thei radiant faces, praising the Lord with all their might and soul and voice, with one accord, till th great volume of thunderous praises blended into a sound as of rushing mighty waters as it rolle majestically Heavenward. It went up as one voice, of one people who were one in heart an adoration of the Most High God and His Glorious Son, Jesus Christ.

It is when praising the Lord thus, as at no other time, my spirit catches the greates revelation-the greatest vision of the mighty, omnipotent King of the Ages, high and lifted up. 'Ti then that the very atmosphere seems electric, charged with the mighty power of the great God, and catch the sound of His chariot wheels leaping o'er the mountains, ever coming nearer as His 'saint continue to adore Him, till I hear the stately steppings of the King in the midst of His hol tabernacle then, as the cloud of glorious adoration still rises from the hearts of the people, I see Hir robed with Honor, crowned with Glory, seated upon a jewelled throne of adoration which His people have builded for Him by their praises.

The Lord inhabiteth the praises of His people.

Where real praise is, there God is.

It is impossible to over-estimate the power, victory, blessing, healing, encouragement and inspiration embodied in this wonderful secret of praising the Lord.

PRAISE THE LORD AT ALL TIMES

"Oh! But you know that I could never put anything on, I never could praise the Lord unless I f-e-e-1 like it," someone exclaims.

Unless you feel like it!! Oh! Is that the gauge by which you measure your offerings of praise?

Is that the foundation upon which your Christian experience is based? My dear Brother, Sister, feelings are a poor and a very uncertain guide upon which to rely when it comes to praising the Lord, or any other Christian experience. Only one man in the Bible that I know of went by feeling; that was dear old Isaac, and you remember how he f-e-l-t the hands and arms of Jacob, his son, and how deceived he was. Oh, dear hearts, praise Him, NOT BECAUSE YOU HAPPEN TO FEEL LIKE IT, but praise Him at "all times," and let His praise "be continually in your mouth."

BECAUSE HE IS WORTHY

Begin to praise Him whether you feel like it or not, and you soon will feel like it. Why, it is impossible for me to lift up my hands and begin to praise and adore my Master without a downpour of His blessing that is as rain to the thirsty fields and flowers, or as the anointing-oil upon my head, running down to the borders of my garments.

"Let everything that hath breath praise the Lord." Why, according to David, the only excuse you have got for not praising the Lord is being out of breath!"

"Oh, Sister, I praise Him in my heart. I could never shout aloud or be demonstrative. It is not my make-up or disposition."

Beloved, when you have put on your beautiful garments of praise (for no matter how homely you may be to the natural eye, you are beautiful to the Lord when you have put on praise as a garment), you are lifted above your own "make-up" and "disposition" and swing far out into the realm of the Spirit. As for praising the Lord in your heart, why, your heart is no different from anyone else's. When it gets just so full of glorious praises and adoration and He becomes so real, so fair as to be altogether lovely, the chiefest of ten thousand to your soul, your heart will run over and you will shout His praises, and your voice will be blended with the voices of all the other redeemed ones and soar upward to the Lamb that sitteth upon the throne.

I was much impressed recently, while in New York, by the notices posted on the subway and places, warning the people of the severe penalty elevated trains and in other prominent public awaiting anyone who should try in any way to break the morale of the soldiers by talking of possible defeat, or failure, or by lauding the strength of the enemy. This should be a warning to Christians also.

DO NOT BREAK THE MORALE OF THE CHRISTIAN ARMY

Two saints attend the same meeting. Probably you have these two saints in your assembly (for almost every assembly has them).

One enters with a long face, takes her seat, looks solemnly about, and if the meetings seems a little stiff or in need of a blessing, or lacking in praise, or "tied up," this dear one, meaning well enough, begins to be burdened and sigh, to pray aloud, or exclaim in this manner:

"Oh, Lord, what is the matter here? Oh, there is such a binding spirit, such a power of darkness. It seems as though the room were filled with demons. Lord, help," etc. Immediately every eye and every thought is directed to the devil, to darkness and binding spirits, and of course (like

Peter when he got his eye on the waves), when we get our eyes on the devil we have them off Jesus.

When we advertise and meditate upon the greatness and strength of the devil, and show fear, we underestimate the power of the great I AM, the Mighty Conqueror who never lost a battle. Such despondency and burdened agonizing is contagious, and soon everyone is moaning and crying and miserable, and it is not until someone begins "seeing and praising Jesus" that the cloud lifts.

The other saint enters the same meeting, where it seems that not one breath of Heavenly gales is stirring, feels the same pressure upon the meeting, and refusing to look at or recognize the enemy, says:

"This is the time to praise our Jesus. This is the time to see our God arise and scatter His enemies. He has told us that he will do great and mighty things if we will but praise Him, and we know that the enemy cannot lodge or abide in an atmosphere that is filled with the praises of the Lord."

This saint straightway begins to shout:

"Hallelujah! We rejoice in Thee! We glory in Thy might, Oh, our King! Victory and honor ever attend Thy troops. Power and dominion envelop Thee. Thy glory and presence fill the Heavens and the earth. It fills my heart just now. It over: flows and fills the room. Why, glory to Jesus! Beloved, the Lord is in our midst. Do you not feel Him? Why, this atmosphere is just like Heaven!"

Such faith and praise is contagious. The fire of unwavering confidence in God that burns within this temple soon leaps over its parapets, spreads first to those in the seats nearby, then on to the farthest corner of the room, inspiring, encouraging, lifting up drooping heads, strengthening feeble knees, and in a moment every eye is fixed on- Jesus, His praises fill the tabernacle, souls are blessed, vessels, are filled to overflowing, the Latter Rain is heard pattering on the roofs, running down the troughs, overflowing the rain -barrels, the dry ground is saturated and the wilderness and the desert places are blossoming as the rose!

What was the difference in the two saints? The one recognized and saw only the power of the devil, and straightway began to bemoan the sad state of affairs, depressing everyone who listened, while the other saw only Jesus in His all-conquering, invincible might and splendor, riding on to sure and certain victory.

MY VISION OF THE DEMONS AND THE ANGELS

The Lord taught me a wonderful lesson sometime ago, demonstrating the majesty and power of praise. I was seated on the rostrum in my tent during the evening meeting. Not only was every seat in the big tabernacle tilled and crowds standing in the aisles, but all about the outside of the tent hundreds and hundreds stood closely packed together. It was the early days of the meeting and conviction had not yet taken the place of curiosity.

Therefore, as a great many of the onlookers were Roman Catholics, and the balance unused to any demonstration of the power of God, the very air was filled with unbelief, scepticism, scoffing and ridicule. The people would listen as long as we sang (or was it because that drowned their murmurings?) But as soon as anyone endeavored to speak, the whisperings and the murmurings would begin until another song was started.

As I stood there on the platform, with my eyes closed, I saw the entire tent surrounded with great black demons, with huge, bat-like wings. Each demon seemed to stand about ten feel tall, and as they stood in a circle, completely surrounding the tent, they were so close together that their wings touched, tip to tip. They stood close to the border of the tent, and with my eyes still closed, my heart began to cry out:

"Oh, Lord, what shall I do?" And He spoke to me in such a real way, ill that calm, undisturbed voice which those who love the Prince of Peace know so well:

"Just begin to praise Me. I will do the fighting. You do the praising."

So I began to praise Him.

"Praise the Lord! The first time I said it I noticed the demons seemed to tremble.

"Praise the Lord!" The second time I shouted it. I am sure my voice was heard above every other sound, and I saw each demon take one step backwards, away from the tent.

"Praise the Lord! Praise the Lord!! Praise the Lord!!!-' Each time I said "Praise the Lord" the demons took another step backward, until I lost all sight of them in the distance.

"Praise the Lord!" The next time I said it I saw in the distance a circular band of angels standing around the tent.

"Praise the Lord! P-R-A-I-S-E T-H-E L-O-R-D!" Each time I praised Him they took one step nearer, another step nearer, still another step nearer, till at last they stood at the very border of the tent, such tall, wonderful-looking angels, with their beautiful white wings spread so wide that the wings of each touched, tip to tip, the ones of the next angel on the right and on the left. Father had sent one of His legions of angels to guard the tent.

Perhaps not another person in the tent saw the vision of this great shining band of angels, yet everyone inside and out must have sensed the presence of the divine, for not only did a great peace steal over my soul, but the whole audience was hushed. When I opened my eyes I could see only the people looking with rapt attention, but closing my eyes again I could see the angels just as plainly as I could see the people.

Is it any wonder that I believe THE POWER OF PRAISE DRIVES BACK THE ENEMY AND BRINGS DOWN THE BLESSING.

Jesus says: "What things soever you desire when ye pray, believe that ye receive them, and ye shall have them."

Now, if we ask God to give us a certain answer to prayer, and we then proceed to believe we have it, it is only polite to begin to thank Him for it, in other words, shoot upward through the prayer zone into the praise zone, and thank God beforehand that, according to His word, it is done.

When contending with sickness, trouble, misunderstanding, discouragement or depression, begin to see Jesus. Praise Him with all your heart, and the upward flight of His praises will lift you as with the wings of a great eagle, above the woes of this earth till sorrow and sighing are lost sight of and consolation and joy unspeakable fill their place as you exalt and magnify the Lamb for sinners slain.

PRAISING HIM IN THE FLESH

"But I do not want to praise Him in the flesh," says someone. Ah, but we walk no more "after the flesh, 'but after the Spirit," and all this poor flesh of mine is fit for anyway is to praise Jesus, and if you never do anything worse in the flesh than to praise the Lord you will never be displeasing in His sight.

When the Comforter abides and has His way, it is so easy to praise Jesus, for "He, when He has come, will glorify Me" and "out of your innermost being shall flow rivers of living water"

BRING THE OFFER OF FRANKINCENSE

You may have but little gold or silver a little of this world's goods to offer but there is no excuse for being sparing or miserly with His praises.

Heap up His praises upon the glowing altar of your soul, and pile His adoration a-top of that, crown Him with glory, laud and magnify His name until His burning praises rise in precious frankincense, as a sweet-smelling savor to be caught in the golden censer of the angel who offers unto the Lord much incense (praise), with the prayers of all saints upon the golden altar which is before the throne. Rev. 8:3.

IN TUNE

Let your heart be tuned up until it shall be as a harp of a thousand strings saved with melody by the fingers of the Holy Spirit.

If you have hung your harp on the willow-tree, if the rust of coldness or self or formality has formed upon the strings, or if they are broken or out of tune, GO GET YOUR HARP!

Take it down from the willows, clean away the rust which has gathered from long disuse, let the Holy Spirit tune up each string until again the music will spring forth at His slightest touch.

Remember it takes but a slight jar to put the most costly harp out of tune; walk softly, dear heart, with unshod feet before Him.

THE FOUR-FOLD MESSAGE OF THE HOUR

(For Fishers of Men)

SALVATION, THE BAPTISM OF THE HOLY SPIRIT, SOON COMING OF JESUS, AND THE PREPARATION OF THE BRIDE

THERE is no time for mincing words or beating round the bush, or sugar-coating the Word of God now.

The time for quick action has come!

This is not a time to be indefinite or vague, or come at the message in a round-about way not a time to come to the door of a man who, unconscious of his danger, rocks in the easy chair of his drawing room, and say:

"Fine day, Sir."

"Good weather we're having."

"Yes, yes, prospect of good crops," etc.

"But the fact is, Sir, I come to bring you a little news don't want to alarm you at all hope you will pardon my intrusion and taking the liberty," etc.

"But I fear you should notify your household and send for assistance, for -er-a I regret to tell you but the whole upper story of your house is on fire and I fear 'tis almost too late to save it."

N-O!! This is a time to ring the alarm with one hand, batter upon the man's door with the other, and shout: "FIRE! FIRE!! F-I-R-E!!!"

So many sermons are preached, so many articles written, that when boiled right down and analyzed, have not enough real warning and invitation to show the sinner his awful condition and invite him to the Savior's feet

Not enough real, definite explanation of the Holy Spirit, and how to receive Him, and the necessity for His incoming, to bring one soul to the place of understanding or seeking for the Spirit-Not enough about the soon coming of Jesus Christ for His waiting church, to explain to that soul how we know He is coming, or how to prepare to meet Him and yet other themes, eloquent, educational, or studious as they may be, fade into insignifance and step aside before this four-fold message of the hour.

The consecrated soul who can preach simple, plain, old-fashioned Salvation, according to John 3:16.

The Baptism of the Holy Spirit, according to Acts 2:4.

The Coming of our Lord, according to Matt. 24, I. Thess. 4:16.

And the Preparation of the Bride, according to I. Thess. 5, becomes at once (in the closing hour of the Church's stay upon earth) a man or a woman with a message.

It is one thing to write, and write, and write, or to talk, and talk, and talk most admirably and interestingly, we grant you, but it is quite another thing in writing or preaching to be a man or a woman with a real message for this hour.

Take down the double-barreled Word of God-take a deliberate aim, and fire straight at a given mark, with a message so simple that, had the sinner (who comes within the reach of your words) never heard of the love, sacrifice, and precious blood of Jesus, or of his own dire need of a Savior, he would know it e'ver you got through A message so plain that had the believer in your midst, like those at Ephesus of old, never heard of the Holy Spirit, there would be enough real definite information in your words to let that seeker know of how our Lord, ascending to His Father, poured out the gift of the Holy Ghost, who when He is come, convicts the sinner of his sin, bears witness with the newly born-again, blood-washed soul that the work is done, baptizes believers with the Holy Spirit, speaking- through them with other tongues, according to Acts 2:4, and is the lifting power which will quicken these mortal bodies when Jesus comes.

So plain and scriptural that your uninformed reader or hearer, who never before had heard the message of the soon coming of the Lord for His waiting church, would have heard, before you words had ceased, what these awful things that are coming upon the earth in these last days mean that you believe Jesus is coming soon your scriptural ground for such a belief, and the signs of the times, linked up with the signs of the Word of God, which confirm your assertion that He is coming BOON.

He would hear, also, of the necessity of getting ready to meet this Jesus in the air, what the preparation of the Bride means, and how it is brought about.

Oh Ye Bride of the Lord

Ye Translation Company

Ye who Love His Appearing poised on one foot, ready for instant flight, your trumpet in your hand for one last warning note to a lost world e'er you depart what will your message be?

Will you come at the real truth in a long, round-about, polite, apologetic way, talking of non-essentials in these last moments? Or will you shout aloud in explicit, clear, definite, concise words, this four-fold message of the hour?

SALVATION

In order to make the message of Salvation so clear and plain that a wayfaring man though a fool, cannot err therein, there are a few definite, scriptural facts that will have to be explained to him.

1. What sin is and God's attitude towards it.

2. How it came about that all were born in sin and shapen in iniquity, and therefore need a Savior.

3. Just what Salvation is; how it is wrought; how to be saved; how to keep saved and what Salvation will do for him.

THE BAPTISM OF THE HOLY SPIRIT

In order to convey a clear, definite conception of the Baptism of the Holy Spirit to a believer, and create a faith and hunger in his heart for this experience, it is necessary to explain clearly the "what saith the Scriptures" upon this subject: 1. Who the Holy Spirit is, and what His Office Work is to the Sinner, to the Believer, to the baptized, preparing Bride.

2. What the Baptism of the Holy Spirit is; how it was received in Bible days, and how the believer of today may know when he receives the Holy Spirit.

3. What is the benefit and necessity of receiving the Holy Spirit? What does He do for the soul in which He has taken His abode, and whom He has made His temple?

THE COMING OF THE LORD

It is not enough merely to make the statement that Jesus is coming soon, and tell the hearer to get ready to meet Him. If you would convince and electrify the unprepared soul into action Be DEFINITE, be EXPLICIT - Tell him the true facts of

1. What are your scriptural grounds for making the statement that Jesus is literally coming back to this earth in clouds of glory for His people?

2. How do you know He is coming soon? What are the signs of His appearing? And which of these signs have been already fulfilled?

3. What will happen when and after He does come?

THE PREPARATION OF THE BRIDE

In admonishing those about you to prepare for the coming of the Lord there is also a great need for the clear, unmistakable directions, given in the Word, to be demonstrated.

1. Who will rise to meet the Lord when He comes? Everyone that professes? The hypocrite?

298

Faultfinder and backbiter? Everyone that claims to be filled with the Spirit? NO?? Then who will go?

2. Whom did the Lord send down into this world (John 16:13, 14) to prepare the Bride? And of what does that preparation consist?

3. What must be the life, conversation, daily walk, clothing, attitude, etc., of the Bride?

Beloved, this Four-Fold Message should bait the hook of every fisher of men; it should load the gun of every hunter who would bring back precious souls for Jesus.

Time is passing the last hours with their golden opportunities are slipping by. Soon our Savior will appear. If you would have souls with which to greet Him, golden sheaves to lay at His feet, be DEFINITE, be ZEALOUS, be INSTANT IN SEASON AND OUT OF SEASON. Whether you in your corner are called upon to write or preach or just to give a plain testimony to those about you, don't ramble vaguely here and there, but for Jesus' dear sake, and the sake of lost souls all about you, be definite and clear, and lift the light embodied in this Four-Fold Message of the Hour.

Part IV

Visions, Prophecies, Messages in Tongues and Interpretation

Given by Sister McPherson

EXPLANATORY NOTE

God, in speaking through the prophet Joel, says:
"And it shall come to pass afterward, that I will pour out my Spirit upon all flesh and your sons and your daughters shall prophesy. And also upon the servants and upon the handmaids will I pour out my Spirit." (Joel 2-28, 29.) The gifts of the Spirit are being restored to the church and amongst their number is the gift of prophecy and also that of tongues and interpretation. (I Cor. 12.)

It is as a direct result of the restoration of these gifts and operations of the Spirit that the following messages and visions are recorded. Sister McPherson claims no authorship, as when these messages were spoken through her, she was completely under the power of the Holy Spirit, her tongue and voice were controlled by the Spirit as though speaking in tongues, only that they came in English. Those who were present copied down the messages word for word as spoken.

Regarding Interpretation, see I Cor. 14:13, 27. "Wherefore let him that speaketh in an unknown tongue, pray that he may interpret. If any man speak in an unknown tongue, let it be by two, or at the most by three, and that by course; and let one interpret."

Poetry or Blank Prose was given in Prophetic song in tongues and interpretation.

"And the same man had four daughters, virgins, which did prophesy." Acts 21-9.

"Then Jeremiah called unto Baruch and Baruch wrote from the mouth of Jeremiah, all the words of the lord, which He had spoken unto him, upon a roll of a book." Jer. 36-4.

The Former and Latter Rain

Tune "Brighten the Corner Where You Are"

It was on the day of Pentecost so long ago,

Christ the Holy Spirit did bestow;

It was with the mighty rushing wind, and tongues of flame,

First fell the promised former rain.

CHORUS

Lift thine eyes, and behold the latter rain, .

Falling today to ripen up the grain;

Jesus is coming soon and with Him we shall reign,

Jesus is coming soon again.

It was after Jesus from death's lonely tomb arose,

Rose triumphant, victor o'er His foes;

He ascended up unto His Father's throne again,

And poured out this glorious former rain.

Then with mighty power and holy boldness did they go,

Precious seed of Jesus Christ to sow;

Sick were healed, lame men leaped, danced, and walked again

When fell that glorious former rain.

Now the great and mighty harvest day is drawing nigh,

And the Lord is pouring from on high

301

Pentecostal showers to ripen up the golden grain.

Have you felt this glorious latter rain?

Still today on hungry, blood washed saints the Spirit falls,

And to you the loving Savior calls,

Just look up in simple, childlike faith, and in My Name,

Receive this glorious latter rain.

O the joy of those endued with power from on high,

As we see our Savior draweth nigh.

When the Spirit comes, we speak in other tongues again,

have you received this latter rain?

RHAPSODY OF PRAISE

At Mt. Forest, Out., Can., August, 1915.

Shout aloud, my soul, and sing

Joyous praises to my King;

Just and holy is His Name,

Shout,' my soul, and sing His fame.

Now my longing, weary eyes,

Wistfully do search the skies,

Looking for my Lord and King,

While my raptured heart doth sing.

To whom shall I compare my Love.

Who fills my heart from Heaven above?

Shout, my soul, and sing His praise,

All throughout eternal days.

Fair to look upon is He

Who from sin hath set me free,

Pure and spotless, kind and true,

And, my friend, He calleth you.

Soon He's coming back again

To call His own with Him to reign.

Shout, my soul, hold not thy peace

Till thy bonds He shall release,

Till I fall before His feet,

And my rapture is complete;

And there, beside the glassy sea,

I'll live with Him eternally.

THE MEETING IN THE AIR

To whom shall I compare my Love

Who came from Heaven above?

Who sent the blessed Heavenly Dove,

Revealing Jesus' holy love.

Chorus:

To whom shall I my Love compare,

The Fairest of the fair;

Soon I His Glory'll share,

In the meeting in the air.

To whom shall I compare God's Son,

Glorious as the noonday sun,

Who bowed His head and cried "'Tis done,"

And final Victory won.

To what shall I compare His might,

As clad in Robes of light,

He rides victorious in the fight,

Dispelling gloom and darkest night.

To what shall I compare thine arm,

Laid bare 'gainst sin's alarm.

To guard His people from all harm,

With its might their souls to charm.

SONG OF PRAISE AND WORSHIP

Who is this clad in the splendor of the Sun?

It is Jesus, the Holy One.

The Rainbow of Peace is under His feet,

And in Him the Godhead Power complete.

Hark the tread of a thousand feet,

Gathering before the mercy seat;

Prostrate before Him there they fall,

Proclaiming Him King and Lord of all.

Lo, He Comes enveloped in Glory's thick cloud,

Mystery and splendor His visage shroud.

One foot on the sea, and one on the land,

He stands with the world in the palm of His hand.

AWAKE, O EARTH! JESUS IS COMING SOON

AWAKE, O earth! Arise thou that slumbereth! Let the eyes of the blind be opened, let the deaf ears be unstopped. Come forth from the grave, O thou who are dead in trespasses and sins. Weep and howl, O thou reveler at thy banqueting hall, for thy day of destruction is at hand. Lo! The voice of thy laughter shall be turned into wailing. Thy dazzling garments of shame shall be removed.

Behold destruction cometh upon the earth, and the hand of Jehovah is heavy upon it. Hearken! The sea groaneth, travailing for the pain which shall shortly come upon thee, O thou wicked nation, which hath forgotten thy God. Yea, the mountains from their snow-capped summits, weep tears for the destruction and the curse of an angry God, that shall descend upon thee as the lightning from a darkened sky. The stars in the Heavens hide their faces before the vials of wrath that shall be poured upon thee.

O thou nations, thou art bathed in iniquity. Yea, O earth, thou art drunken with the wine of thine own iniquity, and with the blood of thy fellow men. Awake and howl and lament aloud, for the day of judgment is near at hand. The sword of Jehovah hangeth over thy head. Misery, devastation and death shall be fulfilled. The earth shall rock and tremble with fear before the approach of the mighty tread of an angry God. The mountains shall melt with fire before the thunder of His voice of wrath. The time of reckoning has come.

In love, in mercy unbounded as the infinity of space, did I shed my blood for thee that thou mightest be saved, but thou wouldst not. This day shall thy blood be shed, yea, it shall cover the fields. Thy garments shall be saturated and heaped with the blood of the nations, who have spurned the blood of Jesus. Lo, the sky has darkened. The Heavens are overcast with the darkness of the frown of God. O thou wicked nation, thou shalt surely die. The way of escape is cut off.

Where is thy hiding place? Or whither shalt thou flee from the wrath of thy Creator? In life thou shalt find no hiding place. Yea, even though thou seekest rest in death, thou shalt not find it.

The hand of Jehovah is upon thee, O land; The hand that was wounded for thee;

The hand that has been outstretched in love, pleading before thee all the days of thy life; The hand upon which I would have engraved thy name;

The hand that would have upheld thee in weakness, and guided thee over the rough and darkened places;

The hand that would have caught thee up and thrust thee into realms above.

The hand which thou hast scorned and spurned and spit upon,

This hand, O nation, have I now turned against thee in wrath and anger.

Thine eyes are blinded that they cannot see.

Thine ears are stopped that they cannot hear.

Through the night of gloom and sorrow peals a sweet voice of love; for a short moment shall I spare it to thee, if perchance that thou mightest listen. An open DOOR have I set before thee, but now the door that is gently and surely closing is still before thee, lest perchance the feet which are hastening to shed blood should turn to enter before it is closed forever, and the gate of mercy which has swung wide before thee all thy days, shall soon be closed. That voice shall soon be hushed and heard no more. The door shall soon be closed and no man shall open it thereafter. The open portals shall soon be locked forever, and none shall enter therein.

O foolish nation, thou who hast chosen the pleasures of this world, when I have pleaded with thee to flee from destruction, to hasten from the valley of death, to flee to the arms of refuge, to hide in the rock that is higher than thou, to flee as a man pursued by sudden death, thou wouldst not hearken. Thou sat thee down in thy gilded banqueting hall, and became drunken with the wine of the devil's pleasures and inducements, and went into slumber.

Lo! The Heavens are filled with the displeasure of thy God. Verily the Heavens which today are filled with clouds of richest blessing ready to drop milk and honey, wine and manna upon the seeking soul, tomorrow shall rain forth with wrath and displeasure, the fire and brimstone of a just and avenging God.

Awake! O thou that sleepest. Cast aside thy garments, O thou drunkard! Flee into the haven of rest, O thou of the bloody sword. Make haste to pass through the door before it is too late. Although the day of God's mercy is almost gone, it is not yet too late.

THE NIGHT IS UPON THEE

Destruction pursueth thee diligently. The lightning of God's wrath shall smite thee. All thy labors and works shall vanish away, and fade as a flower. Thy greatest creation shall I crumble as dust in my hand. Too late shalt thine eyes be opened. Too late shalt thine ears listen for my voice. Too late shalt thy feet search for the narrow path. Too late shalt thou knock at the gate which is barred forever. Too late shalt thou listen for the voice of thy God in Heaven. Thou hast not heeded the voice of my servant which called thee, now will I refuse to listen to thy voice that calleth me.

Nay, though thou fliest from coast to coast, with the speed of an eagle, in search of the word of mercy, thou shalt not find it there. Yea, though thou search diligently from shore to shore, thou shalt not find the narrow way, which today thou despiseth. One short season more have I spared thee. REPENT! REPENT!! REPENT!!! O, thou who hast shunned and forgotten thy God.

REJOICE, O THOU WATCHER IN THE NIGHT

Be glad, O thou of the weeping eye.
Sing aloud, O thou who hast travailed in Spirit.
Dance and sing, O thou redeemed of the King.
Thy day of sorrow is ending.
Thy eternity of joy is dawning.
The night has been long, but the morning cometh.
Thy path has been strewn with thorns, but lo!
I have prepared for thy feet paths of purest gold.
The valley has been dark, but lo!
I come to take thee where darkness shall never enter.

In sackcloth and humility thou hast bowed before me. In radiant robes of light will I transport Thee. Yea, in the twinkling of an eye, shall I change thee. Lift up thine eyes, let them be cast down no more. Lift up thy voice, let it be heard from shore to shore. Lift up Holy Hands, for lo! Thy days of sorrow are ending.

Lo! The King calleth for thee!. Slumber not, neither let thine eyes grow heavy, for lo! He cometh in an hour when ye think not. BEHOLD HE COMETH! Yea, when darkness covereth the earth as a mantle, when wailing, bereavement and sorrow shall be heard in every land, then shall the Son of Man appear, and gathering thee quickly together, all ye who are ready and watching, He will draw thee unto himself. The open gate shall close forever. Doom and destruction shall settle down upon the earth; but unto thee shall I show the glory of the home I have prepared for thee.

Be watchful! Be vigilant! Be careful! Slumber not! For lo! I come quickly.

PROPHECY TO THE NATIONS

HEARKEN to the voice of the Lord, ye nations! Hearken! Give ear, O ye lands!

Lift up your eyes, O ye people, BEHOLD OF THE LORD, for it is seething with the wrath of His indignation. O the seething, boiling cauldron of His wrath! Who hath considered? Who hath understood? He upholds it by His hand, the fires of His fury are kindled underneath it. All the nations that have forgotten God must be thrown into the pot,

His hands are turned against thee, O wicked nations; HIS HANDS loving hands, tender hands, pierced hands. His hands are turned against thee at last. O, His hands. They are now stern hands, strong hands, avenging hands, punishing hands. His hands are upon thee, O earth, in judgment. who can hide from His hands?

Who can conceal themselves from His searching gaze? Though thou hidest in the depths of the ocean, His arm shall reach thee and bring thee back to judgment. Though thou sittest upon the throne, and thy seat is among the haughty; though thou buildest thy nest in the mountain's top with the eagles; though thou gayest I am high, and none shall bring me low; though thou sayest I am secure and none shall make me fall; HIS HAND SHALL LAY THE MIGHTY LOW.

How are the mighty fallen, and the wicked brought to judgment! All shall taste of the cup of His fury, and enter the cauldron, the seething pot of His wrath. The king on his throne, the peasant in the field, the judge on his seat, the prisoner at the bar, the rulers of the lands, and the poor man in his shop, and all they that have forgotten God, shall enter the cauldron of His fury.

The eagle fighting the bull, both shall be cast into the pot together. The eagle with her brood; the lion with her whelps; the unicorn in his power; the beaver in his home; the bear shall be thrown in by His hands; the dragon that seeks to run away shall be gathered into His hands and cast alive into the cauldron. And you, O land of the eagle spread wings, must taste and drink and enter.

All these, the lion, the unicorn, the two eagles, fighting in the field, the beaver, the bear, the dragon, the crescent and the star all must drink, all must be broken and cast down and melted and ended.

Then shall the kingdom of the Lamb the white Lamb, the meek Lamb, the slain Lamb be established. Then shall the lion and the lamb lie down together. Thou hast refused Him in the form of the Lamb, the slain Lamb, but NOW thou wilt receive Him in the form of a lion. He shall rend thee with His teeth, and devour thee with His fury. He sought to conquer thee when He came as a Lamb, now He will conquer thee as the lion of Judah that knows no defeat. All nations shall bow their knee and admit that He is Lord, when He is conqueror. Then shall the lion and the lamb lie down in peace together.

O thoughtless people! O foolish lands, why hast thou not considered? Open thine eyes, behold the wine press of the Lord. He treadeth His wine press in fury. The clusters are gathered from the vine, the clusters from the vine are the nations, they are cast together into the wine press of His wrath. He has risen up to judge the world, the prince of this world is judged.

Who shall stay His step? Who shall cause Him to withdraw His hand? His love have you rejected, His kindness have you spurned. He would have covered you with His mercy and His forgiving love, but you would not. But now He shall cover you with judgment, as the waters cover the sea. O think not that He shall stay His step, His wine press is not yet full.

All nations shall enter, and be judged, and tried, and broken. They refused His broken body and shed blood, now their bodies shall be broken and their bloodshed. He would have taken your place but ye would not. Hear the sound, the rumbling of the earthquakes and the overflowing of the volcanoes; blood and fire and vapor of smoke. Like thunder of the cannon, His voice shall thunder before His army, and when the hills are laid low and the mountains overturned by the root and the hidden things revealed, the high laid low, and the haughty in the dust and all nations brought low, then shall the King come forth in His beauty, with a conquering tread and a marshal step, clad in glory and power.

TO THE SAINTS

His kingly garments are upon Him, His scepter is in His hand. His crown is on His head; the government is upon His shoulders; His face is most fair. In Him is light and truth and beauty.

O, the reins are in His hands, He shall drive aright.

The sun shall withdraw his shining, and the moon shall not need to shine by night, for He is the light of the world and in Him is no darkness at all.

We are now the temple of the Holy Ghost, and the Lamb is the light thereof. A spiritual house of the Lord, O building most precious, I have gathered my stones from the quarry, I have cut them and chiseled them, but O, little people, I want cement to bind my people together.

I must have sand, I must have water, I must have love. Sand is made out of stone ground to powder and sifted most fine. As I put the stones into the crusher, one must crush the other.

309

There is a creaking, a rumbling, and groaning; but IF YOU WILL HOLD STEADY IN MY HANDS I WILL USE ONE STONE TO CRUSH AND GRIND ANOTHER. You may no love each other at the time, but O be patient with my dealings. After I have ground thee and sifted thee fine, you will all come together as fine sand.

I will mix you with the water of salvation. I am the water. O, why can ye not understand my plan? I cannot use big stones or even pebbles in cement; only that which will pass through the sieve. I shall have a people as numberless as the sands of the sea shore. O, I want cement, I will have cement. A PEOPLE CEMENTED TOGETHER IN LOVE. I will put together my spiritual house quickly, when I can get cement of love to bind my lively stones together, saith the Lord of Hosts. Masons do not use a hammer to lay cement. There shall be no sound of hammer to lay cement when I complete my temple.

Behold I come quickly! O let the murmurers murmur no longer. Let the groaning one groan no longer, for soon I will come, for my temple is almost complete. O submit to my will. With mine own hands I have digged thee from my quarry. I have shaped thee and chiseled thee; but if thou wilt not submit to my hands I must lay thee aside in spite of my love for thee and take another who will let me have my way; even as I laid the Jews aside, and chose the Gentiles, for the time i short and I come quickly. I will have a perfect house, my love. HOLD FAST THAT WHICH THOU HAST that no man take thy crown. The number is fixed, and if thou layest down thy crown, another shall take it and put it on. If thou layest aside thy mantle of overcoming, it shall fall upon another.

O consider whose ways are best, your ways or my ways. The Lord is at hand. Be patient yet a little while and He who shall come, will come, and will not tarry. O rejoice! the day of redemption is at hand! The King is coming, coming SOON. HOLD FAST! HOLD FAST! HOLD FAST!

PROPHESY AND VISION

IT was the night, and darkness was upon the face of the earth, yea, gross darkness covered the people. Behold a light coming out of the darkness, a voice calling through the gloom. I lifted my eyes, and beheld the presence of the Most High, the Holy One of Israel, the Lamb without blemish.

His glory, and the brightness round about Him, outshone the brightness of the noonday sun; as He drew near me I hid my face before the radiance of His coming. He spoke, and my soul fell within me at His voice. My strength departed from me, and I fell at His feet as one dead.

I heard His voice saying: "Fear not, Oh, my child, Stand upon thy feet and follow thou Me."

But my strength had departed, and I could not stand. Then put He His arms about me, and behold, we were lifted up from the earth. He carried me in the Spirit and sat me down upon my feet before a small hill, saying: "Hast thou considered this hill of blessing?" Then measured He the hill round about, and I beheld the measure thereof, and it was one hundred cubits. Flowers of praise bloomed on its sides, tiny streams of praise issued there from.

Then caught He me up again in the Spirit, and sat me down upon the earth, at the foot of a very high mountain whose top I could not see, for it was beyond the clouds; its measure could not be taken. An exceedingly high mountain flowing with milk and honey; trees were laden with fruit, whose clusters hung upon the vine, the mountain of the Lord which He builded for His people.

Then said He unto me: "Why have My people stopped at the small mountain of small blessings?

I, even I, have come to lead them forth to My great mountain, from weakness to strength, from defeat to victory, from showers to torrents, from the brooks to rivers. Oh, why have My people not gone on to the fulness? I have said greater things than I do, shall ye do because I go to My Father.

Speak unto My people; cry out: 'Leaving the things that are behind, let us press-on to perfection.'

"Oh, my people, I am longing to show forth My power. I am waiting to do My strange acts. I am waiting for a yielded people, yea, even a worm with which I can thrash a mountain. I seek not wisdom, nor thy strength. I seek humility and yielded hearts."

Then spake the Lord: "Look -at thy side the altar of the Lord which My people have builded for me." I looked, as He commanded, and lo! a bright fire was burning upon the altar; sacrifice and praise, through the Holy Spirit, arose, as a sweet-smelling savor, to the throne. But lo! As I looked, the fire sank lower, and died away in strength 'till only the coals were left.

Then said the Lord, with sadness: "Go, speak unto My people:

"'Wherefore hast thou ceased to offer thyself as a sacrifice, . with thy praise as a sweet-smelling savor, upon My altar? Return thou unto thy first love, unto thy whole-hearted sacrifice, also the sacrifice of praise, and behold, I will send an awakening among the people. The flames shall be kindled upon My altar, saith the Lord.

Behold, the time is short. Whatsoever thou doest, do quickly. Behold, at thy gates lie all manner of precious fruit. Hasten! Hasten! Enter in, My children. Behold, I come quickly, and My reward is with Me. Seek My fulness. Enter thou in, for lo! I come quickly. Even so. Amen".

PERFECT FRUIT

GIVE Me thine ear, O My people. Lend Mo thine ears, for Lo! I would speak unto My children. I would reveal Myself unto Mine anointed.

O My People, behold the vineyard of the Lord.

Behold the Redeemer walking up and down between the trees of His vineyard. He is searching for the perfect fruit. Lo! Here the tree is filled with leaves. But where is the fruit? Here is a tree filled with blossoms, but where is the fruit? O My people! The spring is past, the summer is over, the fall has come. Where is the fruit? Here another tree stands with tiny, immature fruit, but O! the time has come for the perfect fruit.

O, little company! Little flock! Lo, thou hast been considered the least of all, but thou art worthy. O little vineyard, how long have I walked up and down in thy midst. My pruning-knife has been in My hand. I have not spared thee. It has not all been pleasant, but I have been working with thee, little vineyard. But now, hear ye My words: the time has come for the fruit-bearing.

Long have I patiently waited. The spring is over and gone, the summer has come, and the fall is upon us. I am coming soon for developed, pruned and ripened fruit.

I have seen thy patience, and have written it in thy book of My remembrance.

I have seen thy tears, and I have saved them in the sealed vessel of My remembrance.

I have heard thy prayers, and have I not risen up to answer thee? Behold the clouds, the bright clouds of blessing. I have rolled them over thy heads; I am watering thee with the pure water of the Spirit that ye might grow." (O, the sadness on the Master's face! O, the sorrow in the Master's heart! So many trees, so many vineyards, but no ripened fruit).

"O, little people, may I have this corner in the vineyard with the perfect fruit? I have called unto My people in other places, beseeching them to lay all on the altar. I have pled with them many, many years. I have waited, but they have forgotten to seek Me in humility daily. I am waiting for a perfect tree with perfect fruit. Little people, will you also fail Me? O, will you go all the way?"

"O, My people, seek no longer fleshly things; seek not earthly things; but seek thou the things of the Spirit. Be not encumbered with many cares. O, for a people with one accord, in one place, with all things in common, none calling aught they possess their own! How I could show forth My glory. Yea, they would move Heaven and earth with their prayers.

Can you not perceive My plan? Can you not understand My workings? Behold I show you a mystery:

I have called nations from nations.

I have separated people from people.

I have called churches from churches.

I have called out the sanctified from the lukewarm.

I have called out a baptized company from the sanctified.

But now, behold, I do a new work.

I AM SEEKING TO CALL A BAPTIZED PEOPLE FROM A BAPTIZED PEOPLE, WHO WILL GO ALL THE WAY TO THE STANDARD OF MY PERFECTION

All have failed as a complete body to go all the way, and to measure up to the Word; but I will have a people who will not be satisfied with aught but My best perfection, a people who will not slumber nor sleep, but who will watch with Me this one remaining hour. Through this people will I show forth mighty signs and wonders. The people shall marvel before them, saying:

"What manner of people are these?"

They will seem but folly unto the world; but through them shall the wisdom of Jehovah be made manifest.

Weak in themselves, but in Me they shall be strong and do exploits.

Dumb in themselves and their own words, slow to speak, few in words, but they shall speak forth My words in the power and demonstration of the Spirit, O, little, called-out people, I am here tonight.

Have I not called thee out from the people, from earthly bodies, to serve Me? Has it not meant persecution? But thou hast been willing to pay the price thus far. Behold, My heart is pleased with thee; but will you go all the way? Behold, if thou wilt walk with me this way, I will show thee what great things thou must suffer for My name's sake. But I will cause thee to overcome even as I overcame. Thou shalt sit with Me upon My throne even as I sit upon My Father's throne. O keep humble! Keep low at My feet! Trust not in the arm of flesh, even good flesh. Look upon Me. Stand in the bonds of love and unity, with a whole-hearted surrender of everything, and I will do the rest.

Behold great blessings are in store for the overcomers. THE OVERCOMERS. Behold I come quickly to take My perfect fruit and the full overcomers.

VISION AND PROPHECY

THERE came a great voice from Heaven as of a trumpet, crying: JESUS IS COMING SOON GET READY TO MEET HIM.

My soul longed to see His face. My heart had been cleansed by His blood, and the Spirit had entered the tabernacle. I cried out:

"Yea, Lord" and ran to meet Him.

"Get ready! Get ready!" Cried the great voice, again and again. "Get ready! Get ready!!" yet echoed over the hills and through the valleys. "Get ready!"

"O! Lord, Lord!" I cried, "Wherefore sayest thou unto me, 'Get ready?' have I not left all for thee? Didst Thou not wash me in Thy blood? Wherein shall I get ready?"

He held an open Bible before my face and it shone as a mirror. Then showed He me myself, dark and tanned, and uncomely.

"O Lord," I wept, "Have thy way. Get Thou me ready, I pray."

Then I lifted up my eyes and beheld a man, tall of stature, clothed in raiment of light, that shone as the sun. A sharp sword gleamed in His hand. I beheld His brightness, and saw His armour gleaming upon Him. He advanced and drew near me. He towered above me. His beauty was of such brightness my eyes could not gaze upon Him. Then I saw my own imperfections, my blemishes, my failures. I withered under His gaze, and was ashamed in His presence. I wept for my foolish blindness, that had boasted of readiness.

Who can dwell in His brightness without showing a blemish?

"O, Lord" I cried, "I am a failure. I am all blackness. I am undone." Then He spake: "Wilt thou let me have My way? Wilt thou let Me make thee ready, no matter what the cost?"

"O Lord," I cried, "I am utterly unworthy, but have your way."

I saw him in my vision that the open Bible which He held had been transformed into a flashing, two-edged sword. Then He lifted His sword, and placed it upon my lips. It burned as a coal of fire. My lips, my tongue, were utterly consumed. Then He raised His sword and placed it upon My eyes, and I was blinded unto the world and the shortcomings and failures of all mankind.

Then His sword shone as it turned in His hand and He smote off mine ears, so that I could hear no earthly voice, but only His voice, sweet as the rushing of many waters. Again His sword whirled through the sunlight, and this time my head was cut off, that I should think no more in myself.

Then He severed my arms and my limbs, that I should move no more in my flesh.

In my heart I cried: "O! Lord! there will be nothing left of me if You have Your way much longer." My soul failed within me, and I beheld myself as from a distance lying at His feet as one dead, broken in fragments, undone. It seemed that I was utterly undone, and I murmured at His dealings. But He spake and said:

"Thou shalt walk no longer in the flesh, but in the Spirit. Out of death shall come life. This corruption shall put on incorruption. This mortal shall put on immortality. Then shall be fulfilled this saying, "O Death! Where is thy sting? O, Grave! Where is thy victory? That which is flesh must die. Only the Spirit can inherit spiritual life."

Then I looked and behold! A New creation, as of a beautiful woman. I beheld her coming from the West, and walking towards the East. She approached. I beheld her white raiment, dazzling as the snow in the sunshine. Her movements were gracious and tender. Her voice was mellow and full of sweet fragrance. I smelled the fragrance of her garments, as sweet lillies grown in the valleys, and as the rose of Sharon. Her eyes beheld no guile, but they were tender as a dove's eyes. Her lips were pure, and dropped as the honey-comb. No foolishness, no criticism marred their sweetness. No fleshly words, her ears were kept for His alone, her Lover, her Bridegroom, her King.

As she drew nigh, I gazed with amazement into her face, and saw that it was myself. I heard the voice of the Master speaking unto me, saying:

"This is My beloved. How far you have fallen short of the standard of my perfections!"

TO THE SAINTS

O AWAKE! AWAKE! AWAKE!! Thou that sleepest. Jesus is coming soon. Get Ready! Get Ready!! His bride must be without spot or wrinkle or blemish, or any such thing. Her eyes must see Him only. Thy words shall condemn thee if thou speakest ill of thy neighbor. Thine ears shall testify against thee if thou shalt hearken to any voice but His. I will have a separated people, saith the Lord, a people who will walk before Me in holiness, in the beauty of My perfection. Lo! I stand before thee. My sword is in My hand.

Wilt thou let Me have My way? It means death to the natural life, to be spiritual. It means putting off the old man, with the lusts thereof, and being clothed upon with the Heavenly building which is of God.

Beauty for ashes,
Praise for murmuring,
Love for backbiting,
sweetness for unsweetness,
Victory for defeat,
Brightness for shadows.
O beloved, will you let Me have My way?

Over the hills in glory,
Over the mountains bright,
Hear the glad, sweet story,
He cometh with power and might.
Lift up your heads, ye pilgrims,
The Master draweth near;
Weep no more, ye pilgrims,
The Lord is almost here.
AMEN

THE SIEVE OF THE LORD

PROPHECY DURANT, FLA.

BEHOLD, two hands strong hands of the Lord; and in His hands a sieve. He is sifting sifting, sifting His people.

Once they were small, and but as dust then could God use them, but when they ceased to be small and helpless, when they gathered themselves together in separated lumps, they became big and hard and unyielding, and the Lord wept over them. He could no longer mould or shape, o fashion them.

There were the lumps of unbelief, and the lumps of pride. O, those lumps of scepticism those lumps of self and doubts and fears; those lumps of formality and ceremony; God could no put them into the body. He could not form them into that glorious, Bridal Body, for they were no longer yielded and submissive in His hands.

Once they were small, but now harder and larger and wider the lumps had grown, until they were blind, deaf and dumb and slow of understanding Then were formed the lumps o organization and Catholicism. Oh, the stiffness and hardness of those lumps. "I must break them; must smite them with the hammer of My Word. I must have a broken, sifted people through whom I can have My way. I must separate a peculiar people unto Myself."

THE GREAT SIEVE

Behold the hands of the Lord. He put the broken lumps into the great sieve He held in Hi hands. The sieve had large meshes, and as He did shake and begin the work of separation, many o the smaller lumps and dust went through the sieve.

Many hearts were broken and contrite under His dealings; but the bigger lumps of doubt and fears and unbelief, He had to throw them away. He loved His people, but those who would no become broken, He had to throw aside.

Many went through the sieve, in those early days. Many of the smaller lumps passed through the coarse sieve, but they were still hard and lumpy.

THE SECOND SIEVE

So He made another sieve of smaller meshes, and put in His people, who had passed through the first sieve. He shook them and tried them, separated them and sifted them. Man rebelled and refused to go through, so He had to lay them aside.

But some went through this second sieve, and precious were they in His sight.

Those who went through the sieve had to go through the world. They had to let go one another; they had to let go of themselves and of the opinions of people. They who passed throug the sieve had to let go all foolishness and pride.

O, that sifting that separating! The Lord gathered them in His hands. There were still few little lumps. They were still His people; but those who would not believe and be broken, H had to throw aside.

THE FINE SIEVE

Those who had gone through the sieve were not sifted fine enough, nor little enough to b moulded, so the Lord made for Himself a still finer sieve.

Who can understand the plan of the Lord?

Into the finer sieve He put His people, and He is sifting and trying people, who will le Him have His way. All doubts and fears must be eliminated. All selfishness, the old nature, a desire for earthly honor, popularity and recognition, must be taken away. All hardness, stiffness an stubbornness must be taken away. All flesh, even good flesh, must be left behind. All selfis

316

ambitions, all gossip, all earthly, idle words and foolish communication, all falseness and shallowness, and desire for earthly leadership, must be gathered together and cast out.

But His people, He will try again. He will sift them the second, the third time. The fourth time and the fifth time shall He sift His people. Ah! He shall have a people who can go through the finest sieve pass the finest test, whose hearts are broken, whose spirits are mellow and yielded and who are abandoned to His will. He shall gather them together; not a grain shall be lost. But He shall gather His people together from the East and from the West, from the North and from the South from the uttermost parts of the earth He shall gather them in. He shall hold and mould them in the palm of His hand as fine dust.

Once the lumps were large. They were big and great, but He could not use them. His people are a peculiar, sifted, tried people, who are as the dust of His glorious feet; and with that dust He shall form a ~body, even as He did from Adam in the beginning, so shall He form this body. They shall be yielded in His hands; they shall be pliable under His dealings. He shall make them into members of the body and fasten them together with cords of love.

FORMING THE BODY

The Head shall be joined to the neck the neck to the shoulders. The arms shall take their places in the sockets, and they shall not be stiff, but shall be oiled, and soft and mellow with the Spirit.

Their breasts shall be of Faith and Love, and shall be full. All the parts of the Body shall be in their places. The spine shall be formed together, and the loins shall be formed and rest in their sockets.

From yielded dust shall be formed strong limbs-legs as pillars of marble, not to be removed. Of the humble members shall He form the feet; they shall be humble, and bear about the other members, yet without feet the body could not walk.

GIVING LIFE TO THE BODY

Then shall He breathe upon this Body upon His yielded, slain people. He shall breathe life into the nostrils, and the Body shall become a living soul controlled not by self, but by the Spirit. They shall walk not by flesh, but by the Spirit of the Lord. They shall be strong and do exploits. From the Head shall grow the long hair of separation and praise to God not one missing.

COMING FOR THE BODY

Soon He cometh! Ah, soon He cometh this King of glory. Soon shall He part the clouds and descend with a shout. His sifted, humble, tried little people He shall take by the hand, and stand them upon their feet many members, but one Body, and catch them up to reign with Him upon His throne.

O, My people, be little enough to go through the sieve. O, let go everything that would hinder, and go through. Go THROUGH.

WILL THOU WATCH WITH ME ONE LITTLE HOUR?

PROPHETIC SONG

The night is dark. The sun hath long since hid his face.

The Master cometh forth into the garden to pray; He bringeth forth His chosen ones to pray with Him.

O! Dark is the night, their eyes are heavy with slumber.

"Will you watch with Me one little hour?

Will you stay awake and resist the tempter's power?

Will you watch with me this little hour?

Soon the watching will all be o'er."

O hear the Master praying for you;

Praying for a world steeped in sin.

Hear the moaning and the groaning as He travails for the lost.

Weeping, wailing, sobbing, hear the Master now,

As the sweat drops of blood appear upon His brow in the moonlight's glow.

"Will you watch with me one little hour?"

The World has forgotten. See them slumbering...fast asleep.

And still He prays, and still He prays, and cries to God.

Behold the shadows deepen, and the cup is in His hand.

O must He drink it all alone? None to share or bear the burden?

Lo! He is bending over you; He is speaking in your ear.

Canst thou not hear? O, watch and pray, O watch and pray, lest thou should enter into temptation.

"Nevertheless, not my will, but thine be done."

O hear the cry; He is praying for the world.

Wilt thou not watch and pray, until the breaking of the day?

Jesus approacheth again and saith, "Sleep on now and take your rest,

The blessing you might have is fled away.

Alone I prayed with none to stand with Me.

Sleep on, sleep on, and take thy rest."

O, will you too fail Him, will you, too, sleep in slumber deep?

Or will you watch and pray?

'Twill soon be day, and He is coming soon.

Beloved, if ever there was a time for the followers of the Lord to resist the slumber that the enemy would put upon them, and pray, it is now. What a type the sleeping disciples in the garden, and the sleeping virgins with their lamps, are of the church today. The same Jesus who prayed in the garden of old is making constant intercession at His Father's throne today. The same Jesus who besought His disciples to watch with Him and pray that they enter not into temptation, is still calling for intercessors, through whom the Spirit can pray with groanings that cannot be uttered.

It is only a little hour now till He shall appear. Let us be faithful. Awake and pray.

THIS IS THE WAY, WALK YE IN IT

PROPHECY

This is the way, walk ye in it;
Out of defeat, into victory,
Out of the mire, into purity,
Out of darkness, into light,
Out of sin, into Righteousness,

Out of the Valley, into the extended plain, Out of death into Life yea, life everlasting, This is the way, walk ye in it. I am the way, follow thou me; yea, follow in My footsteps.

Lift up your eyes: behold!
Who is tills that cometh with clouds and great glory?
Who is this that rideth upon His horse?
His face shineth as the sun in noonday splendor.
His garments are white and dazzling as the snow: His voice is as the rushing of many waters, His words, sweet and gracious and tender.
Who is this?
His feet shine as burnished brass;
His appearance is as gold in a burning furnace.
Behold He cometh!
He cometh with ten thousand thousands of His saints.
Behold they are coming, riding upon their chariots.
Hear the treading of their horses.
Their spears are gleaming in the sunlight; Their swords are swinging by their sides.
On and on they come.
Behold the Heavens are filled with their glory.
Behold the King cometh with ten thousand times ten thousand of His hosts.
His glory is bright. He is as a burning light; Who shall be able to stand in His presence?
His beauty, who shall declare it?
His beauty, who shall describe it?
Who art Thou whose glory doth fill the Heavens?
Whose light breaketh forth as the morning?
I am the first; I am the last;
I am the beginning; I am the end.
I am the Alpha; I am the Omega;
I am He who was dead, but behold
I am alive forever.
I am HE who passed through defeat, and entered into victory;
I am He who passed through the valley and the shadow of death, into the wide plain forever.
I am He who came through darkness and passed into light.
I am He did swallow up death and brought forth life, yea, eternal life.
I am He, who passed through the mire of this world, with its slander and rebuke, and have been made white and stand in righteousness forevermore.
YEA, AND AS I AM, SO MUST YOU BE ALSO,

That where I am, there may you be forever.
O, Behold, I AM the way, follow thou ME.

320

I AM the Way, follow thou Me.

I AM the Way that leads from earth to Heaven: I AM the Way, the narrow way That leads rom death to Life, from defeat to victory.

Behold the KING is riding forth in His Glory!

For whom art Thou coming, O KING of Heaven and of earth?

I am coming for those who have walked in the way; Who have followed Me; who have een faithful unto death And art alive forevermore."

Who is this that cometh forth out of the wilderness?

She leans upon the arm of her beloved.

There are tears upon her face.

She is foot-sore and weary.

Her back is bowed with a burden.

Her garments are torn and muddied,

But He will give her a white robe of His righteousness.

She climbeth the mountains, and passeth through the valley.

She crosseth the wide, extended field, she journeys o'er the plain.

Before her lies a tunnel, a deep valley bathed with the shadows of night.

She will not falter, even though the way is dark, and the lions roar.

He will not allow her to stumble nor dash her foot against a stone.

He bringeth her through the darkness into the light.

He bringeth her to the boundary line between the two countries.

There she must be searched; there she must be stripped.

She must not bring any message from the country of darkness into the country of light.

ven as your countrymen halt, at the boundary line, all that would enter from the enemy's country, nd search them, so shall she be searched and stripped.

(New garments shall be given her, His righteousness and joy.)

But she will go through, even as He hath said.

I AM the WAY, walk thou in Me and be thou perfect.

Be thou faithful unto death, and I will give thee a crown of life.

Go through. Go through the gates; enter thou in.

Be faithful yet a little longer, the darkness is almost over.

The day of thy humiliation is almost ended.

No more shalt thou be footsore and weary, for I am come to give thee rest.

Even as I washed the feet of the disciples, so shall I wash thy feet,

And I will wipe all tears from all faces.

There shall be no more pain.

Behold, SOON the clouds shall part, and thine eyes shall behold the coming of the KING, aith the Lord.

Behold I come quickly; My reward is with Me;

I neither slumber nor sleep.

Make haste, O beloved of the Lord; He shall remove thy burden and cause thee to shine as the Light forevermore, even the Sun of Righteousness.

This is the WAY, walk ye in it.

Even as I overcame, so must ye overcome.

Even as I was faithful unto death, even the death of the cross,

So must you be, even to the putting away of the old nature, and I will give you eternal fe.

Even as I was misunderstood and mocked, Even as I was cast out of the synagogues.

Even as I was lifted up, a gazing stock, and was spotless, so must ye be.

Even because I AM THE WAY, follow thou Me.

Lift up the hands that hang down, and strengthen the feeble knees.
Be patient yet a little longer, only a little, for behold I come quickly.
O, can you not see?
If you would open your eyes you would see the Heavens are filled with My chariots and My horsemen.
If your ears were open you would hear the rejoicing and victorious shouts of My hosts.
Behold I am coming soon; My victorious armies are with Me; they shall avenge Mine elect.

"O," saith the Lord God Jehovah, "I will avenge Mine elect,"
Soon shall go forth My swift lightning, the lightning of My sword among the nations.
But because thou hast followed Me, thou shalt sit with Me in the Heavens and laugh.

I shall tread My wine-press, and it will be full of the blood of those who rejected Me and thee.

Fear not, My little ones, but GO THROUGH, even as I went through.
He that saveth his life shall lose it; save not thyself.
Behold they will say unto thee, as they said to Me" Save Thyself,"
But go through. Go through.
Vengeance is Mine; I will repay.
Behold I have rolled away the Ked Sea. I have opened a way.
As I rolled back the Red Sea and drowned Pharaoh's hosts of old,
So shall I consume thine adversaries from before thine eyes.
I AM THE WAY
I have made a straight path through the Red Sea, Even through the Red Sea of My Blood
I have made a way.
Pass over, My people.
I have removed the sting of death for thee; for thee there is victory.
I will remove the armies that molest thee, if thou wilt only follow Me.
So many hard things came because thou didst not follow ME.
I have opened a way, follow thou in My footsteps.
I, who have overthrown the walled cities, even I, shall overthrow the wails of opposition
I, who locked the lions' mouths
I, who brake the chains of brass
I, who led armies to victory
O follow thou Me!
Follow Me through into Glory;
Follow Me through the Garden;
Follow Me through the Judgment;
Follow Me through to Calvary;
Follow Me through the tomb;
Follow Me through the resurrection,
And thou shalt follow Me through the translation; Yea, thou shalt follow Me FOREVER,

THIS IS THE WAY, WALK YE IN IT.
AMEN.

THE VINEYARD OF THE LORD

TONGUES AND INTERPRETATION

LIFT up thine eyes and look to the East, to the West, to the North, and to the South; behold the vineyard of the Lord.

His vineyard is before Him; He walketh up and down in the midst of it. Oh, how long, Oh, how long, Oh, how long He has waited for the perfect fruit?

Oh, thou vineyard of the Lord, Jehovah is in the midst of thee. He has never forgotten thee; He has never neglected thee. With His love has He built a wall about thee; He has fenced thee about on every side and sheltered thee from the world. With His own hand has He digged and turned thy soil; by His own power has He sown thy seed, and cared for thy tender plants; He hath watered thee with showers of blessing and times of refreshing from the presence of the Lord.

How earnestly He watched thy budding forth, oh, vineyard of the Lord, when thou didst first receive the former rain! He hath digged about thee; He has caused the sun to shine upon thee; and now behold, He sendeth the latter rain upon thee that thy fruit should come to full perfection, even the perfection of the Lord.

I have let the winds, yea, the North and South winds, blow upon thee that thou might be established, and thy roots sink deep into me. The sap of my life have I sent coursing through thy veins; thy tender leaves have been put forth and developed, and now behold, the time for the ripening of the fruit is here.

The Lord of the vineyard has come forth into His garden to seek precious ripened fruit. He

seeketh the perfect fruit. He turneth to the East, to the West, to the North, to the South. Where, oh, where is the perfect fruit?

Here the fruit is marred, with blemishes upon it. He passeth by. He seeketh not the blemished, but perfect fruit to take to Himself.

Yonder the fruit is small and undeveloped.

Where is the perfect fruit? He seeketh not small and undeveloped, but perfect in measure and stature for Himself.

There the fruit is growing, but so slowly. He is standing, waiting, waiting, looking for the perfect fruit.

He cries unto His vineyard,

Oh, my vineyard, how long, how long, before I shall receive my perfect fruit? Why tarriest thou so long and withholdest thy perfection from me?

Have I withheld my hand from thee? Have I not sent thee the former and latter rain in the first month? Have I not caused the sun to shine on thee by day and the moon to watch thee by night?

And, now, behold, the husbandman, waiting for His Fruit.

Woe unto thee thou barren and unfruitful trees trees! Surely thou shalt be cut off from the garden of living trees, and the place where thou art shall know thee no more. Cursed art thou among trees, for thou hast borne me no fruit.

And thou, trees of the blemished fruit, and the undeveloped fruit, mine eye hath seen thee, mine, eye hath searched thee out.

But Oh! Thou tree of the growing fruit, thou art nearing the days of thy perfection.

Surely thou shalt grow up before me as a tender plant, as a tree planted by the living waters. Thy desire is toward me, my desire is toward thee. And I will gather thee unto myself in the day of thy perfection. AMEN.

THE STORM AND THE WHITE LAMBS

TONGUES AND INTERPRETATION

The clouds are dark. The sky is filled with rolling tempest of darkest clouds. Great bolts and strokes of lightning flash from the Heavens.

The lightnings flash as visible signs of the wrath and fury of Almighty God. Listen! The thunders are rolling and resounding from hill to hill.

Below is a green pasture field, and in its enclosure a beautiful flock of white lambs. Surely they shall know no fear nor terror, for there is One in their midst who holds in one hand His crook, and in the other a cruse of oil.

Some of the lambs leave the enclosure. The lions, the wolves, the hosts of darkness pounce upon them and the place wherein they dwelt knows them no more. O, stay within the enclosure of His will and protecting grace. 'Twill not be long till the Deliverer will come. He sends not His sheep forth to fight wolves; stay thou within the enclosure.

The storm increases, the winds howl, the waves roll, the lightning flashes, the enemy draws nearer, emboldened by the darkness. Whither shall they go? There is no escape to the right nor the left.

There is a barrier before and behind. Stand still, little flock, the indignation of the Lord is being poured out upon the wicked, but He will pass over thee. The storms are raging, but behold the Heavens are rolling apart. There cometh One whose appearance is all glorious, His garments are as robes of light, His face is filled with tenderest compassion. His arms are outstretched

Tis the Shepherd of the sheep.

They are surrounded before and behind on the right and the left, by the hosts of darkness. The lions roar, the serpents hiss, the wolves bare their fangs, the enemy rages against the righteous, but they shall know no terror, for there is an invisible power between them and their enemies.

IT IS THE BLOOD OF JESUS, AND THE POWER OF THE HOLY SPIRIT

Their Leader is with them, even the Spirit, to lead them. A lamb is on his bosom. He speaks to the flock that they should wait and be patient a little longer. The Leader is the Holy Spirit.

Soon will the Shepherd come to gather the sheep of His pasture away from out of the dark and the cloudy day, and take them to that fold where the sun never sets, and they will be with Him, forever.

He poureth in the oil, He bindeth up the wounds, yea, He will heal thee.

Ah, little flock, He cometh, He cometh, ABIDE WITHIN THE POWER OF HIS BLOOD AND SPIRIT. Soon thou shalt hear His voice saying,

"Come home, my sheep, come home." To the world destruction cometh, but to the flock the Shepherd cometh. Look up."

How the hilltops sing together,
Angels strike their harps of gold.
Let His saints all shout together,
In love and praise and joy untold.
Soon He comes o'er hills immortal,
Clad in garments pure and white;
Soon He comes to take His pilgrims,
There to reign in power and might.

MESSAGE GIVEN IN THE SPIRIT

(July 27, 1918)

Behold the day of great darkness, the day of gloominess, of mourning and weeping, the day of wailing, the day of the treading of the wine press is upon thee, O earth. Hearken! Hear the sound of the cannon, the voice of thunder echoing and reverberating through the hills and the mountains.

Behold! The arm of Almighty God is lain bare. His sword is glittering and glimmering in His hand. O, thou earth, filled with unbelief and scoffing, if thine ears had not been stopped thou wouldst have heard the heavy treading of His feet, the falling of His footsteps.

Judgment follows swiftly in His wake. He will recompense, He will repay, He will judge. Had thine eyes not been bound, thou wouldst have seen the clouds rolling over thy lands, black and filled with the lightnings of His wrath. -Ears thou hast had but would not hear. Eyes thou hast had but would not see. The time of thy tribulation has come.

Weep, O lands, and wring thy hands, saith the Lord. Turn unto Me with repentance, with sackcloth and ashes; but thou hath said, "We will dance and make merry, we will sing and drain the wine-cup to its dregs" Too long, too long hast thou sat in the banqueting house. Thou hast desecrated the holy vessels of the Lord. Thou hast used My house, the house of the Lord for merry-making. Thou hast used it to consume it upon thine own lusts. Behold, there cometh forth a hand, it is even now writing upon the wall of thy lands. Behold, thou art weighed in the balances and found wanting. My hands have been outstretched to thee, but thou hast spurned them, thou hast pushed them aside, and now My hands are turned against thee. Thy judgment cometh.

Behold, limb is today being torn from limb, member from member, blood is flowing forth in a crimson stream and encircling the whole earth. Judgments are thundering forth their voices from ten thousand cannons.

Ah! fools, hypocrites, slothful of heart, despisers who wonder and perish. Behold, o'er thy head hangs the great sword suspended by a single thread. Judgment is begun.

In thy midst behold the great wine press. His feet are treading it. Blood is issuing forth, yea, thou hast rejected the blood of My Son Jesus Christ. Now shalt thy blood be shed. Rachel, Rachel weeping for thy children, they are not. Behold the day of the Lord cometh. It is nigh at hand.

Beset on every hand, surrounded on every quarter, threatened from every side, yet His people shall never be ashamed. Protected by His hand they shall abide in the day of His wrath, and He shall take them to Himself purified. Not a hair of their heads shall be destroyed, neither shall the sandals be worn out upon their feet, neither shall spots be found on their garments nor blood upon their hands. Behold, His people stand in the midst of a perverse generation, but they are a sign post, a wonder to all who look upon them.

They are a puzzle to the world, but to Me they are all fair.

Open up thine hearts, for He will cleanse. He will purge, He will purify His temple, He will drive out all that which is unlike Himself, if thou wilt yield to Him. Behold that which has been whispered in the ears, in the closet, shall be made known on the house-tops. Open up thy being to the Lord. Open up the door, my beloved, and He will purge His threshing-floor. He will iron away all thy wrinkles.

325

REIGN, SILENCE, REIGN. PROPHECY.

Nov. 22. 1918

Reign, Silence, reign!
Peace, be still!
Hold thy peace, thou billows of the sea!
Reign for a space of time, O Silence!
Spread thy pinions, one o'er the land, and one o'er the sea.
Hush! Cease thy striving, O thou four winds of the Heaven.
Be still, tempestuous clouds!
Enter thy sheath, O sword!
Be silent, thou thundering cannon!
For the Lord would speak once more to the earth; Once more would He send forth the cry:

BEHOLD THE BRIDEGROOM COMETH, HE IS EVEN AT THE DOOR

Spring forth, ye green blades of the grass, upon the meadows and the hills. Yea, bloom forth, ye hills and valleys. O thou hast been held fast in the grip of War's giant clutch. Bright, crimson drops of blood have been wrung from thy sides and have flowed forth in gory streams.

O, ye torn and devastated forests, be healed of thy wounds for a short space; for the Lord would speak His final word of warning to the earth before the great and notable day of the Lord, for it is near, It Is-Near.

Hold back the winds, O Angels, for a little moment, ere they shall burst in redoubled fury upon the world that has forgotten Christ, our Redeemer, that my children may cry aloud that they may lift up their voices and spare not, that they may proclaim, for a little moment, "the coming of the Lord."

Awake! Awake!! O ye children of the most High God, for in My hands I am holding back the wrath and the indignation, the wars and the pestilences, the plagues, the earthquakes and the suffering, and the fiery indignation that shall soon envelop all those who have forgotten God.

"PEACE" do they cry?
Lo, there is no peace outside of Him who is the Prince of Peace.
"PEACE," do they cry?
But the cries of peace shall fall upon their heads.
Today is the day of salvation.
Proclaim ye the Word.
Yea, declare it from the early morning, even unto the setting of the sun.
Yea, hold not thy peace.

PROCLAIM THE WORD

Cry aloud in the night watches.
Warn the people, warn the people.
Let the message ring forth o'er the land.
Let it echo through the hills.
Let it resound in the valleys,
For the day of the Lord is at hand.
The deliverance of His people hath come.

But, sorrow shall fall upon the heads of those who have forgotten God.

As the avalanche sweeps down the mountain side.
Hear the roaring of His voice?
'Tis the Lord, who is uttering His voice before His army.
He is leading them forth in triumph,
Their's is the crown of glory;
Their's is the victory,
Through Him who has overcome,
Subdued His enemies,
And who shall reign forevermore.

Make haste! Make haste! My little ones.
Make haste! There is no time to spare.
For behold, I am coming soon,
To meet you in the air.

Lift up thy voice, My Love, My Choice,
Unto Me thy praises bring.
Rejoice, My Love, rejoice,
In the praises of your King.

O, SEND FORTH THE MESSAGE.
Shout it from the housetops,
Proclaim it from the steeples,
Declare it in the tabernacles,
Proclaim it in the highways and the hedges,
In the streets and the lanes,
In the city marts, and in the desert lone.
Reign, Silence, reign, a little space, 'till My children shall send forth the last, final call, for
am coming soon. Amen.

LOVE'S PINIONS AND THE CHURCH TRIUMPHANT

Los Angeles, Cal., January 7, 1919

Out of the verdant fields it came, and soared aloft, Above the trees, all laden with thei
fruitage rich and rare.

On milky, snow-white pinions did it soar This dove, so gentle and so pure-Its wing
spread wide, its pinions long; Higher and higher did it rise,

Until it sailed "midst clouds and sunlit skies.

His people, His people are as the dove The pinions upon which they fly are Love.

But now, brought low, O Dove,

Thy pinions clipped; thy wing- feathers plucked;

Thy love destroyed and lost; how canst thou fly aloft, as in the days of yore?

I saw the dove brought low buffeted thrust at, Unable to escape the prodding stick

Of error and false doctrine

With which inquisitive, experimenting children tortured it in passing.

But behold, the feathers have again begun to grow;

Her pinions Spring in snowy whiteness forth-Stronger than before.

Love and praise shall cause thee to arise, And soar into the very skies, My Love.

Let not thy wings be clipped away,

For I am coming soon, at Break of Day.

How canst thou rise to meet Me in the air.

If thy pinions are destroyed, O Love most fair?

The Lord, in the midst of His people, seeks to do a new work, to reveal Himself in migh
and in power. Let, therefore, thy love abound. Love thy God with all thy heart, and thy neighbor a
thyself. Little children, love one another then shall thy wings be spread wide, and thou shalt be
lifted up above the petty things of earth, and thou shalt see the glory of the Lord, and soar throug
the vast expanse of Heaven into His very Presence. Selah!

THE BRIDEGROOM AND THE BRIDE

PROPHECY

Great, Eternal Love of God,
Who shall measure thee?
Divine, Omnipotent, Glorious Love of God,
Who shall fathom thee?

We descend into the depths of the sea, and ask,
"Is God's Love here?" The creatures of the deep all cry aloud and say, "Great, great, great Love of God, it watches over me."
Behold, we ascend into the Heavens, where the birds with outstretched pinions sail through the azure blue. We ask, "Is Thy Love here?" They cry aloud, "Yea, yea, yea, His love upholdeth me."
We climb on into the heights of the ethereal canopy of Heaven, and exclaim:
"Surely, His Love hath not mounted to such heights." But the stars burst forth into singing in their glory, together, and assure us, "Yea, Yea.
It is His great Love that upholds us and causeth us to shine and reflect His glory."
Then down and on, far into the silent wastes of the desert we tread, and our hearts cry:
"Great Love of God, surely it hath not reached this barren land." But the sands cry aloud, "Yea, Yea, He is here with His Love outpoured, and His Love shall cause the desert to bloom as a rose; there shall be pools in the wilderness and floods in the dry lands."
O boundless Love of Thine, Eternal God e'en though the story be told through fathomless, eternal years, 'twill yet be all untold. Thy pinions, and outspread wings reach to the ends of the earth.
Thou dost brood over it as a hen upon her nest.
Thy golden streams of love flow down upon us from every feather. Thy people are protected from the heat of the sun, and from the ragings of storm 'neath the shadow of Thy wings, forever and forever.

With outstretched hand hath He led His people forth,
Through parted floods, dry-shod;
Their enemies hath He consumed before their eyes.
Manna did He pour out from Heaven upon them, Fresh every morning.
Unto a large land did He lead His hosts.
Unto a land which flows with milk and honey A land of pomegranates and vintage of the vine A land of grapes, precious fruitage,
Did He lead His people forth?

Glorious has been their portion,
Righteousness and Peace has been their garment.
Surely His people shall rejoice in Him,
And shall exalt His name forever.

Fair is He, as the morning dawn,
Bright is He, as the noonday sun,
sweet is He, as honey in the comb,
This Jesus, the Lamb of Glory.

Tender is He, as the Mother that holds her babe, Strong is He, as the mountains that guard

thy coasts. Mighty is He, as the sea whose billows break upon thy shores,
Glorious is He, this King of kings the Lord of Hosts.
He it is who led His people forth with singing, He is the Captain of the King's Hosts.
His people shall follow after Him,
And His troops shall shout His praises.

Hark! Hark! He is speaking unto His people r saying, "Dost thou behold this narrow stream shining in the sunlight and lift up thine eyes dost thou behold the great, sweeping expanse of the mighty ocean? Thy present borders are but as the narrow stream, but if thou wilt follow me I will enlarge thy borders; grace and power and glory shall be multiplied unto thee, and as the ocean is more mighty than the stream, so shall thy latter glory be greater than thy former."

"Dost thou behold yonder sapling of the oak? And have you considered the mighty parent oak, rising in lofty maturity far above it? My children are at present but as the sapling nourished by the former and the early latter rain; but O! if they would lift up their heads and open wide their mouths, to receive the latter rain in its abundance, they should be made to grow up and up until their branches should rise above every hindrance, and tower in regal authority over every obstacle. The fowls of the air should nestle amongst its branches, and the herds should lie down in great delight beneath the shadow thereof."

"Dost thou behold the babe, taking its first steps, upheld by its mother's hand? Hast thou beheld the mighty giant striding across the field, upon whose broad shoulders the heaviest burden seems but a feather's weight?

The Body is today as that of a little child beginning to take its first steps forward into the strength and life of the Spirit-controlled realm. But if my people will but look unto Me, and lean no more on the maternal arm of human flesh, I will cause them to tower as a giant; they shall move forward in conquering strides; their reproach shall be taken away from before the heathen, they shall no more ask, "Where is thy God?" but shall say, "We have seen His light from afar off". Then shall the Lord take His Church unto Himself, mighty, strong, conquering, and all-glorious.

The night with its shadows is fleeing away; the sun is rising in splendor o'er the eternal hills, tho day is breaking; the tidal waves of blessing are rolling in; the showers of blessing shall come down in torrents, for behold, midst sunshine and rain the glory of God is rising and bursting upon His people. They shall show forth mighty signs and wonders through His Spirit's power.

Rejoice, O thou Bride of the Bridegroom;

Be glad, O virgins clothed in white;
Rejoice, rejoice, and dry those tears;
For the long, long night is at an end.

See! The light of an eternal dawn is breaking, The Sun of Righteousness is rising with healing in His wings.
Yea, the Sun is rising, even the Sun that shall never set;
The light is breaking, the light that shall never fade away.

Hark! The trumpet is resounding and echoing through the holy mountain of the Lord.
The bugle! Canst thou not hear its clear, swift voice coming o'er the billows?
'Tis echoing down from the land where tears never flow.

Stand, therefore, clad in the robes of love, truth, and praise, thy sandals upon thy feet.
Let thy veil of separation be upon thy face. The Lord cometh quickly for His beloved. .

Thy veiled face is but as a hidden and foolish mystery to the world, But to Me thy face is fair and comely, O chosen one.
Those that love not Me nor thee have cast thy name out as evil, But I have called thee by

My New Name, and thou art Mine.

I have engraven thy name upon the palms of My hands. I have entwined thee in the cords of My heart.

The golden chains upon thy neck, and thy fair jewels, adorn thee, My beloved. Thy rubies are as drops of blood, My blood that was shed for thee; Thy pearls as tear-drops shed by one who walked with Me and fellowshipped My sufferings; Thy diamonds are priceless souls which thou hast won for Me.

Thy heart shall be filled with righteousness, thy face with joy, For thine eyes have caught the earliest rays of dawn. I am coming, little children, I am coming in the morn.

Balm of Gilead, Who art Thou? Thou art the Prince of a mighty host that leadeth His people and healeth them from all their sorrow.

O thou mighty Victor, who cometh with conquering tread, and laden with the trophies of war, Who art Thou?

Thou art our Bridegroom, the King of Righteousness.

O thou Ray of Glory, that shineth down -twixt parted clouds, piercing the darkness of sin's night, and dispelling the gloom of sorrow, Who art Thou?

Thou art the Sun of Righteousness, the Lord of Glory is Thy Name.

O! Radiant Path, that leads from earth to Heaven, O glorious Way, that leads from darkness into light, Who art Thou?

Thou art Jesus, the Way, the Truth, and the Life, and beside Thee there is none other.

O Door, swung wide upon Thy hinges, through Whose portals are revealed blest, sparkling streams and fragrant meadows, Who art Thou?

Thou art the Door, by which, if any man shall enter in, he shall go in and out, and shall find pasture.

O thou Lily of the Valley, thou Rose of Sharon. Thou Bright and Morning Star, thou Fairest of Ten Thousand to the souls of Thy people, Thou art surely our Jesus, the King in royal garments, the Lamb slain from the foundation of the world.

And thou, who comest up out of the wilderness, leaning upon the arm of thy Beloved, thou.

upon whom the first rays of the rising sun are falling in transforming glory, Who art Thou?

Thou art the Church, the chosen bride of the Lamb, the Body of overcomers, the tested, tried people who have passed through the waters and walked through the fire. Thou art the espoused wife of thy Beloved, the Son of the Living God.

What are these white robes that clothe thee, and that shine with righteousness? These are the robes of His righteousness, with which He didst clothe us in the day of our nakedness.

What are these shoes that adorn thy feet, studded with precious jewels and bound with lacings of Love?

These are the shoes of Salvation, with which He hath shod His people whom He leadeth forth.

Her garments are embroidered with the fine needle work, and each stitch is worked in gold, the victor's crown of righteousness shall be placed upon her head, and she shall reign with the King upon His throne.

Come, come, my beloved, the time is short, I long to lead you quickly forth to greater power and victory.

Quicken thy step, O church of the Living God.

Press closer to Me. Lean hard upon Mine arm.

I will lead thee forth to the more excellent glory; Thus shall we hasten on to the end of the way, Till, with My hand I shall sweep back the flaming curtains of eternal dawn, as WE pass through the portals of OUR ETERNAL AND VICTORIOUS DAY. AMEN.

Milton Keynes UK
Ingram Content Group UK Ltd.
UKHW041259121124
2786UKWH00047B/235